The Economics of Corporate Governance and Mergers

The Economics of Corporate Governance and Mergers

Edited by

Klaus Gugler

Department of Economics, University of Vienna, Austria

B. Burcin Yurtoglu

Department of Economics, University of Vienna, Austria

Edward Elgar

Cheltenham, UK • Northampton, MA, USA

Published by
Edward Elgar Publishing Limited
The Lypiatts
15 Lansdown Road
Cheltenham
Glos GL50 2JA
UK

Edward Elgar Publishing, Inc.
William Pratt House
9 Dewey Court
Northampton
Massachusetts 01060
USA

A catalogue record for this book
is available from the British Library

Library of Congress Cataloguing in Publication Data

The economics of corporate governance and mergers/edited by Klaus Gugler, B. Burcin Yurtoglu.
p. cm.
Includes bibliographical references and index.
1. Corporate governance. 2. Consolidation and merger of corporations.
I. Gugler, Klaus. II. Yurtoglu, B. Burcin, 1968–
HD2741.E27 2008
338.6—dc22 2008023879

ISBN 978 1 84720 715 9

Printed and bound in Great Britain by MPG Books Ltd, Bodmin, Cornwall

Contents

Contributors

Karl Aiginger, Austrian Institute of Economic Research, Austria

J. Robert Branston, University of Bath, UK

Gerhard Clemenz, University of Vienna, Austria

Andy Cosh, Centre for Business Research, University of Cambridge, UK

Keith Cowling, University of Warwick, UK

Hans Degryse, CentER, Tilburg University and TILEC, the Netherlands

Engelbert J. Dockner, University of Vienna, Austria

Sonja Fagernäs, University of Cambridge, UK

Andrea Gaunersdorfer, University of Vienna, Austria

Henry Grabowski, Duke University, USA

Paul Guest, Cranfield University, UK and Centre for Business Research, University of Cambridge, UK

Klaus Gugler, University of Vienna, Austria

Alan Hughes, Centre for Business Research, University of Cambridge, UK

Steffen Jørgensen, University of Southern Denmark, Denmark

Margaret Kyle, London Business School, UK

Stephen Martin, Purdue University, USA

Manfred Neumann, Universität Erlangen-Nürnberg, Germany

Hiroyuki Odagiri, Hitotsubashi University, Japan

Steven Ongena, CentER, Tilburg University, the Netherlands and CEPR, UK

Richard Reichel, Universität Erlangen-Nürnberg, Germany

Prabirjit Sarkar, Jadavpur University, India and Centre for Business Research, University of Cambridge, UK

F.M. Scherer, J.F.K. School of Government, Harvard University, USA

Ajit Singh, Queens' College, University of Cambridge, UK

Roger Sugden, University of Birmingham, UK

Günseli Tümer-Alkan, Center for Financial Studies, Frankfurt, Germany and CentER, Tilburg University, the Netherlands

Jürgen Weigand, WHU Graduate School of Management, Germany

Oliver E. Williamson, University of California, Berkeley, USA

B. Burcin Yurtoglu, University of Vienna, Austria

Preface

Over his long and continuing career, Dennis C. Mueller has by any standards had a very important influence on economics in general and industrial organization and public choice literature in particular. While a full account that might do justice to the range and depth of his influence is beyond the scope of this preface (or even this volume), we have at a minimum to mention two main activities through which Dennis has contributed to the scientific community. First of all his publishing record can modestly be described as impressive: in more than 20 books and over 170 papers his contributions range from established textbooks to highly-cited and path-breaking journal articles. Secondly, Dennis has contributed to the enhancement of the economics profession by serving as a founder, president or as an active member of important scientific organizations such as EARIE, Public Choice Society and many others. Another rare competency of Dennis has been to form research groups to address a variety of economic research questions from a cross-national perspective. One element common to almost all of Dennis' contributions can be described as the ability to see patterns in seemingly diverse phenomena and formulate their relationship to fundamental economic concepts. Perhaps equally important is the clarity in his presentation, as simple as possible but no simpler.

We, the editors of this volume, had the good fortune to meet Dennis when we were first year PhD students at the University of Vienna. As always in life, also an element of good luck enabled us to work with Dennis. This has led to a series of jointly-written papers and to the setting-up of a research group in empirical industrial organization at the University of Vienna. The difficulty of this task will be clear to insiders of the Austrian research climate in the 1990s with its binding resource constraints.

Although Dennis officially retires in 2008, those who know him know also that he will never quit as a researcher. Born in 1940, Dennis, after graduating from Princeton University in 1966, worked at the Brookings Institution in Washington, DC. From 1968 to 1976, he was assistant and then associate professor at Cornell University. His first full professorship was at the University of Maryland, College Park (1977–1994); during this time he took on several visiting professorships; most importantly from 1981 to 1983 he was Director at the International Institute of Management at the Wissenschaftszentrum Berlin (WZB). Since 1994, we have been lucky to have him as a full professor of economics at the University of Vienna.

The focus of this book is on corporate governance and mergers. Both of these topics are associated with the work of Dennis in industrial organization, where he has contributed extensively on the theory of firm behaviour, corporate governance, mergers and acquisitions, and competition policy. The contributors to this volume were drawn from those who have been co-authors or collaborators in academic life. We would like to thank all of them. Our thanks are also due to those who would have contributed but were unable to do so within the time limits. Ms Heide M. Wurm provided an invaluable contribution in putting the manuscript together, and to her we owe a special note of thanks.

By putting together this volume, we hope to be able to show at least some fraction of our gratitude to Dennis C. Mueller, an exemplary person and an economist who will certainly have a lasting influence not only on the two of us, but also on many others.

Klaus Gugler
B. Burcin Yurtoglu

1. The economics of corporate governance and mergers

Klaus Gugler and B. Burcin Yurtoglu

1 INTRODUCTION

Over the last two decades, corporate governance (CG) has become an important issue both in the academic literature and in public policy debates. This sudden attention is interesting, because some basic issues related to CG have been raised at least since Berle and Means (1932). Over these last two decades, many issues such as mergers and takeovers, financial structure of the firm, organizational structures, the relationship between performance and ownership have been analysed within the framework of CG. Having said that, it is all the more interesting to note that there is no single definition of CG and the CG problem.

Starting with the influential book by Berle and Means (1932), the attention of academia has focused on a narrow view of CG. According to this view, CG problems in the modern corporation arise when professional managers are not accountable to dispersed shareholders. This view, which corresponds to the principal–agent framework, culminated in the following definition of CG: 'Corporate governance deals with the ways in which suppliers of finance to corporations assure themselves of getting a return on their investment' (Shleifer and Vishny, 1997). Consequently, much of the research on CG took an investor perspective and looked at the ways in which corporate insiders can attract external financing from outside investors.

This narrow view has been criticized and challenged by others who argue that other stakeholders, such as employees, customers, suppliers and communities, have a vested interest in the firm. CG under this broader view refers to the design of institutions to make managers internalize the welfare of all stakeholders in the firm (Tirole, 2001).

The term 'corporate governance' in the narrow sense covers at least three categories of institutional differences: (1) the identities of the owners of corporations, and the size distribution of their ownership stakes; (2) the governance structure of corporations – number, size and composition of monitoring boards; and (3) the legal and political institutions that affect managerial behaviour (Gugler et al., 2003, 2004a and 2004b). One commonly accepted distinction within the corporate governance literature is between 'insider' governance systems, in which ownership stakes are concentrated and the major stakeholders are directly represented on the boards that monitor managers and perhaps in management itself, and 'outsider' governance systems, in which ownership stakes are dispersed, and owners exercise indirect control on management by electing representatives to the monitoring boards, or perhaps by voting on specific proposals of management. The United States and Great Britain are the most important examples of countries with outsider governance systems, and thus this form of governance structure is often called the 'Anglo-Saxon' system, while Germany and Japan are classic examples of insider systems.

While in all these developed countries, the protections offered by the legal system to investors are at a high level, LaPorta, Lopez-de-Silanes, Shleifer and Vishny (1997 and 1998, hereafter LLSV) draw attention to significant differences between civil law and common law systems. According to this line of research, country legal institutions differ from one another with respect to the protections that they afford shareholders. In some countries, for example, shareholders can demand access to the names and addresses of all other shareholders for the purpose of calling a special meeting of the shareholders; in others they cannot. In some countries managers must publish their shareholdings and their compensation packages, in others they do not have to do so. Provisions like these obviously strengthen the shareholders vis-à-vis the management, and help to align shareholder and managerial interests.

In their seminal contributions LLSV (1997, 1998, 2000) examine the content and development of legal institutions in different countries to determine which ones best align shareholder and managerial interests. They conclude that the common law systems found in the Anglo-Saxon countries and former British colonies offer outside and minority shareholders greater protection against managerial abuse of their position than do civil law systems. Within the civil law systems, LLSV distinguish French, German and Scandinavian systems, with the French system offering the shareholders the least protection among the three civil law systems, and the Scandinavian system providing the most protection. LLSV also find that investor protection and ownership concentration are negatively correlated, and weak investor protection and smaller capital markets go hand in hand.

Other scholars have responded critically to the evidence supporting the law and finance view. One of the criticisms is that financial development has changed in important ways over the last century whereas the legal tradition of each country has remained the same (Rajan and Zingales, 2003). This approach puts a much smaller weight on the importance of legal systems, which remain fixed, and highlights the role of political factors that change over time. The 'law and finance' view of LLSV has been quite influential in public policy debates in that it suggested that the exportation of civil law will lead to the protection of minority shareholders and creditors and to the development of financial markets regardless of the political structure. The 'politics and finance' view, on the other hand, suggests that it is the political structure and not legal origin that drives financial development.

Another line of research which supports the 'politics and finance' view has looked at issues concerning the measurement of shareholder rights. For example, Spamann (2006) recodes the 'Antidirector Rights Index' (ADRI) of shareholder protection rules which was originally developed by LLSV (1998) for 46 countries in 1997 and 2005 with the help of local lawyers. ADRI and its more recent version (Djankov et al., 2005) are frequently used as a measure of legal shareholder protection in cross-country quantitative studies. Using the recoded ADRI, Spamann is not able to reproduce some of the important results between measures of shareholder protection and financial development indicators. In a related paper, Lele and Siems (2007) build a different shareholder protection index for the UK, the US, Germany, France and India, and trace the development of the law for over three decades. Their results indicate that in all of the five countries shareholder protection has been improving in the last three decades; that the protection of minority against majority shareholders is considerably stronger in blockholder countries and that convergence in shareholder protection has been taking place since 1993 and has been increasing since 2001. More importantly, the analysis suggests that legal differences between the five countries do not confirm the distinction between common law and civil law countries.

The paper by Sonja Fagernäs, Prabirjit Sarkar and Ajit Singh in Chapter 2 of this volume takes a similar approach and uses the time series dataset developed by Lele and Siems (2007). This dataset of shareholder protection consists of 60 annual legal indicators for the period 1970–2005 for France, Germany, the UK and the US. On the basis of these data the paper examines developments in shareholder protection and reassesses the claims that common law countries have better shareholder protection than civil law countries. It also examines the relationship between legal changes and stock market development. The results cast serious doubt on the claim that common law countries have better shareholder protection which in turn leads to more stock market development.

2 THE AGENCY THEORY OF THE FIRM AND CORPORATE GOVERNANCE

2.1 The Agency Problem and Implications for CG

In the narrow view of CG that we have mentioned earlier, CG is seen as a means to minimize the information problems between insiders (entrepreneur/manager) and outsiders who supply capital.

In the Jensen and Meckling (1976) model of the firm, an owner-manager who decides to issue equity bears all of the agency costs from this action. Potential shareholders, possessed with rational expectations, recognize that the owner-manager will engage in more on-the-job consumption of various sorts, once he is no longer the firm's sole owner, because the costs of such consumption are now shared with the new owners. They lower their bid for the firm's shares, therefore, so that all of the costs of the on-the-job consumption fall on the owner-manager. This reasoning leads to two predictions: first, the greater are agency costs in a country (the weaker are shareholder protections), the less incentive founders of firms have to issue equity. In the extreme, agency costs convert the equity market into Akerlof's (1970) market for lemons, and lead to its disappearance. The first prediction is, therefore, that equity markets will be thinner in countries with poor shareholder protection. The second prediction follows immediately, namely that ownership concentration is higher in countries with poor shareholder protection.

CG under this view is related to mechanisms that try to minimize such problems. The classic mechanisms that have been analysed in the literature include the various incentive mechanisms, and mechanisms through which monitoring and control can be exercised.

2.2 Incentive Mechanisms

Studies that analyse the impact of incentive mechanisms concentrate on the structure of compensation contracts for managers and/or the career concerns of managers. Studies that look at monetary incentives offered to align managerial and shareholder interests often report a large size elasticity of compensation, while the sensitivity of compensation to various (absolute or relative) performance measures is small (see Jensen and Murphy, 1990, and Murphy, 1999, for an overview). While part of the small sensitivity can be explained on the basis of differences in the attitude of managers to risk (Haubrich, 1994) and while some more current research has come up with a much stronger link between performance and pay (Hall and Liebmann, 1998), the implementation of compensation contracts is full of problems, which are partly correlated with managerial discretion (manipulation of accounting data, strategic release of value relevant information, and so on). A recent study by Bertrand and Mullainathan (2001) provides empirical evidence that managers are often rewarded for luck and that the boards of directors and compensation committees contain too many friends of CEOs. The bottom line of this line of research is that incentive contracts are not powerful enough to curb the managerial discretion problems in large corporations.

2.3 The Exercise of Monitoring and Control

In the agency approach active monitoring and control can be exercised through the boards of directors by several large shareholder identities and by large creditors. A further disciplining effect is also expected through the efficient functioning of the market for corporate control.

2.3.1 Boards

Two characteristics of corporate boards have received the most attention: their size and composition. Significant relationships have been found between certain board actions and these characteristics. Board size is inversely related to various measures of firm performance. CEOs are more likely to be removed when their firm is performing badly, if the board of directors is small (Yermack, 1996) and is dominated by outside directors (Weisbach, 1988). Firms with higher proportions of outside directors are less likely to become the targets of hostile takeovers (Shivdasani, 1993) or to undertake acquisitions that are harmful for their shareholders (Byrd and Hickman, 1992), and they have higher profitability (Bhagat and Black, 1998) and are more likely to be sanctioned by the SEC for poor accounting practices (Dechow et al., 1996). The link between CEO pay and firm performance is weaker, the larger the size of the board of directors (Yermack, 1996). These results indicate that the kinds of board actions that should improve a company's performance, are positively related to the proportion of outside directors on the board, and negatively related to its size.

While these results lead one to expect a positive relationship between company performance and the proportion of outside directors on the board, and a negative relationship to its size, surveys of the literature find that 'there is little to suggest that board composition has any cross-sectional relationship to firm performance' (Hermalin and Weisbach, 2003).

One explanation for this somewhat surprising finding may be that having large proportions of outside directors generally worsens the performance of companies, because they lack the detailed knowledge of its operations that insiders have, but that outsiders are more likely to replace bad managers, which increases the performance of a company. The net effect of these two tendencies is to eliminate any systematic relationship between board composition and firm performance.

Oliver E. Williamson's contribution in this volume (Chapter 4) addresses two fundamental questions related to the role of boards in the modern corporation: (1) should boards of directors in the modern corporation be reconstituted as vigilant monitors? and (2) should such boards additionally be active participants in the management of the firm?

Williamson examines the efficiency implications of these questions from the perspective of both CG and organization theory. He reaches the conclusion that there are serious implementation problems with both the vigilant monitoring and active management roles of boards. In addition to that, Williamson points to the necessity of considering the ramifications of these obstacles for the integrity of delegation. Consequently, Williamson argues that the quest for good governance will remain an ongoing challenge in every large corporation and recommends a more systematic examination of the shareholder–management relation as mediated by the board from a credible contracting perspective.

2.3.2 Large shareholders

There has been a considerable amount of research on the impact of different identities of large shareholders on the performance of companies. While the concentration of insider ownership induces an incentive effect, at some level concentrated ownership can induce an entrenchment effect and hence the quest of large shareholders for the private benefits of control can be detrimental to minority shareholders or creditors. The literature provides convincing empirical evidence that large shareholders must have significant levels of cash flow rights to have an incentive to maximize shareholder value. When cash flow rights differ from control rights, as is the case under pyramidal ownership structures in Europe or East Asia, the entrenchment effect is likely to dominate the wealth/incentive effect with the resulting expropriation of minority shareholders. Claessens et al. (2002) show that this is the case in East Asian countries. Further evidence is provided by Gugler et al. (2006) for a large sample of publicly listed firms from the Anglo-Saxon and civil law traditions. A further advantage of the latter study is that the separation of the wealth and entrenchment effects of insider ownership are confirmed using both Tobin's (average) q and for returns on investment (marginal q).

Research on outside blockholders and other activist shareholders shows that they have an impact on firm actions, such as intervening to block or promote a merger. However, there is little evidence that they have any systematic impact on firm performance (Gugler et al., 2004a).

2.3.3 The role of banks

Debt is often viewed as an important disciplining device in CG (as are dividends, see for example Gugler and Yurtoglu, 2003). Debt holders are entitled to repayment of principal at a certain time prior to liquidation and to regular interest payments. Hence, debt can be a good device to extract the free cash flow at the managers' discretion (Jensen, 1986). Additionally, debt provides incentives to managers to generate enough cash flow in order to prevent illiquidity in the future. There are of course also costs of using debt. Myers' (1977) debt overhang problem, and taking excessive risk (Jensen and Meckling, 1976) are among the most important ones.

An excellent overview of these and other related issues is provided by Hans Degryse, Steven Ongena and Günseli Tümer-Alkan in Chapter 5 of this volume. Degryse, Ongena and Tümer-Alkan consider the role played by banks as debt financiers, large shareholders and board members. They also analyse how banks' role differs from other players in the CG of firms.

Their survey shows that banks may play a role in corporate governance as a large shareholder. Their ability to monitor can be constrained by investment regulations which are a function of the legal system. Countries differ in terms of the importance of bank block holdings. For example, bank block holdings are more prevalent in bank-centred economies such as Japan and Continental Europe. Also, banks as long-term shareholders are an important part of the corporate governance mechanism in Germany (Gorton and Schmid, 2000). Whether firm performance is positively affected by bank block holdings remains an open question, however.

Other results presented by Degryse, Ongena and Tümer-Alkan can be summarized as follows: banks improve corporate governance of firms through different complementary mechanisms. This holds in particular in Continental Europe and Japan, where banks, next to being an important debt financier, often also hold large equity stakes of firms, and join the boards of corporations. They find that (i) close bank–firm relationships create shareholder value, increase credit availability and discipline firm managers by preventing them from overinvesting; (ii) bank relationships through debt financing do not necessarily improve firm performance, as banks are able to appropriate some of the benefits of their relationships with firms; (iii) banks as large shareholders generally improve the performance of firms; (iv) appointments of bank directors to firm boards increase with poor stock performance and with earnings losses of firms; and (v) bank board membership improves firm performance, increases executive turnover, but having lenders on board decreases firm debt ratios.

2.3.4 The market for corporate control

Takeovers, mergers and acquisitions and proxy contests are one of the most debated issues in CG. If internal governance mechanisms are ineffective, a hostile takeover can be the last resort to discipline (dismiss) managers (Manne, 1965). Hostile takeovers have been important in the second half of the 1980s in the USA and to some degree in the UK. There is no evidence of hostile takeovers becoming a matter of substantial importance in other countries.

Besides theoretical problems that question the effectiveness of takeovers as control mechanisms (Grossman and Hart, 1980), there is an overwhelming amount of empirical evidence that they do not improve the wealth of the acquiring companies' shareholders (Mueller, 2003; and Moeller et al., 2005). The negative effects of mergers on acquiring company shareholders become much more dramatic measured over long windows after the merger (Rau and Vermaelen, 1998; Gugler et al., 2006). In addition to this, there is not much evidence that the performance in real variables such as profits and market shares improve after mergers (Mueller, 1980; Ravenscraft and Scherer, 1987).

Empirical evidence on these issues is provided by three chapters contained in this book.

Chapter 7 by Stephen Martin provides an up-to-date account of the hitherto five great merger waves. The First Merger Wave of the 1890s predominantly involved large horizontal mergers of many firms at once. Accordingly, they were coined 'merger for monopoly' by George Stigler. Technological changes were also responsible for the Second Merger Wave of the 1920s. The Third Merger Wave in the mid- to late 1960s led to the combination of unrelated lines of businesses, and it is also called the 'conglomerate merger wave'. Internal capital markets were supposed to be superior alternatives to external capital markets. This opinion of the capital markets reversed during the Fourth Merger Wave of the 1980s, where bust-up takeovers led to the divestiture of many of the assets formerly put together. Globalization and technological change are responsible for the Fifth and last Merger Wave of the late 1990s, which is unprecedented in its size and as some observers see it is still ongoing. During all merger waves, however, as Professor Martin intriguingly argues, (excessive?) stock market optimism played a crucial role. After reviewing the evidence on the effects of mergers, the chapter concludes with the following quotation of Dennis Mueller (Mueller, 1977, p. 344):

> It has become customary to close a review of the merger literature by observing that the arguments are still in conflict, the main issues still in doubt, and from this draw the prudent conclusion that policy changes should proceed slowly and cautiously. True, the a priori theories of mergers' causes and effects are still in

> conflict, and will probably always remain so. But the empirical literature, upon which this survey focuses, draws a surprisingly consistent picture. Whatever the stated or unstated goals of managers are, the mergers they have consummated have on average not generated extra profits for the acquiring firms, have not resulted in increased economic efficiency.

Consistently, in Chapter 8 Mike Scherer reports dramatic increases in merger activity in the US and the ensuing exits of large firms through mergers. In particular, large firm exits through merger rose sharply during the 1980s and climbed to the record-setting level of 1.9 exits out of the 100 largest US industrial corporations on average per year between 1993 and 2002. Citing his famous book with David Ravenscraft, *Mergers, Sell-offs, and Economic Efficiency* (1987), Scherer questions positive merger productivity effects. On the contrary, he estimates that the conglomerate merger wave of the 1960s reduced the growth of US real gross national product between 1968 and 1976 by between 0.074 and 0.101 percentage points per year. Reasons include the winner's curse (acquirers bid too much), corporate culture mismatches, incentive failures, or clumsy implementation. Macroeconomic evidence using regressions of percentage productivity growth in the US economy for essentially the whole of last century on GNP growth and aggregate merger activity confirms the notion that mergers do not increase productivity on average.

The findings of the industrial organization literature using accounting data (*ex post* studies) contrast starkly with the findings of the finance literature using stock market data (event studies), since the latter find on average positive effects, at least in the short run. One of the reasons why the finance profession is so keen on mergers is the huge (absolute and relative to other fields such as physical sciences) rise in MBA education teaching on the subject. Thus, the United States created a sizeable professional establishment that sees the making of mergers a significant justification for its existence.

Thus, the conclusions of Scherer are not reassuring: the volume of merger activity has risen, and the disappearance of large industrial firms through merger has reached record levels. High levels of merger activity encourage students of business administration to emphasize merger-making skills in their training, and as they succeed in becoming leaders within the corporate hierarchy, a continuous feedback loop may operate, fostering an attitude that sustains and encourages vigorous merger activity. Last but not least, mergers do not bring substantial efficiency benefits to the economy

Chapter 9 by Hiroyuki Odagiri analyses the impact of mergers on corporate performance among Japanese firms since 1990. It updates the previous study by Odagiri and Tatsuo (1989), and the results suggest that mergers reduce relative profitability, while not impacting labour productivity significantly. Thus, in many cases, it is difficult to expect that mergers improve economic welfare and in fact they are more likely to hurt it. Using the Cournot model, the effects of mergers on economic welfare are summarized. For mergers to increase economic welfare, a substantial efficiency improvement has to be achieved through mergers. From the three main hypotheses discussed, the efficiency-hypothesis, the collusion hypothesis, and the empire-building hypothesis, the evidence favours the empire-building hypothesis. Managerial motives for mergers have also implications for macroeconomic growth. Positive externalities from managerial growth strategies can only be expected from internal growth strategies, possibly from non-horizontal M&A bringing together different capabilities, but not from horizontal M&A. The analysis also has implications for competition policy: the efficiency defence in merger control should only be applied with limits. Particularly problematic mergers in this respect are horizontal mergers of equals.

Next we move to the UK and to Chapter 10 by Andy Cosh, Paul Guest and Alan Hughes. They provide an up-to-date survey of corporate governance reform in the UK, and its implications for *ex-post* merger/takeover performance. Several developments appear particularly worthy of mention. First, there is overwhelming evidence that the proportion of non-executive directors has increased substantially in the UK in the past two decades from an average of about one third in 1980/81 to one half in 1995/96. By 2006, non-executive directors accounted for 60 per cent of the board on average in the top 100 UK-listed companies. Another feature of changes in board structure is the decline in the average board size shown for the largest companies. At the same time, the proportion of firms combining the roles of CEO and Chairman fell from 74 per cent in 1981 to 50 per cent in 1996. Concerning executive remuneration, while the median level of CEO remuneration rose from £222 000 in 1981 to £827 000 in 1996 for a sample of large UK companies, the bonus element of this pay rose from a negligible proportion to 21 per cent by 1996. Amongst the top 100 UK-listed companies in 2006, the median level of CEO remuneration was £1 017 000, and the bonus element had risen to over 35 per cent. The award of stock option and long-term incentive plans that were rare in the early 1980s raises the average pay package of CEOs of FTSE 100 companies to £3.3m and the performance-related element of the whole package increased to about 80 per cent by 2006. Finally, the rising dominance of financial institutions as holders of UK-listed company shares is documented. The proportion of ordinary shares held by financial institutions more than doubled from 30 per cent in 1963 to 62 per cent in 1993. If one adds overseas financial institutions, the holdings of financial institutions have risen from about 30 per cent in 1963 to above 70 per cent since the 1990s.

The authors then go on and ask whether these changes in UK corporate governance regulation and structure had an effect on the quality of decision making, in particular on post-takeover performance. And indeed, acquisitions carried out after Cadbury display more positive announcements and long-run returns, significantly so for the latter. Acquisitions are more profitable following Cadbury for four of the six operating performance measures, significantly so for one of these measures. There is therefore some evidence that takeover performance improves following Cadbury. However, the main performance driver remains CEO ownership, that is, a direct monitoring and incentive device, while executive remuneration, board composition, board size and institutional shareholders remain insignificant.

Chapter 11 by Henry Grabowski and Margaret Kyle is an in-depth study of the pharmaceutical industry by two leading economists in this field. The special problems of the pharmaceutical industry, such as patent expirations and R&D pipeline gaps, high risk and uncertainty associated with clinical studies and economies of scope and scale, are linked to strategic considerations like mergers and alliances. The special problems of this industry make it difficult to find appropriate control groups of firms; in particular, distress is one driving force behind mergers and should be considered. The propensity score method might be one solution.

The main results of a preliminary but highly relevant study on more than 4500 firms covering all (!) initiated new drug projects between 1990 until 2007 are as follows: (1) small and medium-sized firms are significantly less likely to launch their phase III projects relative to large and very large firms; (2) projects initiated after a merger are much more likely to advance from each stage of development. As to the causes of these results the authors pose important new research questions, such as: do mergers combine complementary skills of two firms, leading to better project selection? Do mergers reduce potential competition within a disease area, raise expected profits for a project, and therefore lead to more advancement? Are mergers necessary for the realization of these benefits, or could strategic alliances be used instead?

The consequences of horizontal mergers on firms' profits are traditionally studied within a static Cournot framework and a merger is modelled as an exogenous change in market structure. In an important paper Salant et al. (1983) show that in a static Cournot game with linear demand and cost functions, mergers are unprofitable unless they involve at least 80 per cent of the firms in the industry. This striking result rests on two assumptions. First, Deneckere and Davidson (1985) show that if firms produce differentiated products and set prices instead of quantities, any price increase by the merging firms is matched by the outsiders and hence a merger becomes profitable. Second, the conclusion of Salant et al. is linked to the modelling of the cost structures. If the merging entity can exploit scale economies of the merging firms, cost reductions ensure the profitability of mergers. Perry and Porter (1985) present a model that builds on these arguments: merging firms own a tangible asset, acquired from the merging partners, so that a merged firm can increase output at a given level of average costs and hence benefit from the merger. Dockner and Gaunersdorfer (2001) study exogenous mergers in a dynamic Cournot market. Their conclusion is in sharp contrast to the SSR analysis: if firms compete over an infinite planning horizon, a Markov perfect equilibrium exists in which it is profitable for firms to merge even if there are no scale economies.

A sound understanding of mergers and their consequences on industry and market structure requires, however, a theory of endogenous mergers. In Chapter 12 Engelbert J. Dockner, Andrea Gaunersdorfer and Steffen Jørgensen formulate a two-stage game and propose a dynamic theory of endogenous mergers. In the first stage, an equilibrium ownership structure is determined and in the second stage firms play a dynamic Cournot game in which the planning horizon is infinite. For the special case of a four-firm industry, they prove that in a sub-game perfect equilibrium it is never optimal for a firm to be outside a merger; equilibrium ownership structure always involves mergers.

Chapter 13 by Gerhard Clemenz investigates the impact of vertical mergers between producers and retailers on social welfare and consumer surplus if the goods under consideration display network effects and are not compatible with each other. It brings together two strands of literature, that on vertical integration and that on network goods. The main reason given in the literature for negative effects of vertical integration is the possibility that an integrated firm may be able to raise the costs of its rivals. The chapter offers a new possible reason for a negative effect on consumer surplus. It is shown that vertical integration is indeed harmful for consumers because the integrated firm is able to exploit the network effect in such a way that the other producer is effectively kept out of the market and consumers have to pay higher retail prices. Thus, this chapter fits nicely with Hiroyuki Odagiri's chapter on the effects of horizontal mergers.

Formally the author analyses a model with two producers, each of them producing a network good which is not compatible with the other good. Consumers buy one of the products from a retailer and enjoy utility from a network effect which is increasing in the number of consumers who buy the same brand. There are two retailers who engage in spatial competition which is modelled in the fashion of Hotelling's linear city model.

In the first scenario all four firms are independent. There exist two types of equilibrium. In a symmetric non-standardization equilibrium both brands are sold and have equal market shares. In an asymmetric standardization equilibrium one brand captures the entire market. Due to spatial competition between retailers the price is the same in both equilibria, but consumers are better off in the standardization equilibrium.

In the second scenario each retailer merges with one producer and the two integrated firms compete with each other. In equilibrium each integrated firm sells only its own brand, and if the mergers are *ex ante* profitable then consumers are worse off than in scenario 1.

In the third scenario one retailer merges with one producer, and the two other firms remain independent. If the marginal utility of the network effect is smaller than the marginal travelling costs, then the brand of the integrated firm will take over the entire market, but the independent retailer will be offered a wholesale price that ensures them a profit which is equal to the one they could get if they only sold the other brand. Consumers are worse off than without any vertical integration. If the marginal network utility is larger than the marginal travelling costs, an analogous equilibrium exists, but consumers may be better off than in the symmetric non-standardization equilibrium without any vertical integration. If the network effect is even greater, then the two independent firms will either merge as well or at least act as if they were merged, and in equilibrium only one brand will prevail. Consumers are again worse off than without mergers.

Chapter 14 by Karl Aiginger explores the relation between competition and macroeconomic performance. He collected 13 indicators on the toughness of competition for 29 countries. While some of these indicators come from surveys such as on the legislative regime (intensity of competition, effectiveness of antitrust and so on), other indicators on product market regulation were gathered by OECD experts (time to start a business, state ownership and so on). The author adds *ex post* indicators of the price–cost margins in industries, on aggregate profits, and finally, and as a tribute to the works of Dennis Mueller, on the persistence of profit differences between industries. The usual indicator on trade openness complements the set. Since all indicators relate on a narrow aspect of the broad notion of 'toughness of competition', since they are noisy, and contain measurement errors, he combines the information delivered by the individual indicators by ranking and then averaging them, to arrive at a 'composite indicator on competition'. Economic performance of a country is defined more broadly than usual, combining data on income (per capita level and macroeconomic growth), employment, unemployment (rates and change over ten years) and equity (relation of top 20 per cent income to bottom 20 per cent).

Eleven of the 13 indicators on competition are positively related to performance in the cross-country correlation, with close relations to the assessment of the competition legislation, the extent of state ownership and product market regulation. Most importantly, the relationship between the performance ranking and the combined indicator on competition is proven to be very close. The overall impact of competition seems to be the most important and most robust indicator in explaining performance differences of countries.

3 THE BROADER VIEW OF CORPORATE GOVERNANCE

The CG mechanisms reviewed so far take an agency perspective and consequently most of the literature on corporate governance evaluates the effectiveness of such mechanisms in terms of shareholder value. As indicated by Tirole (2006, p. 65): 'To many noneconomists, economists in this respect appear "oblivious to redistributional issues", "narrow-minded", or "out of touch with social realities".'

While shareholder value maximization can be an appropriate objective function under perfect and complete markets, Allen (2005) argues that in many emerging economies this is not the case and that alternative firm objective functions, such as pursuing the interests of all stakeholders, may help overcome market failures. In these economies other mechanisms such as competition, trust and reputation may be preferable to the use of law to ensure good corporate governance.

A common suggestion is that companies should serve not only the financiers but also internalize the external effects of corporate decisions on other stakeholders (Allen and Gale, 2000).

In Chapter 3, J. Robert Branston, Keith Cowling and Roger Sugden take such a stakeholder perspective and argue that the corporation should be accountable to all parties who are significantly affected by the activities of a corporation. They define corporations as centres of economic planning, which implies that the governance of a corporation is to plan its overall direction, to determine its broad impact and therefore to make its strategic decisions. Interests vary across those concerned about and affected by a corporation's activities and that this variation is reflected in different preferences over strategy. Accordingly, a corporation's impact typically depends upon who governs. The main conclusion of this chapter is that it is a matter of public policy to ensure that corporate governance is in the public interest.

Branston, Cowling and Sugden's chapter calls for an effective democracy in the strategic decision-making processes of corporations. Some of the policy initiatives that might contribute worthwhile steps toward this goal include: (1) the design of suitable company laws, based on widened membership, focusing consecutively on particular economic sectors and specific sets of interested parties; and (2) the creation and empowerment of democratically controlled public bodies.

Studies based on the agency approach to CG suggest that monitoring and control devices are necessary for the efficient functioning of companies. One prediction is that in industries populated by both profit-seeking and nonprofit firms (NPs), the profit-seeking firms should outperform the NPs.

Chapter 6 by Manfred Neumann, Richard Reichel and Jürgen Weigand considers this question, namely whether non-profit firms can compete on an equal footing with profit-seeking firms. In most industrialized countries NPs account for a substantial share of economic activity, and in many cases they are competing with profit-seeking firms. In the present economics literature NPs tend to be viewed to be less efficient than profit-seeking firms. Thus, NPs are frequently predicted to be doomed to failure. So far, this prediction has not come true, however. An outstanding example is the banking industry in Germany. It rests on three pillars: profit-seeking commercial banks; cooperative banks seeking to foster the economic well-being of their members; and non-profit-seeking public sector banks (local savings banks, federal-state central banks and development banks) obliged by law to pursue common goals.

Assuming that NPs strive to just cover long-run costs (including opportunity costs of capital), the chapter derives the following predictions: (1) the NP-bank turns out as the price leader of the market; (2) in the long run the market price is determined solely by average costs of the non-profit firm; (3) total output in the case where both banks maximize profits is lower than in the non-profit equilibrium; and (4) profits of both banks are higher in the case where both banks maximize profits.

The authors find evidence for these predictions. In particular the profitability of German commercial banks is lower than that of their international peers, the market shares of commercial banks increased relative to NP banks over time due to relative efficiency gains, and consolidation via mergers was necessary to achieve economies of scale. Thus there exists a sort of symbiotic relationship between profit-seeking firms and not-for-profit agents, where the development is primarily driven by initiatives from profit-seeking firms.

4 CONCLUSIONS

In summary, the chapters contained in this volume provide an insightful view of the major issues in the economics of corporate governance and mergers.

While some of the chapters highlight the weakness of corporate governance mechanisms as devices to align insider (managerial) and outsider (shareholder) interests such as Williamson's account of the role of boards or Scherer's evaluation of the effectiveness of the market for corporate control, others are more optimistic. For example, Degryse, Ongena and Tümer-Alkan show that banks as large shareholders and creditors may improve corporate governance of firms through different complementary mechanisms.

We believe that two important conclusions can be drawn from this book. First, corporate governance systems that better align shareholders' and managers' interests lead to better corporate performance. Corporate Governance reform in recent years and in many countries indeed improved the system. Thus, it appears that shareholders and the rest of society both benefit from strong(er) corporate governance institutions. It is also important to note that there are a variety of corporate governance arrangements both within and across different countries. Hence, the importance of the corporate governance mechanisms to deal with specific governance problems can vary depending on the institutional background.

Second, there is an important relationship between corporate governance structures and the quality of firm decision making, one of the most important being the decision to merge or take over another firm. Since many mergers still do not deliver the promised benefits, either to shareholders or to society as a whole, the suspicion remains that corporate governance systems and mechanisms are not yet optimal. That many merger decisions were bad very often comes to the surface *after* a merger wave. We are in the midst of one, and it remains to be seen whether this merger wave is different from its predecessors with respect to the success of mergers.

Needless to say, there are many issues that only additional research can illuminate. In this volume, we have collected the state of the art on the major critical issues such as the role of the boards of directors, competition, large shareholders, the market for corporate control and stakeholders. We hope that this volume will also encourage others to evaluate, criticize and refine these and many other unexplored issues in corporate governance research.

REFERENCES

Akerlof, George A. (1970), 'The market for "Lemons": Quality uncertainty and the market mechanism', *Quarterly Journal of Economics*, **84**(3), 488–500.

Allen, F. (2005), 'Corporate governance in emerging economies', *Oxford Review of Economic Policy*, **21**(2), 164–77.

Allen, Franklin and Douglas Gale (2000), 'Corporate governance and competition', in Xavier Vives (ed.), *Corporate Governance: Theoretical and Empirical Perspectives*, Cambridge: Cambridge University Press, pp. 23–84.

Berle, Adolf A. and Gardiner C. Means (1932), *The Modern Corporation and Private Property*, New York: Macmillan.

Bertrand, M. and S. Mullainathan (2001), 'Are CEOs rewarded for luck? The ones without principals are', *Quarterly Journal of Economics*, **116**(3), 901–32.

Bhagat, S. and B. Black (1998), 'The relationship between board composition and firm performance', in K.J. Hopt, H. Kanda, M.J. Roe, E. Wymeersch and S. Prigge (eds), *Comparative Corporate Governance: The State of the Art and Emerging Research*, Oxford: Oxford University Press, pp. 281–306.

Bhagat, S. and B.S. Black (2002), 'The non-correlation between board independence and long-term firm performance', *Journal of Corporation Law*, **27**, 231–73.

Byrd, J.W. and K.A. Hickman (1992), 'Do outside directors monitor managers?: Evidence from tender offer bids', *Journal of Financial Economics*, **32**(2), 195–222.

Claessens, S., S. Djankov, J.P.H. Fan and L.H.P. Lang (2002), 'Disentangling the incentive and entrenchment effects of large shareholders', *Journal of Finance*, **57**(6), 2741–71.

Dechow, P., R. Sloan and A. Sweeney (1996), 'Causes and consequences of earnings manipulations: An analysis of firms subject to enforcement sanctions by the SEC', *Contemporary Accounting Research*, **13**(1), 1–36.

Deneckere, R. and C. Davidson (1985), 'Incentives to form coalitions with Bertrand competition', *The Rand Journal of Economics*, **16**(4), 473–86.

Djankov, S., R. La Porta, F. Lopez de Silanes and A. Shleifer (2005), 'The law and economics of self-dealing', *NBER Working Paper* No. W11883.

Dockner, E.J. and A. Gaunersdorfer (2001), 'On the profitability of horizontal mergers in industries with dynamic competition', *Japan and the World Economy*, **13**(3), 195–216.

Gorton, G. and F.A. Schmid (2000), 'Universal banking and the performance of German firms', *Journal of Financial Economics*, **58**(1), 29–80.

Grossman, S.J. and O.D. Hart (1980), 'Takeover bids, the free-rider problem, and the theory of the corporation', *The Bell Journal of Economics*, **11**(1), 42–64.

Gugler, K. and B.B. Yurtoglu (2003), 'Corporate governance and dividend pay-out policy in Germany', *European Economic Review*, **47**(4), 731–58.

Gugler, K., D.C. Mueller and B.B. Yurtoglu (2003), 'The impact of corporate governance on investment returns in developed and developing countries', *The Economic Journal*, **113**, 511–39.

Gugler, K., D.C. Mueller and B.B. Yurtoglu (2004a), 'Corporate governance and globalization', *Oxford Review of Economic Policy*, **20**(1), 129–56.

Gugler, K., D.C. Mueller and B.B. Yurtoglu (2004b), 'Corporate governance, capital market discipline and the returns on investment', *Journal of Law and Economics*, **XLVII**, 589–633.

Gugler, K., D.C. Mueller and B.B. Yurtoglu (2006), 'The effects of ownership concentration and identity on investment performance: An international comparison', Working Paper, University of Vienna.

Hall, B.J. and J.B. Liebman (1998), 'Are CEOs really paid like bureaucrats?', *Quarterly Journal of Economics*, **113**, 653–91.

Haubrich, J. (1994), 'Risk aversion, performance pay, and the principal–agent problem', *Journal of Political Economy*, **102**, 258–76.

Hermalin, B.E. and M.S. Weisbach (2003), 'Boards of directors as an endogenously determined institution: A survey of the economic literature', *Economic Policy Review*, **9**(1), 7–26.

Jensen, C.M. and W. Meckling (1976), 'Theory of the firm: Managerial behavior, agency cost, and capital structure', *Journal of Financial Economics*, **3**(4), 305–60.
Jensen, M. (1986), 'Agency costs of free cash flow, corporate finance, and takeovers', *American Economic Review*, **76**(2), 323–9.
Jensen, M. and K. Murphy (1990), 'Performance pay and top management incentives', *Journal of Political Economy*, **98**, 225–64.
La Porta, R., F. Lopez-de-Silanes, A. Shleifer and R.W. Vishny (1997), 'Legal determinants of external finance', *Journal of Finance*, **52**(3), 1131–50.
La Porta, R., F. Lopez-de-Silanes, A. Shleifer and R.W. Vishny (1998), 'Law and finance', *Journal of Political Economy*, **106**(6), 1113–55.
La Porta, R., F. Lopez-de-Silanes, A. Shleifer and R.W. Vishny (2000), 'Investor protection and corporate governance', *Journal of Financial Economics*, **58**(1–2), 3–27.
Lele, P.P. and M.M. Siems (2007), 'Shareholder protection: A leximetric approach', *Journal of Corporate Law Studies*, **7**(1), 17–50.
Manne, H. (1965), 'Mergers and the market for corporate control', *Journal of Political Economy*, **73**(4), 110–20.
Moeller, S.B., F.P. Schlingemann and R.M. Stulz (2005), 'Wealth destruction on a massive scale: A study of acquiring firm returns in the merger wave of the late 1990s', *Journal of Finance*, **60**, 757–82.
Mueller, Dennis C. (1977), 'The effects of conglomerate mergers: A survey of the empirical evidence', *Journal of Banking and Finance*, **1**(4), 315–47.
Mueller, Dennis C. (ed.) (1980), *The Determinants and Effects of Mergers: An International Comparison*, Cambridge, MA: Oelgeschlager, Gunn & Hain.
Mueller, Dennis C. (2003), 'The finance literature on mergers: A critical survey', in M. Waterson (ed.), *Competition, Monopoly and Corporate Governance*, Essays in Honour of Keith Cowling, Cheltenham, UK and Northampton, MA, USA: Edward Elgar, pp. 161–205.
Murphy, Kevin J. (1999), 'Executive compensation', in O. Ashenfelter, R. Layard and D. Card (eds), *Handbook of Labor Economics*, vol. 3, Amsterdam: North Holland, pp. 2485–563.
Myers, Stewart (1977), 'Determinants of corporate borrowing', *Journal of Financial Economics*, **5**(2), 147–75.
Odagiri, H. and H. Tatsuo (1989), 'Are mergers and acquisitions going to be popular in Japan too?: An empirical study', *International Journal of Industrial Organization*, **7**(1), 49–72.
Perry, M.K. and R.H. Porter (1985), 'Oligopoly and the incentive for horizontal merger', *American Economic Review*, **75**(1), 219–27.
Rajan, R. and L. Zingales (2003), 'The great reversals: The politics of financial development in the twentieth century', *Journal of Financial Economics*, **69**(1), 5–50.
Rau, R.P. and T. Vermaelen (1998), 'Glamour, value and the post-acquisition performance of acquiring firms', *Journal of Financial Economics*, **49**(2), 223–53.
Ravenscraft, David J. and F.M. Scherer (1987), *Mergers, Sell-offs, and Economic Efficiency*, Washington, DC: Brookings Institution.
Salant, S.W., S. Switzer and R.J. Reynolds (1983) 'Losses from horizontal merger: the effects of an exogenous change in industry structure on Cournot–Nash equilibrium', *Quarterly Journal of Economics*, **98**(2), 185–99.
Shivdasani, A. (1993), 'Board composition, ownership structure, and hostile takeovers', *Journal of Accounting and Economics*, **16**(1–3), 167–98.

Shleifer, A. and R.W. Vishny (1997), 'A survey of corporate governance', *Journal of Finance*, **52**(2), 737–83.

Spamann, Holger (2006), 'On the insignificance and/or endogeneity of La Porta et al.'s "anti-director rights index" under consistent coding', Cambridge, MA: Harvard Olin Fellows Discussion Paper No. 7/2006.

Tirole, J. (2001), 'Corporate governance', *Econometrica*, **69**(1), 1–35.

Tirole, Jean (2006), *The Theory of Corporate Finance*, Princeton, NJ: Princeton University Press.

Weisbach, M.S. (1988), 'Outside directors and CEO turnover', *Journal of Financial Economics*, **20**, 431–60.

Yermack, D. (1996), 'Higher market valuation of companies with a small board of directors', *Journal of Financial Economics*, **40**(2), 185–212.

2. Legal origin, shareholder protection and the stock market: new challenges from time series analysis*

Sonja Fagernäs, Prabirjit Sarkar and Ajit Singh

1 INTRODUCTION

Since La Porta et al. (LLSV) (1998) published a study on the effects of legal origin on shareholder protection (hereafter SP) and financial development, these topics have received considerable attention from economists. The authors found that countries with a common law origin have a higher level of SP than countries with a civil law origin, which in turn in a cross-section explains the different patterns of ownership concentration of companies in these countries. Ownership concentration is found to be lower in countries with a common law origin, explained by the better level of protection offered to minority shareholders.

In a subsequent paper (Djankov et al., 2005), a similar line of reasoning is used to explain a positive correlation between the level of SP and stock market developments, such as those in market capitalization, numbers of initial public offerings and companies listed on the stock exchange. One of the underlying assumptions is that firm financing in the form of equity capital will be higher in countries with better protection. Several authors have since also worked on the links between financial development and legal origin (see for example Beck et al., 2003) or added a limited time dimension to the existing dataset and examined the determinants of SP (see, for example, Pagano and Volpin, 2006). Embedded in the literature on legal origin is the general perception that legal change is likely to be more frequent and the legal system as a whole more adaptable to changing environments in a common law system than in a civil law system. This relies to some extent on the assumption that case law plays a more dominant role in common than civil law systems, which could, however, be questioned.

Indeed, although path-breaking, LLSV's work has not been without controversy. They have been criticized for their legal origin theory, which assumes, without adequate justification, an enormous path dependence lasting hundreds of years. Critics have also taken exception to LLSV's use exclusively of cross-section data throughout their studies. It leads, among other things, to ambiguity about causation. The inter-disciplinary research project, of which this chapter is a part, was designed to address some of these difficulties. The project adopted the strategy of collecting time series data for the four advanced countries – UK, France, Germany and US, which are essentially countries where different legal systems originated (or reached a high level of development), and subsequently spread to developing countries often through colonization and conquest. In a lighter vein, these may be called 'the countries of the original sin' in terms of the LLSV theory.

In more traditional terms, the four countries chosen can also be considered prototypes of a common law country with an equity-finance orientation (US and UK) and debt-finance oriented civil law countries (France, Germany), which also makes for interesting analysis. Additionally, although ownership structures can be expected to change over time, it is generally thought that equity ownership is more concentrated in France and Germany than in the UK and the US.

Not only LLSV's work, but also that of their collaborators as well as their critics, has mostly been cross-sectional, with the outstanding exception of Rajan and Zingales (2003). The last two authors brought an important time series dimension to their cross-country study of capital market developments and showed that contrary to the legal origin theory, there were many 'great reversals' in outcomes which contradicted the theory. For example, before World War I, France had a more developed capital market than the US, while in more recent decades it has been the other way round. This is contrary to the legal origin theory because these origins do not change over time.

The new data which has been examined in this chapter is a product of the above-mentioned research project and consists of 36 years of legal data for 4 countries for 60 variables. This data, which will be described and analysed below in detail, is unique and comprehensive. However, in a longer-term historical perspective, which underlies the legal origin theory, the time series are relatively short, 36 years rather than a century or two.

The aim of this chapter is to use this dataset to examine annual developments in SP in France, Germany, the United Kingdom and the United States since the year 1970 and to assess the relationship between legal and stock market development. The coverage of the legal dataset is much more comprehensive than that of LLSV and tries to accommodate elements of the law of each country. In the light of this new data, the chapter reassesses the claims made that common law countries have better SP than civil law countries, that such law matters for stock market development and describes the developments in different areas of SP in detail. It emerges that existing work creates an inadequate picture of the level and role of SP and that despite differences in legal origin, countries' protection of shareholders changes over time and some convergence in the levels of protection can be seen in recent years.

In short, the main contribution of this chapter lies in its use of the newly available time series data to test the various empirical and analytic propositions advanced in the literature in this area, including notably by LLSV. As we shall see, the time series analysis leads to rather different conclusions from those well established in the literature by cross-section studies. In the light of the nature of the data, the chapter experiments with Principal Component Analysis (PCA) as an aggregation tool and Autoregressive Distributive Lag (ARDL) cointegration analysis to explore long-term equilibrium relationships between the relevant variables.

Section 2 describes the legal data and legal developments in the area of SP as well as the hypotheses tested. Section 3 describes the economic data and model used, section 4 reports the regression result and section 5 concludes.

2 LEGAL DATA AND DESCRIPTIVE ANALYSIS

A detailed description of the construction of the legal data as well as a critique of the original LLSV index can be found in the work of our legal colleagues Lele and Siems (2007). It is based on 'law on the books'. It takes into account company law, and some areas of securities law, although most parts of the latter are excluded. In some areas, only mandatory and not default rules are considered. Corporate governance codes are included as are case law and changes brought about by court decisions. In the case of the US, the coding is based on Delaware law. Self-regulatory listings rules of the stock exchange are also taken into account and in the case of the UK, the City Code on takeovers and mergers is included, although it is not statutory, but compliance is considered a rule.

An explanation of the variables included can be found in the Appendix. There are 60 legal variables for each country, all relating to SP. Each of the variables takes a value between 0 and 1. Many take intermediate values, since it was considered inaccurate and in many cases impossible to describe the level of a certain type of protection simply with a binary variable. A value of 1 relates to the highest level of protection and a 0 to the lowest; so if a country were to have the maximum level of protection, the indicators would sum up to 60. There are two major categories of variables:

protection of the shareholder against management and board, and protection of the shareholder against other shareholders.

This section examines and compares the movements in the legal series over time and between countries. For the purposes of comparison and econometric analysis, some form of aggregation of the variables for each country is required. The aggregation issue will be taken up in the context of the use of PCA for analysing the data.

2.1 Differences in Shareholder Protection: Analysis of Individual Variables

Table 2.1 shows the areas in which legal change occurs in each country. There is a change in roughly a third of the 60 variables in each country over time. One feature that stands out clearly from this analysis is that changes in regulation do not necessarily occur in the same areas of law in each country. This can be seen by looking at the variables for which a standard deviation is calculated, implying that this variable changed over the time period covered.

A look at the means of the variables reveals that countries do protect differently. For instance, concerning agenda-setting power (variable 10), France and Germany have a value of 1, in this case meaning that shareholders do not need to pay for their proposals, whereas this is not the case in the US and the UK, which are assigned a value of 0. Germany has a limit on executive remuneration (variable 28), whereas the other countries do not. In all the others, except the US, the law grants shareholders the first opportunity to buy new issues of shares, and this right can be waived only by the general meeting. All of these refer to cases where there has been no change in regulation over the time. Where there have been changes, the mean takes a value between 0 and 1. The differences in the ways of protecting signal the fact that laws adapt to the economic, industrial and governance structures of the country, and the same laws may be less relevant in one country than in another.

However, areas where the law has changed in all of the four countries relate to board composition, director's compensation, director's disqualification after misconduct, director's duties and compliance with corporate governance codes. Regulations on these tend to be found in corporate governance codes that came into fashion in the 1990s and may well be the clearest unifying feature of SP between the countries. Thus, despite differences, this global phenomenon is clearly reflected in the data. Areas where rules have not changed in the US and UK, but have in both France and Germany concern those on anticipation of shareholder decision, information in the run-up to the general election, no squeeze out and right to exit.

Table 2.1 Means and standard deviation of each variable, 1970–2005*

	I. Protection of shareholder against board and management	France		Germany		UK		US	
		Mean	St. dev.	Mean	St. dev.	Mean	St. dev.	Mean	St. dev.
1	Powers of the general meeting	1.00		1.00		1.00		0.50	
2	Powers of the general meeting	1.00		1.00		1.00		0.50	
3	Powers of the general meeting	1.00		1.00		0.86	0.23	0.50	
4	Powers of the general meeting	0.00		0.33	0.24	0.58	0.50	0.75	
5	Powers of the general meeting	0.50		0.50		0.50		0.00	
6	Powers of the general meeting	1.00		0.50		1.00		1.00	
7	Powers of the general meeting	1.00		0.00		0.86	0.23	0.50	
8	Agenda-setting power	1.00		0.50		0.50		1.00	
9	Agenda-setting power	1.00		1.00		1.00		1.00	
10	Agenda-setting power	1.00		1.00		0.00		0.00	
11	Extraordinary shareholder meeting	0.62	0.18	1.00		0.50		0.00	
12	Extraordinary shareholder meeting	0.00		1.00		1.00		0.00	
13	Anticipation of shareholder decision	0.32	0.24	0.60	0.20	0.75		1.00	
14	Anticipation of shareholder decision	0.56	0.50	0.06	0.16	0.50		1.00	
15	Anticipation of shareholder decision	0.00		0.04	0.14	0.00		0.34	0.13
16	Information in the run-up to the general meeting	0.50		1.00		0.75		1.00	
17	Information in the run-up to the general meeting	0.25	0.25	0.33	0.24	1.00		1.00	
18	Shares not blocked before general meeting	0.56	0.16	1.00		1.00		1.00	
19	Individual information rights	0.31	0.25	1.00		0.00		0.00	
20	Individual information rights	0.42	0.38	0.00		0.00		0.00	
21	Communication with other shareholders	1.00		0.86	0.35	0.50		0.79	0.25

22	Communication with other shareholders	1.00		1.00		1.00		0.19	0.25
23	Board composition	0.53	0.09	1.00		0.17	0.27	0.33	0.24
24	Board composition	0.04	0.14	0.06	0.16	0.13	0.24	0.33	0.24
25	Board composition	0.06	0.21	0.06	0.16	0.30	0.42	0.54	0.32
26	No excessive remuneration for non-executive or executive directors	0.50		0.50		0.53	0.08	0.50	0.09
27	No excessive remuneration for non-executive or executive directors	0.37	0.26	0.29	0.14	0.56	0.16	0.63	0.17
28	No excessive remuneration for non-executive or executive directors	0.00		1.00		0.00		0.00	
29	Performance-based remuneration	0.53	0.51	0.22	0.42	0.28	0.45	1.00	
30	Duration of director's appointment	0.10	0.20	0.06	0.16	0.50		1.00	
31	Duration of director's appointment	0.92	0.12	0.00		0.67	0.15	0.50	
32	Director's duties	1.00		0.50		0.49	0.31	0.74	0.22
33	Director's duties	1.00		1.00		1.00		1.00	
34	Director's duties	0.52	0.07	0.11	0.21	0.30	0.21	0.54	0.09
35	Shareholder supremacy	0.50		0.50		0.50		0.50	
36	Shareholder supremacy	0.62	0.13	0.07	0.18	1.00		0.38	0.12
37	Pre-emptive rights	1.00		1.00		1.00		0.00	
38	Director's disqualification	0.29	0.25	0.36	0.23	0.69	0.38	0.56	0.16
39	Corporate governance code	0.04	0.14	0.11	0.32	0.36	0.49	0.11	0.32
40	Public enforcement of law	0.00		0.00		0.00		0.00	
41	Public enforcement of law	0.00		0.00		0.00		0.00	
42	Public enforcement of law	0.50		0.00		0.50		0.50	
	II. Protection against other shareholders								
43	Quorum	0.83	0.25	0.00		0.00		1.00	
44	Supermajority rights	1.00		1.00		1.00		0.53	0.08
45	One share one vote	1.00		1.00		1.00		1.00	

Table 2.1 (continued)

	II. Protection against other shareholders	France		Germany		UK		US	
		Mean	St. dev.	Mean	St. dev.	Mean	St. dev.	Mean	St. dev.
46	One share one vote	0.50		0.43	0.19	0.00		0.83	0.24
47	One share one vote	0.00		0.19	0.38	0.00		0.83	0.24
48	Cumulative voting	0.00		0.00		0.00		0.00	
49	Voting by interested shareholders prohibited	0.07	0.18	0.50		0.50		0.42	0.19
50	No squeeze out (freeze out)	0.67	0.48	0.86	0.35	0.00		0.00	
51	Right to exit	0.24	0.25	0.00		0.00		0.25	
52	Right to exit	0.43	0.48	0.14	0.35	1.00		0.00	
53	Right to exit	0.00		0.00		0.00		0.00	
54	Disclosure of major share ownership	0.40	0.38	0.42	0.24	0.87	0.13	0.75	
55	Oppressed minority	0.50		0.72	0.25	0.86	0.23	0.58	0.19
56	Oppressed minority	1.00		1.00		1.00		1.00	
57	Shareholder Protection is mandatory	1.00		1.00		1.00		0.44	0.50
58	Shareholder Protection is mandatory	1.00		1.00		0.50		0.00	
59	Shareholder Protection is mandatory	0.00		1.00		0.00		1.00	
60	Shareholder Protection is mandatory	1.00		1.00		0.47	0.12	0.06	0.16
	ALL	32.2	3.7	31.8	2.7	31.5	3.8	29.9	1.6
	Board and management (1–42)	22.5	3.1	21.6	2.0	23.3	3.4	21.2	1.9
	Minority shareholders (43–60)	9.6	0.7	10.3	0.6	8.2	0.4	8.7	0.9

Note: * Standard deviation is shown only when it is not equal to zero (a change occurs over time). See Appendix for exact definitions of the variables in the table.

If there is interest in diversifying ownership, one might expect to see more of an increase in the area of protection against other shareholders in France and Germany, where ownership is traditionally considered less dispersed. This is to some extent supported by the data, since fewer variables in this category change in the UK than in Germany and France, but the same cannot be said about the US. Perhaps unexpectedly, the number of variables with a change has been higher in the two countries where the legal system is traditionally considered more rigid (France, Germany).

In the interest of space, correlations between the legal variables over time in each country are not shown. However, such an analysis reveals some interesting features. In the UK, the correlation between all variables is positive. With the exception of one change in 2005 (director's liability – duty of care), changes in any area of SP have always been positive, and the level of protection has not fallen. This is in contrast with the US, where there are a number of negative correlations, which suggests that SP has risen in some areas and fallen in others. Areas where protection has fallen at any point in time in the US relate to excessive remuneration of CEOs, director's duties, shareholder supremacy, one share-one vote, oppressed minority and mandatory SP. The last three belong to the category of protection against other shareholders, which could be particularly important from a minority shareholder viewpoint. In other areas of law, change has been positive.

France and Germany are intermediate cases, where some negative correlation between variables is observed. Additionally, particularly in Germany, there have been a number of simultaneous changes in SP. In Germany, protection has fallen at any point in time in law that relates to squeeze out, oppressed minority and communication with other shareholders. In France, protection has fallen in the case of no squeeze out, duration of director's appointment and quorum.

2.2 Principal Component Analysis

Confronted with the dataset of 60 variables and only 36 years of observations, an economist's first impulse is to find ways of reducing the dimensionality of the data without sacrificing any essential information. In principle, PCA is ideally suited for this task. It can a) help reduce dimensionality; b) provide a deeper analysis of the structure of co-relations that the dataset contains and c) help with the construction of suitable index numbers for SP.

Principal components are weighted linear combinations of the data, but uncorrelated among themselves. The first component captures the largest share of overall variation in the data, the weights being assigned accordingly. The analysis utilizes either the covariance or correlation matrix of the original data matrix. In our case we have used the covariance matrix. Ideally, the derived components would have a clear interpretation, that is they would reflect a certain type of protection.

In our case, the principal component analysis could be illustrated as follows. We have data x_{ijt} for country $i=1, \ldots, N$, $N=4$, variable $j=1, 2, \ldots, J$, $J=60$, for year $t=1, 2, \ldots, T$, $T=36$ (1970–2005). We want to construct one or more, say R, index numbers as follows:

$$z_{irt} = \sum j a_{rj} x_{ijt} \tag{2.1}$$

where $z_i = X_i a$, z_i is a $T \times R$ matrix of indices, a is a $J \times R$ matrix and X_i is the $T \times J$ matrix for country i for the 60 variables.[1] If we wish to compare the levels of protection for different countries, we need the weights a_{rj} in equation (2.1) to be the same across countries. Alternatively, they could be country-specific, a_{irj} if the principal components analysis is carried out for each country separately. By inspecting the weights (loadings), it may be possible to give an interpretation to each principal component.

A complication of our dataset is that for many variables there is no variation over time within a country, so the rank of the $T \times J$ matrix X_i is $K_i < J$, where $J - K_i$ of the variables in that country do not vary. Since Principal Components (PCs) create indices that explain as much of the variance as possible, they will ignore the J–K variables that do not vary, since they do not contribute to the variance.

To remedy this we carry out PCA for all four countries together, so that weights a_{rj} are the same for each country. For this purpose, we stack the observations vertically to analyse a $(TN) \times J$ matrix $X = [X_1 / X_4]$. In this case, one variable has 144 observations (TN).

There is still the problem that any variable that does not vary either within or between countries, will have a zero weight, but there are far fewer of these than variables that do not vary within countries.

Thus PCA was carried out separately for each country as well as for all countries together. Through the PCA done for each country separately we find that the first three PCs capture most of the time variation in the data, since they together account for at least or over 90 per cent of the variation (see Table 2.2). However, it turned out to be impossible to identify a few variables out of the 60 that would drive variation and give the PCs a meaningful interpretation. It proved similarly difficult to provide a sensible, economic interpretation for the principal components of all countries together, even though the first five principal components accounted for 90 per cent of the total variation.

However, the PC analysis was not totally unproductive. It turns out that the weighted sum of the first three principal components (weighing each

Table 2.2 PCA country by country: Eigenvalues and cumulative proportion of variation explained

PC	Eigenvalue	% of Var. explained	Cum. % explained	Eigenvalue	% of Var. explained	Cum. % explained
		France			Germany	
First PC	1.48	76	76	0.99	72	72
Second PC	0.24	12	88	0.16	12	84
Third PC	0.10	5	93	0.12	8	92
		UK			US	
First PC	1.10	72	72	0.68	63	63
Second PC	0.25	16	88	0.22	20	83
Third PC	0.05	3	91	0.07	7	90

component with the share of variation explained) for individual countries, correlated very highly with the unweighted sum for all 60 variables, the main aggregation device used in this chapter (see the next section). The correlation coefficients were as follows: 0.96 for both France and Germany, 0.99 for the UK and 0.70 for the US. The same holds true of the correlation between the first PC and unweighted aggregate of all 60 variables (0.96 for France, 0.94 for Germany, 0.99 for the UK and 0.59 for the US). Thus, the unweighted sum of SP indicators appears to capture much of the same information as the PCs, and have the advantage that they can be given an interpretation.

2.3 Composing an Aggregate Index of Shareholder Protection

The task of comparing the level and movements in SP in the four countries is simplified if some aggregation procedure is used to arrive at a SP measure. In line with much of the literature, we used the unweighted sum of all variables as an aggregate index of SP. This index, as seen above, is effectively endorsed by the PCA analysis as well.[2]

Figure 2.1 highlights what a simple unweighted sum of all the 60 variables tells us about the level of SP in each country. The aggregate procedure used here assumes that all variables are equally important in explaining protection. This is unlikely to be the case, but assigning a priori weights was considered too arbitrary. France and the UK appear to have seen the largest rises in aggregate protection, starting from a lower level than the two others, but in the latter half of the 1980s climbing higher.

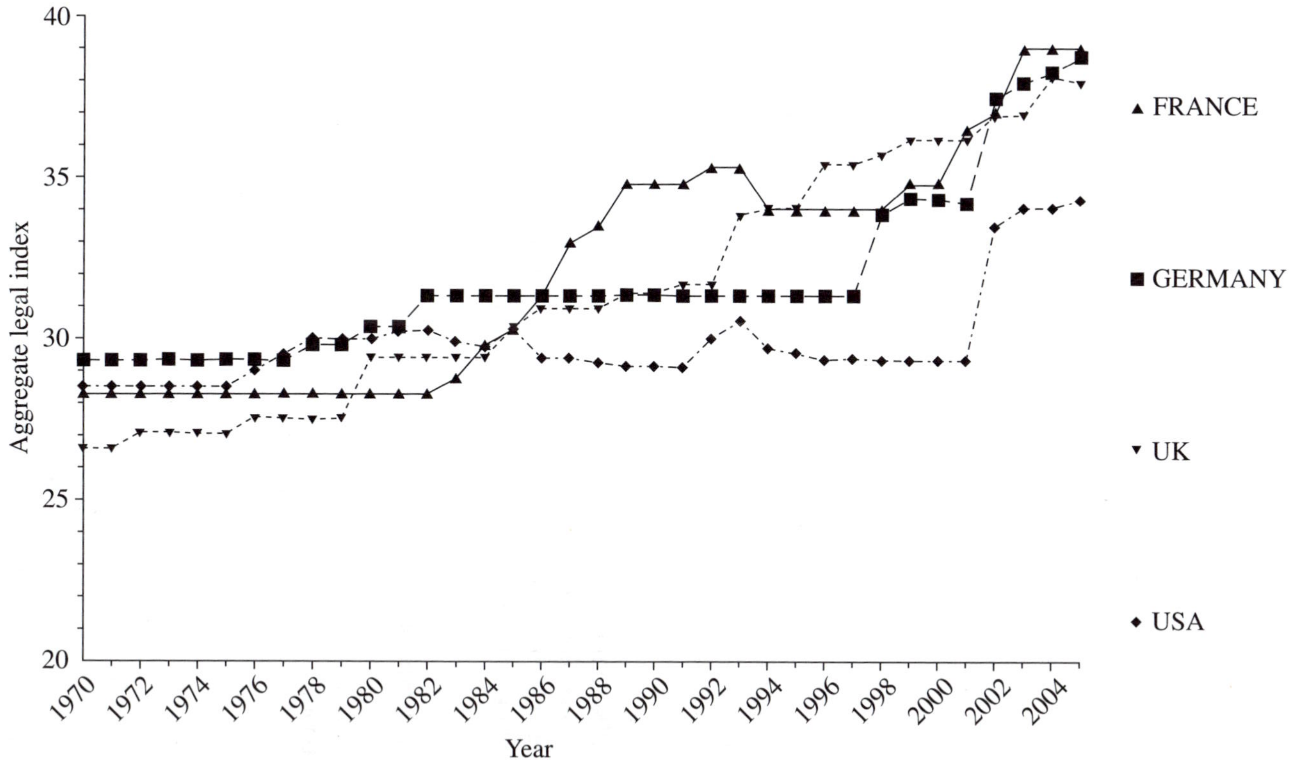

Figure 2.1 Shareholder Protection index, 1970–2005

Table 2.3 Correlation between different variants of protection

France	(a)	(b)	(c)
(a) All (Variables 1–60)	1.00		
(b) Board & Management (Variables 1–42)	0.99	1.00	
(c) Minority Shareholders (Variables 43–60)	0.82	0.74	1.00
Germany			
(a) All (Variables 1–60)	1.00		
(b) Board & Management (Variables 1–42)	0.99	1.00	
(c) Minority Shareholders (Variables 43–60)	0.96	0.94	1.00
UK			
(a) All (Variables 1–60)	1.00		
(b) Board & Management (Variables 1–42)	0.99	1.00	
(c) Minority Shareholders (Variables 43–60)	0.83	0.80	1.00
USA			
(a) All (Variables 1–60)	1.00		
(b) Board & Management (Variables 1–42)	0.89	1.00	
(c) Minority Shareholders (Variables 43–60)	−0.10	−0.54	1.00

Changes in Germany have been less pronounced until the late 1990s, when there are two notable hikes. In the US, the developments in SP have oscillated between rise and fall. The jump in year 2002 is driven mainly by changes in the rules on board composition and director's disqualification after negligent conduct due to the introduction of the controversial Sarbanes–Oxley Act.

We considered two sub-categories of protection by using unweighted sums of different variable combinations: 'protection against board and management' (aggregate of first 42 variables) and 'protection against other shareholders' or 'minority shareholder protection' (aggregate of other 18 variables). Figures 2.2 and 2.3 show the movements in these two sub-categories. Table 2.3 shows the correlation between the different indicators of protection. The correlations between the different variable combinations are generally fairly high and positive in each country, which means that different combinations may in fact give a rather similar picture of the development in SP over time. The clear exception is the US, where protection against other shareholders correlates negatively with other variables. Figure 2.3 shows that it has been falling on several occasions.

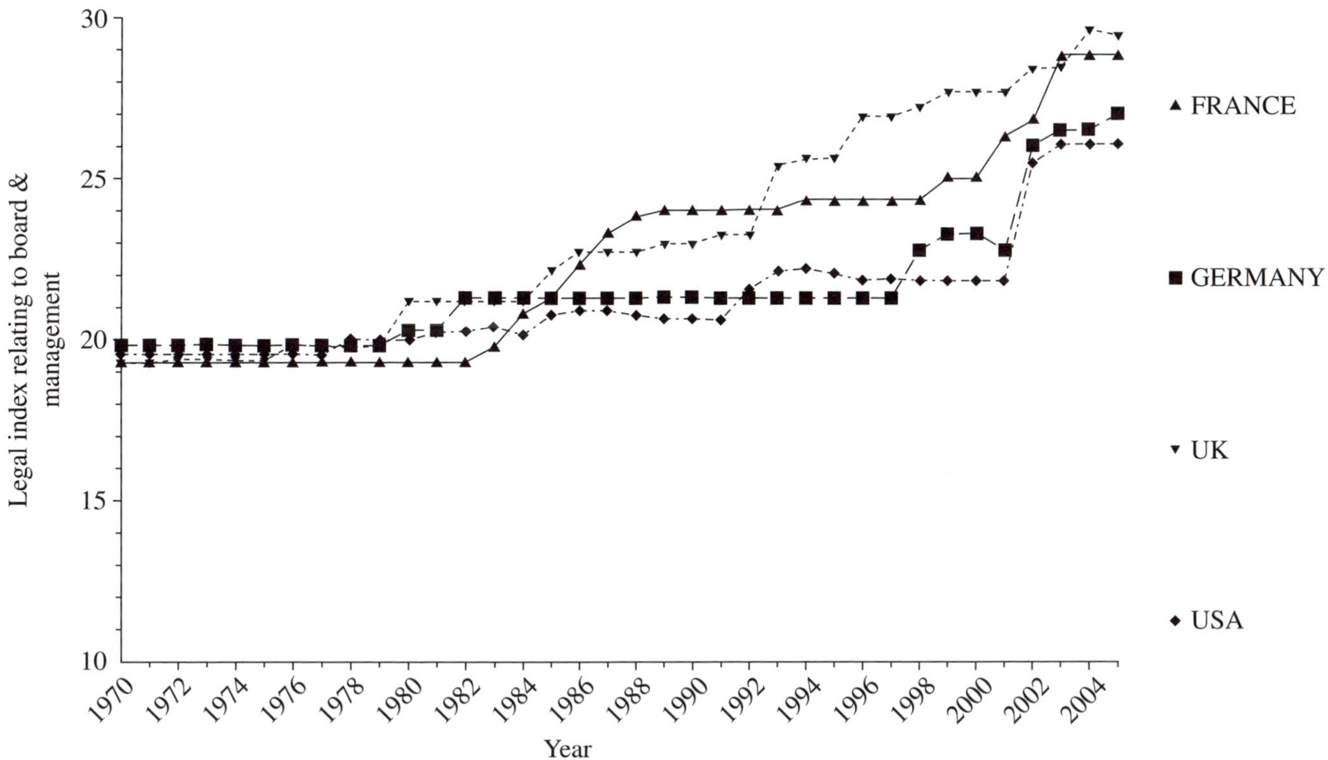

Figure 2.2 Shareholder protection index relating to board and management, 1970–2005

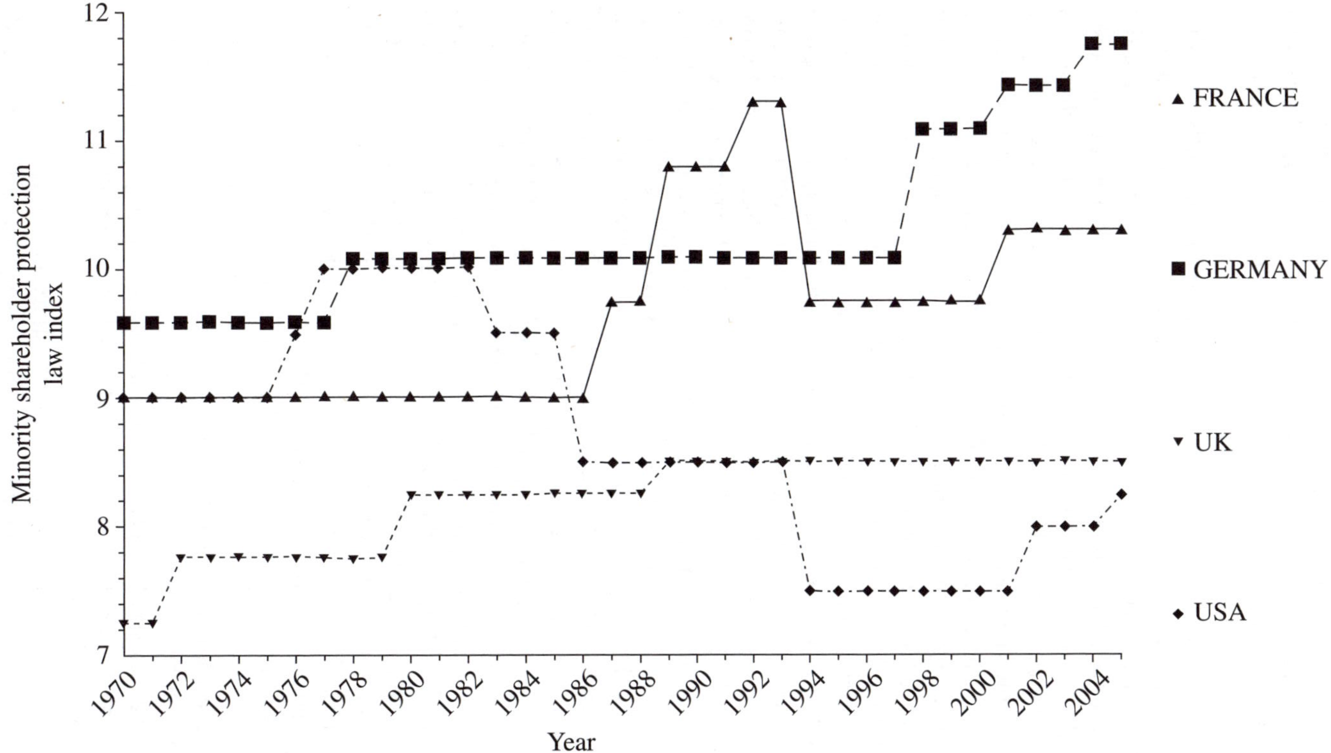

Figure 2.3 Minority shareholder protection index, 1970–2005

The four-country average of aggregate SP has increased during 1970–2005. This is also true for the average of the 42 legal variables relating to board and management, but average minority SP (aggregate of the rest of 18 variables) is stagnant (Figure 2.4).

We have seen that countries protect shareholders differently, but that changes in certain areas have occurred in all of the four countries. Have the levels of SP diverged or converged over time? One way to examine the variation between the four countries is by calculating the coefficient of variation for the values of each legal variable for each year. Due to major changes in the law in France and in the UK and later on in Germany (as shown in Figures 2.1 to 2.3), the coefficient of variation started to rise after the mid-1980s (Figure 2.5). There is some sign of convergence in protection against the board and management after 2002 but it may be too early to call it a trend of convergence. In the field of minority SP, there is a sign of growing divergence.

The original LLSV indicator of SP was based on only 6 variables, and is unlikely to provide an adequate picture of protection in a country. It is available for 49 countries, for a single year, and is calculated as an unweighted mean of several variables. The authors have improved the original indicators recently by constructing a directors' self-dealing index which considers more dimensions of SP and makes use of answers by legal experts to questionnaires (see Djankov et al., 2005). It is still only available for one year. Some of these aspects are also incorporated into the 60 variables used in this study.

Figure 2.1 illustrates that the 60 variable aggregate leads to a rather different conclusion than the one made by LLSV; the relative positions of countries in terms of protection change over time and the US and the UK, the common law countries, do not have a higher level of SP than France and Germany, the civil law countries. On the contrary, the US appears to have the lowest level of aggregate protection since the mid-1980s. Although the definitions of the variables included in our study differ and care was taken to incorporate not only statutory law, but also other aspects, Figure 2.6 shows what the LLSV index might look like if it were calculated with our data.[3] The resulting aggregate looks rather flat, and would provide an inadequate picture of the degree of SP.

The observations made above raise such questions as: why do countries such as France and Germany have a higher level of SP than the UK and US, where stock market development has reached a higher level? Is there an optimal level of protection that has been surpassed? Although the econometric analysis to come cannot fully answer such questions, it will provide some suggestions on the effects on protection on stock market development in the different countries.

The gulf between the cross-section and the time series results is best indicated by a table (Table 2.4) on the quinquennial estimates of the record of SP

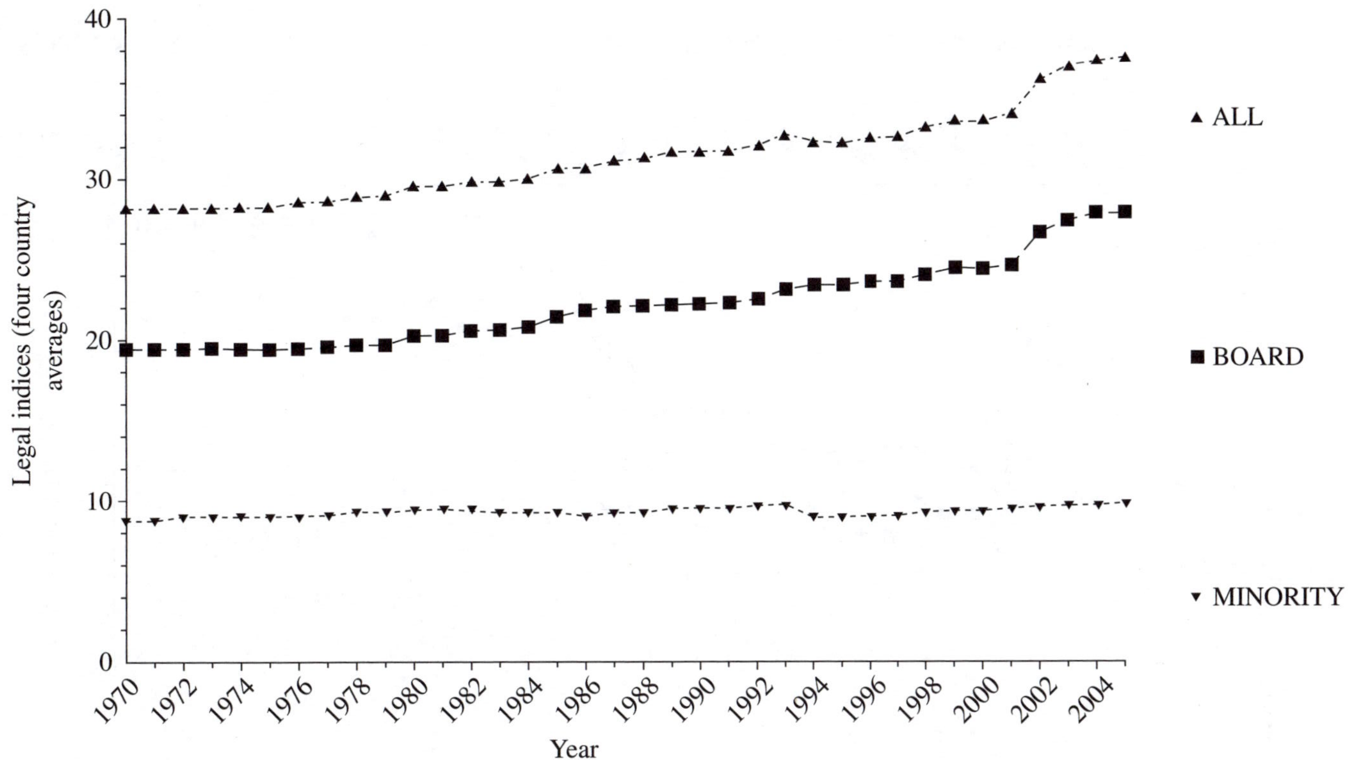

Figure 2.4 Average state of shareholder protection in France, Germany, UK and USA, 1970–2005

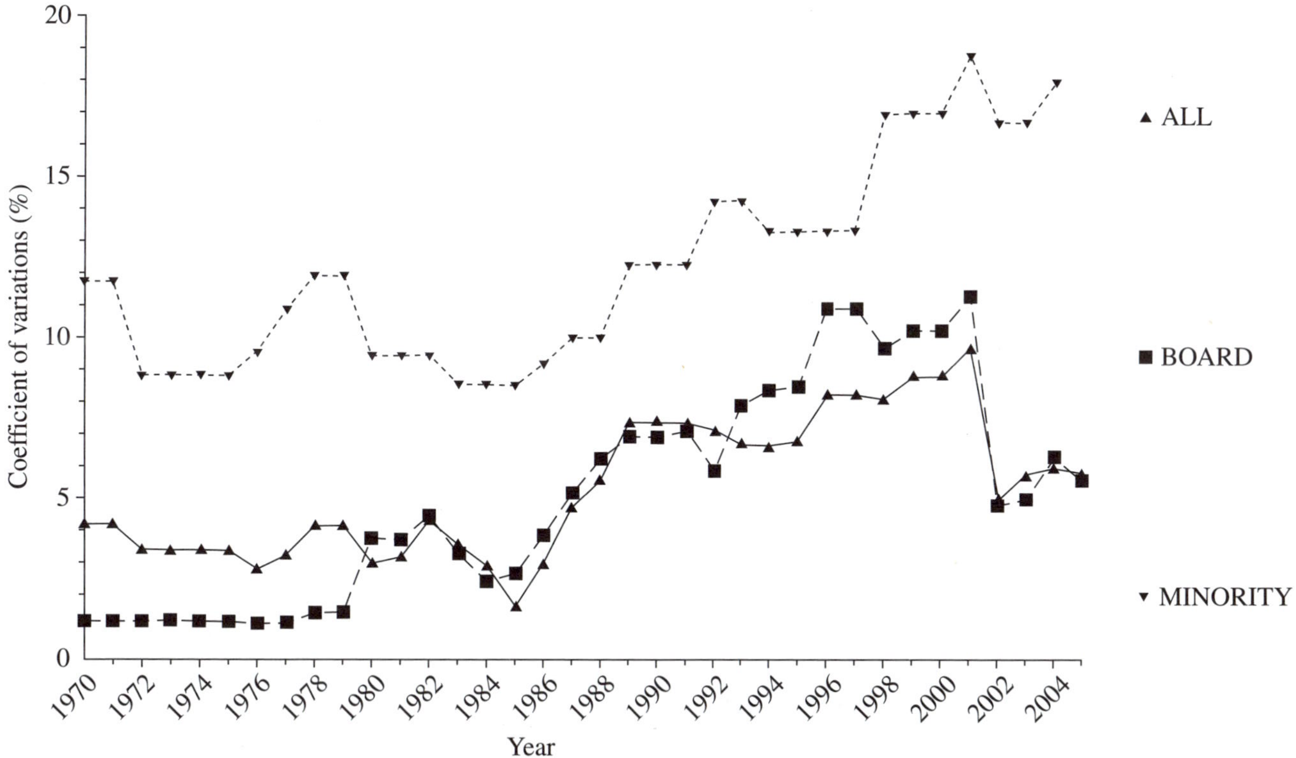

Figure 2.5 *Variations in shareholder protection law among France, Germany, UK and USA, 1970–2005*

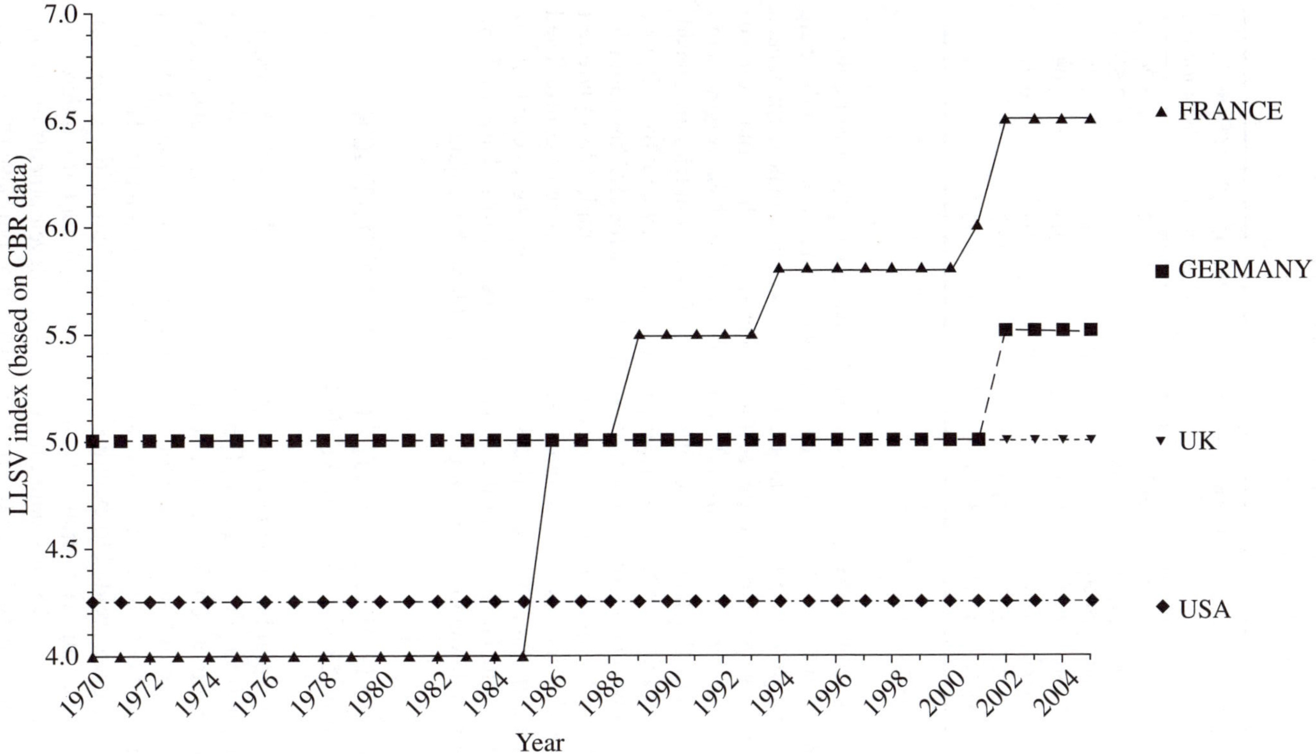

Figure 2.6 LLSV index of shareholder protection, 1970–2005

Table 2.4 Aggregate legal indices of shareholder protection, 1970–2005: 'original sin' countries

Period	USA	UK	Germany	France	Average of 4 countries	Coefficient of Variation (%)
1970–74	28.50	26.80	29.33	28.25	28.22	3.74
1974–79	29.40	27.40	29.53	28.25	28.65	3.53
1980–84	30.00	29.40	30.93	28.65	29.74	3.26
1985–89	29.50	30.88	31.33	32.55	31.06	4.09
1990–94	29.69	32.48	31.33	34.80	32.08	6.69
1995–99	29.39	35.30	32.43	34.15	32.82	7.83
2000–05	32.54	37.00	36.81	37.50	35.96	6.39

Source: Lele and Siems (2007).

observed at each five-year period over the 36-year time span of our dataset. There are seven observations for each country over this period. As these are five years apart the observations arguably are likely to be independent of each other. Comparing the rank order of the predicted with the actual outcome every five years, in all seven cases the predictions of the legal origin theory were rejected by the data. Further, if the Anglo-Saxon countries are considered together and compared with the combined civil law countries (France and Germany), at each of the seven five-year intervals the civil law countries had higher SP than the common law countries. The simple Chi-square test shows that the chances of seven out of seven predictions being contradicted by the data in each of the two cases through sampling fluctuation are extremely small. The null hypothesis that civil law countries have lower SP than common law countries is simply incompatible with the data.

3 SHAREHOLDER PROTECTION AND STOCK MARKET DEVELOPMENT

This section explains the econometric model used and discusses the results. Our concern is the development of the stock market, which is essentially a long-run phenomenon. So we have decided to look for a long-run relationship between shareholder protection and stock market development. Given the small number of countries, instead of pooling the data for all countries together, we have decided to examine the effects of shareholder protection in each of the countries separately, since these are potentially different in the four countries. We have data on stock market development[4] and stock market turnover ratio,[5] over the period 1976–2005, but have data on the legal variables over the period 1970–2005. However, there is only one change in all of the legal variables prior to 1976. So our period of analysis (1976–2005) does not miss much.

With the exception of the US, movements in SP have by and large been positive. Stock market turnover ratio has also risen. This is clearly the case for France and the US (see Figure 2.7), and lately for the UK as well. The German series has an oscillating pattern, with no clear rise in the turnover ratio since the mid-1980s.

As explained earlier, we have decided to use simple unweighted sums of the variables to construct an aggregate measure of shareholder protection. However, we feel that it is important to test whether the two main categories, protection against board and management and protection against other shareholders have different effects. Germany and France are traditionally considered to have more concentrated equity holding, and thus changes in the protection for minority shareholders might produce larger effects than in the UK and the US, where ownership on aggregate is already more dispersed. However, one could also argue that due to such ownership structures, changes in minority protection might be more relevant in the UK and US than in France and Germany.

3.1 Modelling Approach

To examine the long-term relationship between two variables it has now become standard practice to test the stationarity of the variables. Out of all the tests of stationarity, augmented Dickey–Fuller (ADF) tests are the most popular, with many well-known advantages and disadvantages. However, choosing the appropriate order of the ADF test is another problem and different methods of choosing the lag structure of an ADF equation often give different results. Moreover, the distribution of the ADF test statistic is asymptotically true and so the conclusion drawn on the basis of this test for a small sample may not be correct.

Following the methodology followed by Sarkar (2005) we have used the data-dependent General-to-specific (GS) criterion (details in note to Table 2.5) to choose the optimum lag structure of the error process of the Dickey–Fuller equation. The GS criterion is considered to be superior to any predetermined (fixed) lag structure and is also said to be better than various parsimonious information criteria (see Ng and Perron, 1995 and Perron, 1997).

Furthermore, to tackle the problem of small sample the wild bootstrapping method (1000 simulations) is used (with the aid of the EASYREG program) to derive the true probability value of the ADF statistic estimated in each case.

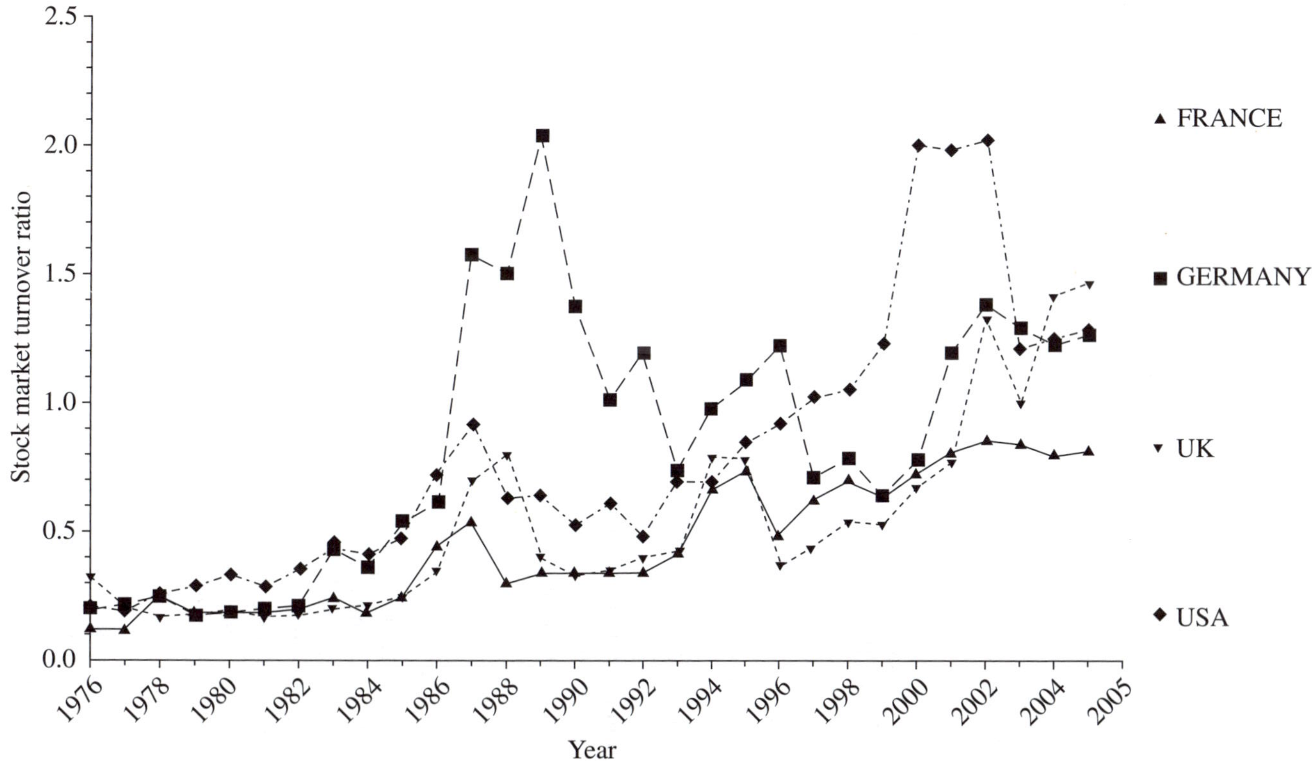

Figure 2.7 Stock market turnover ratio in France, Germany, UK and USA, 1976–2005

Table 2.5 Tests of stationarity of the legal indexes, turnover ratio and nominal GDP, 1976–2005: selected countries

Country/Variables	DF/ADF Statistics[a,b,c]
France	
All (Variables 1–60)	−2.981**(2)
Board & Management (Variables 1–42)	−3.8107**(2)
Minority Shareholders (Variables 43–60)[d]	−1.5814(0)
Turnover Ratio – log values	−4.8996**(1)
Nominal GDP – log values	−4.3709**(0)
Germany	
All (Variables 1–60)[d]	0.9491(4)
Board & Management (Variables 1–42)[d]	1.0616(4)
Minority Shareholders (Variables 43–60)[d]	−0.0422(0)
Turnover Ratio – log values[d]	−1.5773(0)
Nominal GDP – log values[d]	−1.5725(1)
UK	
All (Variables 1–60)	−3.5671**(0)
Board & Management (Variables 1–42)	−3.1126**(0)
Minority Shareholders (Variables 43–60)[d]	−2.3249(0)
Turnover Ratio – log values	−3.1977**(0)
Nominal GDP – log values	−4.7444**(0)
USA	
All (Variables 1–60)[d]	−0.3908(0)
Board & Management (Variables 1–42)[d]	0.0788(0)
Minority Shareholders (Variables 43–60)[d]	−1.0842(0)
Turnover Ratio – log values	−2.4443*(0)
Nominal GDP – log values	−3.8948**(0)

Notes:

a The data-dependent General-to-specific (GS) criterion is used to choose the optimum lag structure of the error process of the Dickey–Fuller equation as advocated by Ng and Perron (1995) and Perron (1997). Under this process, the specific order is chosen out of the general order (we considered here maximum 5 lags) on the basis of the standard t-tests of significance of the lag terms. For instance, if out of 5 lag terms, the 4th lag term is statistically significant but all higher order lag terms are insignificant, we run a 4th order ADF equation and check whether the 4th order lag is significant. If now (say) the 3rd order lag term is significant but the 4th order lag term is insignificant, we fit a 3rd order ADF equation and check the significance of the 3rd order lag term. If the 3rd order lag term is significant, the appropriate ADF model is taken to be of 3rd order. If not, the process continues until we arrive at the zero-order ADF (i.e. DF) equation.

b The null hypothesis of unit root is tested against the trend-stationary alternative. In some cases we have considered mean-stationary alternative marked by d. To tackle the problem of a small sample, we accept or reject the null hypothesis on the basis of 1000 simulations through a bootstrapping method (the errors have been drawn from normal distribution with zero mean and variances squared OLS residuals).

c The order of the test statistic is in parentheses.

d The null hypothesis is unit root tested against mean-stationarity.

** The unit root hypothesis is rejected at 5 per cent level.

* The unit root hypothesis is rejected at 10 per cent level.

This procedure shows (Table 2.5) that the indicator of share market developments such as (log-values of) stock market turnover ratio is trend-stationary for all the countries except Germany.

As for the different aggregates of legal indices considered here, all the categories and the sub-categories for Germany and the USA exhibited non-stationarity because of a number of structural shifts (as can be observed from Figures 2.1 to 2.3). For France and the UK, all the legal variable series except the index for minority SP are trend-stationary (the non-stationarity of the latter is also due to structural shifts as can be observed from Figure 2.3).[6]

In view of these mixed results, we shall use the Autoregressive Distributive Lag (ARDL) approach to cointegration developed by Pesaran and colleagues (Pesaran and Shin, 1999, Pesaran et al., 2001) to ascertain the existence of a long-run relationship between stock market capitalization and different categories of legal indexes governing the share market. This approach accommodates both stationary variables and ones with a unit root. To take into account the level of economic activities of a country as a possible factor influencing the stock market behaviour we have also considered (log-values of) nominal GDP[7] in the ARDL model. These are trend-stationary for all the countries except Germany.

The following ARDL (p, q, r) equation has been fitted with the aid of the MICROFIT programme:

$$X_t = \alpha + \beta t + \sum_{i=1}^{p} \gamma_i X_{t-i} + \sum_{j=0}^{q} \chi_j Y_{t-j} + \sum_{k=0}^{r} \delta_k Z_{t-k} \qquad (2.2)$$

where α is the intercept, β is the coefficient of time, t, X refer to the log values of stock market turnover ratio, Y represents the log value of GDP in local currency and Z represents different legal indices – the sum of all the 60 indicators, the sum of first 42 indicators (concerning the protection against board and management) and the sum of the remaining 18 indicators (concerning the protection against other shareholders). Only one legal index is used per model. Subscripts t, $t-i$, $t-j$, $t-k$ ($i = 1, 2, 3 \ldots p$, $j = 1, 2, 3 \ldots q$ and $k = 1, 2, 3, \ldots r$) indicate different time periods and p, q and r are the lags to be determined.

Following the suggestion of Pesaran and Shin (1999) we have used the Schwarz Bayesian criterion (SBC) to determine the lag-structure of the ARDL (p, q, r) model. The estimates of the long-term coefficients of the legal variables and GDP are reported in Table 2.6.

The basic conclusion that emerges is that on the whole increases in SP do not appear to have a positive link with stock market development as reflected in stock market turnover ratio, irrespective of whether the countries are common law or otherwise. On the contrary, we do find a

Table 2.6 Long-run relationships between shareholder protection law indices and stock market turnover ratio, 1976–2005

Country & Variables	Estimates[1] of long-term coefficients (ARDL model in parentheses)					
	SP-all		SP-board		SP-minority	
France	(2,3,3)		(2,4,3)		(2,3,3)	
ln (GDP)	0.15		−0.02		0.25	
SP	−0.13**		−0.25**		−0.26**	
c	0.16		1.29		−1.23	
t	0.06**		0.1*		0.2*	
Germany	(1,0,0)	(0,0,0)	(1,0,0)	(0,0,0)	(1,0,0)	(0,3,0)
ln (GDP)	−0.48	−1.52	−0.38	−1.47	−0.77	−0.98
SP	0.09	0.05	0.11	0.06	0.54	0.4
c	0.71	−3.85	0.63	−3.97	0.5	−9.74
t		0.37**		0.37**		0.35**
d90		13.39**		13.31**		13.19**
sd90		−0.34**		−0.34**		−0.34**
UK	(0,3,3)		(0,3,3)		(0,5,4)	
ln (GDP)	−2.67*		−3.12*		11.54*	
SP	−0.68**		−0.67**		−14.68**	
c	14.95*		10.71*		75.29**	
t	0.52**		0.54**		−0.53**	
USA	(1,0,0)		(1,0,0)		(1,0,0)	
ln (GDP)	1.24**		1.46**		0.52	
SP	0.1		0.12		−0.33	
c	−8.09**		−10.46**		−2.02	
t						

Note:
* Significant at 5 per cent level (based on asymptotic standard errors).
** Significant at 1 per cent level (based on asymptotic standard errors.
1 The following ARDL (p, q, r) equation has been fitted with the aid of the MICROFIT programme to get the long-run relationship between stock market turnover ratio and the legal variables:

$$X_t = \alpha + \beta t + \sum_{i=1}^{p} \gamma_i X_{t-i} + \sum_{j=0}^{q} \chi_j Y_{t-j} + \sum_{k=0}^{r} \delta_k Z_{t-k}$$

where α is the intercept, β is the coefficient of time, t, X refer to the log values of stock market turnover ratio, Y represents the log values of GDP in local currency and Z represents different legal indices – the sum of all the 60 indicators, the sum of first 42 indicators (concerning the protection against board and management) and the sum of the remaining 18 indicators (concerning the protection against other shareholders). Only one legal index is used per model. Subscripts t, $t-i$, $t-j$, $t-k$ (i =1,2,3. . . p, j= 1,2,3. . . q and k =1,2,3, . . . r) indicate different time periods and p, q and r are the lags. The lag-structure is determined on the basis of Schwartz Bayesian criterion (SBC) and is reported in parentheses. In view of data limitation, the maximum value of the lag considered here is 5.

If the coefficient of time is found insignificant, it is dropped (details of those models are skipped) and the ARDL equation is re-estimated. For Germany, intercept and slope dummies (d90 and sd90, respectively) are added to the ARDL equation to take into account the phenomenon of German unification: d90=0 for 1976–1989 and =1 for 1990–2005; sd90=d90*t varies accordingly. We have also tried dummies for 1991–2005 and the basic conclusion remains unaltered (details are not reported here).

significantly negative relationship between different components of the SP and turnover ratio for both France and the UK. For Germany and the USA we find no relationship.

For Germany our result may be influenced by the phenomenon of the fall of the Berlin Wall (in 1990) and the subsequent German unification (for instance we cannot be sure of what adjustments have been made in the data for stock market capitalization, stock trade and GDP). In order to control for this, we added intercept and time-slope dummies (for the period 1990/91–2005) to the ARDL equation and observed that our finding of no relationship holds (both dummies are statistically significant).

A further interesting aspect of our analysis is that in many of the estimated models, we fail to find a significant direct link between the level of economic activities (as indicated by GDP) and stock market development (as indicated by the turnover ratio). For the USA, however, a positive relationship is found in two out of the three models reported here and for the UK we even get a negative relationship (!) in two models. This requires further investigation beyond the scope of the present chapter.

Thus our ARDL approach casts serious doubt on the proposition that better SP and higher stock market activities are positively linked even in four major developed countries – the so-called legal-origin 'mother' countries. In another study Sarkar (2007) observed no relationship between SP and stock market development in a less developed country such as India over the same period. Perhaps this observation can be generalized for many other developed and less developed countries.

Another issue that is not addressed here but dealt with elsewhere is the lack of long-term relationship between stock market development and growth through capital accumulation (see Sarkar, 2006 and 2007).

4 SUMMARY AND CONCLUSION

Since La Porta et al. (1998) published a study on the effects of legal origin on SP and financial development, these topics have received considerable attention from economists. What the above-mentioned authors captured was a snapshot of the state of regulation in one period in time, and comprehensive time series datasets on legal developments in SP in different countries have been lacking. The research project that this chapter relates to has produced a novel, comprehensive time series dataset of SP consisting of 60 annual legal indicators for the period 1970–2005 for France, Germany, the UK and the US. We have used this dataset to examine annual developments in SP in these countries and reassessed the relationship between legal and stock market development as well as the claims that common law countries have better SP than civil law countries.

If overall SP is measured by an unweighted sum of all of the variables, we see that the relative positions of countries change over time and the common perception that civil law countries (France, Germany) have lower levels of protection than common law countries (US, UK) does not hold. Germany starts out with the highest level of protection, and the UK with the lowest, but towards the end of the period France climbs to the highest position, and the US has the lowest level of protection. Protection for minority shareholders has been stronger in France and Germany than in both the UK and the US since the mid-1980s. With the exception of the US, movements in SP have been mainly positive. Principal component analysis is discussed as an alternative aggregation procedure to unweighted sums in the construction of an indicator of overall protection.

The econometric analysis in this chapter attempts to find long-run relationships between stock market development and SP, separately for each country using annual data for the period 1976–2005. Given the concerns with short time series, we have opted for a simple testing procedure, starting out by examining whether a long-run relationship exists between stock market development indicators such as the stock market turnover ratio and SP. The ARDL method for testing for cointegration is the main tool used. Our study casts serious doubts on a positive long-term relationship between laws protecting shareholders and stock market activity.

NOTES

* It is a pleasure to present this chapter to Dennis Mueller on the occasion of his retirement from his Chair in Vienna. One of us (Singh) has known Dennis for the last thirty years; has collaborated with him on a number of projects over these years; has had many conversations with him; mostly agreed with him but also on occasion disagreed with him. Dennis is the scholars' scholar and has made path-breaking contributions to several fields, including specifically the theory of the firm and the theory of industrial organization. May he continue to be as productive in the future as he has been in the past. This chapter forms a part of the larger ESRC project on Law, Finance and Development at the Centre for Business Research in Cambridge. We are grateful to Professor Ron Smith for valuable comments and to Mathias Siems and Priya Lele for providing us with the data and helpful comments; and to Simon Deakin and John Armor for many useful conversations. However the usual disclaimer applies.

1. Since principal components are not invariant to units of measurement, it is common to standardize the data before calculating it, that is to use the correlation matrix rather than the covariance matrix. In this case, the measures have common units, between 0 and 1, with 1 indicating full regulation, so it seems more sensible not to standardize and to use the covariance matrix.

2. See, however, Pesaran and Smith (2006).
3. The variables included are the legal indices numbering 11, 14, 18, 37, 45, 48, 51 and 56.
4. The data source for stock market turnover ratio is the Financial Structure Dataset of World Bank (see Beck et al., 2000).
5. Stock market turnover ratio is the ratio of the value of total shares traded to average real market capitalization. In our data collected directly from the Financial Structure Dataset, it is calculated using the following method: $T_t/P\_a_t/\{(0.5)^*[Mt/P\_e_t + M_{t-1}/P\_e_{t-1}]$ where T is total value traded, M is stock market capitalization, P_e is end-of period CPI, P_a is average annual CPI.
6. We could have tried Perron tests in view of structural shifts in some variables and might have observed some more variables to be stationary. The methodology followed here and described later does not require ascertaining whether the variables are I (0), I (1) or I (2). So the knowledge of the stationarity property is just a matter of academic interest.
7. The data source for nominal GDP (in local currency) is International Financial Statistics, IMF (available online).

REFERENCES

Beck, Thorsten, Asli Demirgüç-Kunt and Ross Levine (2000), 'A new database on financial development and structure', *World Bank Economic Review*, **14**, 597–605.

Beck, Thorsten, Asli Demirgüç-Kunt and Ross Levine (2003), 'Law and finance: why does legal origin matter?', *Journal of Comparative Economics*, **31** (4), 653–75.

Beck, Thorsten, Asli Demirgüç-Kunt and Ross Levine (2005), 'Law and firms' access to finance', *American Law and Economics Review*, **7**(1), 211–52.

Djankov, S., R. La Porta, F. Lopez de Silanes and A. Shleifer (2005), 'The law and economics of self-dealing', *NBER Working Paper* No. W11883.

La Porta, R., F. Lopez-de-Silanes, A. Shleifer and R.W. Vishny (1998), 'Law and finance', *Journal of Political Economy*, **106**(6), 1113–55.

Lele, P. and M. Siems (2007), 'Shareholder protection: a leximetric approach', *Journal of Corporate Law Studies*, **7**(1), 17–50.

Ng, S. and P. Perron (1995), 'Unit root test in ARMA models with data-dependent methods for the selection of the truncation lag', *Journal of the American Statistical Association*, **90**(429), 268–81.

Pagano, M. and P. Volpin (2006), 'Shareholder protection, stock market development, and politics', *Journal of the European Economic Association*, **4**, 315–41.

Perron, P. (1997), 'Further evidence on breaking trend functions in macroeconomic variables', *Journal of Econometrics*, **80**(2), 355–85.

Pesaran, M.H. and Y. Shin (1999), 'An autoregressive distributed lag modelling approach to cointegration analysis', in S. Strom (ed.), *Econometrics and Economic Theory in the 20th Century: The Ragnar Frisch Centennial Symposium*, Cambridge: Cambridge University Press, pp. 371–413.

Pesaran, M.H. and R. Smith (2006), 'Macroeconometric modeling with a global perspective', *The Manchester School*, **74**(Supplement 1), 24–49.

Pesaran, M.H., Y. Shin and R.J. Smith (2001), 'Bounds testing approaches to the analysis of level relationships', *Journal of Applied Econometrics*, **16**(3), 289–326.

Rajan, R.G. and L. Zingales (2003), 'The great reversals: the politics of financial development in the twentieth century', *Journal of Financial Economics*, **69**(1), 5–50.

Sarkar, Prabirjit (2005), 'Rising manufacture exports and terms of trade: the case study of Korea', *Progress in Development Studies*, **5**(2), 83–8.

Sarkar, Prabirjit (2006), 'Stock market development and capital accumulation in less developed countries', *Working Paper No. 06–06*: Jadavpur University, Kolkata-700032, India (available online at http://ssrn.com/abstract=952154).

Sarkar, Prabirjit (2007), 'Stock market development and capital accumulation: does law matter? A case study of India', paper presented at Queens Seminar (University of Cambridge, 6 February, 2007) available online at http://ssrn.com/abstract=963171.

APPENDIX

Table 2A.1 Shareholder Protection index (variables)

Variables	Description[1]
I. Protection against board and management	
1. Powers of the general meeting[2]	The following variables equal 0 if there is no power of the general meeting and 1 if there is a power of the general meeting. (1) Amendments of articles of association (2) Mergers and divisions (3) Capital measures[3] (4) De facto changes: The decisive thresholds are the sale of substantial assets of the company (e.g., if the sale of more than 50% requires approval of the general meeting it equals 1; if more than 80%, it equals 0.5; and otherwise 0) (5) Dividend distributions: Equals 1 if the general meeting can effectively influence the amount of dividend (e.g., if it decides about the annual accounts and the annual dividend, and if the board has no significant possibility of 'manipulating' the accounts); equals 0.5 if there is some participation of the general meeting; equals 0 if it is only the board that decides about the dividend. (6) Election of board of directors (7) Directors' self-dealing of substantial transactions
2. Agenda-setting power[4]	(8) General topics: Equals 1 if shareholders who hold 1% or less of the capital can put an item on the agenda; equals 0.5 if there is a hurdle of more than 1% but less than 10%; equals 0 otherwise. (9) Election of directors: as above (10) Costs: Equals 1 if shareholders do not have to pay for their proposals; equals 0 otherwise.
3. Extraordinary shareholder meeting[5]	(11) Right: Equals 1 if the minimum percentage of share capital to demand an extraordinary meeting is less than or equal to 5%; equals 0.5 if it is more than 5% but less or equal than 10%; equals 0 otherwise. (12) Enforcement: Equals 1 if shareholders can call the meeting themselves or have a right that the court will enforce it; equals 0 if the court has discretion.
4. Anticipation of shareholder decision	(13) Restrictions on proxy voting: Equals 0 if there are restrictions on who can be appointed or which rights the proxy has so that it is likely that proxy voting does usually not take place; equals 0.5 if there are some restrictions which reduce the relevance of proxy voting; equals 1 if there are no restrictions. (14) Anticipation facilitated: Equals 1 if postal voting or

Table 2A.1 (continued)

Variables		Description[1]
		proxy solicitation with two-way voting proxy form has to be provided by the company; equals 0.5 if two-way proxy form has to be provided but not proxy solicitation; equals 0 otherwise.
	(15)	Costs of proxy contest: Equals 1 if the costs of proxy solicitations are paid by the company or if proxies have the right to have their proposals included in the company's proxy form; equals 0 otherwise.
5. Information in the run-up to the general meeting	(16)	Amendments of the articles of association: Equals 1 if the exact wording has to be sent in advance ('push-system'); equals 0.5 if the shareholders have to request it ('pull-system'); equals 0 otherwise.
	(17)	Mergers: Equals 1 if a special report has to be sent in advance ('push-system'); equals 0.5 if the shareholders have to request it ('pull-system'); equals 0 otherwise.
6. Shares not blocked before general meeting	(18)	Equals 0 if shareholders have to deposit their shares prior to the general meeting and if this has the consequence that shareholders are prevented from selling their shares for a number of days; equals 1 otherwise.
7. Individual information rights	(19)	Right to demand information (1): equals 1 if an individual shareholder or shareholders with 5% or less capital can demand information which will be answered at the general meeting; equals 0.5 if shareholders with 10% or less capital have this right; equals 0 otherwise.
	(20)	Right to demand information (2): equals 1 if an individual shareholder or shareholders with 5% or less capital can demand information independent of the general meeting; equals 0.5 if shareholders with 10% or less capital have this right; equals 0 otherwise.
8. Communication with other shareholders	(21)	Right to access the register of shareholders and (if necessary) beneficial owners: Equals 1 if the right of inspection can be used by a single shareholder; equals 0 if there is no such right.
	(22)	Equals 1 if communication is not affected by proxy rules; equals 0 otherwise.
9. Board composition	(23)	Division between management and control: Equals 1 if there is a two-tier system or at least half of the board members are non-executive; equals 0.5 if at least 25% of the board members are non-executive; equals 0 otherwise.
	(24)	Independent board members:[6] Equals 1 if at least half of the board members must be independent; equals 0.5 if at least 25% of them must be independent or if the independence requirement is very low; equals 0 otherwise.
	(25)	Committees: Equals 1 if companies have to install an audit and a remuneration committee with a majority of independent members; intermediate scores are possible if

Table 2A.1 (continued)

Variables	Description[1]
	the requirement is partial (for instance requires setting up of one of the committees or the independent members of the committees constitute less than a majority); equals 0 if committees are not necessary or if they are not required to have independent members.
10. No excessive remuneration for non-executive and executive directors	(26) General meeting power:[7] Equals 1 if the general meeting has to approve all compensation schemes; equals 0.5 if this is limited (e.g., applies to stock option plans only, or if some directors are excluded); equals 0 otherwise.
	(27) Annual disclosure: Equals 1 if there is full and specific disclosure about the individual remuneration of each director; equals 0.75 if there is information about the individual remuneration of some directors; equals 0.5 if there is disclosure about the top 2 directors (executives); equals 0.25 if there is only disclosure about the overall remuneration; equals 0 otherwise.
	(28) Substantive requirements placing limit for remuneration in order to protect shareholders: Equals 1 if there is a direct regulation; equals 0 otherwise
11. Performance-based remuneration	(29) Equals 1 if performance-based remuneration of directors and managers is fostered (e.g. facilitation of stock options to reward performance); equals 0 otherwise.
12. Duration of director's appointment	(30) Normal duration: Equals 1 if this is one year or less; 0 if this is 5 years or more; equals 0.5 if this is more than 1 but less than 5 years.
	(31) Dismissal feasible: Equals 1 if there are no special requirements; equals 0 if an important or good reason is required; intermediate scores are possible if there are no special requirements but there may be financial burden for the company (e.g. in the form of compensation under a statute or contract or damages for breach of contract or salary under a fixed term contract).
13. Director's duties[8]	(32) Director's liability – duty of care: Equals 0 if there are narrow criteria which virtually exclude liability; equals 0.5 if there are some restrictions (e.g., business judgement rule; gross negligence); equals 1 if there are no or little restrictions regarding business judgement and standard of care.
	(33) Director's liability – duty of loyalty: Equals 1 if there is a duty not to put personal interests ahead of the company; equals 0 otherwise.
	(34) Private enforcement: Equals 0 if this is typically excluded (e.g., because of strict subsidiarity requirement, hurdle which is at least 10%; cost rules); equals 0.5 if there are some restrictions (e.g., certain percentage of share capital (unless the hurdle is at least 10%); cost rules; demand requirement); equals 1 otherwise.

Table 2A.1 (continued)

Variables	Description[1]
14. Shareholder supremacy	(35) General principle: Equals 1 if the board always has to give priority to shareholders' interests; equals 0 if the board have to give priority to the interests of other stakeholders; equals 0.5 in other cases. (36) Takeover law: Equals 1 if there is the principle of strict neutrality in case of takeovers; equals 0.5 if the principle of neutrality is subject to exceptions; equals 0 otherwise.[9]
15. Pre-emptive right[10]	(37) Equals 1 when the law grants shareholders the first opportunity to buy new issues of shares, and this right can be waived only by the general meeting;[11] equals 0 otherwise.
16. Director's disqualification	(38) Equals 1 if negligent conduct can lead to disqualification; 0.5 if directors are disqualified only in specific instances of negligence (e.g., failure of financial reporting); equals 0 if negligent conduct itself is not sufficient for disqualification.
17. Corporate governance code	(39) Equals 1 if companies have to disclose and explain whether they comply with a corporate governance code; equals 0.5 if this is only recommended; equals 0 otherwise.
18. Public enforcement of company law	The following variables equal 0 if there is no power of public authority and 1 if public authority has power. (40) Authorization for director's self dealing of substantial transactions. (41) Authorization for appointment of managers. (42) Power to intervene in cases of prejudice to public interest or interest of the company for instance due to 'mismanagement of company' or in cases of oppression of shareholders.
II. Protection against other shareholders	
1. Quorum[12]	(43) Equals 1 if there is a 50% quorum for the extraordinary shareholder meeting (when it is called for the first time); equals 0.5 if the quorum is 1/3; equals 1/4 if the quorum is 1/4. Equals 0 otherwise.
2. Supermajority requirements	(44) Equals 1 if there are supermajority requirements (e.g., 2/3 or 3/4) for amendments of the articles of association, mergers and voluntary liquidations; equals 0 if they do not exist at all.
3. One share-one vote[13]	(45) Default rule: Equals 1 if this principle exists as a default rule; equals 0 otherwise. (46) Prohibition of multiple voting rights (super voting rights): Equals 1 if there is a prohibition; equals 2/3 if only companies which already have multiple voting rights can keep them; equals 1/3 if state approval is necessary; equals 0 otherwise.

Table 2A.1 (continued)

Variables	Description[1]
	(47) Prohibition of capped voting rights (voting right ceilings): Equals 1 if there is a prohibition; equals 2/3 if only companies which already have voting caps can keep them; equals 1/3 if state approval is necessary; equals 0 otherwise.
4. Cumulative voting	(48) Equals 1 if shareholders can cast all their votes for one candidate standing for election to the board of directors or if there exists a mechanism of proportional representation in the board by which minority interests may name a proportional number of directors to the board (default or mandatory law); equals 0 otherwise.
5. Voting by interested shareholders prohibited	(49) Equals 1 if a shareholder cannot vote if this vote favours him or her personally (i.e., only 'disinterested shareholders' can vote); equals 0 otherwise.
6. No squeeze out (freeze out)	(50) Equals 0 if a shareholder holding 90% or more can 'squeeze out' the minority; equals 1 otherwise.
7. Right to exit	(51) Appraisal rights: Equals 1 if they exist for mergers, amendments of the articles and sales of major company assets; equals 0 if they do not exist at all.
	(52) Mandatory bid: Equals 1 if there is a mandatory bid for the entirety of shares in case of purchase of 30% or 1/3 of the shares; equals 0 if there is no mandatory bid at all.
	(53) Mandatory public offer: Equals 1 if there is a mandatory public offer for purchase of 10% or less of the shares; equals 0.5 if the acquirer has to make a mandatory public offer for acquiring more than 10% but less than 30% of the shares; equals 0 otherwise.
8. Disclosure of major share ownership	(54) Equals 1 if shareholders who acquire at least 3% of the company's capital have to disclose it; equals 0.75 if this concerns 5% of the capital; equals 0.5 if this concerns 10%; equals 0.25 if this concerns 25%; equals 0 otherwise.
9. Oppressed minority	(55) Substantive law: Equals 0 if majority decisions of the general meeting have to be accepted by the outvoted minority; equals 1 if some kind of substantive control is possible (e.g., in cases of amendments to the articles of association, ratification of management misconduct, exclusion of the pre-emption right, related parties transactions, freeze outs); equals 0.5 if this control covers only flagrant abuses of majority power.
	(56) Shareholder action: Equals 1 if every shareholder can file a claim against a resolution by the general meeting because he or she regards it as void or voidable; equals 0.5 if there are hurdles such as a threshold of at least 10% voting rights or cost rules; equals 0 if this kind of shareholder action does not exist.

Table 2A.1 (continued)

Variables	Description[1]
10. Shareholder Protection is mandatory[14]	(57) Exclusion of director's duty of care (see variable 32) in articles: Equals 0 if possible and equals 1 otherwise.
	(58) Rules on duration of director's appointment (see variables 30 and 31): Equals 1 if mandatory and 0 otherwise.
	(59) Board composition (supervisory boards, non-executive directors) (see variables 23 and 24): Equals 1 if mandatory and 0 otherwise.
	(60) Other topics: equals 1 if there is the general rule that company law is mandatory; equals 0 if company law is in general just a 'model off the shelf'; equals 0.5 if there is no general rule.

Notes:

1. Even where the description of the variables does not mention so specifically, we have given intermediate scores wherever necessary.
2. For the power of the general meeting for remuneration see variable 26.
3. The possibility of authorized capital does not lead to a reduction from 1 to 0.5 because the default rule does not change.
4. Variable categories I2 and I3 could also be used as mechanisms for protecting minority from majority shareholders. However, in this study we have considered them as part of protection against directors because the directors are responsible for and decide the agenda and the calling of the shareholders meetings and therefore the legal rules of these variables primarily protect shareholders against directors.
5. See *supra* note 4.
6. To be sure, independent board members may also be a method to protect minority shareholders against majority shareholders. This depends, however, on the definition of 'independence', which is not coded in this variable.
7. For the involvement of boards and committees see generally variable category I9.
8. For approval of directors' conduct by the general meeting, the supervisory board, or independent board members see variable categories I1 and I9; for exclusion of liability in the articles see variable 57.
9. For preventive measures see, e.g., variable category II3.
10. Usually, the directors decide about the issuance of new shares. Pre-emptive right is perceived as an important protection against directors as it prevents them from disregarding the interests of shareholders in general. Of course, in some cases this may also be a method to protect minority against majority shareholders.
11. For the requirements for a waiver (e.g. supermajority, good reason) see variable categories II2, II9.
12. The purpose of requiring a substantial percentage of shareholders to constitute a valid quorum could be to prevent decisions of the general meeting, which are not supported by a significant majority much like the supermajority requirements.
13. Preference shares without voting rights are not addressed because they are feasible in all countries.
14. Note: Variables 57–59 do not code the content of the law (this is already done in variables 23, 24, 30, 31, 32) but only its nature, i.e. whether 'mandatory' or 'default'.

Source: Lele and Siems (2007).

3. Corporate governance and the public interest: the way forward*

J. Robert Branston, Keith Cowling and Roger Sugden

INTRODUCTION

The idea of good governance refers to a wide range of so-called public and private activities, and accordingly to governments, public agencies, corporations and other organizations. Our particular focus is the economics of the modern corporation and the chapter is consequently a contribution to the long-running debate initiated by Berle and Means (1932). Seventy-five years have not dimmed the controversy and topicality of this subject for economies throughout the world.[1] Indeed, the debate on governance was given fresh impetus by the collapse of the US energy corporation Enron in 2001[2] (see for example the reflections of Galbraith (2004, p. 49) on 'the end to corporate innocence'). Questions were asked about shareholders' inability to prevent managers in 'their' corporation from pursuing dubious and illegal strategies. These experiences led to policy queries in other countries, not least in the UK, where further questions were more recently asked of the Royal Dutch Shell Group concerning the role of directors in the over-inflation of oil reserves.[3]

The response to these scandals focused on shareholders being wronged by the criminal or otherwise undesirable activities of the managers/directors of the various companies, and thus on what might be done to prevent such actions in the future. The implication is that corporate governance is primarily concerned with the relationship between shareholders and managers/directors. We would take issue with this response and, in contrast, argue in this chapter that there is a need for accountability to all of the public who have an interest in the activities of a corporation. Merely to increase punishment for managers who fail shareholders is to continue to ignore the significance of the fact that, by design of the US and UK corporate systems, those managers are not supposed to take into account all interests in a corporation's activities. We suggest that these systemic deficiencies point to the fundamental problem of corporate governance today.

The chapter suggests a fundamental change to the focus of industrial economic policy. For all that governance has long been an issue for industrial economists, it has never been the central feature of policy. One reason is that a market-based analysis of the theory and impact of the firm makes markets the principal policy concern – quite appropriately, given its logic – and it cannot give governance that prominence. In contrast, the implication of our analysis is the necessity for governance-centric policy.

The next section outlines corporate governance and the strategic decision-making perspective. It presents a definition of the public interest in corporations and considers the objectives and method of governance-centric industrial economic policy. The third section then concentrates on the details of new policy possibilities. It discusses new legislation on corporations and the role of particular regulations, but lays especial stress on active, effective citizenship. The chapter identifies the communications sector as an area of particular interest. A concluding summary is provided as the final section. Throughout, our comments are illustrated from various industries.

The chapter is UK/US, and particularly UK, in focus although our ideas are broadly applicable beyond this focus. Our aim is to be as practical as possible by offering an outline of a way forward which can guide our policy makers as from today but with a long-term perspective.

GOVERNANCE AND THE CHALLENGE FOR PUBLIC POLICY

Strategy

In mainstream economic theory the firm is conceptualized using a market-centred approach, implying a market-centred view of policy. The starting point for this and perhaps all economic analysis of the firm is Coase (1937). He sees 'markets' and 'firms' as alternative ways to coordinate production. Coase defines a firm (in a pure sense) as the means of coordinating production without using market exchange, and explores why markets are sometimes 'superseded' (p. 390). This definition is in accord with analyses of firms' impact that are also market-orientated and leads to policy conclusions based on market failure (Sugden, 1997). Corporate governance is not a centre of attention in these conclusions.

In contrast, a different reading of Coase (1937) roots his ideas in micro-economic planning within firms (Cowling and Sugden, 1998a). Although Coase observes that coordination by markets entails 'planning by individuals' who 'experience foresight and choose between alternatives', he is particularly interested in 'planning within our economic system which is quite different from . . . individual planning . . . and which is akin to what is normally called economic planning' (pp. 387–8). Indeed, he sees firms as islands of economic planning.

In modern language, the idea of firms as units of planning translates into that of corporations making strategic decisions that give rise to their corporate strategies. In line with Zeitlin (1974), the power to make strategic decisions includes the ability to plan a corporation's relationships with other corporations, its relationships with governments and employees, and its geographical orientation. This focus on strategy points to the modern corporation being viewed as a locus of strategic decision making; following Cowling & Sugden (1987, 1998a), it suggests that a firm is the means of co-ordinating production from a centre of strategic decision making and another way of looking at the strategy-focused theory of the firm is in terms of governance. This is because, again in line with Zeitlin (1974), *to govern* is to control, and to control is to determine broad corporate objectives, which in its turn *is to have the power to make strategic decisions*.

The especial significance of this alternative perspective on the firm is that, unlike mainstream economic theory, it is not associated with a market-centred analysis of impact and policy. Rather, it leads to an understanding of impact based on strategic choice – that is, governance – and it makes governance the centrepiece of policy and the impact of corporations turns on who governs.[4] This outcome is a direct result of adopting the typical economists' assumption that decisions are made in the interests of the decision makers. The implication of this assumption is that a corporation's strategy will be designed and implemented in the interests of those making its strategic decisions. It therefore follows that the impact of a corporation is very much dependent upon who makes such decisions. It is to the evidence presented in extensive previous literature on that issue that we now turn, before looking more specifically at the implications of who governs and thus in more detail at the policy conclusions of the strategic decision-making analysis.

Who Governs and What Are the Implications?

In one respect, literature on the question of who governs a modern corporation provides various answers and considerable debate. In another respect, there is a consensus; control rests with a subset of those having an interest in a corporation's activities.

Most recent literature on corporate governance considers the exact nature of this controlling group by centring the debate on the relationship between shareholders and managers. It seeks to analyse if shareholders can and do exert sufficient control over the managers to ensure that it is their (and not the managers') agenda that the company follows. The literature highlights differences in governance structures across countries. But in reality these differences are shown to have only superficial effects on the make-up of the controlling group: de facto control of the corporation rests between a set of (large) shareholders and the company's senior managers/board.

It would seem that the evidence of the previous literature is that shareholder power rests with an elite in the UK and USA (as it does in Continental Europe and Japan, thanks to their concentrated voting power, in particular; see also Wojcik (2006), who examines corporate governance practice across Europe and finds evidence of convergence to an Anglo-US model). Does this mean that elite shareholders control the firm? In some respects the answer must be that they do, in other respects that they do not.

In theory the elite group of shareholders enjoys formal control of the company. However, as Tirole (2001, p. 17) puts it, 'the allocation of formal control . . . cannot be the full story'. The modern corporation is an immensely complicated (and indeed large) entity and so has to make many strategic decisions. It is unrealistic to expect that all of these decisions are (or can be) made with the understanding of the so-called controlling shareholders, who often face severe information problems. This would seem to indicate that 'players without formal control rights actually enjoy substantial control over their organisations' (Tirole, 2001, p. 17). Shareholders will only be involved (either directly or indirectly) with the most important strategic decisions, which leaves senior managers/the board with a high degree of autonomy and thus de facto control. Only when these individuals deviate significantly from the elite shareholders' wishes will the shareholders pull them back into line and exercise their formal power. Therefore it is likely that de facto control of the modern corporation rests somewhere between a subset of (large) shareholders and the company's senior managers/board.

The significance of identifying those who govern a corporation lies in the fact that interests vary across those concerned about, and affected by, a corporation's activities. This variation would be reflected in differences in the impact of corporations because it would be reflected in different strategic decisions. Zeitlin (1974) recognizes variation in interests when he argues that controlling a corporation actually implies the ability to determine broad corporate objectives *despite resistance from others*, and the consequences have been explored at a systemic level as regards issues concerning (among other things) Pareto efficiency, distribution, employment, trade and technology (see, for example, Cowling and Sugden, 1994, 1998a, 1998b, 1998c).

Consider the activities of a corporate university, an educational organization established by a corporation as part of the corporation, typically operated like other parts and intended to serve the strategic objectives of the corporation. Craig et al. (1999, p. 513) suggest that the

> compatibility of corporate strategies and academic enquiry is contestable; in the corporate university one might well imagine conflict between what scholars consider ought to be enquired into, and what the corporate strategy dictates to be the current action plan. For example, the obvious conflicts between corporate strategies in the tobacco industry and the conduct of research into the health effects of smoking.

Different interests in research activities are also suggested by debates on genetically modified crops and, as yet another example of varied concerns, consider the effects of concentrated strategic decision-making in the communications sector. This sector challenges society's interest in political, economic and social democracy; Williams (1966) observes that the extension of communications is central to increased democracy but that the twentieth century saw the communications sector governed by ever more sectional interests. (Given the importance of this sector and the problem identified, we will return with an extended analysis later in the chapter.)

Strategic Failure and the Public Interest

From recognizing that there are varied interests in a corporation's activities, and that this would be reflected in different strategies, it follows that corporate governance is a central issue for public policy. It has been argued in this section that the modern corporation is governed by a subset of those with an interest in its activities. This group governs in pursuit of its own objectives, opting for strategies that other interested parties would not implement if they were making the decisions. This raises a serious problem if, as a matter of public policy, it is seen as desirable that corporations' activities serve the interests of people more generally; for example, if they are to be governed so as to serve the objectives of varied shareholders, employees and consumers, as well as those affected by the corporations' impact on the environment, democratic processes and so on. The problem is a particular instance of a more general concern that has been previously identified as 'strategic failure, a failure to determine the strategic direction of production . . . in the broader interest – in the interest of the community at large' (Cowling and Sugden, 1999, p. 361). The issue is that the strategy pursued by a typical corporation does not yield the outcomes that are in the broader interest because it is determined by an exclusive subset of economic actors. Most especially, concentration of strategic decision-making power implies a failure to govern production in the public interest.

In focusing on the public interest we are building on the argument in Dewey (1927 [1988]) and Long (1990). For Dewey (1927 [1988]), an act is private when its consequences are essentially confined to the persons directly engaged in it, but if the consequences extend beyond those directly engaged then 'the act acquires a public capacity' (p. 244). He sees (p. 257) the public as those who are 'indirectly and seriously affected for good or for evil' by an act. Drawing on this, Long views the public interest as an evolving consensus among a set of people – a public – regarding the actions of private parties; it is the standard agreed upon by that public and against which those actions can be reasonably assessed. According to him,

> by arriving at some consensus, a moving one, we agree on what is important both for policy and research and the latter becomes a more purposive, disciplined, cooperative endeavour as opposed to a matter of fad, fashion and funding. For public administration and political science, the appropriate standard of evaluation would appear to be the public interest (pp. 170–71).

We would add that it is also an appropriate standard for much of economics. Long argues that the 'consequences of private parties' actions create a public as that public discovers its shared concern with their effects and the need for their control. The public's shared concern with consequences is a public interest' (p. 171). Similarly, we see the public interest in a corporation's activities in general and in its strategies in particular as the agreed-upon, evolving concerns among all of those indirectly and significantly affected by those activities and strategies (wherever they live, whatever their nationality).

To avoid strategic failure, it has been argued in general that an obvious possibility is to search for ways of appropriately involving more and more people affected by strategic decisions in the process of making those decisions; more particularly, to design ways of democratizing governance (Cowling and Sugden, 1999).[5] In line with this, for the particular case of corporations we advocate the search for an effective democracy in their strategic decision-making processes.[6] As an aspect of that, we would argue for the agreed-upon, evolving concerns that are the public interest in corporate strategies to be determined democratically, a point which we explain in more detail below. Our contention is that success in these regards would imply preferable outcomes – from a public perspective – than are currently otherwise being attained. This conclusion follows from the reasoning that we have already presented on the implications of exclusive governance, given what we perceive as the reality of both imperfect competition and imperfect information (about the interests of the public), which are also issues that are explored subsequently.[7]

Competition and the Policy Objective

Such a governance-centric approach to industrial economic policy is at odds with current and previous practice, certainly in Anglo-US economies. In so far as this established practice has a theoretical rationale in economics, its foundation is essentially market failure. Such market-centred approaches give little or no direct importance to strategy; they emphasize the benefits of markets and especially market competition, in contrast to our focus on strategic choice. To the extent that governance is afforded attention, the concern is with private versus public ownership, without appreciating the crucial strategic decision-making issues that sit beneath the private/public superficialities; it is clear the democratization of strategic choice is not an issue that can be reduced to one of ownership.

Nevertheless, we recognize that there are senses in which a market-centred approach may be argued to serve the public interest, even when corporations are governed by sectional interests that are left 'free' from government 'interference'. An argument underlying such a view can be seen in extreme form in an Arrow–Debreu type general equilibrium model (see, for example, Debreu, 1959; Arrow and Hahn, 1971). In this case, the presence of ubiquitous perfect competition ensures Pareto optimal outcomes in situations where producers and indeed all actors pursue their own interests. Less extreme would be the situation where sectional interests govern a corporation but where those with other interests can make takeover bids in a competitive capital market or can establish new, competing corporations. The strategic failure analysis, in contrast, is founded on the significance of *imperfect* competition.

However, recognize the presence of imperfect competition and it may still be argued that the interests of people in general can be served through policies that correct for market failures; this is clear from, for instance, discussions of the 'public interest theory of regulation' (see Hantke-Domas, 2003, for a critical review). A basic reason for this argument is that those policies might be intended to yield outcomes that would be of general benefit, for example the desire for increased productivity. Again, however, there is a stark contrast with the strategic failure analysis.

The prime policy objective in the governance-centric approach is not reducible to rises in per capita incomes or productivity, or even to the attainment of Pareto optimality. It might be that people in general would in fact all see themselves as gaining from such rises, which might therefore be seen as in the public interest. Whether or not this is actually the case would need to be determined democratically; in other words, the interest of the public would need to be arrived at through a democratic process involving everyone in the public (see especially Dewey, 1927 [1988] for a provocative consideration of how this might be achieved in practice). The reason is that, following the analysis of 'economic development' in Sugden and Wilson (2002), the identification of objectives is the most fundamental of strategic decisions in economic activity, and it is neither for those unaffected by the activity to determine those objectives, nor for those affected to be excluded from the decision-making. Rather, the choice needs to be made by a democratic process encompassing all interested parties,[8] otherwise exclusive interests would make the decision following their own preferences and despite the wishes of others. Furthermore, we cannot predict exactly what the democratic outcome would be without the democratic process actually taking place, a point to which we return when discussing possibilities for regulation.

More generally, then, the implication of our discussion is that the prime policy objective of the strategic failure approach is to ensure a democratic strategic decision-making process, including in this a democratic determination of the objectives of economic activity. This is not to imply that effectiveness in meeting the objectives of economic activity is irrelevant; but we are arguing that an assessment of effectiveness can only be made in the context of specified objectives and, if strategic failure is to be avoided, the objectives of economic activity can only be determined through democratic choice.

The Centrality of Voice

To understand what democratic choice really means it is helpful to consider 'exit' and 'voice'. The emphasis on these concepts in the market-centred and strategic failure approaches differs, a contrast that also has important implications for appreciating the policy challenge and correspondingly the policy method. Hirschman (1970) identifies exit as central to market processes and voice as crucial to democracy. He argues that exit is 'neat', 'impersonal' and

> 'indirect' – any recovery on the part of the declining firm comes by courtesy of the Invisible Hand, as an unintended by-product of the customer's decision to shift. In all these respects voice is just the opposite of exit. It is a far more 'messy' concept because it can be graduated, all the way from faint grumbling to violent protest; it implies articulation of one's critical opinions rather than a private, 'secret' vote in the anonymity of the supermarket; and finally, it is direct and straightforward rather than roundabout (pp. 15–16).

His view is that the democratic process of its essence entails 'the digging, the use, and hopefully the slow improvement' of channels of voice, 'essentially an *art* constantly evolving in new directions' (Hirschman, 1970, pp. 17 and 43). Voice is at the heart of strategic failure analysis.

More specifically, the policy challenge for the governance-centric approach is to design a set of initiatives that recognize and nurture the constantly evolving art highlighted by Hirschman (1970), and that maintain an appropriate mix and balance of voice and exit processes. The corresponding policy method is to identify initiatives that might contribute to increased democracy and to see these as part of an evolutionary process in which each step sows seeds that might be nurtured to yield further steps in the future.

INCREASED PARTICIPATION AND EFFECTIVE DEMOCRACY

Corporate Law

In 1998 the Hampel Committee on Corporate Governance rejected the prospect of senior management having a duty towards all interest groups with a stake in a company. The Committee concluded that to make directors responsible to various groups would imply that they 'were not effectively accountable to anyone since there would be no clear yardstick for judging their performance. This is a recipe neither for good governance nor for corporate success' (Hampel Committee Report, 1998, paragraph 1.17).

There is little doubt that many will see it this way. Therefore any discussion of a 'stakeholder' approach to attaining the public interest has to begin to identify a practical way forward that will allow 'good governance' and 'corporate success' within a more democratic framework. We might recall what Oscar Wilde said about (Cole and) Fabian socialism: that he wondered where people would find the time for it. Stakeholder approaches do not mean that everyone is involved in the details of every decision, rather that everyone has the right to a say in decisions that are of great import to them, and that there is a need to consider the design of how this can be achieved efficiently. It is curious that while some consider it appropriate for a corporation to be governed in the interests of only one among a set of stakeholders, the same is not considered appropriate for a nation. Despite the Hampel Committee's conclusion, it is commonly argued that a national government is in some sense accountable to many varied and diverse interests.

It might be argued that a particular way forward would be to introduce directors that represent workers (see, for instance, the Bullock Report, 1977). However, we would view this sort of reform as problematic because it suggests the institutionalizing of divisions that run counter to the search for a democratic consensus based on *all* of the concerns of *all* interested people. First, it would imply that different directors would have responsibilities towards separate and exclusive sets of people. This would certainly encourage directors to think and act in terms of narrow interests, which would be precisely the sort of failure that the search for effective democracy in the strategic decision-making processes of corporations is intended to overcome. Second, it would imply directors having responsibilities towards a particular person only as regards specific issues – such as employment – and not as regards all of that person's concerns with the activities of a corporation. Again, this would imply a division, one that encourages partial rather than rounded development.

In contrast, our intuition is to follow the sort of argument suggested by Sunstein (2001b). He contrasts consumer and political sovereignty, arguing that political democracy requires something other than unfettered pursuit of consumer interests. The crucial point is that people are not merely consumers; rather, they are multi-dimensional. We would stress something similar in the search for an economic democracy. At issue are the interests of people in all of their dimensions, not only as consumers and not only as workers.

With that in mind we suggest that a more appealing possibility for change is to build on the requirement that senior management act in the interests of members by widening membership beyond shareholders, and by conferring all management with duties towards all of those members.

The exact way that the widening of membership is achieved and how company directors are bestowed with attainable duties towards all those members is something that would need imaginative consideration. It would be infeasible to attempt to provide all interests with an appropriate voice in the strategic decision-making process simultaneously, and one option is to focus attention consecutively on particular sectors and sets of interested parties. For example, the effective democratization of governance requires appropriate information and communication among interested parties, itself necessitating a communications sector that is democratically controlled. Communications should therefore be a prioritized sector and we will develop this later. As for different interested parties, one possibility might be to concentrate in the first instance on employees or, depending on the sector involved, the initial focus might be on consumers. Within this there could be further narrowing by concentrating on interests especially committed to a particular corporation, or especially dependent; perhaps employees who have a long association with the company or those who rely heavily on the company's services, for example railway season ticket holders or those captive to a monopoly, such as a water supplier.

There are practical difficulties in developing appropriate processes. One of the most significant is the allocation of votes for electing the board of directors, although recognizing this is *not* to say that we see elections as the essence of democracy – we do not, a point that we will briefly expand upon in due course. Nevertheless, to the extent that elections do matter in the democratization of corporations, the allocation of votes needs to be done in a way that enables real power sharing while ensuring workability. This also needs to take into consideration the possibility of buying votes. Existing English and Scottish law means that buying shares generally implies buying votes and therefore, perhaps, a degree of control over the strategic decision-making process. Again, this is strikingly different from what is widely perceived as appropriate for the governance of a country; the use of money to buy votes in British parliamentary elections was eradicated in the nineteenth century.[9]

Another difficulty is to determine the criteria by which new members are identified. This would not be an easy process. A significant membership fee might be desirable as this might be seen as a cost that only those with a significant interest in the corporation would incur.[10] The fee could take many different forms, for example a one-time payment returnable on the decision to cease being a member. To reduce the exclusion of those with relatively less wealth, the fee might be paid over time, perhaps via a monthly salary contribution. The fee could then be placed in an interest-bearing trust to act like a bank account, giving a guaranteed return disparate from company performance and profits. In this situation, the fee is acting as a bond between the new member and the corporation, whilst maintaining the distinction between shareholder and other members.

It is, however, unrealistic to assume that every interested party would immediately want to become a member of a company. Although the numbers would differ from sector to sector, in many cases only those few with a special interest would exercise their right. This might be seen to imply broad satisfaction, or at least low levels of dissatisfaction, with the company's existing governance. In times of public dissatisfaction we envisage the right to become members being more highly utilized. This shifting balance would be a process that helps affect change; following Hirschman (1970, p. 32), 'a mixture of alert and inert citizens, or even an alternation of involvement and withdrawal, may actually serve democracy better than either total, permanent activism or total apathy'.[11]

We have earlier identified the centrality of voice to the governance approach to the public interest: the ability to become a member is important for giving a voice to those who currently have none, even if it appears that it is not always utilized. For example, it is unlikely that many customers would have become members of British electricity or gas supply companies over the last five years, because there have been low levels of public dissatisfaction with their service. However, given the same rights during the same time period, customers of the private rail companies in Britain would have been far more likely to be active in seeking membership because of the almost universal public dissatisfaction with the performance of these companies during this period.[12] It is also the case that the choice to become a member might be influenced by the quantity and quality of available 'performance' indicators. For electricity and gas, consumers mainly rely on price and the reliability of service, whereas for rail travellers there are far more criteria on which to judge – price, delays, cleanliness of rolling stock, journey times and so on.

These issues highlight the significance of information. Membership cannot be effectively widened if information continues to be restricted; interested parties need information so that they can appropriately access the strategic decision-making process. Policy therefore needs to be directed to ensuring that the appropriate information is widely available. As part of this change one possibility is implied by the proposal for a 'transnational corporations monitoring unit' (Bailey et al., 1994). It is suggested that countries introduce monitoring units 'designed to collect information on transnationals' performance and impact, to prepare accounts and to use these to influence economic policy and attitudes of and towards transnationals' (p. 316). Following Bailey et al. (1999), these units could act as a 'clearing house' where various interested parties pool their information, allowing widespread dissemination and analysis. Such a system could be readily adapted to assist corporate governance in the public interest. It could be invaluable in helping various interested parties gain the information that they need for a real voice in the governance of modern corporations.

This is not to suggest that the passive provision of information is the key issue. We argue that governance in the public interest requires that each member of society be able to think about and therefore participate in the governance process to the extent and level that they freely choose. Each needs to be alert to the need for certain types of knowledge, to be able to exercise their voice in pursuit of that knowledge, and to be able to use that knowledge in expressing their voice on strategic ways forward. In its turn, such active citizenship necessitates appropriate (informal and formal) education and learning for all people. Further, what is required is a focus on relationships among people, with particular stress on communication and on the communities in which they live. That is a clear conclusion from Dewey's (1927 [1988]) analysis of the ways in which the public can be identified and enabled. At issue is the evolution of imaginative ways to nurture and stimulate thought, creativity, deliberation, discussion and interaction, not through committee meetings but rather as integral threads in the fabric of everyday life.

A related issue that policy would need urgently to address is the role of company directors. This would also need to change.[13] Whereas currently in

England directors are effectively responsible only to shareholders, we are advocating that they be responsible to many, more varied concerns; if instead control is to be in the public interest, then their role might more appropriately encompass mediation of conflict. In theory directors in existing law might be said to have one master, although we have seen that shareholders differ in their opinions on strategy. But if directors were to owe a duty to act in the interests of all members and these members had different views on strategy, perhaps a director's explicit role and duty should be to mediate. With this in mind, university business schools could be encouraged to consider the wider public interest when considering good governance; a changing role for directors, including a mediating function across different interest groups, could be an aspect of their learning programmes.

We see an effective democracy as founded upon mutual respect and the search for mutual understanding among its participants. Of course, it also needs to be recognized that the presence of disruptive elements cannot be ruled out. It is in this context that we suggest corporate directors could play a role in drawing out conflicts, providing arenas for discussion and resolution, eliciting compromise and negotiating agreements. They could contribute to making preferences endogenous to the strategic decision-making process, because preferences would be evolving within the process as relationships developed between all the different interested parties. This would be in stark contrast to the assumption of exogenous preferences characterizing Arrow's (1951) impossibility theorem. It might also advance the evolution of economic democracy based on public deliberation, discussion and reason giving.

Regulations to Help Achieve a Democratic Economy

Introducing the sorts of alterations in company law that we have been contemplating might be seen as an overtly radical step. In contrast, new regulations offer possibilities seen as perhaps easier and therefore for more immediate change, although we would emphasize that these cannot be seen as a replacement for policies that directly introduce a genuine democracy. Regulation of free market economies is essentially an arm's-length response to failures in arm's-length relationships, whereas of its essence economic democracy entails inclusive, dynamic processes for shaping preferences and possibilities. When Hirschman (1970) refers to the development of democracy as a constantly evolving art, he is identifying a process that cannot be attained via regulation of an undemocratic process. The democratic process itself implies evolution, change and consequently different outcomes. No arm's-length regulation of an undemocratic process could mirror this, not least because, in its absence, there is no way to know what the democratic process would yield. This is the basic limitation of the regulatory policies advocated by economists: they effect to know what is in the public interest without showing much interest in learning what the public interest might be. This is a neglect of the essence of democracy.

One immediate way forward may be to ensure that democratically controlled public agencies have responsibility and ability to gather information on firms' strategic activity, and to present accounts in light of the public interest. Cost considerations alone would mean that such initiatives would have limited effect; public agencies could not costlessly monitor all strategic decisions of all companies at all times. However, following Bailey et al. (1994), some degree of increased participation in strategic decision-making may be provided, simply as a result of information being made public, and at reasonable cost. Indeed, public agencies have already been given roles to some extent in line with this suggestion. Consider, for example, BSkyB's proposed takeover of Manchester United plc. The bid was referred to (what became) the Competition Commission, whose remit encompassed 'all matters that appear to be relevant in considering the public interest'. For such measures to widen involvement in strategic decision-making with real effect, it is important that the public interest be explicitly identified in terms of all of the members of the public that have concerns in the strategic direction of a company. Serving the public interest needs to be seen in terms of the different interested parties being represented effectively. While each interest in isolation might prefer a different strategic direction, taking account of all interested parties requires the search for compromise and consensus.

However, these are not the considerations that preoccupied the Competition Commission. Policy surrounding the likes of the Commission is nowadays typically labelled 'competition policy', and it is perhaps revealing that when the BSkyB bid was referred, it was reported as exceptional that there were concerns about the wider public interest. Even with such recommendations, in its report the Commission 'based [its] public interest conclusions mainly on the effect of the merger on competition among broadcasters' (Monopolies and Mergers Commission, 1999, p. 4). A preoccupation with competition is more in line with the market failure, market-centred approach to policy. Nevertheless, the Commission's terms of reference were established in quite broad and flexible terms, the concern with public interest apparently allowing a strategic decision-making approach to economic welfare to be pursued. Indeed, this is suggested by the Commission in its investigation of the BSkyB proposal: 'many of the points put to us went well beyond the competition and consumer concerns that normally arise in merger enquiries. However, in considering this merger we are directed . . . to take into account when assessing the public interest "all matters which appear to [us] to be relevant" ' (Monopolies and Mergers Commission, 1999, p. 42).

A broader approach might also be seen as in line with the origins (albeit not current practice) of antitrust regulation in the USA. Friedman (2002, p. 55) reports that the Sherman Act of 1890 'was directed at economic *power*'. He argues that its roots lay in the perception that

> top businesses were big – huge – gigantic; and their tentacles spread over the whole country. It was not just a question of economic efficiency, or higher prices for consumers; it was also the sense of threat, the danger to small business people, to the little shop on the corner. The trust crisis was a culture crisis as much as it was a crisis in prices and business.

Put another way, 'one of the historical foundations on which antitrust policy rested' was 'fear of huge, overwhelming conglomerates, whose power was an evil in itself, a threat to American values' (p. 57).

More generally, we suggest that a policy to complement effective merger control would be the evolution of suitable regulatory offices for particularly important sectors in an economy. These offices could be charged with safeguarding the public interest in all strategic decision-making. Similar to the argument on monitoring, cost considerations alone might mean that it is inappropriate to introduce a regulator for every sector. However, there are precedents, for example the regulatory offices established to oversee aspects of privatized utilities. Although these precedents have a competition focus rather than the broader concerns that we are advocating, they show that our proposals are not as radically different from current practice as to be infeasible in the immediate future, and they suggest that cost considerations are unlikely to be fatal.

Which are the important sectors today where oversight in the public interest is very desirable? Partly it is a matter of the economic and social importance of the sector but partly it is an issue of whether control is vested in particularly few hands; in other words, the necessary and sufficient condition is for a sector to be one which is both economically and socially significant, and where control is vested in particularly few hands. Finance and IT would seem to be fundamental: finance underpins every transformation and IT underpins every modern technology. To talk about threatening the private control of finance would strike at the heart of the capitalist system, but aspects of finance are already the focus of public debate (for example, witness the current concern with private equity capital which has suddenly grown into a dominant position). To talk of IT would strike at the innovatory core of the new economy, which of course impinges on finance as well. It might be considered obvious that the strategy for such fundamentals of the economy should be directed by the public interest. The human genome project is similarly placed.

The Communications Sector

Whilst the increasing concentration of economic power is a general concern for democracy, perhaps the most direct and pervading influence on the effective functioning and growth of a democracy will be felt in the case of the communications sector. Branston and Wilson (2006) highlight how the broadcasting industry is of special importance in this regard, and much of their analysis is readily extendable to the communications sector in general. They suggest (p. 4) that broadcasting is an especially important industry in any economy because of its role in communicating news, ideas, fashions, in providing entertainment and in educating. They argue that broadcasting can directly influence societal welfare through what it produces. Further, and in contrast to most sectors, broadcasting may shape people's perceptions and ideas, even their preferences and behaviour, with implications that stretch to all areas of the economy. Accordingly, they suggest that broadcast media are crucial instruments for enabling and enhancing economic participation. We would go further: their analysis and conclusions are applicable to the entire communications sector.

The basic problem is that despite a recent technological revolution in the communications sector, ownership and control is highly concentrated, and diversity is more apparent than real. The sector is characterized by a highly concentrated structure *within* each form of communication – press, television, sound broadcasting, cinema, books; but also interlocking ownership and control patterns *across* forms of communication – national and local newspapers, newspapers and television, newspapers and local radio, newspapers and books; and vertical links *between* production and distribution, as in cinema. As Raymond Williams (1966), an early commentator on this phenomenon has concluded:

> the extension of communications has been part of the extension of democracy. Yet, in this century, while the public has extended, ownership and control of the means of communication have narrowed. . . . In the modern trend towards limited ownership, the cultural conditions of democracy are in fact being denied; sometimes ironically in the name of freedom (p. 33).

Whilst this was written many years ago, his views are still very much relevant today. For example, in Britain four groups dominate *both* the national popular daily and Sunday newspapers, with one of them also controlling a London evening paper, the most important evening paper in the country.[14]

These same groups are also active in the provinces and in other areas of the communications sector. Consider one of these groups: News Corporation. This large transnational group has interests in the communication sector across the globe and within the UK controls, amongst other things, the largest commercial TV broadcaster (BSkyB), several of the most important national newspaper titles (*The Times*, *The Sunday Times*, *The Sun*, *The News of the World*, and *thelondonpaper*), and a significant book publisher (HarperCollins). It also has further influence through its significant American interests in film and television which sell content into the UK market, and its ownership of the popular MySpace website.[15]

As we have already seen in the earlier part of the chapter, concentration of corporate ownership matters in itself, but as Branston and Wilson (2006) have suggested, this takes on added importance in the communications sector because of the wider implications the sector has for democracy. This type of thinking is evident in the work of Hirsch and Gordon (1975), who argued that the press is fundamentally unrepresentative because the pursuit of profit implies that the interests and views of those with high spending power will command excessive attention since advertising revenue will be directed by the spending power of the audience rather than its size. The so-called quality newspapers will play a leading role: they provide an informed but restricted discussion of public issues and ensure that their affluent readers get an especially powerful voice through the press. This gets reflected in broadcasting and in the popular press, leading to a general conformity in both viewpoint and coverage. With concentrated ownership throughout the communications sector, and with formidable barriers to entry, significant minorities can be safely ignored and minority views can be excluded from any sort of adequate representation in the mainstream output of the industry. As a result it is almost inevitable that the influence of such minorities, or such views, will be effectively curtailed. Whilst individuals within specific social groups may initially be highly variable in terms of values and tastes, extended exposure to a conforming media will tend to move them to conformity – but conformity around the aims and values of those driving corporate strategy, the wealthy and influential.

We can therefore see that an extension of democracy will need to focus on an opening-up of the communications sector to a broader range of ideas and viewpoints. Part of this process will be the aforementioned suggestion of widening company membership to include more voices in the decision-making process. For that to take place in this sector, significant restructuring would be required, and this is something that has been suggested elsewhere.

Raymond Williams (1966) argued that an educated and participating democracy can only be achieved with a communications revolution. People have to grow in capacity and power to direct their own lives which requires, among other things, an extension of expression and exchange of experience which the system of communication provides. He makes some valuable suggestions for the British case which may well have a wider resonance, even today, more than forty years later. In the case of broadcasting and television he argues for the ending of the commercial structures with the close links with the commercial press. In the case of the press he wants to free local newspapers from remote control by large corporations and wants to set up Newspaper Trusts to finance working journalists to produce new local and national newspapers. For the cinema he proposes public production facilities available for use by professional film-makers and the opening up of the cinema circuits for their use. For books, he suggests public funding of a chain of new bookshops and as an alternative to advertising he advocates the funding of the Citizens Advice Bureau to provide information on products and services. To many this will look like pie-in-the-sky or out-of-date thinking, but to others an exciting public prospect. The general thrust seems right in the British case, and we would hypothesize that something like it is needed in many other countries, although one can argue with the detail, even if sympathetic. He is seeking to open up the communications system to new, smaller-scale entrants and at the same time reduce the power of the existing centres of concentration, public or private. Interestingly, from the point of view of acceptability, he goes on to argue that all that is required is some suitable public (or even private?) credit arrangements: these activities can generally be relied on to pay for themselves. If this is more or less true, and we recognize the enormous significance of the system of communications in the development of our democracy, then action of the sort he proposes is surely long overdue. We could then replace the present expansion of the system with 'real growth', offering real choice and variety and moving away from minority control to broad involvement.

CONCLUSION

Following Coase (1937) and Zeitlin (1974), the concepts of strategy and governance are central to understanding modern corporations, their essence, their impact and the design of public policies that affect their activities. Corporations are centres of economic planning; to govern a corporation is to plan its overall direction, to determine its broad impact and therefore to make its strategic decisions. We argue that interests vary across those concerned about and affected by a corporation's activities and that this variation is reflected in different preferences over strategy. Accordingly, a corporation's impact typically depends upon who governs. Our principal conclusion is that it is a matter of public policy to ensure that corporate governance is in the public interest.

Drawing on Dewey (1927 [1988]) and Long (1990), we define the public interest in a corporation's activities and strategies as the democratically agreed-upon, evolving concerns among all of those indirectly and significantly affected by those activities and strategies. We advocate the search for an effective democracy in the strategic decision-making processes of corporations. We explore some of the policy initiatives that might contribute worthwhile steps toward an effective democracy, in the UK but also beyond:

The design of suitable company laws, based upon:

- Widened membership, focusing consecutively on particular economic sectors and specific sets of interested parties.
- Renewed and redirected concern with information, specifically focused on members being alert to the need for certain types of knowledge, able to exercise their voice in the pursuit of that knowledge.
- A role for directors that includes drawing out conflicts, providing arenas or discussion and resolution, eliciting compromise and negotiating agreements.

The creation of democratically controlled public bodies of various forms:

- Agencies with the responsibility and ability to gather information on firms' strategic activity.
- The sort of competition agency to focus monopolies and mergers regulation on an understanding of the public interest that explicitly recognizes the views of all members of the public concerned with the strategic direction of the relevant companies.
- The empowerment of appropriate regulatory offices charged with safeguarding the public interest in particularly important sectors, including communications.

However, it must be stressed that the public interest in corporate governance goes much deeper than laws and regulations. Democracy in essence requires a change in the nature of corporate governance from within, ultimately impossible via legal decree or regulation from without. It is essential to nurture a civic society in which all people develop and penetrate the processes of governance that impinge on their lives. The aim would be to realize a situation in which free citizens have the ability to think about governance processes and therefore to participate in them. It is these citizens that can demand and assure that good governance prevails. They are the key to ensuring that an economy is governed in the public interest.

NOTES

* This chapter is derived from the authors' earlier article 'Corporate governance and the public interest', *The International Review of Applied Economics*, **20**(2), April 2006, 189–212.

1. For example, antitrust actions, privatization policies and takeovers routinely raise disputed and fundamental issues that are central to people's well-being. We would argue that these are essentially issues of corporate governance. To mention one out of any number of examples: has Microsoft been governed with the interests of Internet users appropriately taken into account, given that it denied equipment manufacturers the option of selling with a browserless version of Windows? (See the findings of fact reported in *United States of America* v. *Microsoft Corporation*, Civil Action Number 98-1232 (TPJ), United States District Court for the District of Columbia.)
2. Reported at http://news.bbc.co.uk/1/hi/business/2517389.stm (accessed on 3 December 2002).
3. See *The Financial Times*, 14 April 2004.
4. The argument is not that everything in a corporation is determined solely by strategic decisions. Rather, it is that they are especially important because, by definition, they determine a corporation's broad direction.
5. Evidence in Frey and Stutzer (2000, p. 918) suggests that widening direct involvement in strategic decision-making might in itself increase people's well-being. According to evidence from interview data in Switzerland, 'individuals are *ceteris paribus* happier, the better developed the institutions of direct democracy are in their area of residence'.
6. Jessop (1998, p. 39), in his discussion of 'factors which limit the success of governance in guiding economic development', concludes that 'much literature on economic governance focuses on the modalities rather than objects of governance and thereby ignores the distinctive constraints imposed by the self-organizing dynamic and inter-systemic dominance of capitalism'.
7. We have argued up to now that exclusive governance in pursuit of sectional interests deliberately ignores the public interest. In contrast, to recognize and incorporate the public interest explicitly might be thought self-evidently to imply the likelihood that decisions would be typically more in the public interest than otherwise. A counter to this might be that the public interest could be met via exclusive governance providing there was an appropriate combination of competition and regulation. It is effectively this counter that we will explore and in turn refute in (parts of) the remainder of this section.
8. In its pure form, a democratic choice cannot be confined to interested parties from particular nations; democracy would require the participation of all interested parties, regardless of nationality.
9. This argument is not to deny that influence might be in some sense 'bought' in modern parliamentary elections. For example, donations to finance campaign advertising are presumably designed to affect the way people vote and therefore influence election outcomes.
10. On first impression, requiring a membership fee might be seen as little different to defining company membership exclusively in terms of those buying a share in the company. If both customer and shareholder members are defined (in part) by their willingness to make a financial commitment, why not simplify matters by requiring all company members to have a shareholding, whether or not those members are customers? The reason why not is that customers have interests as customers as distinct from shareholders. There is a similar argument against the view that employees who are also

shareholders – a significant and growing group in, for example, the USA – are appropriately accounted for merely by reason of their shareholdings. See Knight and Sugden (1990) for more details on this and related issues.

11. 'One reason . . . is that the ordinary failure, on the part of most citizens, to use their potential political forces to the full makes it possible for them to react with unexpected vigour – by using normally unused reserves of political power and influence – whenever their vital interests are directly threatened' (Hirschman, 1970, p. 32). Another reason he identifies is that voice needs to be followed by a period in which representatives have time to act.
12. This view of the relative levels of consumer satisfaction is not only available from a typical British consumer of these services, but also evident from industry statistics. See for example, ORR (2007) for performance and complaint statistics for the railways, and Energywatch (2007) and the Energywatch website for a similar overview of the gas and electricity markets.
13. A precedent that we would not advocate be followed in this regard is that of the 'not-for-dividend' organization, Network Rail, which owns the railway infrastructure in Great Britain. This is a very interesting company in that its corporate governance is provided not by shareholders, but instead by a group of members who represent various stakeholders and that are in essence trustees. However, the company is a less than perfect solution to the governance problems we have already identified and so we would not advocate it as a panacea for all to adopt. Whilst a full analysis of the company falls outside the scope of this chapter, an example of one possible problem is that the board of directors has ultimate power over the appointment and removal of the company members, the very group that is supposed to hold the board accountable. There is therefore an incentive and a mechanism to remove those members who make life difficult for the directors, and instead to appoint those who will not, as Hirschman (1970, p. 30) put it, 'kick a fuss'. See Network Rail (2002a and 2002b) for further details on the structure of the company.
14. The four main groups are Express Newspapers (who control *The Daily Express*, *Sunday Express*, *Daily Star* and *Sunday Star*), Trinity Mirror (who control *The Daily Mirror*, *Sunday Mirror*, *People*, *Sunday Mail*, *Daily Record*), The Daily Mail and General Trust (who control *The Daily Mail*, *The Mail on Sunday*, *The London Evening Standard*, *Metro*) and News Corporation (which controls *The Times*, *The Sunday Times*, *The Sun*, *The News of the World*). These four groups and their various titles account for the vast majority of national newspaper sales in the UK (see www.abc.org.uk for detailed circulation figures and ownership information) although there is a fringe of other national newspaper titles which are significant at the higher end of the market.
15. See the News Corporation website (http://www.newscorp.com/) for more details.

REFERENCES

Arrow, K.J. (1951), *Social Choice and Individual Values*, New York: John Wiley and Sons.

Arrow, K.J. and F. Hahn (1971), *General Competitive Analysis*, San Francisco: Holden-Day.

Bailey, David, George Harte and Roger Sugden (1994), *Making Transnationals Accountable: A Significant Step for Britain*, London: Routledge.

Bailey, David, George Harte and Roger Sugden (1999), 'Regulating transnationals: free markets and monitoring in Europe', in Keith Cowling (ed.), *Industrial Policy in Europe: Theoretical Perspectives and Practical Proposals*, London: Routledge.

Berle, Adolf A. and Gardiner C. Means (1932), *The Modern Corporation and Private Property*, New York: Macmillan.

Branston, J. Robert and James R. Wilson (2006), 'Transmitting democracy: a strategic failure analysis of broadcasting and the BBC', University of Bath, School of

Management, working paper 2006.11; http://www.bath.ac.uk/management/research/pdf/2006-11.pdf.

Bullock Report (1977), 'Report of the Committee of Inquiry on Industrial Democracy', London: HMSO.

Coase, R.H. (1937), 'The nature of the firm', *Economica*, **4**, 386–405.

Cowling, Keith (1985), 'Economic obstacles to democracy', in R. C. O. Matthews (ed.), *Economy and Democracy*, London: Macmillan.

Cowling, K. and R. Sugden (1987), 'Market exchange and the concept of a transnational corporation: analysing the nature of the firm', *British Review of Economic Issues*, **9**(20), 57–68.

Cowling, Keith and Roger Sugden (1994), *Beyond Capitalism. Towards a New World Economic Order*, London: Pinter.

Cowling, Keith and Roger Sugden (1998a), 'The essence of the modern corporation: markets, strategic decision-making and the theory of the firm', *The Manchester School*, **66**(1), 59–86.

Cowling, K. and R. Sugden (1998b), 'Strategic trade policy reconsidered: national rivalry vs. free trade vs. international cooperation', *Kyklos*, **51**, 339–57.

Cowling, Keith and Roger Sugden (1998c), 'Technology policy: strategic failures and the need for a new direction', in J. Michie and J. Grieve Smith (eds), *Globalization, Growth and Governance: Creating an Innovative Economy*, Oxford: Oxford University Press.

Cowling, K. and R. Sugden (1999), 'The wealth of localities, regions and nations; developing multinational economies', *New Political Economy*, **4**(3), 361–78.

Craig, R.J., F.L. Clark and J.H. Amernic (1999), 'Scholarship in university business schools: Cardinal Newman, creeping corporatism and farewell to the "disturber of the peace"?', *Accounting, Auditing and Accountability Journal*, **12**(5), 510–24.

Debreu, Gerard (1959), *Theory of Value*, New York: John Wiley.

Dewey, John (1927), *The Public and its problems*, Denver, CO: Holt; page numbers refer to the reproduction in J.A. Boydston (ed.) (1988), *John Dewey. The Later Works Volume 2: 1925–1927*, Carbondale, IL: Southern Illinois University Press.

Energywatch (2007), *Annual Report and Accounts 2006/07*, London: The Stationery Office.

Frey, B. and A. Stutzer (2000), 'Happiness, economy and institutions', *The Economic Journal*, **110**, 918–38.

Friedman, Lawrence M. (2002), *American Law in the 20th Century*, New Haven, CT: Yale University Press.

Galbraith, John K. (2004), *The Economics of Innocent Fraud. Truth for Our Time*, New York: Houghton Mifflin.

Hampel Committee Report (1998), *Committee on Corporate Governance: Final Report*, London: HMSO.

Hantke-Domas, M. (2003), 'The public interest theory of regulation: non-existence or misinterpretation?', *European Journal of Law and Economics*, **15**, 165–94.

Hirsch, Fred and David Gordon (1975), *Newspaper Money*, London: Hutchinson.

Hirschman, Albert O. (1970), *Exit, Voice, and Loyalty. Responses to Decline in Firms, Organizations, and States*, Cambridge, MA: Harvard University Press.

Jessop, B. (1998), 'The rise of governance and the risks of failure: the case of economic development', *International Social Science Journal*, **50**(155), 29–45.

Knight, K.G. and Roger Sugden (1990), 'Efficiency, economic democracy and company law', in Keith Cowling and Roger Sugden (eds), *A New Economic Policy*

for Britain. Essays on the Development of Industry, Manchester: Manchester University Press.
Long, N. E. (1990), 'Conceptual notes on the public interest for public administration and policy analysts', *Administration and Society*, **22**(2), 170–81.
Monopolies and Mergers Commission (1999), *British Sky Broadcasting Group plc and Manchester United plc*, London: HMSO.
Network Rail (2002a), 'Network Rail completes public member selection process', *Network Rail Press Release*, 4 December, PR02078; accessed on 8 January 2003 at http://www.networkrail.com/04-12-02.doc.
Network Rail (2002b), *Memorandum & Articles of Association of Network Rail Limited, Company Number 04402220*, London: Network Rail.
Office of Rail Regulation (ORR) (2007), *National Rail Trends Yearbook 2006/07*, London: ORR.
Sugden, R. (1997), 'Economías multinacionales y la ley del desarrollo sin equidad (Multinational economies and the law of uneven development)', *FACES Revista de la Facultad de Ciencias Económicas y Sociales*, **3**(4), 87–109.
Sugden, R. and J.R. Wilson (2002), 'Economic development in the shadow of the consensus: a strategic decision-making approach', *Contributions in Political Economy*, **21**, 111–34.
Sunstein, Cass R. (2001a), *Designing Democracy. What Constitutions Do*, Oxford: Oxford University Press.
Sunstein, Cass R. (2001b), *Republic.com*, Princeton, NJ: Princeton University Press.
Tirole, J. (2001), 'Corporate governance', *Econometrica*, **69**(1), 1–35.
Williams, R. (1966), *Communications*, London: Chatto and Windus.
Wojcik, D. (2006), 'Convergence in corporate governance: evidence from Europe and the challenge for economic geography', *Journal of Economic Geography*, **6**, 639–60.
Zeitlin, M. (1974), 'Corporate ownership and control: the large corporation and the capitalist class', *American Journal of Sociology*, **79**(5), 1073–119.

4. Corporate boards of directors: a precautionary perspective*

Oliver E. Williamson

The past decade has witnessed a resurgence of interest in corporate boards of directors and corporate governance more generally. Business, economics and law journals as well as the business and popular presses have all participated in this revival. Book length treatises have appeared as well. Partly this flurry of interest has been brought on by corporate governance abuses and disputes over the efficacy of public policy responses thereto, of which the Sarbanes–Oxley Act is most notable. Given the many values at stake, a consensus has been elusive.

This chapter does not attempt a consensus but addresses two questions, the answers to which are pertinent to an accurate understanding of the board of directors: Should boards of directors in the modern corporation be reconstituted as vigilant monitors? Should such boards, additionally or instead, be active participants in the management of the firm? I examine these proposals from an efficiency perspective by applying the lens of contract/governance in combination with organization theory (of a meso-organizational kind) and conclude that (1) serious implementation problems arise with both the vigilant monitoring and active management participation proposals; (2) other purposes served by boards are properly included in the calculus; and (3) the quest for good governance is and will remain an ongoing challenge in every large corporation whatsoever.

I begin in section 1 by examining debt and equity as rules-based and discretionary governance structures, respectively, where the board of directors is interpreted as a means by which to provide credible contracting support for equity investors. Boards in practice, as reported by Myles Mace (1971), are described in section 2. Much of the remainder of the chapter examines and interprets the disparity between boards in principle (as described in section 1) and boards in practice (as described by Mace). Section 3 addresses the problems that would be encountered if concerted efforts were made to implement vigilant monitoring and active participation. Provisional lessons of the foregoing for boards in practice are set out in section 4. The contractual purposes of the board are described as a two-sided credible commitment to both shareholders and the management in section 5, which has additional ramifications for understanding boards in practice. Recent contrarian contributions from the finance literature and by legal scholars are briefly sketched in section 6. Concluding remarks follow.

1 CREDIBLE CONTRACTING

Of the many forms of corporate finance (Tirole, 2006), I focus on the polar forms of debt and equity, where these are described not merely as alternative financial instruments but also as alternative modes of governance. A project financing perspective is adopted. The basic argument is this: (1) different projects pose different contractual hazards; (2) different modes of finance employ different hazard mitigation (governance) mechanisms; and (3) efficiency purposes are served by aligning the contractual needs of projects with the governance attributes of alternative modes of finance.

In general, simple projects will be organized by simple modes of governance, where simple modes of governance tend to be market-like, and more complex modes of governance are more hierarchical. These correspond roughly with rules governance and discretionary governance, respectively. Differences in project complexity depend on the attributes of the projects in question. As viewed through the lens of contract/governance, project complexity varies with the degree to which the identity of the parties is important, where this turns largely on the condition of asset specificity (which is a measure of bilateral dependency) and with the disturbances to which transactions are subject (for which adaptations are needed). Because assets of a transaction-specific kind can be redeployed to alternative uses and users only at a loss of productive value, such transactions pose contractual hazards when subject to consequential disturbances for which advance provision is incomplete or incorrect.

John R. Commons' reformulation of the problem of economic organization, with emphasis on *ongoing contractual relations*, applies: 'the ultimate unit of activity . . . must contain in itself the three principles of conflict mutuality and order. This unit is a transaction' (1932, p. 4). Not only does transaction cost economics name the transaction as the basic unit of analysis, but governance is the means by which to infuse order, thereby to mitigate conflict and realize mutual gains.

As indicated, the finance transaction is examined by adopting a project financing orientation.[1] Thus suppose that a firm is seeking to finance the following projects, where these are arrayed by increasing degrees of nonredeployability: a general-purpose office building located in a population center; a general-purpose plant located in a manufacturing center;

distribution facilities located somewhat more remotely; special-purpose equipment; market infrastructure and product development expenses; and the like. Also assume that the governance structure for debt requires the debtor to observe the following stylized rules: (1) stipulated interest payments will be made at regular intervals; (2) the business will continuously meet certain liquidity tests; (3) sinking funds will be set up and principal repaid at the loan-expiration date; and (4) in the event of default, the debt-holders will exercise pre-emptive claims against the assets in question. If everything goes well, interest and principal will be paid on schedule. But debt is unforgiving if things go poorly. Failure to make scheduled payments results in liquidation. The various debt-holders will then realize differential recovery in the degree to which the assets in question are redeployable.

Debt thus works well for generic projects to which rules-based governance applies. As, however, the condition of asset-specificity increases, the value of liquidation claims declines and the terms of debt finance will be adjusted adversely. Confronted with the prospect that specialized investments will be financed on adverse terms, the firm might respond by sacrificing some of the specialized investment features in favor of greater redeployability. But this entails tradeoffs: production costs may increase or quality may decrease as a result. Might it be possible to avoid these by inventing a new governance structure to which mutual gains (added continuity and adaptability and a lower cost of capital, as supported by added safeguards) can be projected? In the degree to which this is feasible, the value-enhancing benefits of investments in specific assets can be preserved.

Suppose that a financial instrument called equity is invented and assume that equity has the following governance properties: (1) it bears a residual-claimant status to the firm in both earnings and asset-liquidation respects; (2) it contracts for the duration of the life of the firm; and (3) a board of directors is created and awarded to equity that (a) is elected by the pro-rata votes of those who hold tradable shares, (b) has the power to replace the management, (c) decides on management compensation, (d) has access to internal performance measures on a timely basis, (e) can authorize audits in depth for special follow-up purposes, (f) is apprised of important investment and operating proposals before they are implemented, and (g) in other respects bears what Eugene Fama and Michael Jensen refer to as a decision-review and monitoring relation to the firm's management (1983).

The board of directors thus arises endogenously and serves as a credible commitment, the effect of which is to reduce the cost of capital for projects that involve limited redeployability. Not only do the added controls to which equity has access provide added assurance, but equity is more forgiving than debt. Efforts are therefore made to work things out and realize adaptive benefits that would otherwise be sacrificed when disturbances push the parties into a maladapted state of affairs. The upshot is that equity finance has superior continuity and adaptability properties and, because the board of directors serves as a safeguard, is made available on better terms than would (rule governed) debt financing of specific assets.

Interpreting the board of directors as a credible commitment for equity financed investments could nevertheless be challenged. Is there concurrence with this view? What is to be made of the stakeholder (as opposed to the stockholder) perspective? Is the predicted alignment of debt and equity with financial transactions borne out by the data? Also, do boards of directors in practice behave in the manner described? The last of these is discussed in later sections. I comment briefly on the first three here.

Jean Tirole observes with respect to the first that

> The dominant view in economics . . . is that corporate governance relates to the 'ways in which the suppliers of finance to corporations assure themselves of getting a return on their investment.' Relatedly, [corporate governance] is preoccupied with ways in which a corporation's insiders can credibly commit to return funds to outside investors and can thereby attract external financing (2006, p. 16).

This is broadly consonant with the view expressed here (and elsewhere; see Williamson, 1985, 1988). By contrast, the 'stakeholder' view of the board holds that the interests of all corporate constituencies that have a stake in the firm – workers, consumers, other suppliers, the government, and so on – should be represented on the board.

I have examined this stakeholder interpretation of the board elsewhere (Williamson, 1985, chap. 12) and conclude as follows: (1) whether a constituency has a stake depends on whether it makes specific investments in the firm; (2) the contractual relation between the firm and each of its constituencies is crafted at the contractual interface where firm and constituency meet, which is to say that the idiosyncratic needs of each constituency are addressed on their own terms rather than assigned to an all-purpose board; (3) giving the board stakeholder responsibility dilutes its credible contracting support for equity; and (4) describing the purpose of the board in stakeholder terms has the effect of providing the management with an ad hoc rationale to explain any decision whatsoever.[2] Anything goes.

As for corroboration, I would observe that leveraged buyouts are usefully interpreted (in part) as being activated by an excess of equity in relation to debt, in that efficiency can be realized upon substituting debt for equity in firms where the debt–equity ratio is too low, which seems to be borne out by the data (Williamson, 1988, pp. 585–6). Also, a series of empirical studies of debt and equity find a negative correlation between asset specificity and debt (Titman and Wessels, 1988; Balakrishnan and Fox, 1993; Kochar, 1996; Mocnik, 2001).[3] And the recent and carefully executed empirical study by Efraim Benmelech et al. (2005) is corroborative of the proposition that interest rates on commercial property loan contracts increase with the non-redeployability of the assets.

2 BOARDS IN PRACTICE[4]

The foregoing (rather normative) description of the board of directors interprets the board as having been created for and awarded to the equity shareholders. Such boards are presumed to be vigilant monitors and to actively intervene as the occasion warrants. How does this description comport with boards in practice?

Myles Mace's book, *Directors: Myth and Reality* (1971), has the purpose of challenging the myths and telling the reality: 'As a participant on, and observer of, boards of directors for over 25 years, I have developed a healthy skepticism about the prevailing [mythical] concept of the board of directors. Specifically, it seemed important to ask what directors *actually do* in fulfillment of their responsibilities' (1971, p. 8; emphasis added).

His 'final summary' of directors in large and medium sized firms where the CEO and board members own only a few shares of stock is this (Mace, 1971, pp. 205–6):

1. [CEOs] with de facto powers of control select the members of the boards.
2. [CEOs] determine what boards do and do not do.
3. Directors selected are usually heads of equally prestigious organizations with primary responsibilities of their own.
4. Heads of businesses and financial, legal, and educational organizations are extremely busy [people] with limited motivation and time to serve as directors of other organizations.
5. Most boards of directors serve as advisors and counselors to the [CEOs].
6. Most boards of directors serve as some sort of discipline for the organization – as a corporate conscience.
7. Most boards of directors are available to and do make decisions in the event of a crisis.
8. A few boards of directors establish company objectives, strategies, and broad policies. Most do not.
9. A few boards of directors ask discerning questions. Most do not.
10. A few boards evaluate and measure the performance of the [CEO] and select and de-select the [CEO]. Most do not.

Pertaining to item 3 on this list, Mace quotes from one executive as follows (1971, p. 90):

> The board is part of the image of the company. The caliber and stature of the outside board members, both just as names and as people circulating in the business community, contributes to the image of the company. When I look at a company, I look at who is on the board . . . The type of people on a board does, in a series of informal and intangible ways, have a good deal to do with what the character of a company is. Is it a respectable and conservative company, or is it highly speculative? The investing public, you know, really care who is on the board.

Also, Mace observes that one of the functions played by the board with respect to discipline and corporate conscience (item 6) is that the CEO and his subordinates 'know that periodically they must appear . . . before a board of directors consisting of respected, able people of stature [who], no matter how friendly, cause the company organization to do a better job of thinking through their problems and of being prepared with solutions, explanations, or rationales' (1971, p. 180). Mace concludes with a somewhat conflicting description of the board as a corporate conscience (1971, p. 181):

> Usually the symbols of corporate conscience are more apparent than real, and [CEOs] with complete powers of control make the compensation policies and decisions. The compensation committee, and the board which approves the recommendations of the compensation committee, are not in most cases decision-making bodies. These decisions are made by the [CEO] and in most situations the committee and board approval is perfunctory. The [CEO] has de facto powers of control, and in most cases he is the decision maker. The board does, I believe, tend to temper the inclinations of [CEOs] with de facto control, and it does contribute to the avoidance of excesses. Thus it serves the important role of a corporate conscience.

With reference to item 10, Mace identifies two crisis situations where the role of the board of directors is more than advisory. One is if the CEO were to die or become incapacitated; the second is if performance is 'so unsatisfactory that a change must be made' (1971, p. 182) – which recalls Oswald Knauth's view that 'the degree of success that management must produce to remain in office is surprisingly small. Indeed, management must fail obviously and even ignominiously before the dispersed forces of criticism become mobilized for action' (1948, p. 45).

Altogether, Mace's assessment of corporate boards as of 1971 counsels low expectations, to which corporate scandals in the recent past are believed to warrant a downward adjustment. Bengt Holmstrom and

Steven Kaplan, however, hold otherwise: corporate governance underwent significant improvements during the 1980s and 1990s. Thus although Holmstrom and Kaplan are dismayed that so many boards have approved anti-takeover measures, such as poison pills and staggered boards (2003, p. 15), and that some CEO compensation packages are outlandishly generous (p. 14), they have a generally favorable view of corporate governance changes that have taken place since the 1980s. Specifically, whereas it was common for corporate managements to 'think of themselves as representing not the shareholders, but rather . . . [as] "balancing" the claims of all important corporate "stakeholders"' before 1980 when 'only 20% of the compensation of US CEOs was tied to stock market performance' (p. 10), those conditions have changed.

Hostile takeovers and restructuring provided a wake-up call for complacent and inefficient firms in the 1980s, and this restructuring has continued during the 1990s at the initiative of incumbent managements (p. 12). Contributing factors to the more recent restructurings have been the significant degree to which the equity-based compensation of CEOs has increased (to almost 50 per cent of the total compensation of CEOs by 1994) and the increase in share ownership of large institutional investors from under 30 per cent in 1980 to over 50 per cent in 1996 (pp. 12, 14). Indicative of these changes, the Business Roundtable in 1997 changed its position on business objectives to read 'the paramount duty of management and the board is to the shareholder and not to . . . other stakeholders' (p. 13). A downside of the increased executive stock and option ownership is that 'the incentive to manage and manipulate accounting numbers' has also increased (p. 13), to which the practice of post-dating options has recently been uncovered.

Overall, Holmstrom and Kaplan are of the view that corporate governance in the US not only compares favorably with other countries but that it has been getting better. They counsel that it should not be judged on the basis of worst excesses – as at Enron, WorldCom, Tyco, Adelphia, Global Crossing and others (p. 8). Serious abuses notwithstanding, tails do not wag dogs.

3 RESTORING BOARDS TO INTENDED PURPOSES

My purpose here is to examine the ramifications of having boards serve as vigilant monitors and as active participants in the management of the corporation. What would these entail? Are there practical obstacles? Are there conceptual obstacles?

3.1 Practical Obstacles

Board as vigilant monitor

The basic proposition here is this: the board in practice is at a huge disadvantage to the top management of the corporation in information and expertise respects. Thus whereas the management is involved with the corporation on a full-time basis and has the benefit of accounting, legal, financial, engineering, planning and managerial staff expertise to track and interpret the past performance of the firm and develop projections for the future, the membership of the board is part-time and lacks firm-specific knowledge in all of these respects. By default, as it were, the responsibility for measuring and reporting upon past performance and making forecasts and plans for the future falls to the management.

Conceivably, however, these conditions could be rectified. Surely the suppliers of equity finance can direct the firm to provide the funds for the board to hire qualified staff for the board, thereby closing the gap in information and expertise respects. Once, moreover, the board has back-up staff to supply information and expertise, it can participate more knowledgeably in strategic decision making. Indeed, powers could also be devolved upon the shareholders to propose and vote on binding resolutions.[5] Inasmuch as such reforms would appear to entail modest costs and would go a long way toward redressing the problems that beset corporate governance over the past century, what are the obstacles?

One obstacle is that the management and the board may be content with things as they are. Rather than disturb the 'easy life', both prefer to continue with business as usual. Here as elsewhere, however, *significant* inefficiencies invite corrective action by others – in which event competition in the product market (possibly from new entrants) and competition in the capital market (possibly through takeover) will eventually be activated.[6]

Perhaps, however, the main reasons for not involving the board directly in the reading and interpretation of the essential control variables reside elsewhere. One consideration is that, competent though the staff hired by and reporting to the board may be, there is a difference between observing and participating[7] – where the latter is more nuanced. In that event, differences could easily arise that will lead to conflict over the interpretation to be placed upon performance reports. Unless the board insists that its readings and interpretations of performance are final, the differences will need to be reconciled. Either way, managerial incentives are impaired and what could have been a mainly cooperative relation between the board and the management becomes more adversarial in the process.

Sometimes there are no good choices: admonishing the board to serve as a diligent monitor is pointless if the board lacks the requisite information; expecting the management to disclose the relevant information and display the ramifications in an unbiased way collides with the realities of managerial discretion; and providing the board with its own staff to uncover and interpret the data is costly, will never close the information gap, and invites conflict. Consider therefore the recommendation that outside members of the board become more involved as active participants.

Board as active participant

Michael Jensen's discussion of 'the failure of corporate internal control systems' opens with the observation that 'By nature, organizations abhor control systems, and ineffective governance is a major part of the problem with internal control mechanisms. They seldom respond in the absence of a crisis' (1993, p. 852). He thereafter makes a series of observations about boards in practice and subsequently recommends that leveraged buyouts (LBO) and venture capital funds provide the models for effectively redesigning the board in the modern corporation (1993, p. 869):

> LBO associations and venture capital funds provide a blueprint for managers and boards who wish to revamp their top-level control systems to make them more efficient. LBOs and venture capital funds are, of course, the preeminent examples of active investors in recent US history, and they serve as excellent models that can be emulated in part or in total by virtually any corporation. The two have similar governance structures, and have been successful in resolving the governance problems of both slow growth or declining firms (LBO associations) and high growth entrepreneurial firms (venture capital funds).

What are the obstacles, if any, to adopting LBO and venture capital start-up practices in the steady-state modern corporation? While the analogy is not exact, LBOs and start-ups are akin to sprinters whereas the modern corporation is a long-distance runner. It is elementary that altogether different strategies apply to sprinting and long-distance running.

LBOs and start-ups are both variants upon Rudolf Spreckels's remark that 'When I see something badly done, or not done at all, I see an opportunity to make a fortune.' The LBO sees something badly done, mobilizes financing, pays the requisite premium to gain control of the firm, replaces the incumbent management, and reshapes the firm and its financing. Thus debt is substituted for equity, thereby to restore a more efficient mix of debt and equity in relation to the firm's assets,[8] and unrelated or underperforming parts are sold or spun off. The big reward comes when the firm is taken public again.[9] In the interim, the new management and the banks, insurance companies and investment bankers that package the deal are *actively involved* in the management and reshaping of the corporation. Once the firm goes public, the high-powered incentives and the urgency of real-time responsiveness give way to a steady-state modern corporation where managers (rather than financial entrepreneurs) are at the helm, the ownership is more diffuse, and lower powered incentives are employed. (If, in the fullness of time, many of the benefits of LBOs are undone by backsliding, the LBO process could be repeated.)

Start-up firms, especially of a high technology kind, may also be aimed at improvements on something badly done, but more often arise out of perceived opportunities to provide something altogether new (Shane, 2001). These latter are high-risk undertakings that combine venture capitalists with entrepreneurial, technical, and legal talent in a race to be first. High-powered incentives apply and real-time involvement by all of the critical actors (as managers or directors) is practiced.[10] If and as the start-up succeeds, the big rewards are realized when the firm goes public. Thereafter, the firm progressively takes on the characteristics of a business-as-usual enterprise,[11] as more of the action is devolved upon the primary feedback loop and routines set in (as described in the Appendix).

LBOs and start-ups thus differ from mature corporations in consequential ways. The former are evanescent forms of organization for which real-time responsiveness is of the essence and to which concentrated ownership and high-powered incentives are well suited. If and as the project succeeds, the firm takes on the properties of a modern corporation.

3.2 Conceptual Obstacles

Three conceptual considerations that bear on our understanding of corporate boards are discussed here: the remediableness criterion, downside drift and delegation. The first of these holds that hypothetical ideals, always and everywhere, should give way to an examination of feasible alternatives when it comes to public policy in practice – which is implicit in the foregoing and is made more explicit here. Downside drift is an intertemporal regularity that attends 'effective control' in organizations of all kinds, the modern corporation included. Perhaps the most serious obstacle to straight thinking about the corporation, however, is the important but widespread neglect of 'delegation'. Consider each.

Remediableness

The remediableness criterion advises that an extant mode of organization for which (1) no superior *feasible* mode of organization can be described and (2) *implemented* with expected net gains is (3) presumed to be efficient. The import of the remediableness criterion is that it discourages public policy analysis that is based on a comparison of an actual practice with a hypothetical ideal – whereupon the actual practice is judged to be 'inefficient'.

Note that the remediableness criterion is pertinent to the query: have we 'any justification for assuming that those in control of the modern corporation will also choose to operate it in the interests of the shareholders' (Berle and Means, 1932, p. 121)? The normative ideal is that the management should operate the firm in full congruence with the interests of the shareholders. The reality is that this is observed in the breach. The public policy conclusion: a 'market failure' resides therein.

Inasmuch, however, as an actual condition can never be better than and ordinarily will be inferior to a hypothetical ideal, market failures proliferate and hyperactive public policy is the predictable result. Taxes or subsidies or active intervention by the government become ubiquitous. But that defies common sense.

Common sense notwithstanding, the normative tradition in public policy analysis was slow, even loath, to come to terms with the remediableness criterion (Coase, 1964; Demsetz, 1969; Williamson, 1995, 1996; Dixit, 1996) – of which the practice of judging boards to be inefficient because they fail to close an indwelling information deficit is an example. Not only is this mindless (impossible), but it is counterproductive: it invites scorn for best (but limited) efforts of boards to be informed; and it encourages costly excesses of information gathering that will lead to conflict between the board and the management.

The problem with the recommendation that boards become active participants in the management of the firm is that this fails to come to terms with predictable life cycle changes in the corporation (as briefly discussed in 3.1 and as further discussed below) and would compromise the integrity of delegation. Consider each.

Downside drift

One of the lessons of organization theory is that 'organization has a life of its own' (Selznick, 1966, p. 10). Sometimes this occurs spontaneously, as with the 'accidental repartitions' to which Karl Marx referred that get repeated, develop advantages of their own, and gradually ossify (1967, Vol. 1, p. 337). In addition, however, to spontaneous transformations, some transformations are due to the calculated efforts by the leadership to extend and consolidate the natural advantages that leadership confers. The Iron Law of Oligarchy – 'Who says organization, says oligarchy' (Michels, 1962, p. 365) – is mainly a manifestation of the latter.

Albeit a predictable consequence of organization, Robert Michels advises that the lesson of oligarchy is not one of resigned acceptance but rather of judicious mitigation: 'nothing but a serene and frank examination of the oligarchical dangers of democracy will enable us to [mitigate] these dangers' (1962, p. 370). As applied to boards of directors in the modern corporation, the lesson is that out of awareness that management ascendancy is normal and predictable, what mitigation efforts are warranted? Good intentions notwithstanding, efforts to become involved and exercise control are often beset with dysfunctional consequences.

Delegation

'Hierarchy . . . is one of the central structural schemes that the architect of complexity uses . . . [to decompose large systems into] subsystems that, in turn, have their own subsystems, and so on' (Simon, 1962, p. 468), thereby to achieve viability. 'Among possible complex forms, hierarchies are the ones that have the time to evolve' (Simon, 1962, p. 473).

Conscious delegation is one of the properties of hierarchy in formal organizations in business and government, whereby 'Parties higher up the hierarchy . . . delegate functions to parties lower down . . . but parties lower down will not delegate functions to parties higher up' (D. Williamson, 2007, p. 11). Parties lower down nevertheless gain deep knowledge advantages in relation to those above, as a result of which they acquire a degree of autonomy. Also, if parties higher up are large groups (such as voters or shareholders) and work through collective action, delegation from the group to its elected representatives is especially hard to repossess.

Delegation from the shareholders to the management in the modern corporation is accomplished through the board of directors. The benefits of delegation from the board to the management include: (1) delegation is an efficient means by which to assign problems to those with the better training, ability, and/or deeper knowledge of the particulars (to include tacit knowledge acquired through learning-by-doing);[12] (2) delegation enhances incentives by linking compensation and promotions to performance (where an active board would weaken this linkage by obscuring responsibility for performance, be it good or bad); (3) respect for delegation serves as a check upon the 'costs of good intentions' whereby controllers engage in well-intended excesses of control, often with dysfunctional consequences; and, such respect notwithstanding, (4) delegation can be repossessed under extreme circumstances.

The first of these views the firm as a means by which to assemble specialized and complementary expertise by hiring managers and workers with the requisite ability, training and experience and to deepen that experience over time in an interactive way. Managers and workers thereby acquire tacit knowledge of their jobs and those of others with whom they work, both within the firm and with those outside suppliers for which a continuing association yields mutual gains.

Respect for delegation is also a means by which to hold individuals (or interactive groups or divisions) accountable. This in turn means that their compensation, the resources that are allocated to their use, and their promotions can be made contingent on performance. To be sure, performance is a vector, is often interactive with the efforts of a 'team', and results become fully known only with delay. Accordingly, these incentives are muted. Over time, however, delegation is nevertheless a means by which to harness added incentive intensity.

Delegation also serves as a means by which to check over-zealous control. The bureaucratic theories described by James March and Herbert Simon as 'machine models of organization' are pertinent (1958, pp. 36–47).[13] A chronic problem with well-intentioned controllers is that they often have a truncated understanding of the system for which added controls are recommended. In addition to the intended effects, added controls can also have unintended net negative consequences. Greater respect for delegation will serve as a deterrent to over-zealous regulation. Not only would 'excessive interference . . . endanger the division of labor, which is the reason for . . . [appointing managers] in the first place' (Hellwig, 2000, p. 121), but, more generally, the integrity of delegation serves, in effect, as a credible contracting support for the management (more of which later).

4 FIVE PROVISIONAL LESSONS OF THE FOREGOING

Although a lot has transpired since Mace described corporate boards in practice in 1971, his description is broadly applicable to boards in practice today. This will come as bad news to many. Possibly, however, upon making allowance for the practical and conceptual obstacles to activating the board in monitoring and managing respects, what Mace describes is a concession to the realities of what boards should be. That said, there are nevertheless reasons to be concerned.

Of the ten conditions that Mace lists in his summary assessment of boards, the four to which I call special attention are these: (1) the CEO is in de facto control of the operation and composition of the board; (2) outside members of the board are at enormous information and expertise disadvantages to the management; (3) most boards most of the time are responding with nodding approval; and (4) boards are beset by inertia, hence are slow to become active when the corporation experiences adversity. To this, moreover, I would add that (5) the very existence of boards affords an opportunity for the shareholders to 'vote the rascals out'.

4.1 De Facto Control

CEOs who also serve as chair of the board of directors are strategically positioned to entrench their control by appointing sympathetic or compliant members to the board and by controlling the agenda. An obvious composition of the board concern is the ratio of officers to independent board members, but the qualifications and predilections of independent board members are also pertinent. Those with and without business experience and expertise are usefully distinguished.

Other things being equal, independent board members who possess financial or business expertise are better able to relate and have more to offer by way of sound judgment and informed critique than do those who are lacking in these respects. The objectivity of such independent board members can nevertheless be compromised if they are part of what Bang Nguyen-Dang refers to as 'corporate elite's small world . . . [of] cross-directorships' (2005, p. 6).[14] Outside executives who possess the requisite expertise but, because of overlapping interests are 'in this together', lack objectivity and compromise the board.

A second class of problematic board members consists of those who, though lacking in expertise, possess 'gravitas'. Such board members can be expected to be more compliant as (1) the ratio of board payments to their other income is higher, and (2) their susceptibility to indirect rewards – such as 'contributions' to the board member's place of employment (as with eleemosynary institutions) or to favored charities, or out of the prospect of reciprocity (for example, procurement) with the board member's place of employment (Bebchuk and Fried, 2004, pp. 27–8) – is higher.

To be sure, it is altogether understandable that CEOs will seek to appoint internal and outside directors who are perceived to be 'compatible' (Barnard, 1938, p. 224). The possibility that insecure or grasping CEOs will cross the line from constructive support to use obeisance as a selection criterion is where the problem resides. Tirole's succinct summary of the Bebchuk and Fried (2004) critique of the appointment of directors by the CEO applies (2006, p. 32; emphasis added):

> Directors dislike haggling with or being 'disloyal' to the CEO, have little time to intervene, *and further receive a number of favors from the CEO*: the CEO can place them on the company's slate, increasing seriously their chance of reelection, give them perks, business deals (perhaps after they have been nominated on the board, so that they are formally 'independent'), extra compensation on top of the director fee, and charitable contributions to nonprofit organizations

> headed by directors, or reciprocate the lenient oversight in case of interlocking directorates. . . . Directors also happily acquiesce to takeover defenses.

What to do? The obvious corrective would be to prohibit CEOs from serving as chair of the board. That, of course, would have little purpose if the board chair were to be a crony of the CEO. Removing the CEO should also be done mindful of the possibility that the CEO (and the management more generally) would withhold cooperation, thereby to frustrate efforts by an independent chair to be well enough informed to discharge the business of the board effectively. Out of consideration for the importance of the CEO and the board to work in a cooperative manner, having the CEO and an independent member of the board serve as co-chairs warrants consideration.

4.2 Information and Expertise

As discussed in section 3, the board's disadvantages to the management in information and expertise respects are indwelling. The degree of disadvantage is nevertheless variable.

The board's information state can be made worse if the board is misled by a management that deceitfully massages and manipulates the data, of which smoothing performance or, worse, 'hitting the numbers' (thereby to reap incentive compensation benefits) are examples. (The back-dating of options is another more recent example of manipulation, although this is often done with the actual or tacit approval of the board.) By the same token, the board's information state can be improved if the management candidly discloses the relevant data. In principle, accountants and auditors who subscribe to and live up to high standards of professional ethics will relieve propensities of the first kind and reinforce the latter. Legal consequences for orchestrated deceits may be more effective.

The limits of the board in expertise respects is likewise an immanent yet variable condition. Out of respect for the importance of expertise, wasting board appointments on members whose main qualification is that of compliance is especially regrettable.

4.3 Nodding Approval

As discussed in the Appendix, where the relation of the board to the operations of the firm is discussed in conjunction with double-feedback, the natural posture for the board is to respond to acceptable performance with nodding approval. That being both a natural and appropriate state of affairs, the concern is not that this is normal but that this could slip from normal into uncritical acceptance.

4.4 Inertia

The downside of nodding approval is that the board's 'zone of acceptance' gradually expands, to the degree that it fails to act promptly and with urgency when a crisis occurs (to say nothing about being inattentive to early warning signals). Crisis response being a crucial role for the board (item 7 of Mace's summary and the Appendix), creating an early warning capability would seem to have much to recommend it.

Because this entails looking forward rather than backward, it is doubtful that the audit committee would be well-suited. Creating an atmosphere in which board members are expected to 'ask the hard questions' and 'maintain vigilance' but doing this in a way that is both reliable and constructive poses a challenge.

Out of awareness of the hazards of inertia and in recognition that early and effective crisis response is vital to corporate performance, self-confident CEOs might well advise their boards that their main job is to 'keep me on my toes'. Boards that accept that assignment should nevertheless be wary of excesses of involvement. Deliberative discussions on the merits should not become an entree to intrusive involvement. Active intervention is undertaken always and only in response to crises.

4.5 Takeover

In consideration of the difficulties of overcoming the inertial propensities of the board, relying more extensively on competition from the capital market has obvious attractions. This could be reinforced if state regulatory commissions were to adopt default rules that remove poison pills, staggered boards, and other obstacles to takeover – to which Henry Hansmann's treatment (2006) of the efficacy of default provisions in state corporate law is pertinent. Indeed, there may be no more basic function for the board to perform than keeping the gate open so that owners of equity can sell their shares to organized interests that will vote the rascals out.[15]

5 CREDIBLE CONTRACTING REVISITED

As described in section 1, the board of directors is a credible commitment to the suppliers of equity capital. Because, however, this interpretation is severely diminished by the practical limits to which the outside board members are subject in vigilant monitoring and active participation respects, many observers regard the credibility of the board in practice as a pathetic fiction. The remediableness criterion nevertheless counsels moderation. Thus although boards in practice are different from what is described in section 1 and from what many would wish for,[16] this is a condition with which we need to come to terms – awaiting a superior feasible alternative that can be implemented with expected net gains.

There are additional ramifications, moreover, that lead to a more accepting interpretation of boards in practice. As discussed in section 3, the limits of boards in monitoring and managing respects have the effect of supporting the integrity of delegation to the management – which is a benefit and can be thought of as an unintended credible commitment. My purpose here is to consider another possible credibility support: the respect of the board for the legitimacy of the management also serves credible contracting purposes. The concepts of 'informal organization' and the 'economics of atmosphere' are both pertinent.

Very possibly, moreover, credibility supports, or the lack thereof, apply to other aspects of the board–management relationship. If and as a two-sided view of credible contracting deepens our understanding of boards in practice, such considerations should play a more prominent role in the study of corporate governance.

5.1 Informal Organization and Atmospherics

Chester Barnard advises that 'formal organizations are vitalized and conditioned by informal organization . . . [and that] there cannot be one without the other. If one fails, the other disintegrates' (1938, p. 120). He further avers that 'One of the indispensable functions of informal organization in formal organizations . . . [is] that of communication. Another function is that of maintenance of cohesiveness in formal organizations through regulating the willingness to serve and the stability of objective authority' (1938, p. 122).

The economics of atmosphere is also pertinent to an understanding of ongoing contractual relations, where such relations can be devalued by excesses of calculativeness. Thus whereas it is a maxim in economics never to leave any money on the table, that maxim is stood on its head by business people and investment bankers who advise always to leave money on the table. This latter does not in the least reflect their lack of hard-headedness. Rather, if one party is perceived to be bargaining in a relentlessly calculative way, the other can be expected to respond in kind – with the result that the atmospherics are devalued. What could have been a cooperative relation with give-and-take becomes convoluted and costly and may break down altogether.

5.2 Management as a Constituency

Curiously, the contractual relation between the firm and the management is rarely addressed in credible contracting terms. Possibly that is because of the perception that the management, which contracts on behalf of the firm with other constituencies, is already over-represented in the contract between the firm and itself – in that the management is writing a contract (with the consent of a compliant board) with one hand and is signing that contract with the other. If, however, credible contracting is a robust concept and applies to every constituency, then the contract with the management should be examined as well.

The contractual relation between the firm and the management starts with the *formal* employment contract whereby salary, incentive compensation, benefits, severance payments, emoluments, and so on are negotiated. This contract is mediated by the board, which is also, presumably, the forum for resolving disputes. But how does this latter work? What are the mechanisms through which communication is accomplished? What is the legitimacy of the management in board participation respects? In addition to the formal employment contract, the *informal* employment relation evidently comes into play.

Consider therefore two different informal relations between the board and the management. The management enjoys the same de facto controls described earlier for both, but its participation is regarded as illegitimate under one scenario and is accorded legitimacy in the other. What are the ramifications?

I submit that a more contentious relation between boards and managements can be expected to develop under the illegitimacy scenario. Managements whose de facto control is regarded as illegitimate will be more guarded in their communications and their sense of job security will be less. Recognizing that they will face uncertain search prospects in the job market,[17] such managements will renegotiate the contract and will adapt their behavior accordingly. Not only will the added risks be reflected in the compensation package, but they will manage the firm differently. Thus compensation will include added 'hazard pay' and the firm will be managed with reference to a shorter time horizon – since there may be no tomorrow. 'Hitting the numbers' by false and misleading accounting is also encouraged.

Suppose instead that the management is viewed as a legitimate participant on the board, de facto control notwithstanding. In that event, lest their moral involvement deteriorate, 'High level managers and administrators whose decisions cannot be easily or quickly monitored . . . [will be] treated as members of a high trust fraternity' (Fox, 1974, pp. 170–71). Not only do different atmospherics set in if the participation of the management on the board is awarded legitimacy, but the board, in effect, becomes a more credible contracting support for both shareholders and managers, who are in this together.[18] The upshot is that, here as elsewhere, looking ahead and introducing cost effective credible commitments is the source of mutual gains.

To be sure, a more definitive treatment of credible contracting in both delegation and informal/atmospheric/legitimacy respects is needed. More generally, the dialogue on corporate governance will benefit from a more systematic examination of two-sided credible contracting.

6 OTHER CONTRARIAN LITERATURE

The 'standard' view that boards have been hopelessly compromised has been challenged in several recent contributions to the corporate board literature where considerations of feasibility, credibility and mutual gain have been given prominence.

Andres Almazan and Javier Suarez's paper on 'Entrenchment and severance pay in optimal governance structures' (2003) expressly takes exception with the 'standard view in the literature . . . that . . . shareholders should have full control of the board of directors and that any form of CEO entrenchment is necessarily undesirable' (2003, p. 519). They argue that the standard view 'ignores some important interactions between managerial incentive problems and shareholder activism' and thereafter distinguish between strong and weak boards, with emphasis on 'the interaction between CEO compensation and the power that the CEO has, vis-à-vis shareholders, to influence the board of directors over his own replacement' (p. 520). Their main result is that 'some degree of entrenchment can be optimal' (p. 522) – one interpretation of which is that the credible contracting purposes of the board should be enlarged to include the management.

Renée Adams and Daniel Ferreira's paper on 'A theory of friendly boards' (2007) views the board as having the dual role of advisor to as well as monitor of the management and focuses on the tradeoff faced by the CEO in his relation with the board. As they describe it, 'the CEO dislikes monitoring by the board because he values control . . . [but] likes advising by the board because advice increases firm value without interfering with his choices . . . [where] both monitoring and advising by the board are more effective when the board is better informed' (2007, p. 220).

Their key result is that the shareholders may benefit from a CEO-friendly board because the CEO will be more forthcoming under those circumstances (pp. 238–9). Undue friendliness is held in check by their observations that 'many governance mechanisms . . . have a pure monitoring function, for example, takeovers' (p. 235) and by their assumption that 'when a management-friendly board is optimal, one should expect other governance mechanisms to pick up the slack' (p. 242).

The still more recent and unpublished paper by Douglas Baird and Robert Rasmussen (2007) on 'The prime directive' holds that the 'hiring and firing of CEOs is the single most important job that directors face' (2007, p. 923) and makes the argument that because 'boards may be too slow to pull the trigger' (p. 935) we should move 'beyond the conventional forces of corporate law . . . which focuses too narrowly upon the shareholders' (p. 936). Specifically, lenders, especially bankers, should take a leadership role: banks have better information than do directors (p. 936); banks can be more proactive (p. 938); and banks have structures that reduce biases that plague boards (p. 938). The upshot is that if lenders were to 'play a disciplinary role and have de facto power to rid a business of underperforming managers, the less the need to worry that members of the board do not have the stomach for it' (p. 940).

My doubts about the suitability of bankers to take on the role of change agents notwithstanding, both they and I are in broad agreement on the limits of boards. Specifically, they observe that although boards have the formal power 'to be dictators', in fact a 'board's range of action is quite constrained. The directors are part-timers. They have day jobs . . . [and] experience real limits on how much time they can invest in meddling in the affairs of the corporation' (p. 924). Boards commonly lack the requisite information to evaluate management and they have blind spots and biases (p. 935). Also, boards can be captured by the management (pp. 924, 934). The upshot is that boards are poorly qualified to serve as vigilant monitors.

Baird and Rasmussen also make reference to 'life cycle' changes in firms (p. 922) and thereafter distinguish between start-up ventures, where directors are actively engaged and the venture capitalist does not have a collective action problem, and large public corporations, where collective action problems are severe and we should 'not expect too much' from the directors (p. 925).

By reason of these and other limitations of boards, they conclude that 'boards will be too slow to pull the trigger' (p. 935) in terminating CEOs. Even if banks were quicker, any such changes should be done mindful of the effects these could have on the renegotiation of the contract with the management and on the management of the firm (akin to the time horizon effects discussed in section 5). Also, Holmstrom's remarks about quick triggers are pertinent (2005, p. 711):

> Analysts and outside observers, like sports spectators, are quick to leap to conclusions about what should be done when things start to go wrong. They usually want to see the CEO fired much before it happens. Boards are seen as too passive, but the appearance can be deceptive. It takes time and information to figure out what role external factors have played and what responsibility current management carries.

Maybe the information advantages that Baird and Rasmussen ascribe to banks relieve these concerns, but the atmospherics referred to in section 5 remain.

7 CONCLUSIONS

The disparity between corporate boards of directors in principle and corporate boards in practice is widely interpreted as a serious, perhaps *the* defining, illustration of the failures of capitalism. If, therefore, corporate boards have been going from bad to worse, it is all the more urgent to retake control from the management, which has usurped it, and return it to the shareholders (or maybe even the stakeholders), where it belongs. Recommended measures include closing the information gap between the management and the board, thereby to permit more vigilant monitoring of the management, and to encourage active participation by members of the board in the management of the firm.

This chapter examines the disabilities and redeeming features of corporate boards of directors by successively (1) setting out the logic of the board as credible contracting support for the suppliers of equity capital; (2) observing that boards in practice do not live up to that description; (3) inquiring into the factors that are responsible for the limitations of boards as vigilant monitors and as active participants by appealing to organization theory; (4) discussing some of the lessons that reside therein; (5) revisiting the matter of credible contracting to include the formal and informal contract between the board and the management, with the result that the board is given a two-sided credible contracting assignment; and (6) discussing recent literature of a related kind.

Altogether I suggest that the Berle and Means query, to which I referred in section 3.2, got the corporate governance literature off on the wrong foot. Before suggesting that the shareholders have been dispossessed, there is a need to understand the objective limitations of corporate boards by examining the relevant microanalytics through a focused lens. Thus although the observed disparity between boards in theory and boards in practice sometimes represents a breakdown in corporate governance, three additional possibilities warrant consideration: (1) there are serious obstacles to implementing the theory; (2) the theory is wrong; and (3) the theory is right as far as it goes, but it does not go far enough. I focus on (1) and (3) to reach a more accepting interpretation of boards in practice. Not only are there objective obstacles to vigilant monitoring and active participation by the board, but the ramifications of these obstacles for the integrity of delegation need to be factored in. Also, the legitimate involvement of the management on the board is supported by considerations of credible contracting. More systematic examination of the shareholder–management relation as mediated by the board in credible contracting respects is recommended.

Over-reaching by the management is nonetheless a concern for which diligent boards must continuously exercise precaution.[19]

NOTES

* This chapter is based on my article 'Corporate boards of directors: in principle and in practice', which is published in the October 2008 issue of the *Journal of Law, Economics, and Organization*. I am grateful to the *Journal of Law, Economics, and Organization* for permission to reprint this version of the article here. This chapter has benefited from the suggestions of Thomas Campbell, Henry Hansmann, Bengt Holmstrom, Joseph Mahoney, Roberta Romano, Robert Seamans, the referee, and the JLEO Editorial Board. It draws on papers that were presented at the University of Paris X, at the conference on Corporate Social Responsibility and Corporate Governance in Trento, at Concordia University in Montreal, at the 2006 Annual Conference of the International Society of New Institutional Economics, as the 2006 Malthus Lecture at Hatfield, UK, and at the Institutional Analysis Workshop at the University of California, Berkeley.

1. This section is based on Williamson (1988). For a related paper that examines debt financing for different assets, see Andrei Shleifer and Robert Vishny (1992). Note that a governance interpretation of corporate finance provides yet another challenge to the Modigliani–Miller theorem that the cost of capital in a firm is independent of the type of finance.
2. Jean Tirole summarizes (but does not expressly subscribe to) the following objections that have been made of the 'stakeholder-society governance structure' (2006, pp. 59–60);
   (1) 'Giving control rights to non-investors may discourage financing in the first place', since the safeguard for equity is compromised;
   (2) 'Deadlocks may result from the sharing of control';
   (3) Managerial accountability is compromised: 'the socially responsible manager faces a wide variety of missions, most of which are by nature unmeasurable', with the result that 'managers [are] less accountable'; and
   (4) 'It is not obvious that social goals are best achieved by directors and officers eager to pander to their own . . . customers and policy makers.'
3. Evidence that firms engage in 'pecking order' finance (Myers, 1985; Tirole, 2006, p. 238), where internal finance comes first and debt and equity follow, could be interpreted as contrary to the standard transaction cost economics ordering for intermediate product market procurement: try markets, try hybrids, and have recourse to internal organization only as a last resort – for which the corresponding sequence in finance is try debt, try equity, and have recourse to internal finance only as a last resort.

   I do not disagree that behavioral finance is more congruent with the pecking order sequence, but the issues are also more nuanced. For example, internal finance (retained earnings) could be superior, in transaction cost economics terms, for financing newer ventures (for example, R&D), the attributes of which are very difficult to communicate to outside investors.

4. Parts of this section and of section 3.1 draw on sections 4 and 5.2, respectively, of my paper 'Corporate governance: a contractual and organizational perspective' in L. Sacconi, M. Blair, E. Freeman and A. Vercelli, eds, *Corporate Social Responsibility and Corporate Governance* (2008).
5. Lucian Bebchuk has recently recommended that shareholders should be given the power 'to initiate and *vote to adopt* changes in the company's basic corporate governance arrangements . . . [to] include the power to adopt provisions that would allow shareholders, down the road, to initiate and vote on proposals regarding specific corporate decisions' (2005, p. 836; emphasis added). It is his view that increasing shareholder power to intervene in this way will 'improve corporate governance and enhance shareholder value' (2005, p. 836).
6. To be sure, both are lagged responses. If, however, the inefficiencies in question are substantial, such inefficiencies invite their own demise.
7. Note with respect to the acquisition of deep knowledge that this often requires *active* participation, in which event it does not suffice for the board to hire its own specialized staff to report back in its capacity of a 'sophisticated observer'. Thus although learning by observing is instructive, learning by doing is deeper and different. Chester Barnard's remarks about the executive arts are relevant: 'In the common sense, every day, practice of the arts, there is much that is not susceptible of verbal statement – it is a matter of know-how. It may be called behavioral knowledge . . . [and] is nowhere more indispensable than in the executive arts' (1938, p. 291). Also, as Michael Polanyi observes with respect to technology, 'the attempt to analyze scientifically the established industrial arts has everywhere led to similar results. Indeed even in the modern industries the indefinable knowledge is still an essential part of technology' (1962, p. 52). Polanyi also describes 'language [as] an art, carried on by tacit judgments and the practice of unspecifiable skills' to which ongoing experience between speaker and listener is often vital (1962, p. 206).
8. Thus, suppose that the efficient debt to equity ratio undergoes a transformation over the course of time. Specifically (Williamson, 1988, p. 585):

   > Suppose . . . that a firm is originally financed along lines that are consistent with the debt and equity financing principles set out [in Section 1] above. Suppose further that the firm is successful and grows through retained earnings. The initial debt–equity ratio thus progressively falls. And suppose finally that many of the assets in this now-expanded enterprise are of a kind that could have been financed by debt.
   >
   > Added value, in such a firm, can be realized by substituting debt for equity. This argument applies, however, selectively. It only applies to firms where the efficient mix of debt and equity has gotten seriously out of alignment. These will be firms that combine (1) a very high ratio of equity to debt with (2) a very high ratio of redeployable to nonredeployable assets. Interestingly, many of the large leveraged buyouts in the 1980s displayed precisely these qualities.

9. Tirole also describes LBOs as a 'transitory form of organization. LBO sponsors and limited partners want to be able to cash out, in the form of a return to public corporation status or negotiated sales' (2006, p. 48). He furthermore observes that the LBO specialist 'KKR sticks to the companies for five to ten years before exiting' (2006, p. 48).
10. As Jensen observes, 'the close relationship between the LBO partners or venture fund partners and the operating companies facilitates the infusion of expertise from the board during times of crisis. It is not unusual for a partner to join the management team, even as CEO, to help an organization through such emergencies' (1993, p. 870).
11. Henry Hansmann contrasts the use of special charter provisions by venture capital start-up firms that have a relatively short expected life with publicly traded firms that consistently defer to the default terms provided by corporate law (2006, p. 9). Special charter

provisions in venture capital firms are intended to elicit high-powered incentives. Default terms are more well-suited to the business-as-usual enterprise.

12. Recalling Mace's description of many board members as 'heads of prestigious organizations with primary responsibilities of their own' and as 'extremely busy people', involving such people in the ongoing affairs of the firms on whose boards they serve would come at the sacrifice of time to the organizations to which they have principal responsibility. Thus although some of these board members are supremely qualified in technical, organizational, managerial and strategic respects, ongoing operational participation in the affairs of the firms on whose boards they serve is rarely the highest and best use of these talents.
13. Also see Michel Crozier (1963, pp. 178–98).
14. Executive compensation at Verizon is an example, where 'Verizon's compensation committee . . . consists of . . . [four] chief executives or former chief executives', three of whom sit on other boards with the Verizon CEO (Morgenson, 2006, p. A16). This is by no means an isolated example (Bebchuk and Fried, 2004, Chap. 2), moreover.
15. Interestingly, that may already be in progress. As Dennis Berman, Jason Singer and John Wilke put it, 'One after another, the longstanding barriers that protected companies from takeovers are dissolving . . ., [as witness the] unprecedented wave of deal making in which, it seems, few companies are entirely safe' (2007, p. A1) – although they add that possibly this is an ephemeral condition (2007, p. A17).
16. 'If wishes were horses, beggars might ride.' (John Ray, 1670)
17. Executives with investments in non-redeployable (firm-specific) skills are more vulnerable – although many of the skills of management are of a general purpose kind. Ambiguity over the reasons for termination commonly work against the ready re-employment of executives.
18. Parts of this are consistent with management participation on the board of directors that I have described previously (Williamson, 1985, pp. 317–18):

    > So long as the basic control relation of the board to the corporation is not upset, management's participation on the board affords three benefits. First, it permits the board to observe and evaluate the process of decision-making as well as the outcomes. The board thereby gains superior knowledge of management's competence that can help to avoid appointment errors or correct them more quickly. Second, the board must make choices among competing investment proposals. Management's participation may elicit more and deeper information than a formal presentation would permit. Finally, management's participation may help safeguard the employment relation between management and the firm – an important function in view of the inadequacy of formal procedures for grievance.

    But whereas previously I awarded priority to the shareholders, here I introduce the possibility that the legitimacy of the management should be expressly factored in. Note moreover that whereas credible commitments are designed primarily with respect to the distinctive features of each constituency, these are not independent (Williamson, 1985, pp. 318–19).
19. Checks against downside drift mainly entail elevating the status of leading outside board members in relation to the management. Some of the Sarbanes–Oxley efforts to reshape boards and, even more, the Cadbury Report have that purpose. The efficacy of these measures has been questioned, however (Romano, 2005); and a determined CEO can neuter such efforts by nominating those he knows to be compliant candidates. Checks against unduly compliant board service include having an outside member co-chair the board, examining current members with respect to their business competence, overlapping interests between members and management, and the lack of susceptibility to indirect rewards. Also, the integrity of corporate governance is buttressed by keeping the gateway open to competition in the capital market as an instrument of ultimate appeal.

REFERENCES

Adams, Renee and Daniel Ferreira (2007), 'A theory of friendly boards', *Journal of Finance*, **62**(1), 217–50.
Almazan, Andres and Javier Suarez (2003), 'Entrenchment and severance pay in optimal governance structures', *Journal of Finance*, **58**(2), 519–48.
Ashby, W. Ross (1960), *Design for a Brain*, New York: John Wiley & Sons.
Baird, Douglas and Robert Rasmussen (2007), 'The prime directive', *University of Cincinnati Law Review*, **75**, 921–41.
Balakrishnan, Srinivasan and Isaac Fox (1993), 'Asset specificity, firm heterogeneity and capital structure', *Strategic Management Journal*, **14**(1), 3–16.
Barnard, Chester I. (1938), *The Functions of the Executive*, Cambridge, MA: Harvard University Press.
Bebchuk, L.A. (2005), 'The case for increasing shareholder power', *Harvard Law Review*, **118**(3), 833–917.
Bebchuk, Lucian Arye and Jesse Fried (2004), *Pay without Performance: The Unfulfilled Promise of Executive Compensation*, Cambridge, MA: Harvard University Press.
Benmelech, Efraim, Mark Garmaise and Tobias Moskowitz (2005), 'Do liquidation values affect financial contracts? Evidence from commercial loan contracts and zoning regulation', *Quarterly Journal of Economics*, **120**(3), 1121–54.
Berle, Adolph A. and Gardner C. Means, Jr (1932), *The Modern Corporation and Private Property*, New York: Macmillan.
Berman, Dennis, Jason Singer and John Wilke (2007), 'On the prowl: as deal barriers fall, takeover bids multiply', *Wall Street Journal*, 8 May, A1.
Coase, Ronald (1964), 'The regulated industries: discussion', *American Economic Review*, **54**(May), 194–97.
Commons, J. (1932), 'The problem of correlating law, economics, and ethics', *Wisconsin Law Review*, **8**, 3–26.
Crozier, Michel (1963), *The Bureaucratic Phenomenon*, Chicago: University of Chicago Press.
Demsetz, Harold (1969), 'Information and efficiency: another viewpoint', *Journal of Law and Economics*, **12**(1), 1–22.
Dixit, Avinash (1996), *The Making of Economic Policy: A Transaction Cost Politics Perspective*, Cambridge, MA: MIT Press.
Fama, Eugene and Michael C. Jensen (1983), 'Separation of ownership and control', *Journal of Law and Economics*, **26** (June), 301–26.
Fox, Alan (1974), *Beyond Contract: Work, Power, and Trust Relations*, London: Faber & Faber.
Hansmann, Henry (2006), 'Corporation and contract', ECGI Law Working Paper No. 66/2006, Yale Law School, New Haven, CT.
Hellwig, Martin (2000), 'On the economics and politics of corporate finance and corporate control', in Xavier Vives (ed.), *Corporate Governance: Theoretical and Empirical Perspectives*, Cambridge: Cambridge University Press, pp. 95–133.
Holmstrom, Bengt (2005), 'Pay without performance and the managerial power hypothesis: a comment', *Journal of Corporation Law*, Summer.
Holmstrom, Bengt and Steven Kaplan (2003), 'The state of US corporate governance: what's right and what's wrong?', *Journal of Applied Corporate Finance*, **15**(3), 8–20.
Jensen, Michael (1993), 'The modern industrial revolution, exit, and the failure of internal control systems', *The Journal of Finance*, **48**(3), 831–80.

Knauth, Oswald (1948), *Managerial Enterprise: Its Growth and Methods of Operation*, New York: W.W. Norton.

Kochar, Rahul (1996), 'Explaining firm capital structure: the role of agency theory vs. transaction cost economics', *Strategic Management Journal*, **17**(9), 713–28.

Mace, Myles (1971), *Directors: Myth and Reality*, Cambridge, MA: Harvard University Press.

March, James and Herbert A. Simon (1958), *Organizations*, New York: John Wiley & Sons.

Marx, Karl (1967), *Capital*, vol. 1, New York: International Publishers.

Michels, Robert (1962), *Political Parties*, Glencoe, IL: Free Press.

Mocnik, Dijana (2001), 'Asset specificity and a firm's borrowing ability: an empirical analysis of manufacturing firms', *Journal of Economic Behavior and Organization*, **45**(1), 69–81.

Morgenson, Gretchen (2006), 'Advice on boss's pay may not be so independent', *New York Times*, 10 April, p. A16.

Myers, Stuart (1985), 'Comment on investment patterns and financial leverage', in Benjamin Friedman (ed.), *Corporate Capital Structures in the United States*, Chicago: University of Chicago Press, pp. 348–51.

Nguyen-Dang, Bang (2005), 'Investor recognition hypothesis, firm value, and corporate governance: evidence from media coverage of CEOs', Working paper, HEC Paris School of Management.

Polanyi, Michael (1962), *Personal Knowledge: Towards a Post-Critical Philosophy*, New York: Harper & Row.

Romano, Roberta (2005), 'The Sarbanes–Oxley Act and the making of quack corporate governance', *Yale Law Journal*, **114**(7), 1521–612.

Selznick, Philip (1966), *TVA and the Grass Roots*, New York: Harper Torchbooks.

Shane, Scott (2001), 'Technological regimes and new firm formation', *Management Science*, **47**, 1173–90.

Shleifer, Andrei and Robert Vishny (1992), 'Liquidation values and debt capacity: a market equilibrium approach', *Journal of Finance*, **47**(4), 1343–66.

Simon, Herbert (1962), 'The architecture of complexity', *Proceedings of the American Philosophical Society*, **106**(6), 467–82.

Simon, Herbert (1973), 'Applying information technology to organization design', *Public Administrative Review*, **33**(3), 268–78.

Tirole, Jean (2006), *The Theory of Corporate Finance*, Princeton, NJ: Princeton University Press.

Titman, Sheridan and Roberto Wessels (1988), 'The determinants of capital structure choice', *Journal of Finance*, 4**3**(1), 1–19.

Williamson, Dean (2007), 'Ownership, control, and the single entity defense in antitrust: part I', unpublished manuscript.

Williamson, Oliver (1985), *The Economic Institutions of Capitalism*, New York: Free Press.

Williamson, Oliver (1988), 'Corporate finance and corporate governance', *Journal of Finance*, **43**(3), 567–91.

Williamson, Oliver (1995), 'The politics and economics of redistribution and inefficiency', *Greek Economic Review*, **17**(2), 115–36.

Williamson, Oliver (1996), *The Mechanisms of Governance*, New York: Oxford University Press.

APPENDIX: THE BOARD IN RELATION TO DOUBLE-FEEDBACK

W. Ross Ashby's model of double-feedback (1960) and Herbert Simon's examination of the architecture of complexity (1962, 1973) are broadly consonant with the proposition that adaptation is the central problem of economic organization. Ashby established that all adaptive systems that have a capacity to respond to a bimodal distribution of disturbances – some being disturbances in degree; others being disturbances in kind – will be characterized by double feedback. As shown in Figure 4A.1, disturbances of both kinds originate in the environment (E). The feedback divide is this: operating decisions are made and implemented in the primary feedback loop by the reacting part (R) with the benefit of extant decision rules whereas strategic decisions of a more consequential and longer-run kind are processed through the secondary feedback loop, where the essential variables (V) and the step functions (S) are located.

In effect, the reacting part (R) works out of the presumption that successive state realizations are variations in degree to which the application of extant routines will yield an efficacious response. Indeed, the routines employed by the operating part remain unchanged so long as performance falls within the control limits on the essential variables (V) in the secondary feedback loop. If and as, however, performance falls outside of these control limits, the secondary feedback loop interprets this as a disturbance in kind for which new routines (changes in parameter values or new rules) are needed to restore performance to acceptable levels. These changes are introduced into the reacting part as step functions (S). So

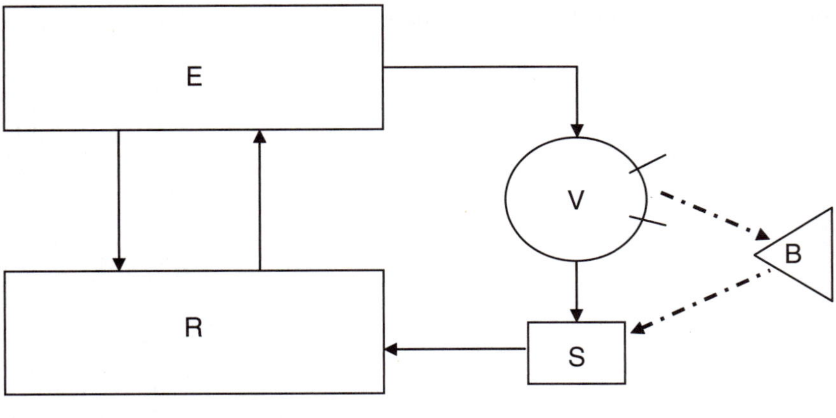

Figure 4A.1 The double-feedback board in practice

described, the primary feedback loop is implementing extant decision rules in real time in a mechanical way whereas the secondary feedback loop is activated by less frequent changes in kind (and possibly with reference to longer-run (strategic) considerations). Evolutionary systems that are subject to such bimodal disturbances will, under natural selection, necessarily develop two readily distinguishable feedbacks (Ashby, 1960, p. 131).

So where does the board of directors appear in the double-feedback scheme of things? The concept of the board as vigilant monitor would presumably locate the board at the essential variables (V), where it would receive and interpret signals that the continuation of business-as-usual is or is not warranted and, if the latter, recommends that fundamental changes be made by the management, which is located at the step functions (S). By reason, however, of the intrinsic limitations of the board in acquiring and interpreting performance information (as discussed in section 3.1), (V) does not seem to be an appropriate location for the board.

The concept of the board as active participant in the management would locate the board at the step functions (S), where the board would participate in the management of the firm in an *ongoing way*. As discussed in section 3.2, however, this would seriously compromise the integrity of delegation and is of doubtful efficacy more generally.

The third interpretation and the one that I recommend is to attach the board to the secondary feedback loop in a peripheral way at (B). The management thus takes and interprets the readings on the essential variables and reports these to the board. If and as the essential variables remain within control limits, the board adopts a posture of nodding approval. If and as, however, a crisis is reported, the board is activated to work with the management to craft a crisis response at the step functions (S). In the limit, but this is outside the model, the management is replaced.

5. Corporate governance: a review of the role of banks*

Hans Degryse, Steven Ongena and Günseli Tümer-Alkan

I INTRODUCTION

In many countries, banks are the most important providers of external finance, in particular for small and medium-sized enterprises (SMEs). Hence, the banks' role in the financing and governance of firms is relevant for the smooth functioning and growth of an economy. Banks not only interact with firms through debt financing, in some countries they also play an important role as firms' large shareholders and board members. The goal of this chapter is to provide an overview of the role of financial institutions in the governance of firms through the different corporate governance mechanisms. We aim to address the question: 'How do banks act as debt financiers, large shareholders, and board members?' Along the way, we also indicate how banks differ from other players' role in the corporate governance of firms.

Banks and firms enter into a relationship to overcome problems of asymmetric information. Without such a relationship firms may be financially constrained. Diamond (1984) shows that the *raison d'être* for financial intermediaries may be the reduction in the cost of monitoring information and therefore the resolution of incentive problems in the *debt markets*. Banks screen firms' loan applications, and monitor firms by designing loan contracts and by interacting frequently. Also, as first argued by Fama (1985), bank loans signal the creditworthiness of firms to other market players, and thereby reduce the information costs for the other contracts. In this chapter, we provide a brief overview of how the existence of bank–firm relationships and the credit market structure affect loan pricing, credit availability and collateral requirements for firms.[1]

When banks acquire private information about firms, they may use this information to extract rents in the future. Known as the 'hold-up problem' in banking literature, firms can partly mitigate this by establishing multiple relationships creating competition among banks or other financiers (von Thadden, 1992). However, an increase in the number of creditors is linked to inefficient renegotiation which disciplines firm managers, since their incentives to strategically default on a loan will be reduced (see Bolton and Scharfstein, 1996; Hart, 1995; and Dewatripont and Maskin, 1995). Moreover, managerial discretion resulting from free cash flow can be mitigated by bank debt as first suggested by Jensen (1986), and empirically tested by Hoshi et al. (1991), Van Ees and Garretsen (1994), Vogt (1994) and Degryse and de Jong (2006), for example.

Banks may play a role in corporate governance as *large shareholders* as well. Depending on the legal system, ownership and monitoring ability of financial institutions can be constrained by investment regulations (Roe, 1990). Countries differ in terms of the importance of bank block holdings. For example, bank block holdings are more prevalent in bank-centred economies such as Japan and continental Europe (Li et al., 2006). Also, banks as long-term shareholders are an important part of the corporate governance mechanism in Germany (Gorton and Schmid, 2000). Whether firm performance is positively affected by bank block holdings remains an open question, however.

Recent work also focuses on how banks influence firms via *board membership*. Kroszner and Strahan (2001), for example, show that the tradeoff between benefits from bank monitoring and the costs of shareholder–creditor conflicts determine the presence of banks on the boards of non-financial firms. Banks tend to be on the boards of large and stable firms that have more collateralizable assets and low reliance on short-term financing. A further distinction is made concerning whether or not banks serve multiple roles in governance. In particular, a distinction is made between banks as lending banks and non-lending banks on the boards of companies in Byrd and Mizruchi (2005). As in Kroszner and Strahan (2001) lenders are least likely to be on the boards when shareholder–creditor conflicts are severe. And Santos and Rumble (2006) find that US banks join the board of a firm when they can control a large voting stake.

As a preview on our findings, we will show that banks improve corporate governance of firms through different complementary mechanisms. This holds in particular in continental Europe and Japan where banks, next to being an important debt financier, often also hold large equity stakes of firms, and join the boards of corporations. We find that (i) close bank–firm relationships create shareholder value, increase credit availability and discipline firm managers by preventing them from over-investing; (ii) bank relationships through debt financing do not necessarily improve firm performance, as banks are able to appropriate some of the benefits of their relationships with firms; (iii) banks as large shareholders generally improve the performance of firms; (iv) appointments of bank directors to firm boards increase with poor stock performance and with earnings losses of firms; and

(v) bank board membership improves firm performance, increases executive turnover, but having lenders on board decreases firm debt ratios.

The remainder of the chapter is organized as follows. In section II, we review selected studies on the impact of banks as debt financiers. We start with the banks' impact on the investment-cash flow sensitivities of the firms and their effect on firm performance. Next we investigate the literature on bank–firm relationships and credit market structure in determining the loan contract terms. In this section, we also briefly review how bank–firm relationships affect firms' stock returns. In section III, we focus on banks as large shareholders of firms, and in section IV on banks as board members. Section V presents some general conclusions.

II BANKS AS DEBT FINANCIERS

A large strand of literature studies how bank debt can play a role in allowing firms to execute investment projects, but also how bank debt can act as a disciplining device, in particular by affecting managerial incentives in a firm. Asymmetric information leads to financing constraints in the form of credit rationing as in Stiglitz and Weiss (1981). When there is excess demand for loanable funds, the interest rate cannot be regarded as a good instrument, since increasing it could induce borrowers to invest in riskier projects. This is the basic explanation of why credit rationing exists, which can also function to prevent managers from investing in risky projects. Bank–firm relationships may help in reducing asymmetric information problems and allow firms to undertake their projects.

There is also a cost side of bank–firm relationships as modelled by Rajan (1992). He shows that there is a tradeoff between bank debt and arm's-length debt. On the one hand, the bank monitors the firm and therefore takes informed continuation decisions giving firms improved incentives. On the other hand, a bank may be tempted to extract benefits by affecting the division of surplus. That is, through information acquisition, the bank gets bargaining power over the firm's profits. One solution to this hold-up problem is suggested by von Thadden (1992) who argues that establishing multiple bank–firm relationships creates competition among banks and limits the rent extraction.

Bolton and Scharfstein (1996) explore the impact of the debt structure on renegotiations in the case of firm default. They argue that an optimal debt structure balances the following effects of multiple banking. First, multiple bank relationships discourage managers from strategically defaulting on a loan. Following a default, the manager will have to pay more to stop the multiple claimholders from liquidating the assets compared to the case with only one creditor. Second, when default is due to liquidity problems, as distinguished by Hart and Moore (1989) and Bolton and Scharfstein (1990), multiple lending is costly since it reduces the expected liquidation value of assets.

Bolton and Scharfstein (1996) explain how the optimal debt structure will depend on firm characteristics and they show that the liquidation value is lower when two creditors are involved. This implies that for firms with low default risk and with low asset complementarity, borrowing from two creditors is optimal. On the other hand, when outside buyers place high valuation on assets, it is more attractive for firms to borrow from one creditor to maximize the liquidation value. Bris and Welch (2005) take a different approach and argue that dispersion weakens creditors, since it is more difficult for dispersed creditors to collect claims in financial distress due to coordination and free-riding costs. Thus a firm that chooses multiple creditors *ex ante* guarantees a better bargaining ability in the case of financial distress *ex post*. In a signalling framework, a higher quality firm chooses fewer creditors, which indicates its confidence in not going bankrupt.

Recent papers by Carletti (2004) and Carletti et al. (2007) have started to explore how the number of bank relationships affects the banks' monitoring incentives. Carletti (2004) analyses why empirical evidence is not always in line with the theories on hold-up and soft budget constraint problems. She argues that firms may benefit from borrowing from two banks to reduce monitoring intensity when one bank would be overmonitoring. Thus, two-bank lending involves lower monitoring but not necessarily higher loan rates than single-bank lending. Her model therefore provides a theoretical background for why multiple-bank lending does not unambiguously increase loan rates or firms' quality. Carletti et al. (2007) explore banks' incentives to finance a firm together with other banks when they have limited lending abilities and when monitoring is important.

A Banks' Impact on Investment-Cash Flow Sensitivities

Firms may face financing constraints such that even those firms with positive net present value projects cannot convince financiers to grant loans, leading to underinvestment (as in Myers and Majluf, 1984). Fazzari et al. (1988) empirically test for potential underinvestment by linking firm investment to the available firm cash flow. The general idea is that without financing constraints, investment and available cash flow should be uncorrelated as firms should execute investment projects independently of their ability to generate cash flow. With financing constraints, however, firms that generate more cash flow will be able to undertake these positive NPV projects and invest more. And indeed, Fazzari et al. (1988) and many follow-up papers find that firms where financial constraints are expected to be binding (i.e., small firms, firms from information-intensive industries, and so on) exhibit greater investment cash-flow sensitivity. This strand of the literature interprets this as evidence for the existence of financing constraints. However, this interpretation has been subject to many discussions in the more recent literature and serious methodological concerns about the underlying cost structure of investment and costs of external financing were raised (see for example Kaplan and Zingales, 1997; Cleary, 1999; and Allayannis and Mozumdar, 2004).

In his seminal paper Jensen (1986) argues that debt prevents firms with large cash flows from investing in negative net present value projects. That is, more debt may limit the overinvestment problem as it redirects the incoming cash flows to the interest payments and debt repayments. Pioneering work has been performed by Dennis Mueller and his co-authors, who have identified the role of the under- and overinvestment problems and their link with investment cash-flow sensitivity. Furthermore, they investigate how legal systems, banks and other governance mechanisms affect the investment cash-flow sensitivity (see Gugler et al., 2007, for example, or Gugler et al., 2004 for an extensive review). Vogt (1994), for example, distinguishes between firms with good and bad prospects using Tobin's q as a proxy, where low q firms are identified as firms facing a managerial discretion problem. Vogt indeed finds that low q firms also exhibit large investment cash-flow sensitivity and interprets this as evidence for the managerial discretion problem.

Here we focus on studies that document a distinct role for financial intermediaries. Van Ees and Garretsen (1994), for example, find evidence for a strong relationship between investments and cash flow of Dutch firms but this investment cash-flow sensitivity is lower for firms having bank–firm ties (including bank debt). In addition, Hoshi et al. (1991) examine how close ties to banks affect investment behaviour of Japanese firms.[2] They show that investment of firms with stronger links to a main bank is less sensitive to liquidity.

Following their approach, another study on listed Dutch firms by Degryse and de Jong (2006) investigates managerial discretion and asymmetric information problems by distinguishing between firms with good and bad prospects using Tobin's q as a proxy. Low q firms are identified as firms facing a managerial discretion problem. The authors find that especially low q firms with higher bank debt have lower investment-cash flow sensitivity, showing that bank debt is a key disciplinary mechanism that reduces managerial discretion and overinvestment problems. Fuss and Vermeulen (2006) examine whether the number of bank relationships affects firms' investment decisions, but they do not find strong evidence for that. Table 5.1 gives a brief summary on the studies examining the role of bank relationships in investment-cash flow sensitivities of firms.

Table 5.1 Impact of bank relationships on investment-cash flow sensitivities

Study	Country, Year Sample, Firm Size	Cash flow sensitivity for investment	
		Number	Affiliation
Houston and James (2001)	US, 1980–1993 250 large	0 / +++ for large projects	
Fuss and Vermeulen (2006)	Belgium, 1997–2002 1448 Med./Large	0	
Fohlin (1998)	Germany, 1903–1913 75 larger		0
Pawlina and Renneboog (2005)	UK, 1992–1998 985 listed		↔
Hoshi et al. (1991)	Japan, 1977–1982 145 listed		0 / +++ for nonaffiliated firms
Van Ees and Garretsen (1994)	Netherlands, 1985–1990 76 listed		0 / +++ for nonaffiliated firms
Degryse and de Jong (2006)	Netherlands, 1993–1998 132 listed		BD: ↔↔↔ for low q firms / BE: 0

Notes:
The table summarizes the results from studies on the impact of the various measures of bank relationships on investment-cash flow sensitivities of borrowing firms. Positive signs indicate that higher levels of the respective measure correspond to higher investment-cash flow sensitivity. The first column lists the *Paper* citation. The second column reports *Country* affiliation and *Year* of the related firms on the first row and on the second row the *Sample size* and an indication of *Firm Size*. The third and fourth columns indicate the sign and significance of the *Impact on Investment-Cash Flow Sensitivities* of changes in the *Number* and bank *Affiliation*. Significance levels are based on all reported exercises and the author's assessment. +++ Positive and significant at 1%, ++at 5%, + at 10%. ↔↔↔ Negative and significant at 1%, ↔↔ at 5%, ↔ at 10%. 0: Included in the specifications but not significant. BD: bank debt/assets. BE: blockholdings by banks.

B Firm Performance

The literature documents various benefits of having bank relationships for firms. Banks reduce asymmetric information problems, increase the availability of capital and affect managerial incentives. The impact is more pronounced in bank-centred economies such as Japan and Germany. Suzuki and Wright (1985), for example, find that bankruptcy risk in Japanese companies is determined by their main bank relationships rather than by financial conditions. The findings by Hoshi et al. (1990) suggest that financial distress is costly for Japanese firms that do not have close relationships to their banks and trading partners.[3]

However, studies on the impact of bank relationships on firm performance give conflicting results. Table 5.2 summarizes the findings of these studies. Weinstein and Yafeh (1998) find that close bank–firm relationships do not lead to higher profitability or growth. They suggest two explanations for their findings. First, the cost of capital of firms increases due to higher interest rates paid to the main bank. This is in line with the argument by Rajan (1992) that banks may extract rents from their clients. Second, banks may be more risk-averse than shareholders. Banks' conservative investment policies discourage firms from investing in risky and profitable projects, thus lowering growth. Kang et al. (2000), on the other hand, find that bank relationships facilitate investment policies that increase shareholder wealth.[4] Studying domestic mergers in Japan, the authors document positive abnormal returns for the acquirer which contradicts previous studies on US mergers. They also report a strong positive association between the abnormal returns and the acquirer's main bank loan ratio.

Degryse and Ongena (2001) show that bilateral bank relationships correspond to higher sales profitability. Using a dataset consisting of Norwegian publicly listed firms, the authors investigate the relationship between the number of bank relationships and sales profitability. They estimate a two-equation model in which firm profitability and bank relationships are jointly determined and they find a negative correspondence between these variables. The results are in line with the model by Yosha (1995) which links multiple relationships to information leakage to competitors and consequently to lower profitability.

Finally, Montoriol Garriga (2006) studies the impact of the number of relationships on firm profitability of Spanish firms. She finds that firms maintaining exclusive bank relationships have lower profitability. This finding suggests that banks are able to appropriate most of the benefits of a close bank–firm relationship.

C Bank Loan, Bank Distress, or Bank Merger Announcements

The value of bank relationships is the subject of several event studies investigating the impact of loan renewal announcements on the abnormal returns of borrowing firms. Another strand of literature examines how bank distress or bank merger announcements can affect the value of a borrowing firm. Table 5.3 summarizes these studies.

In contrast to the studies which do not find significant impacts for other financiers or where other forms of financing may be regarded as 'bad news',

Table 5.2 Impact of bank relationships on firm performance

Study	Country, Year Sample, Firm Size	Measure	Duration	Scope	Number	Affiliation
Foglia et al. (1998)	Italy, 1991–1995 576 + 1295	Firm does not default			↔↔	
Castelli et al. (2006)	Italy, 1998–2000 10 764 (30) empl.	ROA, ROE, Interest over Assets, Sales over Assets	0/+		↔↔	
Montoriol Garriga (2006)	Spain, 2001–2003 41 593 Small	7 Profitability Measures 4 Growth Measures		+++ ↔↔↔	↔↔↔ +++	
Van Overfelt et al. (2006)	Belgium, 1905–1909 569 Large	Market-to-book of equity, ROA, St. Dev. of ROA			↔	++
Agarwal and Elston (2001)	Germany, 1970–1986 1660 largest	Operating income / Sales				0
Degryse and Ongena (2001)	Norway, 1979–1995 1897 listed	Various profitability (Simultaneous equations)	++		↔↔↔	
Suzuki and Wright (1985)	Japan, 1974–1978 56 listed	Firm does not default				MBv: ++
Hoshi et al. (1990)	Japan, 1978–1985 125 listed	Investment, Sales				Group: +++ MBr: ++

Gibson (1995)	Japan, 1992 1355 listed	Investment				0/↔ for 'weaker' banks
Weinstein and Yafeh (1998)	Japan, 1977–1986 6836 large	Ordinary Income / Sales			↔↔↔	↔↔↔
Kang et al. (2000)	Japan, 1977–1993 154 listed	2-Day CARs of acquiring firms				MBr: +++
Limpaphayom and Polwitoon (2004)	Thailand, 1990–1996 1340	Tobin's q			↔↔↔	BD: +++

Notes:
The table summarizes the results from studies on the impact of the various measures of bank relationships on firm performance. Positive signs indicate that higher levels of the respective measure correspond to better firm performance. The first column lists the *Paper* citation. The second column reports *Country* affiliation and *Year* of the related firms on the first row, and on the second row the *Sample size* and an indication of *Firm size*. The third column defines the *Measure of firm performance*. The fourth to seventh column indicate the sign and significance of the *Impact on firm performance* of changes in the *Duration*, *Scope*, *Number* and bank *Affiliation*. Significance levels are based on all reported exercises and the author's assessment. +++ Positive and significant at 1%, ++ at 5%, + at 10%. ↔↔↔ Negative and significant at 1%, ↔↔ at 5%, ↔ at 10%. 0: Included in the specifications but not significant. BD: bank debt/assets. Group: group membership-strong ties to a bank. MBv: size of main bank loans (value). MBr: main bank loan ratio.

Table 5.3 Loan, distress and merger announcement studies

Paper	Country Period	Avg. (Med.) Size, in mln $	Announcement (Events) Affected Borrowers	**2-Day Mean AR, in %** Cross-Sectional Results (Difference?)
Mikkelson and Partch (1986)	US 1972–1982	n/a	Credit Agreements (155)	**0.89*** **
James (1987)	US 1974–1983	L: 675 (212)	Bank Loan Agreement (80)	**1.93*** **
Lummer and McConnell (1989)	US 1976–1986	n/a	Bank Credit Agreement (728)	**0.61*** **
			Revised (357) / New (371)	1.24*** / −0.01 (n/a)
Slovin et al. (1992)	US 1980–1986	E: 281 (68) For initiations	Loan Agreement (273)	**1.30*** **
			Renewals (124) / Initiations (149)	1.55*** / 1.09*** (n/a)
			Small Firms (156) / Large Firms (117)	1.92*** / 0.48 (n/a)
Best and Zhang (1993)	US 1977–1989	n/a	Bank Credit Agreement (491)	**0.32** **
			Renewals (304) / New (187)	1.97** / 0.26 (no)
			Noisy Renewals [a] (156) / Accurate New [a] (187)	0.60** / −0.05 (*)
Billett et al. (1995)	US 1980–1989	E: 316 (79)	Loan (626)	**0.68*** **
			Renewals (187) / New Banks (51)	1.09*** / 0.64* (no)
			Banks' Rating: AAA (78) / < BAA (29)	0.63*** / −0.57 (no)
Fields et al. (2006)	US 1980–2003	E: 738 (136) BA: 1 216 (212)	Bank Loan Renewal (594)	**0.48* **
			1980–1989 (160) / 1990–1999 (291)	0.93** / 0.50 (n/a)
Aintablian and Roberts (2000)	Canada 1988–1995	n/a	Corporate Loan Announcement (137)	**1.22*** **
			Renewal (35) / New (69)	1.26*** / 0.62 *** (*)[a]
Andre et al. (2001)	Canada 1982–1995	n/a	Bank Credit Agreement (122)	**2.27*** **
			Lines of Credit < 1988 (13) / > 1988 (33)	4.82 / 0.32
			Term Loans < 1988 (22) / > 1988 (54)	1.14 / 3.30***

Fery et al. (2003)	Australia 1983–1999	n/a	Signed Credit Agreements (196)	**0.38***
			Published: Single (18) / Multiple (22)	1.62** / 0.89
			Non-Published: Single (56) / Multiple (89)	0.02 / 0.25
Huang and Zhao (2007)	China 2001–2006	A: 316 (154)	Bank Loan Announcements (261)	**−0.50***
Slovin et al. (1993)	US 1984	E: 1085 (692)	Continental Illinois Distress (1)	**−4.16*****
			29 Firms (Direct Lender/Lead Manager)	Firms with low leverage and other banks
Ongena et al. (2003)	Norway 1988–91	S: 400	Bank Distress (6)	**−1.7****
			217 Main Bank firms	Equity-issuing firms w/ undrawn credit (No)
Karceski et al. (2005)	Norway 1983–2000	S: ±500	Completed bank mergers (22)	**0.29, −0.76**, 0.06**
			342 Acquirers, 78 Targets, 1515 Rivals	Firms w/ relationship w/ acquiring banks
Chiou (1999)	Japan 1997–98	A: 3913 (1110)	Daiwa Bank Scandal (1)	**−0.98*****
			32 Main Bank firms	Large firms & w/ no Main Bank
Brewer et al. (2003)	Japan 1997–98	A: 1450	Three Bank Failures (3)	**0.17; −1.32***; −0.49****
			327	Firms with alternative financing (No)
Miyajima and Yafeh (2003)	Japan 1995–2001	A: 2293[a]	Actions (11), Downgrading (5), Mergers (3)	**n/a; −3.1[n/a]; 0**
			9250 + 4016 + 2606	Large, profitable, tech, low debt, bonds (No)
Hwan Shin et al. (2003)	Japan 19.08.99	S: 790 (716)[a]	3-Way alliance (1) 570	**−0.31*****
				Main Bank, high debt, profitable
Bae et al. (2002)	S-Korea 1997–98	BA: 404	Negative Bank News (113) 486	**−1.26*****
				Healthy, unconstrained firms
Sohn (2002)	S-Korea 1998	A: 324[a]	Closure / transfer of five banks (1)	**−4.85*****
			118	Firms with no prior relationship

Table 5.3 (continued)

Paper	Country Period	Avg. (Med.) Size, in mln $	Announcement (Events) Affected Borrowers	**2-Day Mean AR, in %** Cross-Sectional Results (Difference?)
Djankov et al. (2005)	Indonesia Thailand S-Korea 1997–99	n/a	Closures (52) Foreign Sales (209) Domestic Mergers (92) Nationalizations (94)	**−3.94***** **−1.05*** **−1.27** **3.14***** Large Firms (No)

Notes:
The table lists the main findings of event studies tracing the impact of bank loan, bank distress, or bank merger announcements on the stock prices of borrowing firms. The first column provides the *Paper* citation. The second column reports the *Country* affiliation of the affected firms and the *Period* during which the announcements were made. The *Average (Median) Firm Size* column lists both the size measure and the average (median) size of the firms in millions of US$. The fourth column reports on the first row the type of *Announcement* and the number of *Events* and on the second row the *number of Affected Borrowers*. The final column provides on the first row a *Two-Day Mean Abnormal Return*, in most cases over either [−1,0] or [0,1] interval, in per cent. If two-day CARs are not reported over either interval, the shortest reported interval including either one of these two-day periods is used. The second row provides a breakdown of the announcements in key categories reported in the paper (in parentheses we report whether the differences in mean abnormal returns between reported groups of announcements are significantly different from zero) or key results from any cross-sectional exercises reported in the paper as an answer to the question 'Which firms suffer the least?' Between brackets we report if abnormal returns differ between affected and unaffected firms (i.e., firms not borrowing from the affected bank at the time of the announcement).

A: assets. [a] Authors' calculations. Avg.: average. [b] Their Table 1b does not specify which firm size measure is used (the usage of market equity is possibly implied in the text). n/a: not available. BA: book assets. E: market equity. Med.: median. Mln: million. S: sales. w/: with. *** Significant at 1%, ** significant at 5%, * significant at 10%.

Source: Ongena and Smith (2000) and Degryse and Ongena (2007).

such as issuing stock, loan announcements generally have a positive impact on borrowing firms' stock returns. Mikkelson and Partch (1986) and James (1987) are the first papers documenting positive and significant abnormal returns for firms that announce bank loan agreements. The findings are in line with Fama (1985), who argues that bank loans signal the creditworthiness of firms. However, Lummer and McConnell (1989) find significant stock price reactions only in case of loan renewals. They distinguish loan announcements as loan initiations and loan renewals since the information content of these two groups may differ. On the other hand, no other study was able to support their findings. To summarize, all studies report a positive impact on firms' stock prices except the recent paper by Huang and Zhao (2007). The authors argue that under poor governance debt is no longer a disciplining device. Instead, managers can use it in their own interests rather than the interests of shareholders. The paper reports negative abnormal returns for Chinese firms with low governance quality and that borrow from banks with weak monitoring ability.

Billett et al. (1995) explore the effect of lenders' credit ratings on the borrowing firms' equity returns and find evidence for a positive relationship. Slovin et al. (1993) find evidence for a negative impact of bank insolvency announcement on firms' stock prices that have a relationship with the bank. Several studies examine the impact of bank distress as well as bank mergers on borrowing firms' stock returns. Although the magnitudes of the coefficients differ across studies, the findings again confirm the value of bank relationships to firms.

D The Role of Bank Relationships and Credit Markets in Determining Credit Conditions

1 Impact of bank relationships

There is a long line of research examining the role of bank–firm relationships in credit conditions such as credit availability, cost of credit and collateral. The studies measure bank–firm relationships with the duration, number and/or scope of bank–firm relationships. Degryse and Ongena (2007) provide a detailed review of these studies, and Table 5.4 presents an overview of the findings.

The impact of the number of relationships and duration on the cost of credit shows mixed results, which suggests that European firms pay higher loan rates to their relationship lenders whereas it is the opposite in the US. For the impact of the scope on loan rates, the majority of studies find a negative coefficient. However, one should be careful in interpreting and comparing the results since the proxies used for the cost of credit may differ across studies.

Table 5.4 Duration, number and scope of bank relationships and the cost of credit, collateral and the availability of credit

Panel A	Paper	Source Year	Observations Firm Size	**Cost of Credit,** in basis points	Duration Δ=1 year	Number Δ=1 bank	Scope Δ=1
US	Bodenhorn (2003)	1 Bank 1855	2616 s	Loan rate – A1 commercial paper	−2.9**		
	Petersen and Rajan (1994)	NSSBF 1987	1389 s	Most recent loan rate (prime on RHS)	3.7	32.1***	0.8 [che]
	Berger and Udell (1995)	NSSBF 1987	371 s	Line of credit – Prime rate	−9.2**		
	Uzzi (1999)	NSSBF 1987	2226 s	Most recent loan rate (prime on RHS)	−1.3**		−4.2**
	Blackwell and Winters (1997)	6 Banks 1988	174 s	Revolver – Prime rate	−0.9		0.0
	Berger et al. (2002)	NSSBF 1993	520 s	Line of credit – Prime rate	−5.3**		
	Brick and Palia (2007)	NSSBF 1993	766 s	Line of credit – Prime rate	−2.4**	−18.8	
	Hao (2003)	LPC 1988–99	948 l	Facility coupon + fees – LIBOR		8.0***[lf]	
	Bharath et al. (2007)	LPC 1986–2001	9709 l	Facility coupon + fees – LIBOR			−6.6***[a]
Canada	Mallett and Sen (2001)	CFIB 1997	2409 s	Loan interest rate	0		0
Italy	Conigliani et al. (1997)	CCR 1992	33 808 m	Loan interest rate	−14.1***[cl]	−2***	

	Ferri and Messori (2000)	CCR 1992	33 808 m	Loan interest rate	nw: −19.1* ne: −13.5[n/a] so: 9.6[n/a]	nw: −0.3 ne: 0.7[n/a] so: −13.6*[a]	
	D'Auria et al. (1999)	CCR 1987–94	120 000 l	Loan interest rate – Treasury Bill rate	2.5***	−1.3***	
	Angelini et al. (1998)	Survey 1995	2232 s	Line of credit	ccb: −1.8 oth: 6.4***	−10.0***	
	Cosci and Meliciani (2002)	1 Bank 1997	393 s	Interest Payments – Total Debt		−0.2	
	Pozzolo (2004)	CCR 1992–96	52 359	Loan interest rate	43***		
Spain	Hernandez-Canovas and Martinez-Solano (2006)	Survey 1999–2000	184 s	Avg. cost of bank finance – Interbank	5*	60*	8.5
France	Ziane (2003)	Survey 2001	244 s	Credit interest rate	−20.2	51.4	20.1*
Belgium	Degryse and Van Cayseele (2000)	1 Bank 1997	17 429 s	Loan yield till next revision	7.5***		−39.3***
	Degryse and Ongena (2005)	1 Bank 1997	15 044 s	Loan yield till next revision	11.0***		−40.7***
Germany	Harhoff and Körting (1998)	Survey 1997	994 s	Line of credit	1.7	−0.2	
	Elsas and Krahnen (1998)	5 Banks 1996	353 ml	Line of credit – FIBOR	0.3		−4.8
	Machauer and Weber (1998)	5 Banks 1996	353 ml	Line of credit – interbank overnight	−0.3	0.0	1.3
	Ewert et al. (2000)	5 Banks 1996	682 ml	Line of credit – FIBOR	0.7***	0.6	−22.1
	Lehmann and Neuberger (2001)	Survey 1997	318 sm	Loan rate – Refinancing Rate	1.8[a]		−5.6

Table 5.4 (continued)

Panel A	Paper	Source Year	Observations Firm Size	**Cost of Credit**, in basis points	Duration Δ=1 year	Number Δ=1 bank	Scope Δ=1
	Lehmann et al. (2004)	Survey 1997	W: 267 sm E: 67 sm	Loan rate – Refinancing Rate	w: 1.6 e: −0.5		w: −2.0 e: 20.3
Finland	Peltoniemi (2004)	1 Bank 1995–2001 1 Non-bank	279 s 576 s	Effective loan rate	−12*** −2*		6.6[a1]
Japan	Weinstein and Yafeh (1998)	JDB 1977–86	6836 l	Non-bond interest expenses – Debt			53***
	Miarka (1999)	1985–1998	1288 sm	Interest Rate on Borrowing			−22.2***
	Shikimi (2005)	JADA 2000–02	78 695	Loan Rate – Prime rate		18***	
	Kano et al. (2006)	SFE 2002	1960	Maximum Loan Rate < 1 Yr	No / −3.5***[s]		No / 4**[a s]
Thailand	Menkhoff and Suwanaporn (2007)	9 Banks 1992–96	416 l	Loan Rate – Min. overdraft rate	−0.9	−6.5**	−22.0**
Argentina	Streb et al. (2002)	CDSF 1999	8548	Highest overdraft interest rate		6.9***	−69.0***
Chile	Repetto et al. (2002)	SBIF 1990–98	20 000	Interest rate paid	−65.1**[cl]	−47.0**	−26.5
57 countries	Qian (2007)	LPC 1980–2004	3608 l	Drawn All-in Spread		−28.7***[a]	

Panel B	Paper	Source Year	Observations Firm Size	**No Collateral,** in %	Duration Δ=1 year	Number Δ=1 bank	Scope Δ=1
US	Bodenhorn (2003)	1 Bank 1855	2616 s	No guarantors	2.6**		
	Berger and Udell (1995)	NSSBF 1987	371 s	No collateral	12.1**		
	Chakraborty and Hu (2006)	NSSBF 1993	983 s	No collateral L/C	2* [a]	−1.2 [a]	−7.4 [al]
			649 s	No collateral non L/C	−1[a]	−1.4 [a]	3** [al]
	Hao (2003)	LPC 1988–99	948 l	Not secured		1[lf]	
	Roberts and Siddiqi (2004)	LPC 1988–2003	218 l	No collateral		−0.0 [a]	
Italy	Pozzolo (2004)	CCR 1992–96	52 359	No real guarantees	−17***	5***	
				No personal guarantees	14***	1***	
France	Ziane (2003)	Survey 2001	244 s	No collateral	8.3	−2.3**	−2.8*
Belgium	Degryse and Van Cayseele (2000)	1 Bank 1997	17 429 s	No collateral	4.2*		−64.5***
Germany	Harhoff and Körting (1998)	Survey 1997	994 s	No collateral	7.0**	−10.0**	
	Machauer and Weber (1998)	5 Banks 1996	353 ml	Unsecured % of credit line	−0.1*	0.6**	−9.4***
	Elsas and Krahnen (2002)	5 Banks 1996	472 ml	No collateral			−17.6**
	Lehmann and Neuberger (2001)	Survey 1997	318 sm	No collateral	−0.8[a]		−4.1***
	Lehmann et al. (2004)	Survey 1997	W: 267 sm E: 67 sm	No collateral	w:−1.6*** e:5.2**		w:−15*** e:−12.9**
Finland	Peltoniemi (2004)	1 Bank 1995–2001	562 s	No collateral	−2 [a]		50*** [al]
Japan	Kano et al. (2006)	SFE 2002	1960	No collateral	−*		−**
Thailand	Menkhoff et al. (2006)	9 Banks 1992–96	416 l	No collateral	1	23**	−33**

Table 5.4 (continued)

Panel C	Paper	Source Year	Observations Firm Size	**Availability of Credit**, in %	Duration Δ=1 year	Number Δ=1 bank	Scope Δ=1
US	Petersen and Rajan (1994)	NSSBF 1987	1389 s	% Trade credit paid on time	2.3**	−1.9**	
	Uzzi (1999)	NSSBF 1987	2226 s	Credit Accessed	−0.1		0.5
	Cole (1998)	NSSBF 1993	2007 s	Extension of credit	5.0***	−12.0***	−22.0[che]
	Cole et al. (2004)	NSSBF 1993	585 s	Extension of credit by small banks	−0.0	−1.1	5.9**[che]
	Scott and Dunkelberg (2003)	CBSB 1995	520 s	Single credit search	21.5***	−25.7***	
Italy	Angelini et al. (1998)	Survey 1995	2232 s	No rationing	7.0**	−6.4**	
	Cosci and Meliciani (2002)	1 Bank 1997	393 s	1 – [Credit used / Credit offered]		23.3**	
	Guiso (2003)	SMF 1997	3236 s	No loan denial	0.8	0.0	−0.1
France	Dietsch (2003)	1993–2000	2 530 353	Loans / Turnover	2.7**[a]	1.5**[a]	10.1**
Belgium	de Bodt et al. (2005)	Survey [f] 2001	296 s	No rationing	20.0**[a]	−22.0**	
Germany	Lehmann and Neuberger (2001)	Survey 1997	318 sm	Credit approval	0.1***[a]		0.9***
Japan	Shikimi (2005)	JADA 2000–02	78 695	Debt / Assets		18***	
	Kano et al. (2006)	SFE 2002	1960	No loan denial	0.0		0.0/++ **[s]
Thailand	Menkhoff and Suwanaporn (2007)	9 Banks 1992–96	4161	Ratio L/C / (liabilities + L/C)	0.3	0.0	9.6***
Argentina	Streb et al. (2002)	CDSF 1999	8548	Unused credit line Ratio		−2.7***	21.4

	Bebczuk (2004)	UIA 1999	139	Probability of obtaining credit	no		
Chile	Repetto et al. (2002)	SBIF 1990–98	±20 000	Debt / Capital	1.7**	11.9**	−45.4**

Notes:
The table reports the coefficients from studies on the impact of the duration, scope and number of bank relationships on the cost of credit. The first column lists the *Country* affiliation of the related firms and the second column provides the *Paper* citation. The third column reports the data *Source* and *Year(s)*, the fourth column the number of *Observations* and an indicative *Firm Size* (small, medium and/or large). The fifth column gives a precise definition of the *Dependent Variable* and the next three columns indicate the impact on the dependent variable of an increase in *Duration* (by one year), *Number* (by one relationship) and *Scope* (from 0 to 1) of bank relationships. Coefficients and significance levels are based on the reported base specification. All coefficients for logged Duration or Number measures are averaged over the [1,4] interval.
[a] Authors' calculations. [a1] for a doubling from 10 to 20 bank services taken. CBSB: Credit, Banks and Small Business Survey collected by the National Federation of Independent Business. ccb: Credit granted by Chartered Community Banks to CCB members. CCR: Central Credit Register. CDSF: Center of Debtors of the Financial System at the Central Bank of Argentina. CFIB: Canadian Federation of Independent Business. [che] Checking account at the bank. [cl] based on contract length. [d] based on a dummy. [f] French-speaking part. JADE: Japanese Accounts and Data on Enterprises. JDB: Japan Development Bank. l: large. L/C: Line of Credit. LPC: Loan Pricing Corporation Dealscan database.
[lf] Number of lenders in facility. m: medium. NSSBF: National Survey of Small Business Finances. ne: Northeast. nw: Northwest. oth: All other credit. RHS: Right Hand Side. s: small. so: South. SBIC: Small Business Investment Companies. SBIF: Chilean Supervisory agency of Banks and Financial Institutions. SFE: Survey of the Financial Environment. SMF: Survey of Manufacturing Firms. [s] Result only for small banks / firms without audits and low banking market competition. *** Significant at 1%, ** significant at 5%, * significant at 10%.

Source: Degryse and Ongena (2007).

Table 5.4, Panel B and Panel C display the results of the impact of bank–firm relationships on the collateral and credit availability respectively. Most of the studies find that a decrease in the number of banks (or increase in the duration) decreases the probability of pledging collateral and it also increases the availability of credit. A recent paper by Tirri (2007) finds a positive relationship between the number of lenders and the availability of credit when correcting the potential endogeneity of the firm's decision of whether to rely on multiple relationships through a two-stage conditional maximum likelihood estimation technique. However, in contrast to other studies the proxy for credit availability is a binary variable. Moreover, the number of bank relationships below three cannot be observed in the data. Another potential endogeneity problem when investigating the impact of bank–firm relationships on credit conditions is that contract terms are jointly determined in a loan contract (Brick and Palia, 2007).

2 Impact of credit market structure

The credit market structure plays an important role in determining competition on banking markets. Many studies analyse the impact of market concentration on loan rates or credit availability. Market concentration is typically measured by the Herfindahl–Hirschman Index (HHI). Table 5.5 displays an overview of the studies including cost of credit and credit availability as dependent variables (Degryse and Ongena, 2003).

The majority of the studies find that market concentration increases loan rates. In the US for example, a 0.1 increase in the HHI increases the loan rates between 12 to 55 basis points (Hannan, 1997; and Cyrnak and Hannan, 1999). Petersen and Rajan (1995) on the other hand find a negative coefficient especially for young firms. They also find evidence for easier access to credit in concentrated banking markets. Most studies also document a positive impact of market concentration on credit availability, whereas Angelini et al. (1998) and Shikimi (2005) do not find any significant effect.

Recent work investigates how the existence of public and private information-sharing mechanisms between banks determines the debt capacity of firms and the role and value of bank–firm relationships (see, for example, Jappelli and Pagano, 1993; Padilla and Pagano, 1997, 2000; or Bouckaert and Degryse, 2006, for theoretical insights). Djankov et al. (2007) and Sorge and Zhang (2006) find that firms in countries where banks do share information enjoy a greater debt capacity and have a larger proportion of long-term debt available, respectively. Brown et al. (2007) test the impact of information sharing on the credit market performance in the transition countries of Eastern Europe and the former Soviet Union. They find that information sharing is associated with improved availability and lower cost of credit to firms, especially for opaque firms. In

Table 5.5 Impact of market concentration on loan rates and credit availability

Paper	Data Source & Years # Observations in Regressions Observation Type	Concentration in Bank Markets Geo Span: Avg. Pop. / Area Average HHI	Loan Rate or Credit Measure Impact of Concentration **Impact of ΔHHI = 0.1, in Basis Points**
Hannan (1991)	STB ± 8250 US firms	Bank deposits 4725 HHI: 0.14	Loan rate Mostly Positive **−6 to 61*** **
Petersen and Rajan (1995)	NSSBF 1987 ± 1400 US small firms	Bank deposits ± 2 250 000[a] HHI: 0.17[a]	Most recent loan rate (prime rate on RHS) Mostly Negative, especially for Young Firms 0 yrs: **−170****, 10 yrs: **−3**, 20 yrs: **46**[a]
Hannan (1997)	FRB Survey 1993 1994 / 7078 US banks	Bank deposits ± 2 500 000[a] HHI: 0.14	Small business floating loan rate Positive **31***** (unsecured), **12***** (secured)
Cavalluzzo et al. (2002)	NSSBF 1993 ± 2600 US small firms	Bank deposits ± 2 500 000[a] HHI: 0.14	Most recent interest rate on line of credit No effect, but positive for Hispanics All: **−8**, Hispanic: **124****
Cyrnak and Hannan (1999)	FRB Survey 1996 511 / 2059 US banks	Bank deposits ± 2 750 000[a] HHI: 0.16	Small business floating loan rate Positive **55***** (unsecured), **21***** (secured)[1]
Sapienza (2002)	Credit Register 107 501 Italian firms	Bank loans 600 000[a] HHI: 0.06	Loan rate – prime rate Positive **59*****
Degryse and Ongena (2005)	One Bank 15 044 Belgian small firms	Bank branches 8632 HHI: 0.17	Loan rate Mostly Positive **−4 to 5*****
Fischer and Pfeil (2004)	Survey 1992–1995 [s] 5500 German banks	Bank branches n/a HHI: ± 0.20 (West) / ± 0.30 (East)	Bank interest margins Positive **20***

Table 5.5 (continued)

Paper	Data Source & Years # Observations in Regressions Observation Type	Concentration in Bank Markets Geo Span: Avg. Pop. / Area Average HHI	Loan Rate or Credit Measure Impact of Concentration **Impact of ΔHHI = 0.1, in Basis Points**
Kim et al. (2005)	Central Bank of Norway 1241 Norwegian firms	Bank business credit 250 000[a] HHI: 0.19	Credit line rate – 3 month money market rate Insignificantly Positive **3**[b]
Claeys and Vander Vennet (2005)	Bankscope 1994–2001 2279 Banks 36 European Countries	Bank loans 30 000 000[a] HHI: 0.10	Bank net interest margin Positive (West) / Often Negative (East) West: **14***** to **23*****; East: −**110***** to **190*****
Corvoisier and Gropp (2002 and 2001)	ECB 2001 ±240 EU countries-years	Bank loans 30 000 000[a] HHI: 0.13	Country-specific loan rate margin Positive **10** to **20****[c] and **50*****[d]
Petersen and Rajan (1994)	NSSBF 1987 ± 1400 US small firms	Bank deposits ± 2 250 000[a] HHI: 0.17[a]	% Total Debt / Assets Positive **36*****
Petersen and Rajan (1995)	NSSBF 1987 ± 1400 US small firms	Bank deposits ± 2 250 000[a] HHI: 0.17[a]	% Trade credit paid before due date Positive, especially for Young Firms **140***** to **280*****,[p] ≤10 yrs: **175**** to **740**,[r] >10 yrs: **150*** to **0**[r]
Cavalluzzo et al. (2002)	NSSBF 1993 ± 2600 US small firms	Bank deposits ± 2 500 000[a] HHI: 0.14	Various credit availability measures No effect overall but significant positive effects for African Americans and Females
Zarutskie (2004)	SICTF 1987–1998 ± 250 000 US firms-years	Bank deposits ± 2 250 000[a] HHI: 0.19	% Outside Debt / Assets Positive **19** to **77*****

Scott and Dunkelberg (2001)	CBSB 1995	Bank deposits	No credit denial
Scott (2003)	± 2000 US small firms	± 2 500 000[a] HHI: 0.19	Positive + to +++[e]
Angelini et al. (1998)	Survey 1995 2232 Italian small firms	Bank loan Median: <10 000 HHI: 0.42	Perceived Access to Credit No effect **0**
Shikimi (2005)	JADE 2000–2002 28 622 Japanese small firms	Credit N/a CR3: 0.44	% Debt / Assets No effect **0**

Notes:
The table lists the main findings of selected empirical work investigating the impact of bank market concentration on bank loan rates and measures of bank credit availability. The measure of concentration in all studies is either the Three-Bank Concentration ratio (CR3) or the Herfindahl–Hirschman Index (HHI), which can be calculated by squaring the market share of each bank competing in the market and then summing the resulting numbers (0 < HHI < 1).

[a] Authors' calculations or estimates. [b] For HHI increasing from 0.09 to 0.19. [c] Their models 2 and 5. CBSB: Credit, Banks and Small Business Survey collected by the National Federation of Independent Business. [d] Coefficients in regressions for short-term loans in their models 3, 5, and 6. [e] Based on the COMPETITION variable, not on the HHICTY. JADE: Japanese Accounts and Data on Enterprises. NSSBF: National Survey of Small Business Finance. [p] Linear approximation using their Table IV coefficients and assuming that the mean HHI below 0.1 equals 0.05 and above 0.18 equals 0.59. [r] Linear approximation assuming that the mean HHI below 0.1 equals 0.05 and above 0.18 equals 0.59, based on means and medians in their Table V. SBIF: Chilean Supervisory agency of Banks and Financial Institutions. SICTF: Statistics of Income Corporate Tax Files. STB: Federal Reserve's Survey of the Terms of Bank lending to business. yrs: years. 0: Included in the specifications but not significant.
*** Significant at 1%, ** at 5%, * at 10%. +++ Positive and significant at 1%, ++ at 5%, + at 10%. ↔↔↔ Negative and significant at 1%, ↔↔ at 5%, ↔ at 10%.

Source: Degryse and Ongena (2007).

an experimental study, Brown and Zehnder (2007) analyse the disciplining effect of credit registries on repayment behaviour of borrowers. Their results suggest that credit reporting is valuable in markets where banking relationships are not prevalent. However information-sharing mechanisms have little value when firms do have relationship lenders.

III BANKS AS LARGE SHAREHOLDERS

It is not always easy to distinguish between the different roles that banks play in corporate governance of firms. Especially in continental Europe and Japan, banks control firms through all mechanisms: debt financing, large ownership stakes, and positions on supervisory boards.[5] In this section, we summarize the studies that focus on the governance mechanism applied by banks as large shareholders. Table 5.6 gives a brief summary on the findings of these studies.

Berlin et al. (1996) model the optimal bank equity stake in a borrowing firm when the firm's uninformed stakeholders depend on the bank to inform them if the firm is financially distressed. The model shows that the banks must hold either a very small or very large share to ensure that it reveals truthful information; that is, not forming a coalition with the firm's owners to seek unnecessary concessions when the firm is healthy or to claim that the firm is healthy when the firm is distressed.

However, the legal system constrains banks' role in the corporate structure as argued by Roe (1990). The Glass–Steagall Act and Bank Holding Company Act of 1956 prohibit US banks and bank holding companies from owning large equity stakes in non-financial companies. The Gramm–Leach–Bliley Act repealed the Glass–Steagall Act in 1999. Although the act brought some changes, it did not remove the restrictions on banks in owning non-financial corporations.[6] Roe (1990) explains these restrictions as the pervasive mistrust of financial power and the lobbying of interest groups for the restrictions. Due to legal restrictions on banks' equity ownership of non-financial firms in the US, the studies typically analyse European countries and Japan where banks play an important role as large shareholders of firms.

Using cross-country data, Li et al. (2006) examine which macro government factors affect institutional ownership decisions. They find that countries with strong shareholder rights and effective legal enforcement have a greater extent of block holdings. They explain their findings as evidence for the tradeoff between the benefits and costs of shareholder monitoring. In strong governance environments, monitoring costs are reduced, which leads to increased level of block holdings and institutional monitoring. However,

Table 5.6 Impact of bank equity ownership

Paper	Country	Source, Year Sample, Firm Size	Measure	Impact on Dependent Variable
Gorton and Schmid (2000)	Germany	1975 + 1986 283 + 280 large	Market-to-book of equity	+++
Lehmann and Weigand (2000)	Germany	1991–96 361	ROA	++
Edwards and Nibler (2000)	Germany	1992 156 large	Market-to-book of equity	++
Meyer and Prilmeier (2006)	Germany	1997–2006 92 large	(*Banks' Sale of Firms' Stake*) On Abnormal Returns	+++
Pawlina and Renneboog (2005)	UK	1992–98 985 listed	Investment-cash flow sensitivity	↔
Van Overfelt et al. (2006)	Belgium	1905–09 569 large	Market-to-book of equity, ROA	0
Suzuki and Wright (1985)	Japan	1974–78 56 listed	Firm does not default	0
Hoshi et al. (1990)	Japan	1978–85 125 listed	Investment, Sales	0
Gibson (1995)	Japan	1992 1355 listed	Investment	0/↔ for 'weaker' banks
Morck and Nakamura (1999)	Japan	1981–87 383 large	Various performance measures	0/↔
Morck et al. (2000)	Japan	1986 373 large	Tobin's q	↔↔↔
Limpaphayom and Polwitoon (2004)	Thailand	1990–96 1340	Tobin's q	+++

Table 5.6 (continued)

Paper	Country	Source, Year Sample, Firm Size	Measure	Impact on Dependent Variable
Azofra-Palenzuela et al. (2007)	Spain	1999–2002 142 listed	ROA	BB: ↔↔ BNB: + NBB: +++
Franks and Mayer (2001)	Germany	1989–94 75 large	Board turnover	+ for poor performance firms
Agarwal and Elston (2001)	Germany	1970–86 1660 largest	Operating income / Sales Cost of Credit Availability of Credit	0 + ↔
Garcia-Marco and Ocana (1999)	Spain	1991–94 129 large	Credit Availability	++

Notes:
The table summarizes the results from studies on the impact of bank equity ownership on various measures, mainly firm performance. The first column lists the *Paper* citation on the first row and the *Country* affiliation of the related firms on the second row. The second column reports on the first row the data *Source* and *Year* and on the second row the *Sample size* and an indication of *Firm Size*. The third column defines the *Measure of* the dependent variable. The fourth column indicates the sign and significance of the *Impact on Firm Performance* of changes in the *Bank Ownership*. +++ Positive and significant at 1%, ++ at 5%, + at 10%. ↔↔↔ Negative and significant at 1%, ↔↔ at 5%, ↔ at 10%. 0: Included in the specifications but not significant. BB, BNB and NBB are dummy variables for banks as one of two largest shareholders (bank and bank; bank and no-bank; no-bank and bank).

this relation is weak in the case of banks. Due to bank–firm relationships, banks' ownership decisions seem to be less affected by macro governance factors when compared to other blockholders, argue these authors.

Morck et al. (2000) analyse the relation between firms' ownership structure and firm value in Japan. They find a non-linear relationship between the equity ownership by main banks and firms' Tobin's q. At low levels of bank ownership, an increase in bank equity stakes leads to a decrease in Tobin's q. However, at high levels of ownership, this impact is either mitigated or reversed. The authors also find evidence that at low to moderate levels of ownership, banks' power to extract rents increases. They argue that their findings may explain both the benefits and costs of bank equity ownership. However, there is a concern of a potential endogeneity problem of bank ownership which the authors do not control for.

Banks' influence is also prevalent in the German financial system. German universal banks can own blocks of equity and vote shareholders' votes in proxy. Proxy-voting is a mechanism that enables banks to exercise voting power in stockholders' meetings. For that reason, if there are voting restrictions, banks can outvote non-bank blockholders using proxy votes. Gorton and Schmid (2000), for example, investigate the impact of banks' equity control rights, banks' proxy-voting rights and the concentration of control rights on firms' performance measured as market-to-book value of equity. The findings suggest that firm performance improves with concentrated equity control rights. The impact is much stronger with bank equity control rights than the one with non-bank blockholders. Edwards and Nibler (2000) perform a similar analysis on Germany and find that large bank equity stakes have a positive impact on market-to-book value of equity. The estimated coefficient is similar in size to the coefficients of two other types of large shareholders, that is individuals or families and foreign firms. Thus the authors argue that bank equity ownership does not have greater effects on firm performance than those of other types of large shareholders. But both studies differ. One difference corresponds to the measurement of bank equity control rights. Edwards and Nibler (2000) distinguish between large banks and other banks when examining the impact of bank equity control rights. However, both studies document a positive effect of bank equity stakes on the performance of large listed firms. This suggests that banks are not only important for SMEs, but also for larger firms in Germany that have access to other sources of finance.

Another study investigating the ownership of German corporations is by Franks and Mayer (2001). They take a different approach and examine the association between board turnover and performance of firms with different ownership structures. The findings suggest that firms with poor performance have a higher board turnover. There is also some evidence of higher board turnover in loss-maker firms than in non-loss-maker firms where banks have large equity stakes. This is in line with the view that banks have a distinct role in exerting a disciplinary function. However, regression results imply little or no relation between types of ownership and board turnover even when pyramiding structure is taken into account. The authors conclude that the static relationship of ownership in Germany is similar to the one in the UK and the US. But they report differences in dynamic relations such as transfer of ownership as observed in the market of share blocks that operates for corporate control.

IV BANKERS ON BOARDS

Gilson (1990) examines changes in corporate ownership and control in publicly traded US firms that default on their debt. The author finds that in the case of bankruptcy or restructuring of a firm, the corporate control shifts from the management and the board towards blockholders and creditors. Moreover, the percentage of equity stakes owned by blockholders and banks increases as well. Alternatively, banks place their representatives on the board of the distressed firm directly. 'Bankers on board' is not an unusual practice and does not necessarily require financial distress of a firm. In this section, we give a brief summary of studies that investigate the role of banks on boards of non-financial firms.

Table 5.7 summarizes the results from studies on the impact of banks as board members on different performance measures. Papers on European firms document positive influence of bank board membership on firm profits (see Van Overfelt et al., 2006; and Lehmann and Weigand, 2000). Byrd and Mizruchi (2005) investigate the impact on debt ratios of US firms. They find that having lenders on the board has a negative impact on both debt ratio and equity values of firms. However, when the probability of financial distress is high and when other banks are appointed to the board, they provide certification and expertise, and firm debt ratios rise. In this case, the multiple roles of banks in governing firms is clearly visible. On the other hand, lenders tend to avoid board appointments when the cost of board monitoring is higher than the benefits. In that case other bankers may replace the lenders.

Also other studies investigate the determinants of appointments of bank directors to corporate boards (see Kaplan and Minton, 1994; Kroszner and Strahan, 2001; and Santos and Rumble, 2006). Table 5.8 displays the findings of these studies. Kaplan and Minton (1994), for example, explore both the determinants and implications of appointments of bank and corporate directors in Japanese firms. They find that appointments of bank directors increase with poor stock performance and with earnings losses. In

Table 5.7 Impact of bank control through board membership

Paper	Country	Source, Year Sample, Firm Size	Measure	Impact on Dependent Variable
Byrd and Mizruchi (2005)	US	1980–91 456 largest	Market equity / assets	↔↔
Şişli Ciamarra (2006)	US	2002 and 2004 403 listed	Cost of Credit Availability of Credit	↔↔ +++
Van Overfelt et al. (2006)	Belgium	1905–09 569 large	Market-to-book of equity, ROA, St. Dev. of ROA	++ ↔↔
Agarwal and Elston (2001)	Germany	1970–86 1660 largest	Operating income / Sales Cost of Credit Availability of Credit	0 + ↔
Lehmann and Weigand (2000)	Germany	1991–96 361	ROA	++
Van Ees and Garretsen (1994)	Netherlands	1985–90 76 listed	Investment-cash flow sensitivity	0 / +++ for nonaffiliated firms
Suzuki and Wright (1985)	Japan	1974–78 56 listed	Firm does not default	0
Gibson (1995)	Japan	1992 1355 listed	Investment	0/↔ for 'weaker' banks
Kaplan and Minton (1994)	Japan	1980–88 119 large	Executive turnover	+++

Notes:
The table summarizes the results from studies on the impact of banks as board members on different performance measures and/or credit conditions. The first column lists the *Paper* citation on the first row and the *Country* affiliation of the related firms on the second row. The second column reports on the first row the data *Source* and *Year* and on the second row the *Sample* size and an indication of *Firm Size*. The third column defines the *Measure of* the dependent variable. The fourth column indicate the sign and significance of the *Impact on Firm Performance* of changes in the *Bank Ownership*. +++ Positive and significant at 1%, ++ at 5%, + at 10%. ↔↔↔ Negative and significant at 1%, ↔↔ at 5%, ↔ at 10%. 0: Included in the specifications but not significant.

Table 5.8 Determinants of the presence of bankers on board

	Paper	Kaplan and Minton (1994)	Morck and Nakamura (1999)	Gorton and Schmid (2000)	Santos and Rumble (2006)	Kroszner and Strahan (2001)	Byrd and Mizruchi (2005)
	Country	Japan	Japan	Germany	US	US	US
	Sample Years	1980–88	1981–87	1975 + 1986	2000	1992	1980–1991
	Number of Observations	933	2371	138	27 051	430	456
	Firm size	Large	Large	Large	Large	Large	Large
	Measure	Probability of bank appointment	Probability of bank appointment	Fraction of board seats held by banks	Presence of a bank on board	Presence of a bank on board	Presence and Number of bankers on board
Relation	Scope		+				
Firm	Size			↔	++	+++	0
	Growth	0	↔				0
	Profitability	↔↔	↔↔		+		
	Stock return	↔↔↔					
	Risk					++/↔↔	↔↔
	Cash Flow		↔				0
	Intangibility					↔↔↔	0
	Debt		0		+	0	
	Bank Debt	+++	+++				
	Short-Term Debt					↔↔	0

	Bank Debt by Largest Lender	++			
	Group member	0			
	Concentration of Ownership / or Control Rights	0	0		
	Board size				↔ +++
Bank	Equity Control Rights		+++		
	Voting Rights		++	+	

Notes:
The table summarizes the results from studies on the determinants of the presence of banks on the boards of firms. The first column lists the variable names. The other columns contain the results from the respective papers. The *Paper* citations are on the first row. The second row lists the *Country* and the third row the *Sample Years*. The fourth row reports the *Number of Observations* and the fifth row the *Firm size*. Other rows list the sign and significance levels of the coefficients on the independent variables as reported in the paper. +++ Positive and significant at 1%, ++ at 5%, + at 10%. ↔↔↔ Negative and significant at 1%, ↔↔ at 5%, ↔ at 10%. 0: Included in the specifications but not significant.

addition, executive turnover increases following the appointments of outsiders. They also find that firm performance slightly improves after appointments. The authors apply their analysis to a sample of US firms as well. The comparison of the results confirms that banks play a more important role in monitoring and disciplining the firms in Japan than the banks do in the US. Banks and corporate shareholders in Japan seem to substitute the role of takeovers in the US.

Also Kroszner and Strahan (2001) examine what determines the presence of banks on the boards of corporations by focusing on the potential conflicts of interest between lenders and shareholders and on lender liability. They find that banks are present on the boards of large and stable firms that have higher proportions of tangible assets but lower proportions of short-term debt. The relationship between firm risk and the presence of a bank on the board is found to be non-monotonic. This result suggests that banks are less likely to join the boards of a firm that would actually benefit most from bank monitoring when they are concerned about conflicts of interest. The paper also documents that only a few main lenders are represented on corporate boards in the US. Instead, banks prefer to lend to firms in industries where their executives have board membership. The authors argue that the conflicts of interests between lenders and shareholders could be mitigated if banks were allowed to hold equity of a firm, which is prohibited in the US as explained in the previous section.

However, banks can make equity investments through their trust business. Consequently, they can control large voting stakes of firms by separating cash rights from voting rights, as argued in Santos and Rumble (2006). These authors analyse the implications of having voting rights for banks and whether it can explain banks' presence on corporate boards. They show that banks tend to join the boards of firms in which they (that is, their bank holding company) control a large voting stake. In contrast to previous literature that documents the limitations of banks' role in the US, the paper documents that US banks may indeed have an influence on corporate governance of firms.

V CONCLUDING REMARKS

This chapter provides an overview of the different roles banks play in the corporate governance of firms. Banks interact with firms through different mechanisms and can influence corporate control in this way. Especially in bank-centred economies such as continental Europe and Japan, this influence is more pronounced where banks, in addition to being an important debt financier, are allowed to hold large equity stakes of firms.

Moreover, banks join the boards of corporations and for example, in Germany, they control firms through the proxy-voting mechanism.

As important providers of finance, banks reduce information asymmetry, solve incentive problems in debt markets, signal the quality of a firm to other financiers and increase credit availability. Banks also discipline firm managers by preventing them from investing in negative NPV projects. However, the literature documents mixed findings for the impact of bank relationships on firm performance. Another strand of literature explores the impact of loan announcements on the abnormal returns of borrowing firms. While most studies do not find significant impacts for other financiers, most studies report a positive impact on stock prices for bank–firm relationships, confirming the value of bank relationships to firms.

Banks' influence as large shareholders of firms is also investigated by the literature (Gorton and Schmid, 2000; Edwards and Nibler, 2000; Morck et al., 2000; and Franks and Mayer, 2001). Studies find either a positive or a nonlinear relationship between bank equity stakes and the performance of firms. Moreover, when banks have large equity stakes in loss-making firms, corporate board turnover is significantly higher than it is for family-owned firms, which again confirms the disciplinary role of banks. Alternatively, banks may join the boards of distressed firms. However, if there is a lending relationship between the bank and the firm, banks tend to avoid being on the board when cost of board monitoring is high (Byrd and Mizruchi, 2005; and Kroszner and Strahan, 2001).

In sum, banks control firms through several complementary governance mechanisms but depending on the country in varying degrees of intensity. Jenkinson and Ljungqvist (2001) argue that as banks reduce their stakes in firms, cases of hostile takeovers will increase in Germany. This view is in line with Kaplan and Minton (1994) who argue that banks and corporate shareholders in Japan substitute the role of takeovers in the US. However, Ivashina et al. (2006) document another disciplining role of US banks. Banks seem to affect the probability of takeovers via a lending-related information channel. They find that bank lending intensity has a significant and positive effect on the probability of a firm becoming a target. Their findings suggest that the role banks play in the governance of corporations may have many unexpected dimensions and that more research is warranted.

NOTES

* Günseli Tümer-Alkan gratefully acknowledges financial support from the European Corporate Governance Training Network (ECGTN).

1. See Degryse and Ongena (2007), for example, for an extensive review of these issues.

2. Here, 'close ties' also include equity ownership. In bank-centred economies like Japan and Germany, banks interact with firms through several mechanisms at the same time.
3. Many firms in Japan have close relationships with a main bank, which is part of a large industrial structure known as *keiretsu*.
4. We will analyse the impact of bank relationships on firm stock returns in detail in the next section.
5. In Japan, banks are not allowed to hold more than 5 per cent of a firm's shares. However, Li et al. (2006) find that many bank shareholdings are above this limit. Indeed, the bank trust divisions are not subject to this restriction.
6. Gilson (1990) finds that over the period of financial distress of US firms that default on their debt, the percentage of equity stakes of creditors rises. However, according to the law, this stock must be divested within two years.

REFERENCES

Agarwal, R. and J.A. Elston (2001), 'Bank–firm relationships, financing and firm performance in Germany', *Economics Letters*, **72**, 225–32.

Aintablian, S. and G.S. Roberts (2000), 'A note on market response to corporate loan announcements in Canada', *Journal of Banking and Finance*, **24**, 381–93.

Allayannis, G. and A. Mozumdar (2004), 'The impact of negative cash flow and influential observations on investment-cash flow sensitivity estimates', *Journal of Banking and Finance*, **28**, 901–30.

Andre, P., R. Mathieu and P. Zhang (2001), 'A note on: capital adequacy and the information content of term loans and lines of credit', *Journal of Banking and Finance*, **25**, 431–44.

Angelini, P., R. Di Salvo and G. Ferri (1998), 'Availability and cost of credit for small businesses: customer relationships and credit cooperatives', *Journal of Banking and Finance*, **22**, 925–54.

Azofra-Palenzuela, V., F.J. López Iturriaga and F. Tejerina-Gaite (2007), 'Banks as shareholders: the Spanish model of corporate governance', in Frank J. Columbus (ed.), *Corporate Governance: Issues and Challenges*, Nova Science Publishers.

Bae, K.H., J.K. Kang and C.W. Lim (2002), 'The value of durable bank relationships: evidence from Korean banking shocks', *Journal of Financial Economics*, **64**, 181–214.

Bebczuk, R.N. (2004), 'What determines the access to credit by SMEs in Argentina?', Universidad Nacional de la Plata, Working Paper.

Berger, A.N. and G.F. Udell (1995), 'Relationship lending and lines of credit in small firm finance', *Journal of Business*, **68**, 351–81.

Berger, A.N., R.J. Rosen and G.F. Udell (2002), 'Does market size structure affect competition? The case of small business lending', Board of Governors of the Federal Reserve System, mimeo.

Berlin, M., K. John and A. Saunders (1996), 'Bank equity stakes in borrowing firms and financial distress', *Review of Financial Studies*, **9**, 889–919.

Best, R. and H. Zhang (1993), 'Alternative information sources and the information content of bank loans', *Journal of Finance*, **48**, 1507–22.

Bharath, S., S. Dahiya, A. Saunders and A. Srinivasan (2007), 'So what do I get? The bank's view of lending relationships', *Journal of Financial Economics*, **85**(2), 368–419.

Billett, M.T., M.J. Flannery and J.A. Garfinkel (1995), 'The effect of lender identity on a borrowing firm's equity return', *Journal of Finance*, **50**, 699–718.
Blackwell, D.W. and D.B. Winters (1997), 'Banking relationships and the effect of monitoring on loan pricing', *Journal of Financial Research*, **20**, 275–89.
Bodenhorn, H. (2003), 'Short-term loans and long-term relationships: relationship lending in early America', *Journal of Money, Credit, and Banking*, **35**, 485–505.
Bolton, P. and D.S. Scharfstein (1990), 'A theory of predation based on agency problems in financial contracting', *American Economic Review*, **80**, 93–106.
Bolton, P. and D.S. Scharfstein (1996), 'Optimal debt structure and the number of creditors', *Journal of Political Economy*, **104**, 1–25.
Bouckaert, J. and H. Degryse (2006), 'Entry and strategic information display in credit markets', *Economic Journal*, **116**, 702–20.
Brewer, E., H. Genay, W.C. Hunter and G.G. Kaufman (2003), 'The value of banking relationships during a financial crisis: evidence from failures of Japanese banks', *Journal of Japanese and International Economies*, **17**, 233–62.
Brick, I.E. and D. Palia (2007), 'Evidence of jointness in the terms of relationship lending', *Journal of Financial Intermediation*, **16**(3), 452–76.
Bris, A. and I. Welch (2005), 'The optimal concentration of creditors', *Journal of Finance*, **60**, 2193–212.
Brown, M. and C. Zehnder (2007), 'Credit reporting, relationship banking and loan repayment', *Journal of Money, Credit and Banking*, **39**(8), 1883–1918.
Brown, M., T. Jappelli and M. Pagano (2007), 'Information sharing and credit: firm-level evidence from transition countries', CSEF Working Paper, no. 178.
Byrd, D.T. and M.S. Mizruchi (2005), 'Bankers on the board and the debt ratio of firms', *Journal of Corporate Finance*, **11**, 129–73.
Carletti, E. (2004), 'The structure of bank relationships, endogenous monitoring, and loan rates', *Journal of Financial Intermediation*, **13**, 58–86.
Carletti, E., V. Cerasi and S. Daltung (2007), 'Multiple-bank lending: diversification and free-riding in monitoring', *Journal of Financial Intermediation*, **16**(3), 425–51.
Castelli, A., G.P. Dwyer Jr. and I. Hasan (2006), 'Bank relationships and small firms' financial performance', Federal Reserve Bank of Atlanta, Atlanta.
Cavalluzzo, K.S., L.C. Cavalluzzo and J.D. Wolken (2002), 'Competition, small business financing, and discrimination: evidence from a new survey', *Journal of Business*, **75**, 641–80.
Chakraborty, A. and C.X. Hu (2006), 'Lending relationships in line-of-credit and nonline-of-credit loans: evidence from collateral use in small business', *Journal of Financial Intermediation*, **15**, 86–107.
Chiou, I. (1999), 'Daiwa bank's reputational crisis: valuation effects on bank–firm relationships', New York University Stern School of Business, mimeo.
Claeys, S. and R. Vander Vennet (2005), 'Determinants of bank interest margins in central and Eastern Europe: a comparison with the West', Ghent University, mimeo.
Cleary, S. (1999), 'The relationship between firm investment and financial status', *Journal of Finance*, **54**, 673–92.
Cole, R. (1998), 'The importance of relationships to the availability of credit', *Journal of Banking and Finance*, **22**, 959–77.
Cole, R.A., L.G. Goldberg and L.J. White (2004), 'Cookie-cutter versus character: the micro structure of small business lending by large and small banks', *Journal of Financial and Quantitative Analysis*, **39**, 227–52.

Conigliani, C., G. Ferri and A. Generale (1997), 'The impact of bank–firm relations on the propagation of monetary policy squeezes: an empirical assessment for Italy', *Banca Nazionale del Lavoro*, **202**, 271–99.

Cosci, S. and V. Meliciani (2002), 'Multiple banking relationships: evidence from the Italian experience', *Manchester School*, **70**, Supplement 1, 37–54.

Corvoisier, S. and R. Gropp (2001), 'Contestability, technology, and banking', European Central Bank, mimeo.

Corvoisier, S. and R. Gropp (2002), 'Bank concentration and retail interest rates', *Journal of Banking and Finance*, **26**, 2155–89.

Cyrnak, A.W. and T.H. Hannan (1999), 'Is the cluster still valid in defining banking markets? Evidence from a new data source', *Antitrust Bulletin*, **44**, 313–31.

D'Auria, C., A. Foglia and P.M. Reedtz (1999), 'Bank interest rates and credit relationships in Italy', *Journal of Banking and Finance*, **23**, 1067–93.

De Bodt, E., F. Lobez and J.C. Statnik (2005), 'Credit rationing, customer relationship, and the number of banks: an empirical analysis', *European Financial Management*, **11**(2), 195–228.

Degryse, H. and A. de Jong (2006), 'Investment and internal finance: asymmetric information or managerial discretion?', *International Journal of Industrial Organization*, **24**(1), 125–47.

Degryse, H. and S. Ongena (2001), 'Bank relationships and firm performance', *Financial Management*, **30**, 9–34.

Degryse, H. and S. Ongena (2003), 'Distance, lending relationships, and competition', Center for Economic Studies – KU Leuven & CentER – Tilburg University, Discussion Paper.

Degryse, H. and S. Ongena (2005), 'Distance, lending relationships, and competition', *Journal of Finance*, **60**(1), 231–66.

Degryse, H. and S. Ongena (2007), 'Competition and regulation in the banking sector: a review of the empirical evidence on the sources of bank rents', CentER – Tilburg University, mimeo.

Degryse, H. and P. Van Cayseele (2000), 'Relationship lending within a bank-based system: evidence from European small business data', *Journal of Financial Intermediation*, **9**, 90–109.

Dewatripont, M. and E. Maskin (1995), 'Credit and efficiency in centralized and decentralized economies', *Review of Economic Studies*, **62**, 541–55.

Diamond, D. (1984), 'Financial intermediation and delegated monitoring', *Review of Economic Studies*, **51**, 393–414.

Dietsch, M. (2003), 'Financing small businesses in France', *European Investment Bank Papers*, **8**, 93–119.

Djankov, S.D., J. Jindra and L. Klapper (2005), 'Corporate valuation and the resolution of bank insolvency in East Asia', *Journal of Banking and Finance*, **29**, 2095–118.

Djankov, S., C. McLiesh and A. Shleifer (2007), 'Private credit in 129 countries', *Journal of Financial Economics*, **84**(2), 299–329.

Edwards, J. and M. Nibler (2000), 'Corporate governance in Germany: the role of banks and ownership concentration', *Economic Policy*, **15**(31), 237–67.

Elsas, R. and J.P. Krahnen (1998), 'Is relationship lending special? Evidence from credit-file data in Germany', *Journal of Banking and Finance*, **22**, 1283–316.

Elsas, R. and J.P. Krahnen (2002), 'Collateral, relationship lending, and financial distress: an empirical study on financial contracting', Center for Financial Studies, mimeo.

Ewert, R., G. Schenk and A. Szczesny (2000), 'Determinants of bank lending performance in Germany', *Schmalenbach Business Review*, **52**, 344–62.
Fama, E. (1985), 'What's different about banks?', *Journal of Monetary Economics*, **15**, 29–40.
Fazzari, S.M., R.G. Hubbard and B.C. Petersen (1988), 'Financing constraints and corporate investment', *Brookings Papers on Economic Activity*, **1**, 141–206.
Ferri, G. and M. Messori (2000), 'Bank–firm relationships and allocative efficiency in northeastern and central Italy and in the south', *Journal of Banking and Finance*, **24**, 1067–95.
Fery, J., D. Gasborro, D.R. Woodliff and J.K. Zumwalt (2003), 'Market reaction to published and non-published corporate loan announcements', *Quarterly Review of Economics and Finance*, **43**, 1–10.
Fields, L.P., D.R. Fraser, T.L. Berry and S. Byers (2006), 'Do bank loan relationships still matter?', *Journal of Money, Credit, and Banking*, **38**, 1195–209.
Fischer, K.H. and C. Pfeil (2004), 'Regulation and competition in German banking', in J.P. Krahnen and R.H. Schmidt (eds), *The German Financial System*, Frankfurt: Oxford University Press, pp. 291–349.
Foglia, A., S. Laviola and P. Marullo Reedtz (1998), 'Multiple banking relationships and the fragility of corporate borrowers', *Journal of Banking and Finance*, **22**, 1441–56.
Fohlin, C. (1998), 'Relationship banking, liquidity, and investment in the German industrialization, *Journal of Finance*, **53**, 1737–58.
Franks, J. and C. Mayer (2001), 'Ownership and control of German corporations', *Review of Financial Studies*, **14**(4), 943–77.
Fuss, C. and P. Vermeulen (2006), 'The response of firms' investment and financing to adverse cash flow shocks – the role of bank relationships', European Central Bank, Working Paper Series 658.
Garcia-Marco, T. and C. Ocana (1999), 'The effect of bank monitoring on the investment behavior of Spanish firms', *Journal of Banking and Finance*, **23**, 1579–603.
Gibson, M.S. (1995), 'Can bank health affect investment? Evidence from Japan', *Journal of Business*, **68**, 281–308.
Gilson, S.C. (1990), 'Bankruptcy, boards, banks, and blockholders: evidence on changes in corporate ownership and control when firms default', *Journal of Financial Economics*, **27**, 355–87.
Gorton, G. and F.A. Schmid (2000), 'Universal banking and the performance of German firms', *Journal of Financial Economics*, **58**, 29–80.
Gugler, K., D.C. Mueller and B.B. Yurtoglu (2004), 'Corporate governance around the world', *Oxford Review of Economic Policy*, **20**(1), 129–56.
Gugler, K., D.C. Mueller and B.B. Yurtoglu (2007), 'Corporate governance and the determinants of investment', *Journal of Institutional and Theoretical Economics*, **163**(4), 598–626.
Guiso, L. (2003), 'Small business finance in Italy', *European Investment Bank Papers*, **8**, 121–47.
Hannan, T. (1997), 'Market share inequality, the number of competitors, and the HHI: an examination of bank pricing', *Review of Industrial Organization*, **12**, 23–35.
Hannan, T.H. (1991), 'Bank commercial loan markets and the role of market structure: evidence from surveys of commercial lending', *Journal of Banking and Finance*, **15**, 133–49.

Hao, L. (2003). 'Bank effects and the determinants of loan yield spreads', York University, mimeo.

Harhoff, D. and T. Körting (1998), 'Lending relationships in Germany – empirical evidence from survey data', *Journal of Banking and Finance*, **22**, 1317–53.

Hart, O.D. (1995), *Firms, Contracts, and Financial Structure*, Oxford: Oxford University Press.

Hart, O.D. and J. Moore (1989), 'Default and renegotiation: a dynamic model of debt', Cambridge: MIT, Department of Economics, manuscript.

Hernandez-Canovas, G. and P. Martinez-Solano (2006), 'Banking relationships: effects on the debt terms of the small Spanish firms', *Journal of Small Business Management*, **44**, 315–33.

Hoshi, T., A. Kashyap and D. Scharfstein (1990), 'The role of banks in reducing the costs of financial distress in Japan', *Journal of Financial Economics*, **27**, 67–88.

Hoshi, T., A. Kashyap and D. Scharfstein (1991), 'Corporate structure, liquidity, and investment: evidence from Japanese industrial groups', *Quarterly Journal of Economics*, **106**, 33–60.

Houston, J. and C. James (2001), 'Do relationships have limits? Banking relationships, financial constraints and investment', *Journal of Business*, **74**, 347–74.

Huang, W. and S. Zhao (2007), 'When debt is bad news: market reaction to debt announcements under poor governance', University of Toulouse, mimeo.

Hwan Shin, G., D.R. Fraser and J.W. Kolari (2003), 'How does banking industry consolidation affect bank–firm relationships? Evidence from a large Japanese bank merger', *Pacific-Basin Finance Journal*, **11**, 285–304.

Ivashina, V., V.B. Nair, A. Saunders, N. Massoud and R. Stover (2006), 'Bank debt and corporate governance', EFA 2004 Maastricht Meetings Paper No. 4601.

James, C. (1987), 'Some evidence on the uniqueness of bank loans', *Journal of Financial Economics*, **19**, 217–35.

Jappelli, T. and M. Pagano (1993), 'Information sharing in credit markets', *Journal of Finance*, **48,** 1693–718.

Jenkinson, T. and A. Ljungqvist (2001), 'The role of hostile stakes in German corporate governance', *Journal of Corporate Finance*, **7**, 397–446.

Jensen, M.C. (1986), 'Agency costs of free cash flow, corporate finance, and takeovers', *American Economic Review*, **76**, 323–9.

Kang, J., A. Shivdasani and T. Yamada (2000), 'The effect of bank relations on investment decisions: an investigation of Japanese takeover bids', *Journal of Finance*, **55**(5), 2197–218.

Kano, M., H. Uchida, G.F. Udell and W. Watanabe (2006), 'Information verifiability, bank organization, bank competition and bank–borrower relationships', Wakayama University, mimeo.

Kaplan, S.N. and B.A. Minton (1994), 'Appointments of outsiders to Japanese boards: determinants and implications for managers', *Journal of Financial Economics*, **36**, 225–58.

Kaplan, S.N. and L. Zingales (1997), 'Do investment–cash flow sensitivities provide useful measures of financing constraints?', *Quarterly Journal of Economics*, **112**, 169–215.

Karceski, J., S. Ongena and D.C. Smith (2005), 'The impact of bank consolidation on commercial borrower welfare', *Journal of Finance*, **60**, 2043–82.

Kim, M., E.G. Kristiansen and B. Vale (2005), 'Endogenous product differentiation in credit markets: what do borrowers pay for?', *Journal of Banking and Finance*, **29**, 681–99.

Kroszner, R.S. and P.E. Strahan (2001), 'Bankers on boards: monitoring, conflicts of interest, and lender liability', *Journal of Financial Economics*, **62**, 415–52.

Lehmann, E. and D. Neuberger (2001), 'Do lending relationships matter? Evidence from bank survey data in Germany', *Journal of Economic Behavior and Organization*, **45**, 339–59.

Lehmann, E. and J. Weigand (2000), 'Does the governed corporation perform better? Governance structures and corporate performance in Germany', *European Finance Review*, **4**, 157–95.

Lehmann, E., D. Neuberger and S. Rathke (2004), 'Lending to small and medium-sized firms: is there an east–west gap in Germany', *Small Business Economics*, **23**, 23–39.

Li, D., F. Moshirian, P. Pham and J. Zein (2006), 'When financial institutions are large shareholders: the role of macro corporate governance environments', *Journal of Finance*, **61**(6), 2975–3007.

Limpaphayom, P. and S. Polwitoon (2004), 'Bank relationship and firm performance: evidence from Thailand before the Asian Financial Crisis', *Journal of Business Finance and Accounting*, **31**, 1577–600.

Lummer, S.L. and J.J. McConnell (1989), 'Further evidence on the bank lending process and the capital market response to bank loan agreements', *Journal of Financial Economics*, **25**, 99–122.

Machauer, A. and M. Weber (1998), 'Bank behavior based on internal credit ratings of borrowers', *Journal of Banking and Finance*, **22**, 1355–83.

Mallett, T. and A. Sen (2001), 'Does local competition impact interest rates charged on small business loans? Empirical evidence from Canada', *Review of Industrial Organization*, **19**, 437–52.

Menkhoff, L. and C. Suwanaporn (2007), 'On the rationale of bank lending in pre-crisis Thailand', *Applied Economics*, **39**(9), 1077–89.

Menkhoff, L., D. Neuberger and C. Suwanaporn (2006), 'Collateral-based lending in emerging markets: evidence from Thailand', *Journal of Banking and Finance*, **30**, 1–21.

Meyer, S. and R. Prilmeier (2006), 'The market vs. banks – an event-study perspective on the value creation of banks as blockholders in Germany', European Business School, mimeo.

Miarka, T. (1999), 'The recent economic role of bank–firm relationships in Japan', WZB, Discussion Paper.

Mikkelson, W.H. and M.M. Partch (1986), 'Valuation effects of security offerings and the issuance process', *Journal of Financial Economics*, **15**, 31–60.

Miyajima, H. and Y. Yafeh (2003). 'Japan's banking crisis: who has the most to lose?', Center for Economic Institutions, Working Paper.

Montoriol Garriga, J. (2006), 'The effect of relationship lending on firm performance', Universitat Pompeu Fabra, Barcelona, mimeo.

Morck, R. and M. Nakamura (1999), 'Banks and corporate control in Japan', *Journal of Finance*, **54**, 319–39.

Morck, R., M. Nakamura and A. Shivdasani (2000), 'Banks, ownership structure, and firm value in Japan', *Journal of Business*, **73**, 539–67.

Myers, S.C. and N. Majluf (1984), 'Corporate financing and investment decisions when firms have information that investors do not have', *Journal of Financial Economics*, **13**, 187–221.

Ongena, S. and D.C. Smith (2000), 'Bank relationships: a survey', in P. Harker and S.A. Zenios (eds), *The Performance of Financial Institutions*, London: Cambridge University Press, pp. 221–58.

Ongena, S., D.C. Smith and D. Michalsen (2003), 'Firms and their distressed banks: lessons from the Norwegian banking crisis (1988–1991)', *Journal of Financial Economics*, **67**, 81–112.

Padilla, J.A. and M. Pagano (1997), 'Endogenous communication among lenders and entrepreneurial incentives', *Review of Financial Studies*, **10**, 205–36.

Padilla, J.A. and M. Pagano (2000), 'Sharing default information as a borrower discipline device', *European Economic Review*, **44**, 1951–80.

Pawlina, G. and L. Renneboog (2005), 'Is investment-cash flow sensitivity caused by agency costs or asymmetric information? Evidence from the UK', *European Financial Management*, **11**(4), 483–513.

Peltoniemi, J. (2004), 'The value of relationship banking: empirical evidence on small business financing in Finnish credit markets', University of Oulu, academic dissertation.

Petersen, M.A. and R.G. Rajan (1994), 'The benefits of lending relationships: evidence from small business data', *Journal of Finance*, **49**, 3–37.

Petersen, M.A. and R.G. Rajan (1995), 'The effect of credit market competition on lending relationships', *Quarterly Journal of Economics*, **110**, 406–43.

Pozzolo, A.F. (2004), 'The role of guarantees in bank lending', Ente Luigi Einaudi, mimeo.

Qian, J. and P.E. Strahan (2007), 'How law and institutions shape financial contracts: the case of bank loans', *Journal of Finance*, **62**(6), 2803–34.

Rajan, R. (1992), 'Insiders and outsiders: the choice between relationship and arm's length debt', *Journal of Finance*, **47**, 1367–400.

Repetto, A., S. Rodriguez and R.O. Valdes (2002), 'Bank lending and relationship banking: evidence from Chilean firms', Universidad de Chile, mimeo.

Roberts, G.S. and N.A. Siddiqi (2004), 'Collateralization and the number of lenders in private debt contracts: an empirical analysis', *Research in Finance*, **21**, 229–52.

Roe, Mark J. (1990), 'Political and legal restraints on ownership and control of public companies', *Journal of Financial Economics*, **27**, 7–41.

Santos, J.A.C. and A.S. Rumble (2006), 'The American keiretsu and universal banks: investing, voting and sitting on non-financials' corporate boards', *Journal of Financial Economics*, **80**, 419–54.

Sapienza, P. (2002), 'The effects of banking mergers on loan contracts', *Journal of Finance*, **57**(1), 329–67.

Scott, J.A. (2003), 'Soft information, loan officers, and small firm credit availability', Temple University, mimeo.

Scott, J.A. and W.C. Dunkelberg (2001), 'Competition and credit market outcomes: a small firm perspective', Temple University, mimeo.

Scott, J.A. and W.C. Dunkelberg (2003), 'A note on loan search and banking relationships', Temple University, mimeo.

Shikimi, M. (2005), 'Do firms benefit from multiple banking relationships? Evidence from small and medium-sized firms in Japan', Hitotsubashi University, Discussion Paper.

Şişli Ciamarra, E. (2006), 'Monitoring by affiliated bankers on board of directors: evidence from corporate financing outcomes', New York University, mimeo.

Slovin, M.B., S.A. Johnson and J.L. Glascock (1992), 'Firm size and the information content of bank loan announcements', *Journal of Banking and Finance*, **16**, 35–49.

Slovin, M.B., M.E. Sushka and J.A. Polonchek (1993), 'The value of bank durability: borrowers as bank stakeholders', *Journal of Finance*, **48**, 289–302.

Sohn, W. (2002), 'Banking relationships and conflicts of interest: market reactions to lending decisions by Korean Banks', Columbia University, mimeo

Sorge, M. and C. Zhang (2006), 'Credit information quality and corporate debt maturity: theory and evidence', World Bank Working Paper, 12/2006.

Stiglitz, J. and A.M. Weiss (1981), 'Credit rationing in markets with imperfect information', *American Economic Review*, **71**(3), 393–410.

Streb, J.M., J. Bolzico, P. Druck, A. Henke, J. Rutman and W.S. Escudero (2002), 'Bank relationships: effect on the availability and marginal cost of credit for firms in Argentina', UCEMA, Working Paper.

Suzuki, S. and R.W. Wright (1985), 'Financial structure and bankruptcy risk in Japanese companies', *Journal of International Business Studies*, **16**(1), 97–110.

Tirri, V. (2007), 'Multiple banking relationships and credit market competition: what benefits the firm?', Intesa Sanpaolo – Research Department, mimeo.

Uzzi, B. (1999), 'Embeddedness in the making of financial capital: how social relations and networks benefit firms seeking financing', *American Sociological Review*, **64**, 481–505.

Van Ees, H. and H. Garretsen (1994), 'Liquidity and business investment: evidence from Dutch panel data', *Journal of Macroeconomics*, **16**(4), 613–27.

Van Overfelt, W., J. Annaert, M.D. Ceuster and M. Deloof (2006), 'Do universal banks create value? Universal bank affiliation and company performance in Belgium, 1905–1909', University of Antwerp, mimeo.

Vogt, S.C. (1994), 'The cash flow/investment relationship: evidence from US manufacturing firms', *Financial Management*, **23** (Summer), 3–20.

von Thadden, E.L. (1992), 'The commitment of finance, duplicated monitoring and the investment horizon', London: ESF-CEPR.

Weinstein, D.E. and Y. Yafeh (1998), 'On the costs of a bank centered financial system: evidence from changing main bank relationships in Japan', *Journal of Finance*, **53**(2), 635–72.

Yosha, O. (1995), 'Information disclosure costs and the choice of financing source', *Journal of Financial Intermediation*, **4**, 3–20.

Zarutskie, R. (2004), 'New evidence on bank competition, firm borrowing and firm performance', Duke University, mimeo.

Ziane, Y. (2003), 'Number of banks and credit relationships: empirical results from French small business data', *European Review of Economics and Finance*, **2**(3), 32–48.

6. Competition between profit seekers and non-profit firms: the case of German banking

Manfred Neumann, Richard Reichel and Jürgen Weigand

1 INTRODUCTION

In most industrialized countries non-profit firms (NPs) account for a substantial share of economic activity. In many cases they are competing with profit-seeking firms. In the present economics literature NPs tend to be viewed to be less efficient than profit-seeking firms. Thus, NPs are frequently predicted to be doomed to failure. So far, this prediction has not come true, however. An outstanding example is the banking industry in Germany. It rests on three pillars: profit-seeking commercial banks, cooperative banks seeking to foster the economic well-being of their members, and non-profit-seeking public sector banks (local savings banks, federal-state central banks, and development banks) obliged by law to pursue common goals. In the present chapter we wish to examine the competitive interplay of these banks and evaluate their economic performance and ability to survive.

The chapter is organized as follows. In section 2 we briefly discuss the characteristics of the German banking sector. The different pillars also reflect different ownership and governance structures. The interesting question is how these differences in the underlying goal of a bank, namely profit maximization vs. furthering the common weal, as reflected in the banks' governance approach impact the market outcome. Therefore, section 3 presents a Cournot-type model of competition between profit-seeking and non-profit-seeking banks. We show that in a competitive (non-cooperative) market equilibrium, profit seekers and non-profit banks will co-exist. Section 4 corroborates with empirical evidence the two main conclusions of the model: (1) Non-profit-seeking savings banks act as price-leaders, and competition with them depresses the profitability of commercial banks; (2) relative cost determine market shares in the market for loans to non-banks. The chapter closes with a discussion of challenges and prospects of future developments.

2 BANKING IN GERMANY

2.1 Industry Structure

The German banking sector can be classified according to the scope of bank activities and how banks are governed. Governance – to be discussed in detail below – is concerned with ownership and identity of owners. In the governance dimension, usually three pillars are being distinguished, private commercial banks, cooperative banks (*Genossenschaftsbanken*), and public sector banks, such as savings banks (*Sparkassen*) and regional banks (*Landesbanken*).

With respect to scope it is reasonable to distinguish between universal banks and specialized banks. German universal banks usually offer a broad portfolio of products, including commercial and investment banking, asset management and mortgages. They are engaged in cross-selling (including insurance) and take profitable advantage of it. The group of universal banks comprises commercial banks, savings banks and cooperative banks. Specialized banks have a specific focus, such as building societies and mortgage institutions which finance private building, or special institutions which focus on structural development or trade financing.

In contrast to profit-seeking private commercial banks, public savings banks are legally obliged to further the common weal, and cooperative banks seek to enhance the economic performance of their members. Cooperative banks jointly own (at present two) central banks to cope with business, the size of which is too large to be handled by a single cooperative bank. Likewise, public savings banks are associated with regional banks (*Landesbanken*), run jointly by the government of federal states and communal savings banks to provide similar services to savings banks as in the case of cooperative banks and, in addition, to serve as 'house banks' for the government of the respective federal states. Within all three pillars banks run institutions to provide ancillary services, such as investment funds, mortgage banking, building societies and insurance.

In May 2007, the group of universal banks accounted for about 75 per cent of the banking sector's total assets, as Table 6.1 reveals. Table 6.1 also shows that in particular the number of savings banks and cooperative banks has substantially declined recently.

Despite this recent decline in the number of banks, empirical evidence indicates that the German banking sector is still fragmented, in comparison

Table 6.1 Banking groups in Germany: number of banks and total assets

Banking groups	May 2007			May 2000		
	Number of banks	Assets in billion €	Per cent of total assets	Number of banks	Assets in billion €	Per cent of total assets
Commercial banks	255	2221.1	30.0	289	1690.3	28.3
Of which:						
'Big Banks'	5	1403.2	19.0	5	943.3	15.6
Branches of foreign banks	93	155.4	2.1	87	121.7	2.0
Public sector banks	460	2494.3	33.6	578	2095.8	35.1
Landesbanken (Regional banks)	12	1482.7	20.0	13	1178.8	19.7
Sparkassen (savings banks)	448	1011.6	13.6	565	917.0	15.4
Cooperative banks	1258	857.1	11.5	2004	736.1	12.3
Central institutions	2	247.2	3.3	4	214.1	3.6
Cooperatives	1256	609.9	8.2	2000	522.0	8.7
Specialized banks	64	1847.6	24.9	76	1449.5	24.3
Of which:						
Mortage banks	22	854.2	8.2	31	864.9	14.5
Building societies	26	609.9	8.2	32	148.0	2.5
Total	2037	7420.1	100	2947	5971.7	100

Source: Deutsche Bundesbank, Bankenstatistik, Monatsbericht, July 2007, p. 24*, historical data from time series available at: http://www.bundesbank.de/statistik/statistik_banken.php, own calculations.

to other countries.[1] The combined market share of the big banks, as measured by the share in total assets at the national level, is about 20 per cent. The combined share in total assets of the banking industry held by local savings banks amounts to roughly 14 per cent, whereas their regional head organizations – the twelve *Landesbanken* – commanded roughly one-fifth of the market. The cooperative banks occupy some 8 per cent and their central institutions are holding 3 per cent of the banking market.

The drawback of these as indicators of market shares is that reliable data for Germany is only available at the national market level. Moreover, the big banks have an international scope of activities, whereas the cooperatives and savings banks operate only at the regional or local level. It is the big banks who are undoubtedly in the lead of cross-border asset and depository transactions. Industry analysts estimate their market share for cross-border traffic to be in the neighbourhood of about 40 to 50 per cent. At the regional or local level, the picture is different. Cooperative and savings banks dominate the retail markets, especially with respect to loans to small and medium-sized firms, mortgage financing for private home building, consumer credits, but also insurance products due to extensive cross-selling. Casual evidence suggests that the market structure in local areas often resembles an asymmetric or sometimes even symmetric duopoly, consisting of one cooperative bank and one savings bank. Both banking groups ban spatial within-group competition through exclusive territory guarantees. For the savings banks this is called *Regionalprinzip* (regional protection). According to internal statistics of the Deutsche Bundesbank, 44 per cent of the deposits of private persons are in the accounts of German savings banks, 28 per cent rest with cooperative banks, and only 11.3 per cent are entrusted to the big commercial banks.[2] This implies some market power and customer loyalty for savings and cooperative banks at the local level. More recently market power of this kind has come to be somewhat diluted by online banking offered by banks outside the respective region.

Table 6.2 lists the Top 10 banks in Germany for the year 2006. Banks differ significantly in size, legal form and governance structure across groups. The group of commercial banks is led by the so-called 'Big Banks' – *Deutsche Bank*, *Dresdner Bank* (recently a 100 per cent subsidiary of the Allianz insurance group), *Commerzbank* and *HVB* (just recently taken over by the Italian banking group Unicredito).

Looking at competitors at the European level such as HSBC, RBS, and others, such as City Bank, the German commercial banks – even Deutsche Bank – are lightweights compared to scale. Unsurprisingly, they are on the radar screen as potential takeover targets.

The inter-group financial relationships are summarized in Table 6.3 for commercial banks, savings banks and cooperative banks, with their respective central institutions.

Two facts merit special mention. First, the share in loans to non-banks for savings banks and cooperative banks exceeds their share in total assets. Second, the inflow of funds (deposits from non-banks and outstanding securities) was larger than the loans to non-banks both for savings banks and *Landesbanken* (1525 vs. 1313) and cooperative banks and their central institutions (548 vs. 474). Apparently, these banks have been forced to channel inflows of funds to other domestic banks or abroad. Presumably this has rendered their use to them less remunerative or more risky and has enabled commercial banks to increase their share in total assets.

2.2 Goals, Corporate Governance and Performance

Whilst commercial banks aim at maximizing profits, savings banks and coperative banks are non-profit firms. Rather than seeking to attain

Table 6.2 The top 10 banks in Germany

Rank	Bank	Total assets in 2006 in mill. €	Change to 2005 in %	Branch offices	Staff	Banking group
1	Deutsche Bank AG, Frankfurt/M.	1 126 230	13.5	1 717	68 849	Commercial
2	Commerzbank AG, Frankfurt/M.	608 339	36.8	1 106	35 975	Commercial
3	Dresdner Bank AG, Frankfurt/M.	497 287	8.0	952	27 625	Commercial
4	DZ Bank AG, Frankfurt/Main	438 984	9.3	31	24 055	Cooperative
5	Landesbank Baden-Württemberg, Stuttgart	428 253	5.8	223	12 252	Public sector
6	KfW Bankengruppe, Frankfurt/Main	359 606	5.4	3	3 697	Public sector
7	HVB Group, München	358 299	−27.4	788	25 738	Commercial
8	BayernLB, München	353 218	3.6	1	10 080	Public sector
9	WestLB AG, Düsseldorf	285 287	−3.1	40	6 149	Public sector
10	Eurohypo AG, Frankfurt/M.	224 332	−4.2	26	2 404	Commercial

Source: Deutscher Bankenverband, http://www.germanbanks.org, 2007.

maximum profits they are obliged to abide by their mission, that is, to further the common weal in the case of savings banks and to enhance economic welfare of their members in the case of cooperative banks, without incurring losses. In the long run they must cover costs, where costs include opportunity costs of capital. This, again, depends on the level of risks incurred in lending. Moreover, in the short run savings banks and cooperative banks may earn windfall profits which indicate opportunities to expand activities. Although savings banks and cooperative banks, in principle, may finance an expansion of their activities by fresh capital supplied by their respective shareholders, that is, communities in the case of savings banks and members in the case of cooperatives, expansion of activities is ordinarily financed by retained earnings.

Table 6.3 Inter-group financial relationships, June 2007

Banks (number)	Size* (share in per cent)	Loans to		Deposits from		
		banks	non-banks	banks	non-banks	Outstanding securities
All banks	7410 (100)	3043	3859	2085	2794	1737
Commercial banks (254)	2185 (29.5)	896	1069 (27.7)	776	884 (31.6)	244
Landesbanken (12)	1478 (19.9)	804	590 (15.2)	528	355 (12.7)	461
Savings banks (448)	1017 (13.7)	240	723 (18.7)	203	660 (23.6)	49
Cooperative centrals (2)	253 (3.4)	170	60 (1.6)	148	38 (1.3)	43
Cooperative banks (1256)	613 (8.3)	156	414 (10.7)	79	428 (15.3)	39

Notes: * Total assets in billion Euro (percentage of total).

Source: Deutsche Bundesbank, Monatsbericht August 2007, pp. 24*–25*.

2.2.1 Governance

Corporate governance is concerned with the question of how the management of a firm is to be induced to serve the interests of the respective owners. The main characteristic of the modern corporation is that its owners delegate the authority over corporate assets to non-owning managers.[3] The separation of ownership from control allows managers to behave opportunistically. Running the company leaves managers better informed than distant shareholders. The information advantage provides managers with substantial residual control rights which they may exploit by pursuing their own agenda (for example consuming perks, building empires), undisturbed by shareholders, rather than employing assets productively to maximize shareholder value. The exploitation of managerial discretion results from misaligned incentives ('agency conflict') and gives rise to inefficient outcomes.[4] These issues have been discussed in the literature primarily for profit-seeking firms. They also apply *mutatis mutandi* for cooperative (Boettcher, 1981) and public firms.[5]

Commercial banks, as well as cooperative banks and savings banks, have a two-tier system of management. It consists of the executive board (*Vorstand*) and a supervisory board (*Aufsichtsrat*) in the case of commercial and cooperative banks and a supervisory council (*Verwaltungsrat*) in the case of savings banks.[6] Members of the supervisory board are voted into office by shareholders and their role is to monitor the executive board to take care of the interests of owners and of stakeholders in the case of public savings banks. There are three mechanisms to ensure that the management abides by the goals of the firm: (1) prudential regulation by government agencies to ensure stability of financial markets; (2) the market for corporate control in the case of profit-seeking firms and monitoring by outside auditors which are entrusted by the respective association of savings banks and cooperative banks: (3) competition in the markets of products sold. In the case of savings banks and cooperative banks, monitoring is not confined to ensuring that accounting standards are observed, but it also sees that the legally stated goals are attained.

2.2.2 Performance of German banks

In examining the comparative performance of banks it has frequently been assumed that with respect to market behaviour, profit-seeking commercial banks on one hand and public savings banks and cooperative banks on the other do not display substantial differences. Whether this is true, has to be seen. Anyway, it would be erroneous to infer from the observation that savings banks and cooperative banks behave similarly in the market, that both have aligned themselves to profit-seeking banks, as suggested by the German Monopolkommission (2000, p. 80). On the contrary, as will be shown in due course, it is just the other way around. Commercial banks have aligned their behaviour to savings banks, as far as their domestic business is concerned. First however, we will look at some facts.

The economic performance of banks has come to be evaluated by the *cost–income ratio*, whereby costs are measured as current operating costs and income as current net revenue from commissions and interest. Obviously, the cost–income ratio does not provide a complete picture of the true cost–income situation of a bank, in particular because the opportunity cost of capital is not considered. Opportunity costs include a compensation for risk taking. Therefore, the cost–income ratio can be expected normally to fall short of unity even if economic profit is zero.[7] Figure 6.1 shows the more recent development of the cost–income ratio in German banking for the three banking groups, commercial banks, savings banks and cooperative banks, separately.

The level of costs appears to differ across the banking groups, as implied by Figure 6.2 which depicts the ratio of administrative costs to total assets. Cooperative banks show the highest ratio, followed by savings banks and commercial banks.

In the previous literature this finding has been interpreted as revealing 'expense preference' by non-profit firms (Verbrugge and Jahera, 1981; Akella and Greenbaum, 1988; Purroy and Salas, 2000) and shirking

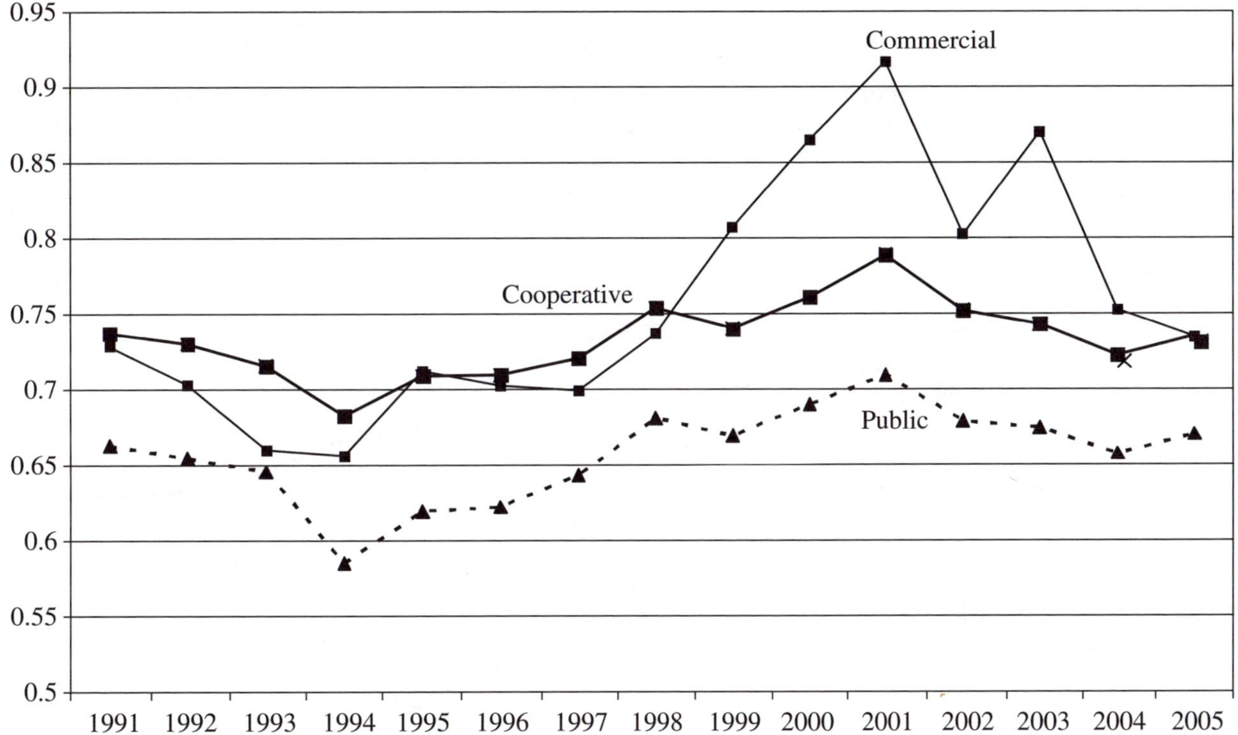

Figure 6.1 *Cost–income ratios of German banking groups*

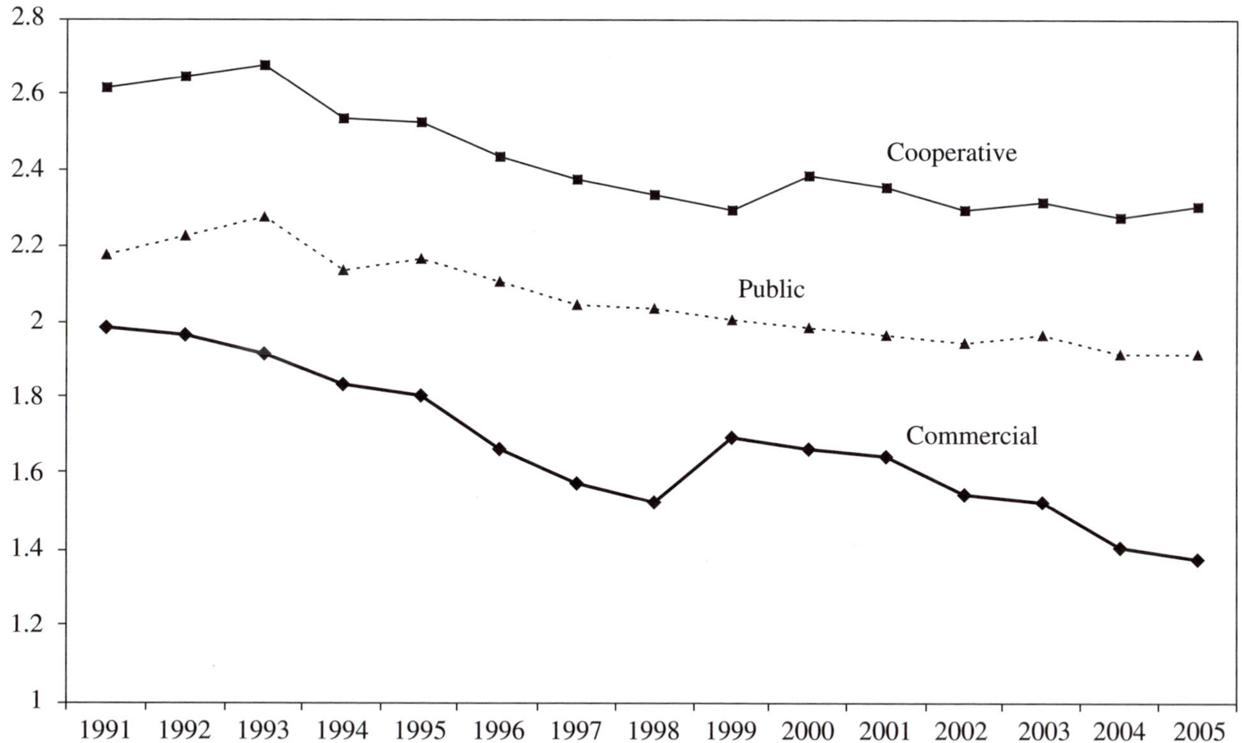

Figure 6.2 *Ratio of administrative costs to total assets for German banking groups*

(Alchian and Demsetz, 1972, p. 789). This critical appraisal, however, is not generally justified.[8] A higher level of administrative costs in relation to total assets may very well follow from efforts of the management of non-profit firms to satisfy demands of their customers, that is, the preferences of the beneficiaries, rather than the preferences of managers.

3 THE MODEL

To examine the outcome of competition between profit-seeking commercial banks and non-profit banks, that is, savings banks and cooperative banks, by abstracting from details of the institutional structure of banking in Germany, we first consider a duopoly where a profit-seeking commercial bank is competing with a non-profit savings bank or cooperative bank.

3.1 Duopoly

We assume a homogeneous market for a particular product since in the financial sector for any given risk class products are in fact homogeneous and carry a single price.[9] The inverse demand function is $p = a - Q$, where $Q{:} = q_s + q_b$. We thus assume banks to compete by setting quantities.

Regarding the relationship between cost and output we have to distinguish the short run from the long run. In the short run, average costs may be assumed to increase more than proportionally upon an increase in output because of scarce resources and the necessity to acquire financial funds at rising costs.[10] In the long run, in principle average costs may decline because of economies of scale. Available empirical evidence, however, casts doubt on the prevalence of economies of scale in banking, as far as the administrative costs are concerned.[11]

Let short-run costs be $C(q_i) = c_i q_i + (\alpha_i/2)q_i^2$, $i = s, b$, where s denotes a savings bank or cooperative bank and b denotes a commercial bank. In the long run α_i is assumed to be zero. Hence, in the long run average costs are assumed to be constant and equal to marginal costs, whilst in the short run both marginal and average costs may increase due to limitation of own resources or the necessity to pay higher prices for acquired resources.

The savings bank chooses output such as to enhance the economic welfare of the public in the case of public savings banks, and members in the case of cooperative banks. This requires price to equal marginal costs, $p = C'(q_s)$. In the long run, where marginal costs equal average costs, this yields zero profit. In the short run, however, price may exceed average costs so that profits are positive. The philosophy of non-profit firms would then induce the management to use retained profits to finance an expansion of their activity so that eventually marginal costs again become equal to average costs and profits are zero.

The savings bank chooses the output such that $a - q_s - q_b = c_s + \alpha_s q_s$ and the profit-seeking commercial bank maximizes profits, which requires marginal revenue to equal marginal costs, that is, $a - q_s - 2q_b = c_b + \alpha_b q_b$. The Cournot equilibrium is thus determined by the set of equations

$$\begin{pmatrix} 1+\alpha_s & 1 \\ 1 & 2+\alpha_b \end{pmatrix} \begin{pmatrix} q_s \\ q_b \end{pmatrix} = \begin{pmatrix} a - c_s \\ a - c_b \end{pmatrix}$$

Solutions are

$$q_s^* = \frac{(a-c_s)(1+\alpha_b) - (c_s - c_b)}{\Delta^*}, \tag{6.1}$$

$$q_b^* = \frac{(a-c_b)\alpha_s + (c_s - c_b)}{\Delta^*} \tag{6.2}$$

and

$$Q^* = \frac{(a-c_s)(1+\alpha_b) + (a-c_b)\alpha_s}{\Delta^*} \tag{6.3}$$

where $\Delta^* := 1 + 2\alpha_s + \alpha_b + \alpha_s\alpha_b$.

By contrast, in the long run

$$q_s^{**} = (a - c_s) - (c_s - c_b), \tag{6.4}$$

$$q_b^{**} = (c_s - c_b), \tag{6.5}$$

and

$$Q = a - c_s, \tag{6.6}$$

such that the commercial bank can survive in the market only if its average costs are lower than the average costs of the savings bank. Furthermore, total output and the resulting market price depend only on the average costs of the savings bank. Strikingly, the savings bank turns out as the price leader of the market. In the short run, however, the outcome depends also on how fast average costs rise upon an increase in output.[12]

By comparison consider the case where both banks maximize profits. In this case a Cournot equilibrium yields individual output

$$q_i^C = [(a - c_i)(1 + \alpha_j) - (c_i - c_j)]/\Delta^C,\ i, j = s, b$$

and

$$Q^C = [(a - c_s)(1 + \alpha_b) + (a - c_b)(1 + \alpha_s)]/\Delta^C$$

where now

$$\Delta^C := 3 + 2\alpha_s + 2\alpha_b + \alpha_s\alpha_b$$

Obviously, output of both banks is lower than in the non-profit equilibrium and the market price is higher.

The comparison yields the following conclusions.

(i) In the long run the market price is determined solely by average costs of the non-profit firm.
(ii) Total output in the case where both banks maximize profits is lower than in the non-profit equilibrium.
(iii) Profits of both banks are higher in the case where both banks maximize profits.

3.2 Oligopoly

We continue by looking at the case of a homogeneous product with n non-profit banks and m commercial banks. Hence total output sold in the market is

$$Q = \sum_{i=1}^{n} q_s^i + \sum_{j=1}^{m} q_b^j$$

Within each group all banks have identical costs. In the long run, assuming, as in the previous section, all savings banks choose quantities of supplies such that the price equals average costs and all commercial banks maximize profits, one obtains equilibrium conditions (Neumann and Reichel 2006, pp. 256f.) for the long run,

$$\begin{pmatrix} n & m \\ n & m+1 \end{pmatrix} \begin{pmatrix} q_s \\ q_b \end{pmatrix} = \begin{pmatrix} a - c_s \\ a - c_b \end{pmatrix}$$

which yield market shares of savings banks and commercial banks, respectively,

$$\frac{nq_s}{Q} = 1 - \frac{m(c_s - c_b)}{a - c_s} \tag{6.7}$$

$$\frac{mq_b}{Q} = \frac{m(c_s - c_b)}{a - c_s} \tag{6.8}$$

Thus the cumulative market share of commercial banks depends on their number, given the difference in average costs. Hence, horizontal concentration among commercial banks yields a fall in their cumulative market share unless their costs decrease. Similarly, for savings banks, horizontal concentration does not affect their cumulative market share unless they are able to lower their costs more than commercial banks.

4 EMPIRICAL EVIDENCE AND EVALUATION

Two main conclusions can be drawn from the models. First, since non-profit savings banks are price leaders, the profitability of commercial banks is depressed following from the competition with savings banks. Second, market shares in the loan market depend on relative costs.

4.1 Profitability of Commercial Banks

An international comparison reveals the profitability of German banks to fall substantially short of the profitability of banks in comparable industrial countries, such as the UK and the USA. Comparison in detail and for different groups of banks is somewhat difficult because the profitability of banks displays considerable volatility. Still, a first instructive picture is given by profits before taxation and administrative costs in the case of big banks, as shown in Table 6.4.

In Germany profits of commercial banks are substantially lower than in comparable industrial countries. Since costs have been higher in these countries,[13] the higher profitability can hardly be attributed to better economic performance. The superior profitability of commercial banks in the US and UK in particular appears to follow from market power. These findings may suffice to support the prediction of our model that the profitability of commercial banks is severely depressed by the competition of non-profit banking, that is, of savings banks and cooperative banks. Our interpretation of the evidence is also supported by witness of an insider. Mr Stephan Green of the British HSBC was asked in a press interview, whether his bank would be planning to enter the German market. His answer was strongly in the negative, saying that the German market is saturated by the supply of savings banks and cooperative banks so that commercial banks have no chance to be profitable.[14]

Table 6.4 Profitability of big banks: profits before taxation and administrative costs as percentage of average balance sheet, 2004–2006

Countries (number of banks considered)	2004		2005		2006	
	Profits	Costs	Profits	Costs	Profits	Costs
USA (10)	1.84	3.46	1.89	3.25	1.83	3.10
UK (9)	0.95	1.69	0.87	1.58	0.98	1.68
Germany (9)	0.13	1.41	0.37	1.15	0.47	1.19
France (6)	0.65	1.49	0.67	1.94	0.86	1.43
Italy (5)	0.87	2.83	1.05	2.11	1.15	2.54

Source: Fitch Ratings (BIS 77th Annual Report 2006/2007, p. 139).

Table 6.5 Market shares in per cent

	Total assets		Loans to non-banks	
	1995	2007	1995	2006
Commercial banks	25.1	29.5	25.8	27.7
Savings banks	20.1	13.7	22.7	18.7
Cooperative banks	11.8	8.3	13.4	10.7

Source: Deutsche Bundesbank, Monatsberichte September 1995, pp. 20*f., September 2007, pp. 24*f.

4.2 Market Shares Depending on Relative Costs

The development of market shares is succinctly stated in Table 6.5.

Both the share in total assets and of loans to non-banks have increased for commercial banks and have strongly declined for savings banks and cooperative banks.

First, during the same time, where the market share of savings banks and cooperative banks declined, the administrative costs as a percentage of total assets, as shown in Figure 6.2, went down in relation to the respective ratio for savings banks and cooperative banks. According to our model one would thus expect the market share of commercial banks to increase.

Second, the demand for loans from banks has presumably declined following a slowing down of domestic investment activity as a result of globalization and outsourcing and a decline in domestic home building financing, which has been an important field of activity for savings banks and cooperative banks. As can easily be ascertained from equations (6.7) to (6.8), a decline in demand following from a downward shift of the demand function, that is, a decrease of a, yields an increase in the market share of commercial banks and consequently a decrease in the market share of savings banks and cooperative banks.

4.3 Mergers and Market Shares

Following mergers, the number of banks in all three groups has substantially declined, as shown in Table 6.6.

We could not find any direct relationship between mergers and the development of market shares in the loan market which might be attributed to economies of scale concerning administrative costs. Economies of scale in particular fields of business, like consumer credit and computer services, have rather induced outsourcing in specializing entities which are sometimes run as joint ventures.

Still, a relationship between mergers and market shares may follow from the necessity of banks to cope with risk. The ongoing rise in firm size in industry, following mergers and the concomitant increase in horizontal concentration, has given rise to an increase in the size of individual loans demanded. To maintain diversification in the portfolio and a sound relation of extended loans to equity (in particular required by prudential regulation in Basel II) and thus to control risk, banks had to grow larger. The alternative would have been joint loans with neighbouring banks or the respective central institutions. Transaction costs to be incurred in this case would have impeded competitiveness.

Table 6.6 Number of surviving banks, June 1995, 2000, 2007

Banking group	1995	2000	2007
Commercial banks	336	289	255
Public-sector banks	640	578	460
Cooperative banks	2635	1970	1258
Total number of banks	3665	2913	2037

Source: Deutsche Bundesbank, Monatsberichte September 1995, p. 20*, September 2000, p. 24*, August 2007, p. 24*.

5 SUMMARY AND CONCLUSIONS

Non-profit firms (NPs) account for a substantial share of economic activity in most industrialized countries. In many instances, NPs compete with profit-seeking firms. Contrary to the traditional view in economics, NPs seem to be able to coexist with profit seekers in a competitive environment even in the longer run. The present chapter therefore uses theoretical analysis to examine competition between profit seekers and NPs. We show in a Cournot competition model that in non-cooperative market equilibrium NPs and for-profit firms can coexist. To confront our model's predictions with the empirical facts, we consider the German banking industry.

Banking in Germany is evolving on a trajectory determined by two major trends. First, the presence of the non-profit sector yields a depressing influence on profitability of commercial banking which entails a welfare enhancing effect. Second, the opportunities inherent in the non-profit sector are not fully exploited. Presumably following from insufficient size of savings banks and cooperative banks and weak vertical relationships, inflows of funds into the non-profit sector must be channelled via commercial banks into productive investments of non-banks. Apparently, the Landesbanken and the central institutions of the cooperative sector were unable to accomplish what savings banks and cooperative banks could not do. This seems to call for further mergers in the non-profit sector. It also leads us to question the efficiency of corporate governance in this sector. For commercial banks profitability provides an unequivocal and reliable guide to evaluating economic performance. Profitability signals opportunities for private success. Under competitive conditions these opportunities are likely to yield an enhancement of economic welfare. For the non-profit sector an equivalent yardstick is missing. The consequences are twofold.

First, being satisfied with just covering costs has a ring of passivity. The firm seeks to adjust itself to market conditions as they are. This creates a challenge to profit-seeking competitors, as shown in the present chapter. This very challenge, if it is accepted and answered successfully by profit-seeking rivals, gives them a chance to survive and creates itself a challenge to non-profit agents, if the profit-seeking firm succeeds in reduceing costs by innovating activities. Thus there exists a sort of symbiotic relationship between profit-seeking firms and not-for-profit agents, where the development is primarily driven by initiatives from profit-seeking firms.

Second, although rent-seeking within the non-profit sector is kept at bay by the rivalry of profit-seeking competitors, the missing unequivocal yardstick of success is likely to engender problems. The management of a non-profit firm must anticipate whether and to what extent it lives up to the expectations of owners in the case of cooperatives, and of representatives of the public in the case of public savings banks. To be successful in this respect is more difficult the larger the decisive body of representatives is. This gives rise to a dilemma between preventing inefficiencies and rent-seeking, if the enterprise is too large, and forsaking economies if the firm is too small. Concerns in the membership of cooperatives about being exploited by the management of a large corporation are a hindrance for a cooperative bank to achieve a sufficient size by merger. The same applies similarly for public savings banks run by communities.

NOTES

1. Hempell (2002, p. 34) provides concentration measures for German banking in the 1990s derived from Deutsche Bundesbank's internal banking statistics which include data on all German banks. She calculated simple concentration indices such as C3 as well as the Herfindahl–Hirschman Index HHI. Banks' individual market shares were measured by the ratio of the individual bank's total assets to the sum of all German banks' total assets. Although the HHI increased from 1993 to 1998 from 111 to 140, reflecting the ongoing consolidation process, the absolute size of the HHI was very low compared to values found for other countries (see, for example, Stiroh and Strahan, 2003, for the US). A similar picture shows for the C3 which was about 12 per cent in the analysed time period.

   See Krahnen and Schmidt (2004) for a recent survey of the German financial system. Brunner et al. (2004) and Koetter et al. (2004) provide surveys of the German banking industry and empirical comparisons to other countries.
2. Reported in 'EU unzufrieden mit Sparkassenmodell', *Financial Times Deutschland*, 30 January 2007, p. 26.
3. See the seminal work of Berle and Means (1932), Mueller (2003) and Tirole (2006, ch. 2) for a most recent review on corporate governance.
4. See in particular Jensen (1986, 1993); also Fama (1980), Fama and Jensen (1983), Bebchuk and Fried (2004).
5. See Canoy et al. (2001), Macey and O'Hara (2003), and Levine (2004) for a detailed discussion on the governance of banks.
6. Some critics have demanded that the two-tiered system should be replaced by the Anglo-Saxon one-tier model. However, according to the evaluation of Shleifer and Vishny (1997, p. 737) 'the United States, Germany, Japan, and the United Kingdom have some of the best corporate governance systems in the world, and the differences between them are probably small relative to their differences from other countries.'
7. It would be misleading therefore to infer just from a cost–income ratio falling short of unity that the respective banks achieve a price–cost margin in excess of zero implying that they are enjoying monopolistic market power.
8. Regarding the claim of Alchian and Demsetz it has been shown by Mesters (1993) that in the US the mutual S&Ls were on average less inefficient than stock S&Ls.
9. Barcena-Ruiz (2007) has studied a model with a private and a public firm where products are heterogeneous and firms compete with prices, without however giving any hints where the model can be assumed to apply.
10. Carbo et al. (2002) found marginal costs to exceed average costs in a large sample of European savings banks in 1989–96.
11. See Boot (2004, p. 145). It is quite reasonable to assume that up to a minimum efficient size average costs decrease. Beyond this level, they are presumably bound to increase, at

least in the short run. In fact, for German cooperative banks Lang and Welzl (1996) found evidence of diseconomies of scale.

12. It may be noted that in the case where two or more savings (or cooperative) banks with different cost levels are competing, their equilibrium level of output is different. The savings bank with lower costs attains a larger market share than savings banks with higher costs.
13. The cost figure for the USA may be out of line because US banks, in the wake of the only recently repealed Glass–Steagall Act, presumably are still predominantly commercial banks, whilst European banks are universal banks, comprising both commercial and investment banking.
14. Interview in *Wirtschaftswoche*, 15 December, 2005, No. 51, p. 66. Contrary to the claim that the dominant position of German savings banks would inhibit commercial banks to expand their activities, it should be remembered that the market share of savings banks lies in the range of 14–20 per cent (Table 6.5).

REFERENCES

Akella, A.A. and S.I. Greenbaum (1988), 'Savings and loan ownership structure and expense preference', *Journal of Banking and Finance*, **12**, 419–37.

Alchian, A.A. and H. Demsetz (1972), 'Production, information costs and economic organizations', *American Economic Review*, **62**, 777–95.

Bárcena-Ruiz, J.C. (2007), 'Endogenous timing in a mixed duopoly: price competition', *Journal of Economics*, **91**, 263–72.

Bebchuk, Lucian A. and Jesse M. Fried (2004), *Pay without Performance: The Unfulfilled Promise of Executive Compensation*, Cambridge, MA and London: Harvard University Press.

Berle, Adolf and Gardner Means (1932), *The Modern Corporation and Private Property*, New York: Macmillan.

Boettcher, Erik (1981), 'Genossenschaften I: Begriff und Aufgaben', in *Handwörterbuch der Wirtschaftswissenschaft*, vol. 3, Stuttgart, Tübingen and Göttingen: Fischer, Mohr, Vandenhoeck & Ruprecht, pp. 540–56.

Boot, Arnoud (2004), 'Financial services: consolidation and strategic positioning', in M. Neumann and J. Weigand (eds), *The International Handbook of Competition*, Cheltenham, UK and Northhampton, MA, USA, Edward Elgar, pp. 133–72.

Brunner, A., J. Decressin, D. Hardy and B. Kudela (2004), *Germany's Three-Pillar Banking System. Cross-Country Perspectives in Europe*, Occasional Paper 233, International Monetary Fund, Washington, DC.

Canoy, M., R. de Mooij, J. Lemmen, M. van Dijk and J. Weigand (2001), *Competition and Stability in Banking*, CPB Special Study, CPB Den Haag, November.

Carbo, S., E.P.M. Gardener and J. Williams (2002), 'Efficiency in Banking: Empirical Evidence from the Savings Bank Sector', *Manchester School*, **70**(2), 204–28.

Fama, E. (1980), 'Agency problems and the theory of the firm', *Journal of Political Economy*, **88**, 288–307.

Fama, E. and M.C. Jensen (1983), 'Separation of ownership and control', *Journal of Law and Economics*, **26**, 301–25.

Hempell, H.S. (2002), *Testing for Competition Among German Banks*, Discussion paper 04/02, Economic Research Centre of the Deutsche Bundesbank, Frankfurt.

Jensen, M.C. (1986), 'Agency costs of free cash flow, corporate finance and takeovers', *American Economic Review*, **76**, 323–9.

Jensen, M.C. (1993), 'The modern industrial revolution, exit, and the failure of internal control systems', *Journal of Finance*, **48**, 831–80.

Koetter, M., T. Nestmann, S. Stolz and M. Wedow (2004), *Structures and Trends in German Banking*, Kiel Working Paper No. 1225, Kiel Institute of World Economics.

Krahnen, Jan P. and Reinhard H. Schmidt (eds) (2004), *The German Financial System*, Oxford: Oxford University Press.

Lang, G. and P. Welzel (1996), 'Efficiency and technical progress in banking: empirical results for a panel of German cooperative banks', *Journal of Banking and Finance*, **20**, 1003–23.

Levine, R. (2004), *The Corporate Governance of Banks: A Concise Discussion of Concepts and Evidence*, World Bank Policy Research Working Paper 3404, Washington, DC.

Macey, J. and M. O'Hara (2003), 'The corporate governance of banks', *Federal Reserve Bank of New York Economic Policy Review*, April, pp. 91–107.

Mesters, L.J. (1993), 'Efficiency in the savings and loan industry', *Journal of Banking and Finance*, **17**, 267–86.

Monopolkommission (2000), *Wettbewerbspolitik in Netzstrukturen*, Gutachten 1998/1999, Baden-Baden: Nomos Verlag.

Mueller, Dennis C. (2003), *The Corporation – Investment, Mergers and Growth*, London: Routledge.

Neumann, M. and R. Reichel (2006), 'Struktur der deutschen Bankwirtschaft', *Jahrbuch für Wirtschaftswissenschaften – Review of Economics*, **57**, 247–72.

Purroy, P. and V. Salas (2000), 'Strategic competition in retail banking under expense preference behaviour', *Journal of Banking & Finance*, **24**, 809–24.

Shleifer, A. and R. Vishny (1997), 'A survey of corporate governance', *Journal of Finance*, **52**, 737–83.

Stiroh, K.J. and P.E. Strahan (2003), 'Competitive dynamics of deregulation: evidence from US banking', *Journal of Money, Credit and Banking*, **35**, 801–28.

Tirole, Jean (2006), *Theory of Corporate Finance*, Cambridge, MA: MIT Press.

Verbrugge J.A. and J.S. Jahera, Jr (1981), 'Expense-preference behavior in the savings and loan industry', *Journal of Money, Credit and Banking*, **13**, 465–76.

7. Mergers: an overview

Stephen Martin

I am the very model of a modern merger-wavicle,
I have dimensions horizontal, vertical, and conglomerical,
I know the kings of industry, and I quote the fights historical
From U.S. Steel to DaimlerChrysler, in order divestiturical;
I'm very well acquainted, too, with matters mathematical,
I understand equations, both the simple and quadratical,
About the CAP-M I'm teeming with a lot o' news,
With many cheerful facts about random walks on the loose.

(With apologies to Gilbert and Sullivan)

1 INTRODUCTION

The singular of data, Stigler among others is supposed to have said, is anecdote. By the same token, the plural of anecdote is data. At this writing, business history has been good enough to furnish us with five anecdotes about mergers in developed economies, in the form of the five merger waves recorded between the turn of the nineteenth century and the turn of the twentieth century. It is possible to take the view that each merger wave is sufficiently different from the others to require individual study (Markham, 1955, p. 154). Yet one may hope that (like waves in the ocean) although each merger wave is in some aspects unique, merger waves as a class have enough elements in common to permit generalization about mergers as a phenomenon.

That is the approach taken here. In section 2, I review each of the five merger waves of the last hundred-plus years. In sections 3 and 4 I distill the things economists have had to say about what seem to be the common characteristics of the mergers that make up these merger waves.

2 MERGER WAVES

2.1 Timing

In Congressional Testimony, Yellen (1998) begins with the Great Merger Wave of the 1890s and moves on to those of the Roaring 20s, the Go-Go 60s, the Deal Decade 80s, and then to a fifth merger wave, ongoing at the time of her testimony (as it is at the time of this writing). Allowing for the fact that World War II may have diverted the attention of the US business community from its customary activities,[1] one might conclude that a merger wave comes along every 20 years or so.

There is general consensus about the broad outlines of the timing of the merger waves. The First Merger Wave is usually bracketed by depressions in 1893 and 1903. Butters et al. (1951, p. 288) write 'The whole movement reached its peak in 1901 with the formation of the billion-dollar United States Steel Corporation and finally ended like the first with the sharp depression of 1903 and the *Northern Securities* decision in early 1904.'[2] The Second Merger Wave is usually pegged as starting in 1919, the first full year after World War I, or sometime during the 1920s, when the economy had picked up from a 1921 depression. Nelson (1959, p. 5) writes that 'The second large movement took place in the years 1926 through 1930', and it now seems clear that the October 1929 stock market crash and beginning of the Great Depression signalled the end of the Second Merger Wave.[3]

The Third Merger Wave, distinctive in a number of respects, was also compressed in time, starting in 1964 or 1965 and ending by 1970 or 1971. It took little more than half a decade. Ravenscraft (1988, p. 19) has the Fourth Merger Wave, which on many levels served to undo the Third, starting in 1981. For Hogan and Huie (1992, Section II.D), '[t]he fourth wave of M&A activity developed slowly in the late 1970's and reached full flower a decade later'. The early 1990s now appear to be a trough in US merger activity (Scherer, 2006, Figure 1). From this trough, US merger activity rose continuously through 11 September 2001, plummeted abruptly, and returned just as abruptly to its previous level. Whether or not there would have been a lull in the Fifth Merger Wave if the 9/11 attacks had never happened,[4] it seems likely that the Fifth Merger Wave, like the First, will be regarded as one merger movement with two peaks.

2.2 First: Turn of the Nineteenth Century

What we now tend to refer to as the First Merger Wave was known to its contemporaries as 'Great', not only because it was larger than anything in their experience, but also because it transformed the landscape of the American economy. Depending on how size is measured, the third and later merger waves may have been larger than the first,[5] but none left so enduring an imprint.

The backdrop against which the First Merger Wave played itself out is familiar from the work of Chandler (1965; 1977, Part II). In the two decades after the American Civil War, railroads integrated what had been semi-autonomous regional economies into a continent-wide single market and also served as the proving ground for management techniques able to satisfactorily organize the activity of firms that commanded resources on a hitherto unknown scale.

The mergers that made up the first wave were predominantly horizontal, and involved many firms. They typically created survivor firms that were dominant in their industries (Butters et al., 1951 p. 288, footnote omitted):

> By [early 1904] over 300 industrial combinations, representing consolidations of about 5,000 distinct plants and covering most major lines of productive industry, had been formed. . . . these combinations controlled fully 40% of the manufacturing capital of the country with 78 of these consolidated corporations controlling one-half or more of the country's total production in their respective fields, and with 26 controlling 80% or more.

For a sample of 93 mergers, Lamoreaux (1985, p. 2) similarly reports that 'seventy-two controlled at least 40 percent of their industries and forty-two at least 70 percent'.

The timing of the First Merger Wave cannot be explained by market integration alone; market integration was substantially complete a decade or more before the First Merger Wave started. US railroad construction peaked in 1887 (Harley, 1982, Figure I and p. 814). State laws that might otherwise have obstructed the free flow of goods within the United States were struck down in 1890,[6] the same year that the Superintendent of the Census recognized the closing of the American frontier (Turner, 1893).

To an economist, the integration of regional markets into a larger whole naturally suggests the possibility that firms operating in industries where the technology displays economies of large-scale production will expand output, lowering operating cost and making it profitable to supply a larger geographic market. But the work of O'Brien (1988) suggests that horizontal economies of scale cannot explain the First Merger Wave. Production in many of the industries caught up in the merger wave did entail economies of scale, but those economies had been largely realized two decades or more before the merger wave began (1988, pp. 645–6, footnote omitted):[7]

> almost two-thirds of the increase in factory size that was to take place between 1869 and 1929 had occurred by 1889 – well before the beginning of the merger

> wave. . . . American industrial structure evolved largely because of the technological and organizational innovations of the 1870s and 1880s . . . the great merger wave cannot be explained by unreaped economies of scale.

Contemporary observers were not short of explanations for the merger wave. Among those summarized by Homan are that merger was favoured at the end of the nineteenth century (1935, p. 115):

- because antitrust law was cordial to merger, hostile to collusion;
- by business experience with harsh competition during the recent depression;
- by development of a financial market that 'could absorb securities upon an unprecedented scale';
- by imitation of the success of a few early mergers;[8] and
- because of 'promoters and financiers who stood to gain from promoters' fees and underwriting operations'.

The first point[9] is that in an infancy of listless enforcement, Section 1 of the Sherman Act was interpreted to strictly prohibit collusion,[10] while Section 2 was rendered impotent against large-scale mergers.[11] The second point is that a business community of highly individualistic First Gilded Age entrepreneurs had been made more receptive to the idea of merger by the fierce price competition that prevailed during the 1893 depression.[12] The idea that tough competition encourages market concentration, whether effected by merger or otherwise, survives generally (Symeonidis, 1998, 2002), and in somewhat refined form as regards the First Merger Wave. We return to this idea below.

Homan's first point is about public policy toward product market structure. His second point is about the conduct of firms on the supply side of a product market. His final three points refer to the impact of financial market characteristics on firms' incentives to merge. The third point is simply that by the late 1890s, New York City had become a financial centre that facilitated mergers.[13] With the First Merger Wave, industrial securities succeeded railroad securities as an effective device to raise large amounts of financial capital from the private sector, amounts far exceeding what the largest partnership could hope to put together. Further, the existence of a market for securities made it possible to carry out mergers while using an amount of capital far smaller than the value of the assets involved. When, as was often the case, the owners of firms being consolidated accepted payment in shares of stock in the post-merger firm, no actual cash payment was required. What sellers of assets were taking in payment was claims on future dividend payments.

In practice, most payments to firms entering into a merger involved a mixture of cash and financial instruments. For example, Navin and Sears

(1954, Table 1) estimate that payments to shipping lines entering the International Mercantile Marine Company (IMM) in October, 1902 were $50 million in cash, $60 million in preferred stock and $60 million in common stock. The cash expense of carrying out the merger was $652 429, the largest part of this being a British tax on the transfer of securities (Navin and Sears, 1954, p. 311). Navin and Sears (1954, p. 313) make a 'conservative valuation of the component properties of the merger as of December, 1902' of about $75 million, which they argue 'should be compared not with [$170 million] but with [$83.7 million], the cost in cash plus the anticipated opening market value of the securities issued in payment'.[14]

The existence of an organized financial market also made it possible for the promoters of mergers to be paid (Navin and Sears, 1954, p. 311, footnote omitted):

> For their part in raising $50,000,000 in cash, the partners of J.P. Morgan & Company received a managers' fee of 5,000 shares of preferred stock and 50,000 shares of common. Since the preferred stock was expected to sell for about $85 and the common for about $35, the anticipated market worth of the Morgan firm's fee may be set at $2,175,000.

The IMM never prospered,[15] and for most of those who sold their firms to it for the promise of future dividends, it became an early example of 'wealth destruction on a massive scale',[16] an outcome that was not all that uncommon during the First Merger Wave. Somewhat less common was that J.P. Morgan & Company also lost money, in an amount that Navin and Sears (1954, p. 324) estimate at between $1 and $1.5 million.[17]

The weight of Stigler's authority is as great in discussion of mergers as it is with most topics of industrial organization, and the rise of a modern capital market is one of the two institutional innovations he cites in explanation of the timing of the First Merger Wave. The other is the limited-liability corporation (Stigler, 1950, p. 28):[18]

> Our theory is that mergers for monopoly are profitable under easy assumptions that were surely fulfilled in many industries well before the mergers occurred. The only persuasive reason I have found for their late occurrence is the development of the modern corporation and the modern capital market. In a regime of individual proprietorships and partnerships, the capital requirements were a major obstacle to buying up the firms in an industry, and unlimited liability was a major obstacle to the formation of partnerships.

Stigler, too, highlighted the role of promoters (1950, p. 30):[19]

> I am inclined to place considerable weight upon one other advantage of merger: it permitted a capitalization of prospective monopoly profits and a distribution

> of a portion of these capitalized profits to the professional promoter. The merger enabled a Morgan or a Moore to enter a new and lucrative industry: the production of monopolies.

Later commentators have accepted the key role of the promoter in whipping merger waves along.[20] Since a strong case can be made that the New York financial market was less well developed than that in London,[21] and with a view to laying the groundwork for discussion of debates about empirical estimates of the effects of mergers, it is worthwhile citing Hannah's (1974, p. 8, footnotes omitted) explanation of the way systematic differences in information created a place for the merger promoter:

> Given the imperfections of information in the late Victorian capital market and the speculation that these encouraged, the expectations of existing owner-managers of private firms, based as they were on accumulated experience and close personal knowledge of the trade, were rather more stable than the profit expectations of holders or potential holders of publicly quoted shares. In a period when stock market prices were volatile and companies in manufacturing industry had only recently gained quotations in significant numbers, there was great scope for the company promoter to boost expectations from merger issues artificially and to increase his own profits accordingly. There is ample evidence of the major role of the promoting houses in creating excessively optimistic expectations among the investing public, most notably in the case of merger issues, and it is not unreasonable to suppose that peak levels of share prices indicate the periods in which such exaggerated expectations were at their maximum level. It is thus especially at times of high share prices that we would expect a large discrepancy to appear between the valuations placed on their firms by owner-managers and the net present values of the profits expected from the same firms by shareholders. Significantly it was at such times that the sales of many private businesses to promoting syndicates, intent on floating them collectively as a merger issue, were made.

Product-market considerations were present, as Homan (1935) emphasized. Lamoreaux (1985, p. 87) emphasizes the combination of intense competition and heavy fixed cost as inducements to merge:[22]

> Manufacturers formed consolidations to escape the severe price competition that developed during the depression of the nineties in certain types of industries: capital-intensive, mass-production industries in which firms were closely matched and in which expansion had been rapid on the eve of the Panic of 1893. In these industries, not only did firms have extensive capital investments, but also they were new firms and thus most likely to be pressured by high fixed charges.

Nothing prevents simultaneous pursuit of multiple goals, and turn-of-the-nineteenth century mergers may have been motivated as much by a desire to rationalize the organization of production. One motive behind the

1899 formation by merger of the American Steel and Wire Company, which had 'a near monopoly in the manufacture of barbed wire' (McFadden, 1978, p. 483) was to escape the press of competition. But it also led to steps to increase efficiency (McFadden, 1978, pp. 486–7):

> They were also able to initiate better management and personnel practices, and to close down more costly operations. Five uneconomical plants, for example, were closed down almost immediately in various parts of the country. The uniting of wire companies with several steel companies also extended vertical integration, as the new firm also controlled substantial holdings in coal and iron ore resources, operated a fleet of lake ore steamers, and increased its wire rod capabilities substantially, all of which provided extensive economies in the manufacturing process of wire products of all kinds.

But this was by no means a necessary consequence of merger. Utton (1972, p. 54) writes that two persistent problems of UK mergers of the period were overcapitalization and coordination of post-merger activities. The two problems were related, in that it was often necessary to pay generously to induce the participation of firms that were well inside the efficiency frontier but whose presence outside the combination would thwart the goal of containing competition. This led to overcapitalization. Once the bit players were in the operation, however (Utton, 1972, p. 54):[23]

> In view of the sheer number of concerns involved in many of the amalgamations, it is not surprising that administrative problems were fairly common. The difficulty was to co-ordinate the price and production policies of many formerly independent concerns which were used to different methods and were of differing levels of efficiency.

Nelson's comment on the impact of the First Merger Wave on performance was (1966, pp. 65–6):

> Arthur Stone Dewing once made a study of the financial record of several large consolidations created at the turn of the century, during the frenzied years of trust-building. His frequently quoted conclusion was that 'the trusts turned out ill'. What he described was essentially a record of overcapitalization and the wholesale issuance of stock, actions which led many mergers to painful reorganizations. With today's economy in mind, we can correctly say that Dewing wrote about another time, long past, and that nothing as extreme is likely to recur.

Publications lags being what they are, this must have been written before the Third Merger Wave revealed its nature.

Although the distinctive characteristic of the First Merger Wave was large 'horizontal' mergers (Stigler, 1950) – 'merger for monopoly' – the firms formed during the First Merger Wave that maintained their dominant positions did so because they integrated 'vertically'. When vertical integration, which assured access to essential inputs and secured distribution outlets, was made the basis for large-scale production, it allowed efficiency advantages that rivals could not match (Chandler, 1977, p. 339, pp. 364–5). It was the realization of cost advantages that was key to enduring market leadership (Lamoreaux, 1985, p. 139):

> If a consolidation had an advantage in costs over its rivals, it could set prices at the limit value and maintain indefinitely both its market share and its ability to forestall price cutting by independents. If the consolidation was no more efficient than its rivals, it would gradually lose its position of dominance and, with this, its ability to set prices for the industry.
>
> . . . the latter result was more common.

2.3 Second: The Roaring 20s

The Second Merger Wave, like the First, was preceded by technological changes that permit competition on a larger stage, and, at least for consumer goods, the cultivation of product differentiation – the arrival of the automobile and commercial radio (Markham, 1955, p. 172):

> This new transportation system tended to break down small local markets in two ways: it provided sellers with a new means for extending their sales area, and it made consumers considerably more mobile. The 1920's also marked the rise of the home radio, a medium particularly amenable to advertising national brands.

Financial markets contributed to the 1920s merger movement, as they had to the one before (Thorp, 1931, p. 85):

> One important element which stimulates the merger movement in time of prosperity is the condition of the money market. Many mergers, and some acquisitions, involve the flotation of new securities. In periods like 1928 and early 1929, when there is almost an insatiable demand for securities, the merger movement will be certain to flourish. Its most active sponsor is the investment banker.

The relaxed attitude of antitrust enforcement agencies during the 1920s may also have been a factor (Watkins, 1935; Eis, 1969, p. 290; Martin, 2008, Section 2.3).

In terms of the incidence of mergers, Eis (1969, p. 273, p. 275) confirms Stigler's (1950, p. 32) observation that food industries were well represented in the Second Merger Wave.[24] Stigler also observes that follow-up mergers in industries that had been featured in the First Merger Wave transformed them from declining-dominant-firm markets to oligopolies (while mergers in the food sector often created local oligopolies). Stigler attributes this difference between the First and Second US merger waves to antitrust policy (1950, p. 32): 'the ghost of Senator Sherman is an ex officio member of the board of directors of every large company'. Eis' judgement is more nuanced: he finds (1969, pp. 277–8) evidence that the spectre of antitrust action may have influenced the merger activity of firms that had been the target of prior antitrust prosecution, not otherwise.

2.4 Third and Fourth: The Conglomerate 60s and the UnConglomerate 80s

The natures of the 1960s and 1980s merger waves were quite different, but they are linked at a fundamental level. The Third Merger Wave was a spike in merger activity, taking off in 1965, peaking in 1968, and falling back to the 1965 level by 1972 (Steiner, 1975, p. 5). Not only was it compressed in time, but its composition differed from those of its predecessors. Pure conglomerate mergers, combining firms with neither horizontal nor vertical relationships, rose from 14.2 per cent of large US mergers in 1956–59 to 21.2 per cent in 1964–67, then jumped to 43.6, 38.1, 32.5 and 43.4 per cent in 1968, 1969, 1970 and 1971, respectively. The share of conglomerate mergers in large-firm US mergers in 1972 was back down to 19.9 per cent (Steiner, 1975, Table 1-4).

US antitrust policy was put forward as a partial explanation for the rise of conglomerate mergers (Mueller, 1969, Section 5). Sceptics pointed to financial markets as well (Malkiel, 2007, p. 57):

> Although antitrust laws at that time kept large companies from purchasing firms in the same industry, it was possible for a while to purchase firms in other industries without interference from the Justice Department. The consolidations were carried out in the name of synergism. Ostensibly, mergers would allow the conglomerate to achieve higher sales and earnings than would have been possible for the independent entities alone.
>
> In fact, the major impetus for the conglomerate wave of the 1960s was that the acquisition process itself could be made to produce growth in earnings per share. Indeed, the managers of conglomerates tended to possess financial expertise rather than the operating skills required to improve the profitability of the acquired companies.

Conglomerate mergers, like all others, might be pursued in the name of profit (Mueller, 1969, p. 643):

> If firms maximize profit, mergers will take place only when they produce some increase in market power, when they produce a technological or managerial economy of scale, or when the managers of the acquiring firm possess some

> special insight into the opportunities for profit in the acquired firm which neither its managers nor its stockholders possess.

One might be inclined to doubt the possibility that a conglomerate merger would create or reenforce market power, but one should not discount the idea entirely. Multimarket diversification may make tacit collusion an equilibrium outcome (Scott, forthcoming). Reciprocity[25] may also be an issue in the effects of conglomerate mergers.

If management is a fixed and lumpy asset, a firm may have unused 'managerial capacity'. A conglomerate merger might in principle be a way to spread such a fixed management cost over greater (diversified) firm output, reducing management cost per unit of revenue. Alternatively, a merger might be a way for a more efficient management to displace a less efficient management; this way lies the theory of the market for corporate control.

The 'market for corporate control' idea relies on an efficiency motive based on information differences. The management of firm A realizes (or believes) that it can run firm B more efficiently than the incumbent management of firm B. The shareholders who are the owners of firm B are not aware of the efficiency differential, at least, not until they are alerted to its existence by the takeover bid.[26]

Mergers and takeovers might be based on information differences that have nothing to do with efficiency. The managers of firm A might realize that shares of firm A stock are momentarily overvalued, or that shares of firm B are undervalued, or both. If the shareholders who own firm B are unaware of the valuation differentials, firm A can acquire control of firm B at a bargain rate.[27]

Diversification, to the extent that it reduces the variance in a firm's income flow, may reduce its costs of capital. This is an efficiency advantage rooted in financial markets. But if diversification is accomplished by means of conglomerate mergers that increase the firm's fixed interest payment obligations, the reduction in risk that would otherwise come with diversification might be neutralized (Mueller, 1977, p. 322).

A financial-market efficiency put forward for multidivisional-form firms, which would include but not be limited to appropriately organized conglomerates, was the internal capital market (Williamson, 1975). Since a firm's management would (so the story went) have differentially-superior information, it could harvest cash flow from mature divisions in markets with limited opportunities for value-maximizing investment and allocate funds to cash-starved divisions operating in markets with better investment prospects.

If one admits the possibility that managers pursue their own goals, then mergers that do not have value-maximization as a goal may appear. Hubris, empire-building and growth-maximization may all motivate mergers, including conglomerate mergers.[28]

Hogan and Huie (1992, Section I.D[29]) cite lax antitrust enforcement under the Reagan Administration as one reason for the fourth merger wave. They also mention financial market factors: 'Pursuit of the [leveraged buyout] as a novel form of corporate reorganization by issuing junk bonds to finance the takeover.' They describe the Fourth Merger Wave as distinctive for the large numbers of firms and the values involved in takeovers, as well as the appearance both of hostile takeovers and of defensive takeover tactics. But they also note what is generally regarded as the unique aspect of the Fourth Merger Wave, the prevalence of bust-up takeovers designed to restructure firms, divest assets, and undo the conglomerate mergers of the 1960s. By the 1980s, it appeared, what in the 1960s had been seen as advantages of conglomerate firms were no longer there (Bhide, 1990, p. 71):

> In fact, most large corporations have come to insist upon an arm's-length relationship between their units. They have learned that whatever benefits might be gained by coordinating the activities of multiple units (such as economies of scale in production or purchasing) are more than offset by internal bickering, delays, and the difficulty of allocating costs and revenues. Consequently, over 80 percent of large and medium-sized companies are organized into independent strategic business units or profit centers that have limited dealings with one another. And those transactions that do take place between units are often conducted as if they were between independent firms, using market-based transfer pricing methods.

Internal capital markets, in operation, seemed to suffer from handicaps. Stewart and Glassman (1988a, p. 86) include among these 'curtailing an unproductive reinvestment of cash flow' and 'eliminating subsidies for underperforming businesses', which would seem to cut out the heart of the original argument for an internal capital market as a resource allocation mechanism.

Conglomerate diversification, it was said, would allow a firm to even out fluctuations in its income stream and so enjoy a lower cost of capital. A prerequisite for this is that financial markets are able to evaluate conglomerate performance. Stewart and Glassman (1988b, p. 81) offer the following on this point:

> Several years ago, at a roundtable discussion our firm sponsored covering effective financial communication with investors, an investment banker suggested that conglomerates sold at a discount because securities analysts found them difficult to follow. Michael Sherman, head of investment strategy for Shearson Lehman Brothers, bristled. 'It's not that conglomerates are difficult for analysts to understand. We worry that conglomerates are difficult for management to understand,' he countered.

This would seem to leave two possibilities open, the first that financial analysts had difficulty understanding conglomerate operations, the second that business executives had difficulty managing them. Neither possibility speaks well for the conglomerate firm.

Financial markets reacted accordingly (Hubbard and Palia, 1999, p. 1131, footnote 1, references omitted):

> In the post-1980 period, diversified firms had lower Tobin's q values than a comparable portfolio of stand-alone firms . . . , a lower imputed stand-alone value of assets, sales, and earnings than a portfolio of stand-alone firms . . . , and a lower level of total factor productivity . . . [There was] a return to firm focus and specialization in the 1980s, . . . diversifying bidders earned lower abnormal returns on announcement of an acquisition than bidders making related acquisitions. Further, divesting firms in the 1980s earn positive abnormal returns on announcement of the divestiture . . . , and are more likely to divest unrelated businesses.

The question remains why firms and financial markets participated in a conglomerate merger wave in the 1960s and a deconglomerate merger wave in the 1980s.[30] Matsusaka (1993, pp. 376–7) suggests three possibilities. The first is that conglomerate mergers were value-maximizing in the 1960s and that something changed between the 1960s and the 1980s, so that bust-up mergers were value-maximizing in the 1980s. Matsusaka contrasts the tough horizontal and vertical merger antitrust policy of the 1960s with the 'lax enforcement in the 1980s under the Reagan administration'. Matsusaka and others suggest that financial markets simply became relatively more efficient between the 1960s and the 1980s. As Hubbard and Palia put it (1999, p. 1133):

> We suggest that diversified firms were perceived ex ante by the external capital markets to have an informational advantage, because external capital markets were less well developed. For example, relative to the current period, there was less access by the public to computers, databases, analyst reports, and other sources of company-specific information; there were fewer large institutional money managers; and the market for risky debt was illiquid. Accordingly, diversified firms were allocators of capital and provided financing expertise to companies whose management they retained for operating expertise.

Alternatively, Matsusaka suggests, the conglomerate industry may have been like any other profitable new industry that is not protected by barriers to entry. Early conglomerates had latched on to a good thing, and for a while it was very profitable to be a conglomerate. Imitators followed, and the rate of return to being a conglomerate went down.[31]

Or it could be that (Matsusaka, 1993, p. 377) 'the market simply made a mistake about diversification'. The typical conglomerate firm may have been just as inefficient, relative to more focused enterprises, in the 1960s, as it came to be perceived as being in the 1980s.[32] On this view the conglomerates, as Arthur Stone Dewing said of the trusts, 'turned out ill'.

2.5 Fifth: Turn of the Century

Three of the four factors Yellen (1998) includes among common explanations for the merger wave that was in full swing at the end of the twentieth century were present in earlier merger waves as well. These are falling regulatory barriers, technological change and a high stock market. Her fourth factor is globalization. Black, too, comments on the worldwide scope of the merger movement (2000, p. 800):

> In contrast, the current wave has a distinctly international flavor. Many of the signature transactions – including Daimler's acquisition of Chrysler to form DaimlerChrysler and Vodafone's acquisition of Mannesmann – were either entirely outside the United States or involved a non-US party. The $180 billion Vodafone–Mannesmann transaction, between two non-U.S. firms, is the largest in history.

Globalization is itself a consequence of falling trade barriers and technological change. Just as the wider markets that contributed to the First and Second US Merger Waves were created by technological changes, so too were the global markets of the twenty-first century. And the dramatic unravelling of a signature international merger suggest that international financial markets are no more immune to mistakes than were (are) national financial markets.

3 MERGER CAUSES

What light do five merger waves shed on the causes of mergers? Mergers may be undertaken to increase firm value. Horizontal mergers may be profitable because they increase static market power. Horizontal mergers that increase static market power may also yield social efficiency gains, to the extent that they permit and are followed by the rationalization of production. Static market power alone is unlikely to endure in the absence of strategic entry-deterring behaviour or efficiency advantages that permit limit pricing.[33] In early merger waves, vertical integration was a source of efficiency advantages in some industries. The same technological advances that, some suggest, have vastly increased the information-processing capabilities of twenty-first-century financial markets may also have increased the relative efficiency of vertical disintegration in production; the jury remains out on this question. In any case, there appears to be less to the conglomerate firm than met the eye during the Third Merger Wave.

Technological and institutional changes that widened markets were fundamental factors in the First, Second and Fifth Merger Waves. If production involves fixed costs, the equilibrium number of firms in a larger integrated market is less than the sum of the equilibrium numbers of firms in pre-integration markets (Martin and Valbonesi, 2007). To reach an efficient market structure in a larger market implies some firms must exit. If investment in fixed assets is not sunk, adjustment to the new equilibrium can be smooth. If investments are sunk, they cannot be liquidated and their value moved to other markets. Interest on inherited debt may throw owners into bankruptcy, but the assets will remain in the market: that is the nature of sunk investment. In this kind of market, merger may well be as graceful a way as possible for market structure to reach a new equilibrium.[34]

Mergers may be undertaken for reasons that have nothing to do with the increase of firm value. Managers may pursue growth. Financial agents may extract very real profits during periods of irrational exuberance. The cautions that are part of Yellen's summary are entirely appropriate (1998; emphasis added):

> The main reason managers give for undertaking mergers is to increase efficiency. And studies show that, on average, the combined equity value of the acquired company and the purchasing company rises as a result of the merger. However, *an increase in shareholder value can arise for reasons other than greater efficiency – such as increased market power* and the resulting ability to increase profits by raising prices. And the separation of ownership from control in the modern corporation means that *mergers may serve the interests of managers more than shareholders* (e.g., empire building, increased salary associated with running a larger firm). Finally, *even if mergers are designed to enhance efficiency, they often don't work* and can instead create inefficiencies (see the merger of the Union Pacific and Southern Pacific railroads in 1995 as a notable example of such an outcome).

4 MERGER EFFECTS[35]

Industrial economists and financial economists instinctively analyse the effects of mergers in different ways. Industrial economists quite naturally study the effects of mergers on sales, on profit, on efficiency, and so on, by examining the impact of mergers on sales, on profit, on efficiency, and so on.[36] There are genuine measurement, modelling and analytical difficulties associated with these research efforts, and these should not be minimized. But for industrial economists, this is the direct approach.

Financial economists analyse the effects of mergers on performance by examining the impact of the merger on the stock market value of the firms involved in a narrowly defined event window around the time the merger becomes public knowledge. What Caves (1989, p. 153) calls the conventional wisdom resulting from such studies is uniform:

> Acquisitions always entail a large gain for the target firm's shareholders over the market value of the freestanding entity. The proportional gain if anything has been rising over time and amounts to a premium of 30 percent for the change in corporate control via tender offer or takeover, 20 percent via merger . . . The average return to the bidding firm's shareholders is less clear. Some studies have found small but statistically significant gains, others small losses. It seems safe to conclude that the bidder's shareholders approximately break even. Indeed, they have been doing worse and worse over time.

If the acquired firm's shareholders gain substantially while the acquiring firm's shareholders break even, the net effect of the merger on shareholders' wealth is positive (Caves, 1989, p. 153; Scherer, 2006, p. 331). One might then question whether acquiring firms are, on average, being managed in *their* shareholders' interest. The common result of studies that examine stock-market returns over a longer post-merger period is as follows (Scherer, 2002, p. 9):

> Study after study has shown that, although the acquiring company's common stock prices experience on average zero cumulative abnormal change in short time 'windows' around merger announcements, they tend, relative to market movements generally, to decline by impressive and statistically significant magnitudes in the one to three years that follow substantial merger activity.

Meanwhile, direct studies of the impact of mergers on performance fail to find the benefits that, event studies indicate, financial markets anticipated (Caves, 1989, p. 164):[37]

> these results seem to add substantially to the negative evidence on the ex post efficiency of mergers. In particular . . . they indicate substantial declines in the real productivity of acquired assets, not merely that acquirers fail to create enough value to justify their acquisition premia.

The premise of event studies is that financial markets efficiently distil all available information, making the stock market price a valid indicator of the market's evaluation of a firm's expected present discounted value. But Scherer (2002, p. 9) quotes Fischer Black (1986) to the effect that even in an efficient financial market, there can be substantial and persistent departures of current stock price from value:

> [W]e might define an efficient market as one in which price is within a factor of 2 of value, i.e. the price is more than half of value or less than twice value. The factor of 2 is arbitrary, of course. Intuitively, though, it seems reasonable to me, in the light of sources of uncertainty about value and the strength of the forces tending to cause price to return to value. By this definition, I think almost all markets are efficient almost all of the time. 'Almost all' means at least 90%.

All five merger waves were tinged with what contemporary observers took – often *ex post*, and often to their regret – to be the enthusiasm of the moment. If the event study methodology is applied to the First Merger Wave, the results show that those mergers, too, created value for owners (Banerjee and Eckard, 1998). Given that all existing evidence points to the presence of substantial imperfections in financial markets at that time,[38] and given the verdict on *ex post* performance that 'the trusts turned out ill', one might be forgiven for concluding that a finding that mergers from the First Merger Wave were efficient calls the validity of the methodology into question more than demonstrating the result.

On balance, Mueller's (1977, p. 344) conclusion remains unshaken:

> It has become customary to close a review of the merger literature by observing that the arguments are still in conflict, the main issues still in doubt, and from this draw the prudent conclusion that policy changes should proceed slowly and cautiously. True, the a priori theories of mergers' causes and effects are still in conflict, and will probably always remain so. But the empirical literature, upon which this survey focusses, draws a surprisingly consistent picture. Whatever the stated or unstated goals of managers are, the mergers they have consummated have on average not generated extra profits for the acquiring firms, have not resulted in increased economic efficiency.

NOTES

1. Some, controversially, claimed to see signs of a US merger boomlet in the late 1940s, and concern about an immediate postwar merger wave was one factor leading to passage, in 1950, of the Celler–Kefauver Act. If the boomlet was there, it subsided; Markham (1955, p. 179) calls it 'a ripple'.
2. Utton (1972, p. 52) has a British merger wave peaking in the years 1895–1902. Hannah (1974, Figure 1, Table IV) identifies a trough in British merger activity in 1892 or 1893, with a peak in 1898 or 1899 (in both cases, the precise year depending on whether one looks at number of mergers or number of firm disappearances by merger), and falling to a trough in 1901. Kling (2006, p. 675) documents a German merger wave beginning in 1898 and 'centered on a peak in 1906' (2006, p. 675).
3. Some mergers that had been put in motion in 1929, before the crash, were carried out in 1930. That the depression called a halt to the merger wave was not universally recognized by contemporary observers; see Thorp (1931, p. 87).
4. *The Economist*, Internet edition, 27 September 2001, 'Wait and see': 'Some of these companies may be using the attacks as a convenient excuse for a decision [not to pursue an announced merger] that would have been taken anyway.'

5. If size is measured in constant dollar value of acquisitions, the First Merger Wave dwarfs the Second and is itself dwarfed by the Third and later waves (Scherer, 2006, Figure 1). If size is measured by value of assets acquired as a fraction of US GNP, the First Merger Wave is substantially larger than the Second and Fourth (the only ones for which data are illustrated; Golbe and White, 1988, Figure 9.8). Given the international character of the Fifth (at this writing, ongoing) Merger Wave, normalization by US GNP would overstate merger wave size with respect to an appropriate measure of overall economic activity.
6. Minnesota *v*. Barber 136 U.S. 313 (1890). See McCurdy (1978).
7. Chandler (1977) points to economies permitted by the combination of backward and forward vertical integration and economies of throughput in continuous-process industries. We take this up below.
8. Hannah (1974, p. 2) suggests that UK demand for stock was promoted by prominant early combinations 'the spectacular success of promotions such as the Guinness and Coats flotations, of 1886 and 1890 respectively, further boosted public demand for manufacturing issues'.
9. See Bittlingmayer (1985).
10. *Addyston Pipe & Steel* 85 F. 271 (6th Cir., 1898), 175 U.S. 211 (1899).
11. *E.C. Knight (Sugar Trust)* 156 U.S. 1 (1895). This decision was effectively reversed by *Northern Securities* 193 U.S. 197 (1904).
12. Cook and Cohen (1958) cite intense short-period competition as a cause of mergers in three of their case studies of mergers in six UK industries. Their time periods include that of the first US merger wave, but are generally much longer, with exact periods varying from case study to case study. Utton (1972, p. 2) refers to 'severe short term price competition' in the presence of excess capacity as 'an argument which recurs again and again' in the run-ups to mergers during the first British merger wave.
13. On the development of financial markets generally, see Baskin (1988), Baskin and Miranti (1997), and in connection with the First Merger Wave, Navin and Sears (1955), Nelson (1959, pp. 89–100).
14. See their footnote 35 for a breakdown of the calculations yielding the value $83.7 million.
15. In addition to Navin and Sears (1954), see Fields (1932a, b).
16. Apologies to Moeller et al. (2005).
17. On the House of Morgan, see De Long (1991).
18. Hannah (1974, p. 2) cites the same two factors as preconditions for the turn-of-the-nineteenth century UK merger wave.
19. Markham (1955, p. 162, fn. 49), who notes that not all large mergers at the turn of the nineteenth century led to enduring monopoly, refers to 'producers of mergers' rather than 'producers of monopolies'.
20. See Seager and Gulick (1929, p. 64), Butters et al. (1951, pp. 310–11, quoting Seager and Gulick to support their own view); Mueller (1977, p. 315); McFadden (1978, p. 486); Cheffins (2002, p. 50). There is related literature on the connection between business cycles and mergers (generally held to be positive), on which, see Nelson (1966), Hannah (1974, p. 7), and for sceptical views, Markham (1955, pp. 146–54, Penrose (1959 [1980]), pp. 240–42.
21. Davis (1966, p. 272) relies on lesser development of US than UK financial markets to explain the relatively greater scale of US than UK mergers:

    > It appears, therefore, that the difficulties inherent in acquiring external finance in the United States in the nineteenth century provide an explanation for the basis of the fortunes of certain American entrepreneurs and suggest at least one reason why that economy was characterized by increasing concentration in the growth sectors. In the case of the UK, on the other hand, adequate financial markets appear to have yielded much smaller returns to financial manipulation, and firms without good financial contacts were much less heavily penalized in the search for funds for expansion. As a result, concentration when it did occur tended more to reflect product rather than financial market considerations.

22. See similarly O'Brien (1988, p. 649).
23. For another UK example, see Reader (1976): the firm that became Metal Box formed by merger in 1922 as (p. 39) 'a very cosy affair'. For the Board of Directors, (p. 40) 'It was no part of their purpose to interfere in the management of each other's enterprises: far less to extinguish their independence in the manner of the "rationalizers" of the day . . .' Rationalization did not occur until the 1930s, in face of the dual threats of depression and American competition. For a US example, see Whitney's (1958, Chapter 10) discussion of the US Cast Iron Pipe and Foundry Company, created by merger of the firms involved in the *Addyston Pipe and Steel* cartel (and other firms) between the time the Circuit Court of Appeals handed down its decision condemning the cartel and the time the US Supreme Court confirmed that decision. It did not rationalize its operations until some 25 years after it was formed.
24. Together with the food group, Eis reports that primary metals, petroleum refining, chemicals, and transportation equipment accounted for the bulk of merger activity.
25. FTC *v*. Consolidated Foods Corp. 380 U.S. 592.
26. If the market for corporate control explanation of conglomerate mergers is to apply, the management of the acquired firm must be displaced (Mueller, 1969, p. 659, footnote omitted):

    > While to many it may seem implausible that managers with no familiarity with a company's operations or industry could run it or recognize its opportunities for profits better than the firm's own managers or stockholders, no one can say for certain that this is not so. In light of the crucial importance of the existence of these supermanagement capabilities on the part of the acquiring firm's management in conglomerate mergers, it is interesting to note that some of the most aggressive conglomerate merger firms look for companies whose managements are able and willing to continue to run the acquired company after it has been assimilated into the conglomerate's corporate structure.

27. See Malkiel (2007, Chapter 3) for numerous case studies that seem best explained by differential awareness of market misvaluations.
28. Mueller (1969). Malkiel (2007, pp. 60–61) writes that the Automatic Sprinkler Corporation 'offers a good example of how the game of manufacturing growth was actually played during the 1960s. Between 1963 and 1968, the company's sales volume rose by more than 1,400 percent. This phenomenal record was due solely to acquisitions.
29. There are no page numbers on the digital edition of this paper to which I have access.
30. It has long been recognized that mismatches between the efficient scale of operation of complementary production processes might be an efficiency explanation for splitting off what had been part of an integrated operation as a distinct entity (Jewkes, 1952, p. 248; Robinson, 1958, p. 20). This organizational explanation can explain a divestiture; whether it can explain a wave of divestitures is a research question (Lamoreaux et al., 2003).
31. For this explanation to be correct, in equilibrium external capital markets and internal capital markets would allocate capital, at their respective margins, with equal effectiveness. Then one would have to suppose that the 1960s merger wave went 'too far', and that after a wave of divestitures, one would see a balanced rate of formation of diversified and focused firms. In any case, the imitation and entry explanation seems inconsistent with the idea that internal capital markets subsidize underperforming businesses.
32. Exceptional individuals may earn rents to great ability in the operation of conglomerates, as in any other endeavour. See Scherer's (2002, pp. 19–20, footnote omitted) analysis of the success of one 1960s conglomerate:

    > the founder and long-time chief executive officer of Teledyne, Henry Singleton, was a managerial genius. He was extremely intelligent, and he had the knack of bringing into his fold and motivating similarly able managers. Shortly after he retired from active management of Teledyne in 1989 . . . the company's performance plummeted. Also, Teledyne concentrated many of its investments in high-technology fields, where Singleton, who had a Ph.D. in science and who loaded his board of directors with

science and engineering Ph.D. holders, had comparative advantage. Thus, Teledyne was more like a modern-day high-technology venture capital portfolio fund than an operator of run-of-the-mill companies.

33. That limit pricing is possible does not mean it will be a value-maximizing long-run strategy (Gaskins, 1971). But if an incumbent enjoys no efficiency advantage over potential entrants, limit pricing is not possible at all.
34. See Lamoreaux (1985) on the First Merger Wave.
35. For surveys, see Caves (1989), Scherer (2002, 2006) and Mueller (2003).
36. See Gugler et al. (2003) for an example.
37. Caves refers specifically to the findings of Mueller (1985) and Ravenscraft and Scherer (1987).
38. In 1899, Henry O. Havemeyer, President of the American Sugar Refining Company (the *Sugar Trust* of U.S. *v.* E.C. Knight), testified as follows before the Congressional Industrial Commission (Glover, 1954, p. 357):

    Q. You think, then, that when a corporation is chartered by the State, offers stock to the public, and is one in which the public is interested, that the public has no right to know what its earning power is or to subject them to any inspection whatever, that the people may not buy this stock blindly?
    A. Yes; that is my theory. Let the buyer beware; that covers the whole business. You can not wet nurse people from the time they are born until the time they die. They have got to wade in and get stuck, and that is the way men are educated and cultivated.
    Q. Then, you think that they have a right to charter corporations and allow them to offer stock to the people – to the whole community – and that the community then has no right to a knowledge of what the earning power of that stock is?
    A. Precisely.

REFERENCES

Banerjee, A. and E.W. Eckard (1998), 'Are mega-mergers anticompetitive? Evidence from the first great merger wave', *Rand Journal of Economics*, **29**(4), 803–27.

Baskin, J.B. (1988), 'The development of corporate financial markets in Britain and the United States, 1600–1914: overcoming asymmetric information', *Business History Review*, **62**(2), 199–237.

Baskin, Jonathan Barron and Paul J. Miranti, Jr. (1997), *A History of Corporate Finance*, Cambridge: Cambridge University Press.

Bhide, A. (1990), 'Reversing corporate diversification', *Journal of Applied Corporate Finance*, **3**(2), 70–81.

Bittlingmayer, G. (1985), 'Did antitrust policy cause the Great Merger Wave?', *Journal of Law and Economics*, **28**(1), 77–118.

Black, B.S. (2000), 'The first international merger wave (and the fifth and last US wave)', *University of Miami Law Review*, **54**, 799–818.

Black, F. (1986) 'Noise', *Journal of Finance*, **41**, 529–43.

Butters, J. Keith, John Lintner and William L. Cary (1951), *Effects of taxation: corporate mergers*, Boston, MA: Harvard University, Graduate School of Business Administration.

Caves, R.E. (1989), 'Mergers, takeovers and economic efficiency: foresight vs. hindsight', *International Journal of Industrial Organization*, **7**(1), 151–74.

Chandler, Alfred D. Jr. (1965), *The Railroads: The Nation's First Big Business*, New York: Harcourt, Brace & World, Inc.

Chandler, Alfred D. Jr. (1977), *The Visible Hand: The Managerial Revolution in American Business*, Cambridge, MA: Harvard University Press.

Cheffins, Brian R. (2002), 'Investor sentiment and antitrust law as determinants of corporate ownership structure: the great merger wave of 1897 to 1903', Berkeley Program in Law & Economics, Working Paper Series, Paper 77, 15 December, http://repositories.cdlib.org/blewp/art77.

Cook, P. Lesley and Ruth Cohen (1958), *Effects of Mergers*, London: George Allen & Unwin Ltd.

Davis, L. (1966), 'The capital markets and industrial concentration: the US and UK, a comparative study', *Economic History Review*, **19**(2), 255–72.

De Long, J. Bradford (1991), 'Did J.P. Morgan's men add value?', in Peter Temin (ed.), *Inside the Business Enterprise*, Chicago and London: University of Chicago Press, pp. 205–36.

Eis, C. (1969), 'The 1919–1930 merger movement in American industry', *Journal of Law and Economics*, **12**(2), 267–96.

Fields, M.J. (1932a), 'The International Mercantile Marine Company – an ill-conceived trust', *Journal of Business*, **5**(3), 268–82.

Fields, M.J. (1932b), 'The International Mercantile Marine Company – an ill-conceived trust (concluded)', *Journal of Business*, **5**(4), 268–82.

Gaskins, Darius W. Jr (1971), 'Dynamic limit pricing: optimal limit pricing under threat of entry', *Journal of Economic Theory*, **3**, September, 306–22.

Glover, J.D. (1954), *The Attack on Big Business*, Boston, MA: Division of Research, Graduate School of Business Administration, Harvard University.

Golbe, Devra L. and Lawrence J. White (1988), 'A time-series analysis of mergers and acquisitions in the U.S. economy', in Alan J. Auerbach (ed.), *Corporate Takeovers: Causes and Consequences*, Chicago and London: University of Chicago Press, pp. 265–302.

Gugler, K., D.C. Mueller, B.B. Yurtoglu and C. Zulehner (2003), 'The effects of mergers: an international comparison', *International Journal of Industrial Organization*, **21**, 625–53.

Hannah, L. (1974), 'Mergers in British manufacturing industry, 1880–1918', *Oxford Economic Papers*, **26**(1), 1–20.

Harley, C.K. (1982), 'Oligopoly agreement and the timing of American railroad construction', *Journal of Economic History*, **42**(4), 797–823.

Hogan, S.D. and M.C. Huie (1992), 'Bigness, junk and bust-ups: end of the fourth merger wave?', *Antitrust Bulletin*, **37**(4), 881–956.

Homan, Paul T. (1935), 'Trusts', in Edwin R. A. Seligman (ed.), *Encyclopedia of the Social Sciences*, vol. 15, New York: Macmillan, pp. 111–15.

Hubbard, R.G. and D. Palia (1999), 'A re-examination of the conglomerate merger wave in the 1960s: an internal capital markets view', *Journal of Finance*, **54**(3), 1131–52.

Jewkes, J. (1952), 'The size of the factory', *Economic Journal*, **62**(246), 237–52.

Kling, G. (2006), 'The long-term impact of mergers and the emergence of a merger wave in pre-World War I Germany', *Explorations in Economic History*, **43**(4), 667–88.

Lamoreaux, Naomi R. (1985), *The Great Merger Movement in American Business, 1895–1904*, Cambridge: Cambridge University Press.

Lamoreaux, N.R., D.M.G. Raff and P. Temin (2003), 'Beyond markets and hierarchies: toward a new synthesis of American business history', *American Historical Review*, **108**(2); (http://www.historycooperative.org/journals/ahr/108.2/lamoreaux.html).

Malkiel, Burton G. (2007), *A Random Walk Down Wall Street*, New York and London: W. W. Norton & Company.
Markham, Jesse W. (1955), 'Survey of the evidence and findings on mergers', in *Business Concentration and Price Policy*, Princeton, NJ: Princeton University Press, pp. 141–82.
Martin, S. (2008), 'The goals of antitrust and competition policy', Working Paper 2007-003, Center for International Business Education and Research, Krannert School of Management, Purdue University, July; forthcoming in Wayne Dale Collins, (ed.), *Issues in Competition Law and Economics*, American Bar Association.
Martin, Stephen and Paola Valbonesi (2007), 'Equilibrium state aid in integrating markets', September.
Matsusaka, J.G. (1993). 'Takeover motives during the conglomerate merger wave', *Rand Journal of Economics*, **24**(3), 357–79.
McCurdy, C.W. (1978), 'American law and the marketing structure of the large corporation, 1875–1890', *Journal of Economic History*, **38**(3), 631–49.
McFadden, J.M. (1978), 'Monopoly in barbed wire: the formation of the American Steel and Wire Company', *Business History Review*, **52**(4), 465–89.
Moeller, S.B., F.P. Schlingemann and R.M. Stulz (2005), 'Wealth destruction on a massive scale? A study of acquiring-firm returns in the recent merger wave', *Journal of Finance*, **60**(2), 757–82.
Mueller, D.C. (1969), 'A theory of conglomerate mergers', *Quarterly Journal of Economics*, **83**(4), 643–59.
Mueller, D.C. (1977), 'The effects of conglomerate mergers', *Journal of Banking and Finance*, **1**, 315–47.
Mueller, D.C. (1985), 'Mergers and market share', *Review of Economics and Statistics*, **47**, 259–67.
Mueller, Dennis C. (2003), 'The finance literature on mergers: a critical survey', in Michael Waterson (ed.), *Competition, Monopoly and Corporate Governance*, Cheltenham, UK and Northampton, MA, USA: Edward Elgar, pp. 161–205.
Navin, T.R. and M.V. Sears (1954), 'A study in merger: formation of the International Mercantile Marine Company', *Business History Review*, **28**(4), 291–328.
Navin, T.R. and M.V. Sears (1955), 'The rise of a market for industrial securities, 1887–1902', *Business History Review*, **29**(2), 105–38.
Nelson, Ralph L. (1959), *Merger Movements in American Industry*, Princeton, NJ: Princeton University Press.
Nelson, Ralph L. (1966), 'Business cycle factors in the choice between internal and external growth', in William W. Alberts and Joel E. Segall (eds), *The Corporate Merger*, Chicago and London: University of Chicago Press, pp. 52–70.
O'Brien, A.P. (1988), 'Factory size, economies of scale and the great merger wave of 1898–1902', *Journal of Economic History*, **48**(3), 639–49.
Penrose, Edith (1959 [1980]), *The Theory of The Growth of the Firm*, Oxford: Basil Blackwell; first edn 1959, second edn 1980.
Ravenscraft, David J. (1988), 'The 1980s merger wave: an industrial organization perspective', in Lynne E. Browne and Eric S. Rosengren (eds), *The Merger Boom*, Federal Reserve Bank of Boston, pp. 17–37.
Ravenscraft, D.J. and F.M. Scherer (1987), *Mergers, Sell-Offs, and Economic Efficiency*, Washington, DC: Brookings Institution.
Reader, W.J. (1976), *Metal Box: A History*, London: Heinemann.

Robinson, E.A.G. (1958), *The Structure of Competitive Industry*, Cambridge: Cambridge University Press.

Scherer, F.M. (2002), 'The merger puzzle', in Wolfgang Franz, Hans Jürgen Ramser and Manfred Stadler (eds), *Fusionen*, Tübingen: Mohr Siebeck, pp. 1–22.

Scherer, F.M. (2006), 'A new retrospective on mergers', *Review of Industrial Organization*, **28**(4), 327–41.

Scott, John T. (forthcoming), 'The multimarket contact hypothesis', in Wayne Dale Collins (ed.), *Issues in Competition Law and Policy*, American Bar Association, Antitrust Section.

Seager, Henry R. and Charles A. Gulick, Jr (1929), *Trust and Corporation Problems*, New York and London: Harper & Brothers Publishers.

Steiner, Peter O. (1975), *Mergers: Motives, Effects, Policies*, Ann Arbor, MI: University of Michigan Press.

Stewart, G.B. III and D.M. Glassman (1988a), 'The motives and methods of corporate restructuring', *Journal of Applied Corporate Finance*, **1**(1), 85–99.

Stewart, G.B. III and D.M. Glassman (1988b), 'The motives and methods of corporate restructuring', *Journal of Applied Corporate Finance*, **1**(2), 79–88.

Stigler, G.J. (1950), 'Monopoly and oligopoly by merger', *American Economic Review*, **40**(2), 23–34.

Symeonidis, George (1998), 'The evolution of UK cartel policy and its impact on conduct and structure', in Stephen Martin (ed.), *Competition Policies in Europe*, Amsterdam: North-Holland.

Symeonidis, George (2002), *The Effects of Competition: Cartel Policy and the Evolution of Strategy and Market Structure in British Industry*, Cambridge, MA and London: MIT Press.

Thorp, W.L. (1931), 'The persistence of the merger movement', *American Economic Review*, **21**(1), 77–89.

Turner, Frederick Jackson (1893), 'The significance of the frontier in American history', Report of the American Historical Association for 1893, pp. 199–227.

Utton, M.A. (1972), 'Some features of the early merger movements in British manufacturing history', *Business History*, **14**(1), 51–60.

Watkins, Myron W. (1935), 'Trusts since 1910', in Edwin R. A. Seligman (ed.), *Encyclopedia of the Social Sciences*, **15**, New York: Macmillan, pp. 115–22.

Whitney, Simon N. (1958), *Antitrust Policies: American Experience in Twenty Industries*, New York: The Twentieth Century Fund.

Williamson, Oliver E. (1975), *Markets and Hierarchies: Analysis and Antitrust Implications*, New York: The Free Press.

Yellen, Janet L. (1998), 'Testimony', Senate Judiciary Committee, 16 June 1998; downloaded 8 October 2007 from http://judiciary.senate.gov/oldsite/yellen.htm.

8. A new retrospective on mergers*

F.M. Scherer

1 INTRODUCTION

For at least three decades Dennis Mueller and I have plowed parallel furrows on a question of considerable importance: the economic consequences of mergers. (At Princeton during the 1960s we worked in another common field: the economics of research and development.) Both of us have been skeptical of the conventional corporate finance wisdom insisting that most mergers are value-enhancing. As I return once more to merger questions after a lapse, I have three itches that still need scratching. First, during the past several years merger activity has revived strongly and bids fair to reach the highest levels ever recorded. It is time to take a new look at the trends. Second, the debate over the success of mergers continues. And third, I have become intrigued about how mergers and their consequences are being treated in business schools. This chapter addresses all three themes, with emphasis on the US experience, although similar developments are visible in Europe.

2 RECENT TRENDS

After a brief slump connected with the 2001–02 stock market crash, merger activity has rebounded. Figure 8.1 extends to 2006 a statistical series begun in the first (1970) edition of my industrial organization textbook. It is a series of splices, beginning with Ralph Nelson's series for 1895–1920 and then extending the series, expressed in billions of constant 1972 dollars, with adjustments for Tobin's q and data source coverage.[1] Thus, more than a century of US merger activity is tracked. One sees clearly the great merger wave in the early years of the twentieth century, the more modest 1920s boom, the largely conglomerate wave of the 1960s, the resurgence in the 1980s, the continuing growth during the 1990s, the early twenty-first century slump, and then renewed growth.

Even more striking is the extent to which companies have disappeared through merger from periodic lists of the largest 100 US 'industrial' (preponderantly, manufacturing and mining) corporations. Figure 8.2

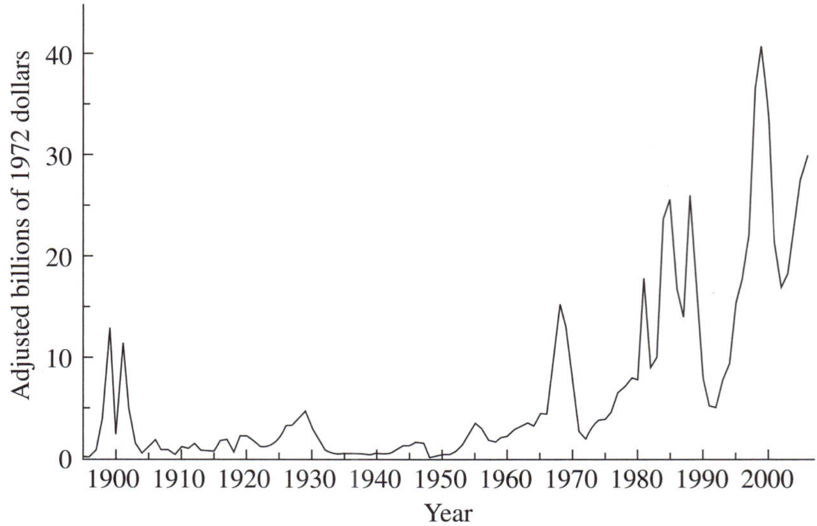

Figure 8.1 Spliced index of merger activity over a century

presents the data for eight discrete time intervals covering most of the twentieth century.[2] After a long hiatus influenced at first by the Great Depression and World War II (evidently, there are some things more important than making mergers – such as winning a war) and then by vigorous antitrust enforcement, large-firm exits through merger rose sharply during the 1980s and then climbed to the record-setting level of 1.9 exits on average per year between 1993 and 2002.

3 EFFICIENCY EFFECTS?

My most systematic attempt to assess the efficiency effects of mergers was the book with David Ravenscraft, *Mergers, Sell-offs, and Economic Efficiency* (1987). It was in my opinion the best single scholarly work I have published during my long career. I take pride in it because it addressed an important topic – the massive merger wave that peaked during the 1960s; because it exploited the most comprehensive, narrowly disaggregated accounting data ever brought to bear on the question of merger causes and effects – four years of Federal Trade Commission Line of Business data, supplemented by 15 case studies; and because I was fortunate to have an especially able co-investigator, David Ravenscraft. We worked on the project for more than three years, estimating from our combined results that manufacturing sector inefficiencies following in the wake of the conglomerate merger wave reduced

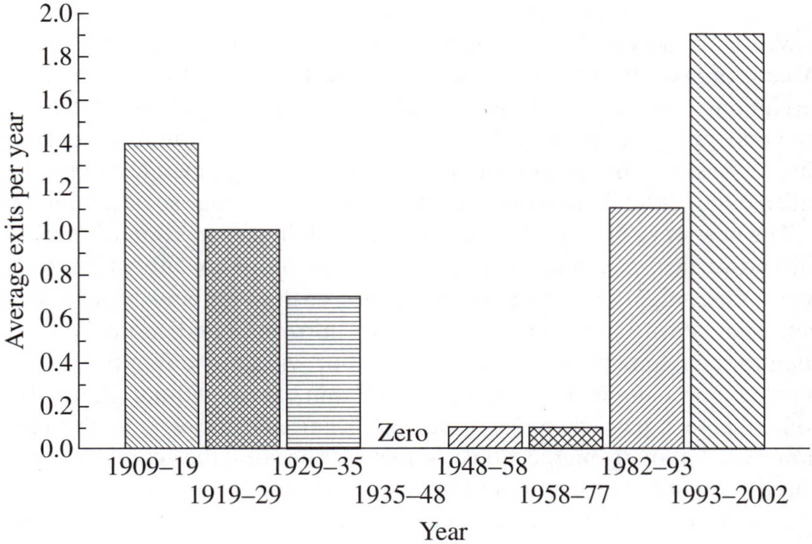

Figure 8.2 Trends in merger-related exits from the top 100 industrials

the growth of US real gross national product between 1968 and 1976 by between 0.074 and 0.101 percentage points per year.[3]

When we completed our book manuscript, it was sent out by Brookings Institution for peer review. As is common in such cases, Brookings asked us to suggest reviewers. Here Dennis Mueller came into the picture again. As we made early conference presentations anticipating our findings, finance specialists regularly took pot shots at them. But we considered the composite of our results to be bullet-proof, so I suggested as one of the reviewers a leader of the school skeptical of assertions that mergers might on average be profit- and efficiency-reducing. Weeks and months went by, and our Brookings editor reported that the book was being delayed because one peer reviewer had not delivered on his agreement to provide an evaluation. Finally, we were asked to suggest an alternative reviewer. We named Dennis, and he came back quickly with a recommendation. As usual, we did not and still do not know what he said, but the book was accepted for publication on an accelerated schedule. Shortly after the book's publication, finance specialists began to concede that the largely conglomerate merger wave of the 1960s and 1970s had been marked by widespread failure. Yet by and large, our research has been ignored, especially by the corporate finance specialists who do much of the research on mergers. They almost never cite our book. Being ignored is one of the worst things that can happen to a scholar. It's worse than being criticized.

There are some plausible explanations for the neglect the Ravenscraft–Scherer merger research has experienced. Each merger wave in American history had unique characteristics. The wave of the 1960s, which left among other things a legacy of sell-offs during the 1970s and 1980s, was preponderantly conglomerate, bringing together entities in quite different lines of business. By the time our book appeared, conglomerate mergers had fallen out of fashion, in part because they were on average so disappointing.

The new wave of the 1980s involved a much higher fraction of horizontal and vertical mergers, facilitated in part by more lax antitrust enforcement. One might expect opportunities for cost saving and benefits from complementarity to be much stronger for horizontal and vertical mergers than for conglomerates, and so the record of widespread failure we documented may simply have become irrelevant. It is without doubt that some mergers, perhaps many, yield significant efficiencies. It is also clear, however, that many mergers fail – sometimes because the acquirers experienced a winner's curse and bid too much, sometimes because of corporate culture mismatches, incentive failures, or clumsy implementation. What is uncertain is where the balance lies. In my principal publication returning more recently to the merger question, I summarized several large-scale studies, some by management consulting firms, that found widespread disappointment and failure in the record of more recent mergers.[4] In a survey earlier this year,[5] *The Economist* recalled that the only one of its weekly covers to be selected in an American editors' poll as one of the 40 best magazine covers of the past 40 years was one from 1994 headed 'The trouble with mergers' and showing two camels in flagrante delicto.[6] According to the more recent (2006) survey:

> The article that went with it explained why most mergers go wrong. But mergers have become no more extinct than camels. Last year was a bumper one for cross-border acquisitions in Europe, and in America the value of telecoms deals alone was over $100 billion. Nevertheless, it remains extremely difficult to make mergers work.

Similiarly, a leading German newspaper, calling attention to the new boom in merger activity, asked rhetorically, 'Haven't managers learned? Haven't dozens of studies shown that in truth two out of three mergers only destroyed value?'[7] And a prominent *New York Times* columnist wrote in 2007, '[F]ew management actions have done as good a job of destroying value as have mergers and acquisitions. Some work out fine, but many do not.'[8] It seems clear that the problem of failed mergers has by no means disappeared since the period on which Ravenscraft and I focused.

Another reason for the neglect of our work by financial specialists is that we inhabit separate, distinct, and scarcely communicating methodological worlds. Ravenscraft and I analyzed accounting data. They have their difficulties, to be sure, but we deployed a substantial array of controls to adjust for systematic biases. The finance specialists emphasize 'event studies', determining how stock market investors respond in a typically short time window around the announcement of a merger. The most typical finding has been that the stock of the target company rises significantly, largely because a takeover premium is expected, while the stock price of the acquiring company changes insignificantly. A plus added to a zero is a plus, signifying the enhancement of economic value. And if antitrust enforcers are doing their job properly, the change cannot be attributed to enhanced monopoly power, so the gains must stem from the realization of efficiencies and/or complementarities.

There are two main problems with this approach, which I have explored at greater length in a (2002) article. Finance specialists live or die on the basis of their belief in efficient markets, asserting that at any moment in time markets impound all the information available on the evolution of future events.[9] If combined stock prices rise in the few days surrounding a merger announcement, it must be because rational stock market investors anticipate future earnings gains. Skepticism toward this view is suggested *inter alia* by evidence from numerous studies that over the longer run of one to three years after major mergers, the 'abnormal' returns of the merged firm tend to decline.[10] Finance specialists who defend mergers as value-enhancing on average tend to dismiss these results as an anomaly, non-causal, or (in a startling non sequitur) as inconsistent with the axioms of market efficiency combined with the assurance that mergers are value-enhancing.

The other problem is that the company leaders who decide whether to initiate mergers believe, or at least claim to believe, that stock markets are not so efficient that they cannot be outwitted through superior analysis or insider information. It is almost universally accepted that stock prices follow random walks. Figure 8.3 shows four simulated random walks, adhering closely to random walk parameters defined by Fisher Black (1986) in his presidential address to the American Finance Association.[11] If a would-be acquirer in Firm 1 can see through the random walk and recognize that his firm's stock is randomly overvalued at 200 days after the simulation began and that Firm 2's stock is randomly undervalued, the makings of a profitable acquisition exist. The key question is whether real-world decision-makers can see through random valuation errors to engage in such analyses. Abundant clinical evidence suggests that they do, or at least believe that they can. Finance specialists disagree, and therein lies a fundamental methodological disagreement.

4 WHAT BUSINESS SCHOOLS TEACH AND WHY

Recently I have been puzzling actively over something that had been subliminal for a long time. I received my MBA from the Harvard Business School in 1958. Reflecting on my two-year course of study, I could recall only one case study (assigned in the second-year core Business Policy course) focusing mainly on a merger – the merger between Merck and Sharpe & Dohme in 1953. Consulting with colleagues from that era, I found that they recalled no formal merger cases and certainly no emphasis on mergers in the overall curriculum. Perhaps we have reached an age at which we remember little from our ancient past. But to juxtapose the possibly imperfect recollection of our past experience against the present, I first searched the list of case study titles in the Harvard Business School's computerized list of the case studies it had available in 2005. Thirty-one had titles containing the word 'merger'; 11 the word 'takeover'; 37 'acquisition'; and seven 'M&A'. Three courses offered during the 2005–2006 academic year focused directly on M&A-like questions: 'Acquisitions and Alliances', 'Creating Value through Corporate Restructuring', and 'Negotiating Complex Deals and Disputes'. Several other courses had clear M&A components. A friend on the faculty of the Stern School of Business at New York University reported that the mergers and acquisitions course

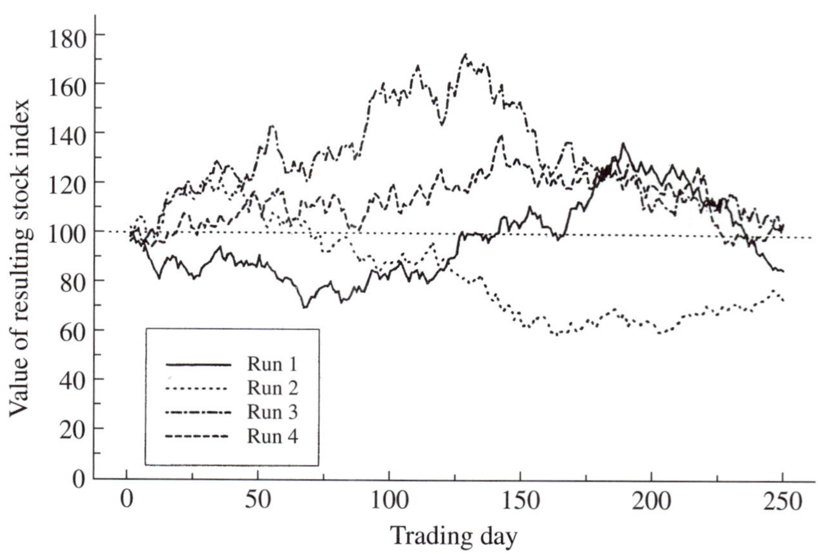

Note: Seed = 100; daily standard deviation = 2.5 percent

Figure 8.3 Plot of four random walks

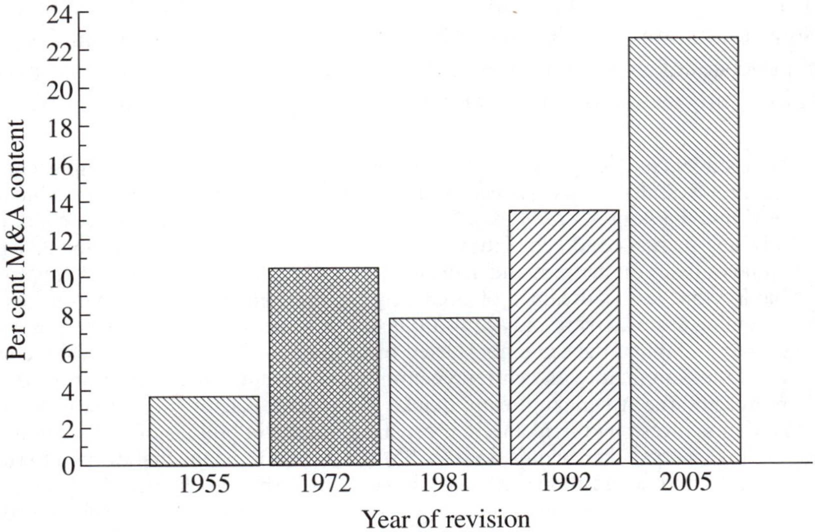

Figure 8.4 Merger and acquisition content in editions of a leading finance casebook

was one of the most popular electives, offered in two distinct flavors, one taught by an experienced merger-maker and one by a scholar.

Memories deceive, so I sought more solid quantitative evidence on trends. One of the few textbooks we used in our first year at the Harvard Business School was a collection of case studies, *Case Problems in Finance*. We purchased for use in our studies the 1955 revised edition, edited by HBS faculty members Pearson Hunt and Charles Williams. The collection has been updated under diverse editors, typically with HBS affiliations, through twelve editions. Figure 8.4 shows various collections' content devoted to mergers and acquisitions as a percentage of total pagination (counted up to the first index page). Merger content rose from 3.7 per cent, expansively defined,[12] in the 1955 edition to a peak of 22.6 per cent in the 2005 edition. The only break in the series is the decline for the 1981 edition, following a merger slump, from the higher value for 1972 in the wake of the 1960s conglomerate merger boom.

In the 1958 edition of the authoritative Paton and Dixon accounting textbook, only 3½ pages out of 792, or 0.4 per cent, dealt with merger and acquisition accounting. There was a vast increase in the number of pages devoted to merger questions between the fourth edition of the *Accountant's Handbook*, published in 1956, and the ninth edition, published in 1999.

The increased orientation of business schools toward M&A activity pleases students, and indeed, it may reflect sensitivity to students' demands in the tough competition among business schools for attractive students. Some quotations from Ridgway (2005) on the aspirations, studies, and work experiences of undergraduates at Pennsylvania's Wharton School – ranked consistently as the top undergraduate business program – are indicative:

> [The students] quickly discover that the only thing more prestigious than becoming an investment banker is becoming an investment banker at the most elite of deal-making houses – Goldman Sachs (p. 31) . . . Goldman has been a leader in advising mergers and acquisitions (p. 32) . . . Lazard was renowned for its legendary advice on mergers and acquisitions (p. 41) . . . Parr embodied the type of banker that Jessica dreamed of becoming . . . the man credited for sparking and executing more mergers and acquisitions than anyone else in the industry's history (p. 45) . . . When the economy started picking up in the mid to late 1990s, concentrations in finance and entrepreneurial management, with all their promise of power and the American dream, quickly became intoxicating to many Wharton students. Investment banks were prospering, raking in billions of dollars in fees for huge mergers and acquisitions (p. 95) . . . 'I want to be the first woman to run mergers and acquisitions at some large bank', she proclaimed (p. 117) . . . 'Investment banking is unparalleled in terms of the amount of responsibility you get at such a young age', she said. 'Plus there's an adrenaline rush. I want to pick up the *Wall Street Journal* one day and see a deal that I did' (p. 119).

Studying corporate finance in particular, said by Ridgway (2005, p. 26) to be the major favored by two-thirds of Wharton undergraduates, was seen to be the leading pathway into M&A work. In sharp contrast, and quite consistent with my experience at Harvard, is Whyte's (1956, pp. 75, 68) characterization of business students' aspirations a half century ago:

> Those who mark down finance as a choice are also staff-minded. Few ever mention speculating or investing in stocks and bonds. Their interest in finance is administrative rather than accumulative; they are primarily interested in credit, mortgage loan work, trust and estate work, and financial analysis. . . . Placement officers find that of the men who intend to go into business . . . less than 5 percent express any desire to be an entrepreneur. About 15 to 20 percent plan to go into their fathers' business. Of the rest, most have one simple goal: the big corporation.

Attitudes have changed in part because opportunities and market demands have changed. But in addition, it must be admitted that M&A is one of the most interesting, intellectually challenging topics taught in business schools. When I think back upon my MBA studies, I realize that, although quite fundamental, the material we covered was humdrum – the basics of accounting, channels of distribution, how to choose effective advertising media, how top-level functional managers coordinate their activities, how to motivate subordinates, and – yes, we spent three hours on the matter – how to place a workpiece squarely in the jaws of a milling machine. How much more excitement there is in 'doing the numbers' to estimate the internal rate of return from a big proposed merger, devising takeover strategies and financial incentives to force merger despite the reluctance of well-known corporate leaders, and structuring merger partners' payments to minimize taxes!

In this I am not simply fabricating comparisons out of thin air. Recently Harvard's Kennedy School, whose reformed curriculum in the early 1970s was strongly influenced by business school models, surveyed thousands of alumni to ascertain their views on the quality of their educational experience.[13] On the excellence of their KSG training in relevant concepts and skills, those who graduated between 1984 and 1994 ranked 'systematic thinking about problems' first, 'economics' second, and 'cost–benefit analysis' third. With the three lowest rankings among 23 categories were 'managing people', 'organizing/mobilization', and 'leadership'. It is easy to impress one's students about quantitative analyses that have crisp, definitive right and wrong answers. It is much harder to teach the soft arts of leadership and motivation, although, I should add, some Kennedy School faculty members do so superbly.

There is more to the story. In 1958, the year I received my MBA, 4041 master's degrees in business subjects, including 474 in accounting, were conferred by US institutions of higher learning.[14] Those who received MBAs were an elite group. Those who took jobs in big business could expect to be put on the fast track, observed, and groomed for higher-level responsibilities by top management. In the year 2000, 112 258 master's degrees in business studies were awarded by US schools. Receiving an MBA is far from an elite distinction, and although there is sorting based upon the much-publicized quality of the program from which a young person graduates, there are many more people one must overtake to move up in the corporate hierarchy. Working on an important acquisition helps one stand out.

A brief digression: from the numbers in the previous paragraph, one can calculate an average growth rate for MBA degrees of 7.92 per cent per year. The comparable rates for US master's degrees in some other fields of direct interest to business were as follows:

Engineering	3.62 %
Physical sciences (incl. chemistry)	1.11 %
Mathematics	2.42 %
Biology and other life sciences	3.46 %

The changes over time are summarized in Figure 8.5. In 1958, the number of business master's degrees was 35 per cent of the combined number of master's degree recipients in these four S&E fields; in the year

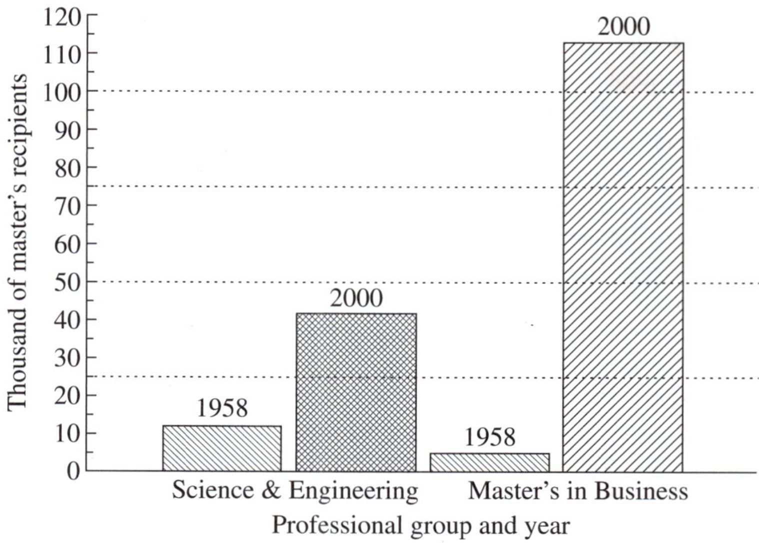

Figure 8.5 Comparison of the number of S&E and Business master's graduates

2000, the proportion was almost exactly the reverse.[15] At least in part because business graduates' salaries tend to be higher than those of technically educated individuals, the United States has been increasing its stock of individuals trained in the techniques of business administration much more rapidly than it has been augmenting the number of people trained in the scientific underpinnings of the important things business firms do to satisfy consumer demands and raise productivity.[16]

Given the increased numerical competition among MBA holders, it is only sensible for business school students to study subjects that will win them high-visibility jobs immediately and/or bring them quickly to the attention of top managers. As we have seen from the Wharton School study, investment banking, whose forte is M&A, is one such fast track – a particularly well-paid one. (It was not so when I graduated from Harvard Business School.) If a new MBA joins a large non-financial corporation, the assignment most likely to bring one into the thick of conducting big, high-visibility projects and attract the attention of top managers is to work in a business development or finance group analyzing possible avenues to growth through mergers and acquisitions. Plodding away as an accountant, salesperson, foreign exchange specialist, advertising account assistant, or production foreman is a ticket to permanent obscurity as one of Whyte's (1956) 'organization men'.

Thus, we in the United States have created a sizeable professional establishment that sees as a significant justification for its existence the making of mergers. Business school curricula emphasizing mergers are a reaction to corporate sector demand, but the supply in turn reinforces the demand. That would be troubling enough, if business program training provided the members of that establishment with deep insight into the consequences of what they are doing. But there are grounds for skepticism. As Ridgway (2005, p. 114) quotes one interviewee in her Wharton study:

> 'Investment banking is a narrow skill set', he explained. 'It's crunching numbers and modeling. You don't get what is behind the numbers we're analyzing. The bottom line is that what you're doing is just working with numbers. You can't see how they fit into the bigger picture. I personally feel that those numbers are worthless, especially with investment banking.'

I believe that from all this I see why my book with David Ravenscraft has received little attention from finance academics, most of whom are employed by business schools. Our finding that mergers during the 1960s and 1970s were on average efficiency-reducing and similar conclusions from other more recent studies challenge one of their most popular educational offerings. It is like telling Ford Motor Company that its SUVs have a high propensity to roll over, or like telling Coca-Cola that its Coke Classic contributes to obesity and eventual diabetes. It can hardly expect to receive an enthusiastic reception.

5 MERGERS AND PRODUCTIVITY GROWTH

The emphasis of fast-track business school graduates on merger-making would be unproblematic if, in contrast to what Ravenscraft and I found, mergers of recent vintage were indeed efficiency-enhancing rather than merely boosting managerial egos and compensation.[17] I remain open to proof of that proposition. As one small step toward a further exploration of the issues, I used the century-long data series graphed in Figure 8.1 for a statistical test of relationships between aggregate merger activity and private non-farm sector productivity growth.[18]

Merger activity was initially measured as year-to-year changes from the previous year's value. The series of year-to-year percentage changes is extremely noisy and skewed toward high values. Therefore, logarithms (to base 10) were taken of the merger level values in Figure 8.1 and year-to-year first differences $\delta LOGMERG_0$ were computed. (The zero subscript denotes a change from previous to current year merger activity.) The distribution of $\delta LOGMERG$ differed insignificantly from normal. The results reported here differ little when regressions were run in the unlogged variables. Because the US economy was dominated by war production and subsequent inflation during World Wars I and II, the years 1917 through 1920 and 1940–1946 are excluded from all analyses.

We begin by addressing the classic hypothesis that merger cycles are positively correlated with, and presumably influenced by, stock market fluctuations. Where $\delta S\&P_0$ is the year-to-year percentage change in the Standard & Poor's stock price index and δGNP_0 is the percentage change in real gross national product (or in later years, real gross domestic product), the fitted regression equation is:

$$\delta LOGMERG_0 = -0.033 + 0.0036\ \delta S\&P_0 + 0.0082\ \delta GNP_0; \quad (8.1)$$
$$[1.12] \quad [1.99] \qquad\qquad [1.25]$$

$$R^2 = 0.094;\ N = 97;$$

with t-ratios reported in subscripted brackets. The conventional wisdom is supported, although only weakly. When the data are limited to the post-World War II years 1947–2003, the GNP variable is statistically significant while the S&P variable, though positive, falls into insignificance.

We now focus on $\delta PRODY_0$, which is the percentage change in output per labor hour in the non-farm business sector or, prior to 1941, using the Kendrick series, for the private domestic economy. If mergers have a positive impact on productivity, it should take a year or so for the effect to materialize, so three prior years of the $\delta LOGMERG_0$ variable are used. There might arguably be an impact in the year of merger, if for example layoffs are effected shortly after mergers made during the earlier months of a calendar year. Here, however, we must be careful of confounding effects from another variable. It is well known under a phenomenon described as Verdoorn's law that productivity growth is higher when real GNP growth is higher.[19] We control for the contemporaneous Verdoorn effect with δGNP_0. To minimize an autocorrelation problem, all regressions are computed using a Cochrane–Orcutt correction.

For the entire data series (excluding wartime observations) with productivity data from 1899 to 2004, the fitted regression omitting current-year merger activity is:

$$\delta PRODY_0 = 1.62 - 0.52\ \delta LOGMERG_1 - 0.004\ \delta LOGMERG_2 \quad (8.2)$$
$$[5.21] \quad [0.41] \qquad\qquad [0.00]$$

$$- 1.41\ \delta LOGMERG_3 + 0.226\ \delta GNP_0; \qquad R^2 = 0.112;\ N = 95;$$
$$[1.19] \qquad\qquad [3.55]$$

where subscripts on the $\delta LOGMERG$ variables indicate the number of years lagged. The Verdoorn hypothesis is supported. All three signs on the mergers productivity effect are negative, but none is statistically significant. When the current-year merger variable is added, the regression is:

$$\delta PRODY_0 = \underset{[5.07]}{1.63} + \underset{[1.39]}{1.87}\,\delta LOGMERG_0 - \underset{[0.84]}{1.17}\,\delta LOGMERG_1 \quad (8.3)$$

$$+ \underset{[0.21]}{0.28}\,\delta LOGMERG_2 - \underset{[1.03]}{1.26}\,\delta LOGMERG_3 + \underset{[2.95]}{0.201}\,\delta GNP_0;$$

$$R^2 = 0.101;\ N = 93.$$

Now the signs alternate. Harmful collinearity between the $\delta LOGMERG_0$ and δGNP_0 variables is implied by the reduced t-ratio on δGNP_0 and the fall in R^2. The algebraic sum of the four merger impact coefficients is negative. When the four lagged merger terms were combined into a single rectangular lag variable, the regression coefficient was −0.78, with a statistically insignificant t-ratio of 0.37.

If we turn now to the data from 1947 to 2004 only, which may reflect a new and more enlightened era of merger-making, the analogue of regression (2) is:

$$\delta PRODY_0 = \underset{[0.77]}{0.29} - \underset{[0.98]}{1.18}\,\delta LOGMERG_1 + \underset{[0.43]}{0.53}\,\delta LOGMERG_2 \quad (8.4)$$

$$+ \underset{[0.83]}{0.98}\,\delta LOGMERG_3 + \underset{[7.16]}{0.615}\,\delta GNP_0; \qquad R^2 = 0.504;\ N = 57.$$

The sum of the merger impact coefficients, all insignificant, is positive but small. The Verdoorn hypothesis is strongly supported. With a contemporaneous merger activity variable added, the regression is:

$$\delta PRODY_0 = \underset{[0.68]}{0.26} - \underset{[1.09]}{1.35}\,\delta LOGMERG_0 - \underset{[0.82]}{1.02}\,\delta LOGMERG_1 \quad (8.5)$$

$$+ \underset{[0.32]}{0.39}\,\delta LOGMERG_2 + \underset{[0.78]}{0.93}\,\delta LOGMERG_3 + \underset{[7.23]}{0.64}\,\delta GNP_0;$$

$$R^2 = 0.502;\ N = 56.$$

Here the merger variables are more negative, but insignificant, as is a rectangular lag combining all four lagged merger variables.

In sum, the regression analysis provides no significant support for the hypothesis that more intense merger activity leads to higher productivity growth at the national level with a lag of zero to three years. To be sure, these results should not be the last word on a controversial subject. The level of aggregation is high, and both the merger and productivity series are the result of splices. Productivity is notoriously difficult to measure, and it is driven by multiple forces, most notably by the research and technological development performed by scientists and engineers whose numbers have risen much more slowly than the number of MBAs. At most, the results can be read as a mild caveat to the assertion that mergers yield important productivity benefits to the US economy.

6 CONCLUSION

My return to the merger scene is not reassuring. The volume of merger activity has risen, and the disappearance of large industrial firms through merger has reached record levels. High levels of merger activity encourage students of business administration to emphasize merger-making skills in their training, and as they succeed in becoming leaders within the corporate hierarchy, a continuous feedback loop may operate, fostering an attitude that sustains and encourages vigorous merger activity.

One would like to believe that mergers bring substantial efficiency benefits to the economy, but on this point, the balance of evidence remains tenuous. Mainly through technological innovation based upon the human capital that the United States cultivated domestically and attracted from abroad, the twentieth century has been the American century. Continuation depends upon providing strong inducements for young people to pursue careers in science and engineering and maintaining sufficiently diverse centers of industrial initiative, allowing one hundred flowers to bloom. For the new century, my task is to get out of the way. But I worry about what kind of economic environment we pass on to subsequent generations.

NOTES

* This chapter is drawn with permission and some changes from an article by the same name in the *Review of Industrial Organization*, vol. 28 (June 2006).

1. For the most detailed description of splicing methodology, see Scherer (1980, p. 120). Data following discontinuation of the Federal Trade Commission large manufacturing and mining merger series after 1988 are spliced, with considerable downward adjustment, from various issues of the W.T. Grimm & Co. *Mergerstat Review*, combined with Q-ratio data kindly provided by Professor Tobin.
2. Disappearance data for the first five time intervals are from Collins and Preston (1961). They are supplemented by my own tabulations using *Fortune* magazine's largest corporation lists. Banking, insurance, trade and other service sector companies have been systematically excluded from the tallies.
3. Ravenscraft and Scherer (1987, pp. 202–203).

4. See Scherer (2002, p. 5). A more detailed survey of the same literature by Pautler (2002) concluded that 'Mergers and acquisitions are risky undertakings that achieve the primary goals of the surveyed managers substantially more than half the time, but are only successful in a more quantitative financial sense (i.e., raising shareholder value relative to pre-deal levels) about 30 to 55 percent of the time.'
5. 'A survey of the company', *The Economist*, 21 January, 2006, p. 8.
6. 'The trouble with mergers', *The Economist*, 10 September, 1994.
7. 'Jeden Tag ein neuer Deal' ('Every day a new deal'), *Die Zeit*, 9 March, 2006, p. 23 (my translation). The article goes on to observe, 'These are the questions of yesterday' due to new rules of the game, including 'cool and systematic' pre-merger calculations.
8. Floyd Norris, 'Owners lose as bosses win in bad mergers', *New York Times*, 20 April, 2007, p. C-1.
9. See, for example, Jensen (1988, p. 26).
10. See, for example, the survey by Dennis Mueller (2003).
11. Details are provided in Scherer (2002).
12. If a case study concerning an involuntary sell-off required under the Public Utilities Holding Company Act is excluded, the figure falls to 2.8 per cent.
13. John F. Kennedy School (2005, p. 85).
14. The data are from the 'earned degrees conferred' tables of the *Statistical Abstract of the United States* for 1960 and 2002.
15. Degrees in the four S&E fields were 36 per cent of the business master's degrees for the year 2000. If we add master's degrees in computer and information sciences – a category not counted separately in 1958 – the combined fraction for five S&E fields in 2000 rises to 49 per cent.
16. For an analysis of domestic and foreign science and engineering education trends, see Scherer (1999, Chapters 6 and 7).
17. On compensation, see, for example, Gretchen Morgenstern, 'What are mergers good for?' *New York Times Magazine*, 5 June, 2005, pp. 56–62; and 'Fat merger payouts for CEOs', *Business Week*, 12 December, 2005, pp. 34–37.
18. The productivity variable is spliced together from various editions of the *Economic Report of the President* and US Department of Commerce (1966), p. 189. All first differences were computed between years from a continuous series.
19. See Verdoorn (1949) and (for an emphasis on short-run cyclical phenomena) Gordon (1979).

REFERENCES

Black, Fisher (1986), 'Noise', presidential address to the American Finance Association, *Journal of Finance*, **41**, 529–43.

Collins, N.R. and L.E. Preston (1961), 'The size structure of the largest industrial firms', *American Economic Review*, **51**, 986–1011.

Gordon, R.J. (1979), 'The "end-of-expansion" phenomenon in short-run productivity behavior', *Brookings Papers on Economic Activity*, **1979**(2), 447–61.

Hunt, Pearson and Charles M. Williams (1955), *Case Problems in Finance* (revised edition), Homewood, IL: R.D. Irwin.

Jensen, M. (1988), 'Takeovers: their causes and consequences', *Journal of Economic Perspectives*, **1**, 21–48.

John F. Kennedy School of Government, Harvard University (2005), *Report of the Teaching Programs Review Committee*, Cambridge, MA.

Mueller, Dennis (2003), 'The finance literature on mergers: a critical survey', in Michael Waterson (ed.), *Competition, Monopoly and Corporate*

Governance, Cheltenham, UK and Northampton, MA, USA: Edward Elgar, pp. 161–205.

Paton, W.A. and R.L. Dixon (1958), *Essentials of Accounting*, New York: Macmillan.

Pautler, P.A. (2002), 'The effects of mergers and post-merger integration: a review of business consulting literature', draft paper, Federal Trade Commission.

Ravenscraft, David J. and F.M. Scherer (1987), *Mergers, Sell-offs, and Economic Efficiency*, Washington, DC: Brookings Institution.

Ridgway, Nicole (2005), *The Running of the Bulls: Inside the Cutthroat Race from Wharton to Wall Street*, New York: Gotham Books.

Scherer, F.M. (1980), *Industrial Market Structure and Economic Performance*, 2nd edn, Chicago: Rand-McNally.

Scherer, F.M. (1999), *New Perspectives on Economic Growth and Technological Innovation*, Washington, DC: Brookings Institution.

Scherer, F.M. (2002), 'The Merger Puzzle', in Wolfgang Franz et al. (eds), *Fusionen*, Tübingen: Mohr Siebeck, pp. 1–22.

US Department of Commerce, Bureau of the Census (1966), *Long Term Economic Growth 1960–1965*, Washington, DC.

Verdoorn, P.J. (1949), 'Fattori che regolano lo sviluppo della produttivita del lavoro', *L'Industria*, **1**, 45–53.

Whyte, William H. (1956), *The Organization Man*, New York: Simon & Schuster.

9. Mergers and efficiency: theory, empirical evidence and competition policy in Japan*

Hiroyuki Odagiri

Economic consequences of mergers have always been one of the major research interests for Dennis Mueller. When he edited a special issue on mergers in the *International Journal of Industrial Organization*, he stated that

> With respect to mergers . . ., disagreement exists over (1) whether mergers are adequately explained by a profits maximization assumption, (2) whether mergers generate net private returns which are positive, zero, or negative, (3) whether mergers generate social returns that go beyond their private returns, and if so what sign do they have, and (4) whether merger policy should stimulate more mergers, or try to curtail them (Mueller, 1989, p. 1).

Being skeptical of the efficiency arguments of mergers, he said that 'Whether the large number of unprofitable mergers is due to managerial hubris or managerial pursuit of goals other than stockholder welfare, these mergers arise because of the considerable discretion managers have in this area. Policies to reduce the number of efficiency reducing mergers should seek to curb managerial discretion' (ibid., p. 7). Once he even proposed that 'A policy for preserving this system without sacrificing economic efficiency would be a flat ban on mergers subject to an efficiencies defense' (Mueller, 1986, p. 234).

Whether or not one agrees with this recommendation, everyone would agree that these issues have recently become even more pertinent as mergers have become commonplace. This applies particularly well in Japan where the number of M&A cases has increased more than six times in the last two decades according to Recof, a private consulting firm: see Table 9.1. Although the increase in merger cases has been modest, acquisitions (of majority shares), business purchases (for example, purchases of plants and divisions), capital participation (that is, minority acquisitions) have increased rapidly, particularly since the end of 1990s. M&As by foreign firms (out-in M&As) also increased significantly.

Table 9.1 The number of mergers and acquisitions in Japan, 1986–2006

		By type					By nationality			
Year	Total	Mergers	Acquisitions	Business purchase	Capital participation	Increased ownership	In-In	In-Out	Out-In	Out-Out
1986	418	30	169	59	156	4	223	178	14	3
1987	382	20	156	44	160	2	206	156	18	2
1988	523	33	186	102	201	1	218	285	14	6
1989	645	34	317	57	236	1	245	380	12	8
1990	754	44	371	63	270	6	268	459	19	8
1991	638	55	235	78	267	3	309	292	19	18
1992	483	38	198	66	174	7	254	179	29	21
1993	397	34	171	61	120	11	234	108	26	29
1994	505	39	181	101	181	3	250	187	33	35
1995	531	33	196	97	198	7	255	208	33	35
1996	621	56	230	102	213	20	320	227	31	43
1997	753	75	235	136	277	30	452	215	53	33
1998	834	68	278	213	247	28	488	213	85	48
1999	1169	107	379	269	363	51	719	247	129	74
2000	1635	96	447	335	716	41	1066	361	175	33
2001	1653	80	499	381	627	66	1189	282	159	23
2002	1752	85	596	432	555	84	1352	258	131	11
2003	1728	70	638	423	473	124	1352	211	158	7
2004	2211	70	829	477	664	171	1681	315	206	9
2005	2725	88	1108	409	901	219	2130	399	179	17
2006	2775	87	1146	465	879	198	2175	412	171	17

Notes:
In-In: Japanese firms acquiring Japanese firms.
In-Out: Japanese firms acquiring foreign firms.
Out-In: Foreign firms acquiring Japanese firms.
Out-Out: Japanese subsidiaries abroad acquiring foreign firms or foreign firms acquiring Japanese subsidiaries abroad.

Source: Recof.

Accordingly, a heated discussion is now going on between the Ministry of Economy, Trade and Industry (METI), which stresses the usefulness of M&As for industrial re-structuring to deal with 'increasing global competition',[1] and the Fair Trade Commission (FTC), which stresses merger regulations as a competition policy. At the heart of this discussion is exactly the questions Mueller raised above, in particular, whether mergers are undertaken to improve efficiency (on which Mueller was doubtful), whether mergers do in fact improve efficiency (on which Mueller was again doubtful), and whether a merger policy should accept efficiency defense (on which Mueller seems in favor).

The present chapter aims to investigate these questions both theoretically and empirically.[2] In section 1, I will show that in a symmetric Cournot oligopoly without entry and without collusion, a merger is unprofitable unless it results in efficiency gains. In section 2, I offer three hypotheses to explain why firms nevertheless intend to merge. In section 3, I investigate theoretically a case in which such efficiency gains are attained to the effect of lowering the marginal cost of merger firms. If the efficiency gains are substantial, the profits of merger firms can increase. If these gains are even more substantial, it is also possible that the equilibrium price will go down after the merger, increasing consumers' surplus. In reality, however, few of the empirical studies I survey in section 4 confirmed that mergers enhanced efficiency. In section 5, I turn to the discussion of a managerial theory of the firm, in which managers are assumed to maximize the growth of the firm subject to valuation constraint. I will argue that this growth-maximization behavior can contribute to macroeconomic growth: importantly, however, two conditions have to be met; first, firms invest in R&D and, second, growth is pursued internally – not with M&As but with internal investment in physical and knowledge capital. Finally, in section 6, I will survey merger guidelines of the US, EU and Japan regarding efficiency defense and, as a conclusion, will argue in favor of a cautious attitude towards using efficiency gains as a defense for horizontal mergers.

1 MERGERS IN A COURNOT OLIGOPOLY MODEL

Let me begin by analyzing the effect of mergers theoretically using a simple Cournot oligopoly model.[3] Suppose that there are n firms before the merger, each producing q_i units of output. For simplicity, assume a linear model in which the marginal cost is constant and the inverse demand function is

$$p = a - bQ \tag{9.1}$$

where a and b are positive constants, p the price, and $Q = \sum_{i=1}^{n} q_i$. If the marginal cost c is common across firms, we have the following symmetric Cournot equilibrium:

$$q^0 = \frac{S}{n+1},\quad Q^0 = \frac{nS}{n+1},\quad p^0 = c + \frac{bS}{n+1},\quad \pi^0 = \frac{bS^2}{(n+1)^2} \tag{9.2}$$

where $S = (a-c)/b$, π is per-firm profit and superscript 0 indicates a pre-merger equilibrium. Figure 9.1 illustrates this equilibrium. The area marked as *CS* indicates consumers' surplus and the area marked as *PS* indicates producers' surplus, namely industry profits (assuming the absence of fixed costs) that equal $n \times \pi^0$.

Now suppose that two of the n firms merge to become a single firm. With everything else unchanged, we now have a $(n-1)$-firm symmetric Cournot equilibrium; hence, by replacing n in Equation (9.1) with $n-1$,

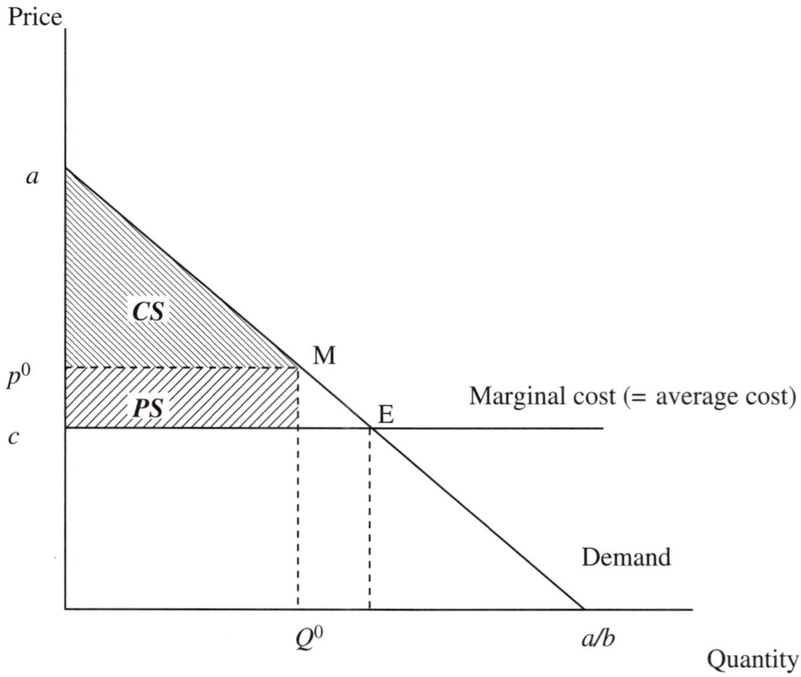

Figure 9.1 Pre-merger equilibrium

and denoting the post-merger equilibrium by superscript 1, we have the following equilibrium conditions:

$$q^1 = \frac{S}{n}, \quad Q^1 = \frac{(n+1)S}{n}, \quad p^1 = c + \frac{bS}{n}, \quad \pi^1 = \frac{bS^2}{n^2} \tag{9.3}$$

Obviously,

$$q^1 > q^0, \quad Q^1 < Q^0, \quad p^1 > p^0, \quad \pi^1 > \pi^0 \tag{9.4}$$

That is, the price rises, causing a decrease in consumers' surplus. The profit of a non-merger firm increases. In contrast, the profit of merger firms decreases. This proposition is confirmed because the combined profits of the two pre-merger firms, $2\pi^0$, is more than the post-merger profits π^1, provided $n \geq 3$, that is, unless the merged firm becomes a monopoly firm.

It is true that the profit rate on sales increases because the profit margin per unit of output, $p-c$, increases. However, with the decrease in output from $2q^0$ to q^1, the amount of profits decreases, reducing the total shareholder wealth. Thus, insofar as the firms maximize the shareholder wealth, there is no incentive for a merger.

This simple result may appear odd because, if the two former firms – now two divisions or two factories within a merged firm – act as if they were independent, they seemingly would be able to earn at least $2\pi^0$. This conjecture, however, ignores an important consequence of a merger to be called the internalization of business-stealing effects. Consider a simple case illustrated in Figure 9.2. At a crossroad, there are four stores competing against each other. When Store A lowers its price or intensifies its marketing effort, it can increase its revenue, first, by enlarging the market demand and, secondly and probably more effectively, stealing customers from competitors (B, C, and D), as shown by arrows in the figure. This is the *business-stealing effect*.[4]

Now suppose that A and B merge. A can still steal business from C and D, which is a gain to the merged firm. A can also steal business from B; however, A's gain is B's loss and, since they are now within the same firm, there is no gain at the firm level. That is, between A and B, the business-stealing effect is *internalized*, with no contribution to the firm as a whole. Consequently, A (and B) have a smaller incentive to lower the price or intensify the sales effort than C and D, and will gradually reduce their market share. In equilibrium, A and B combined must have the same market share as C or D, as shown by Equation (9.3) above. The profits of the merged firm are smaller than the pre-merger level, whereas those of non-merger firms are larger.

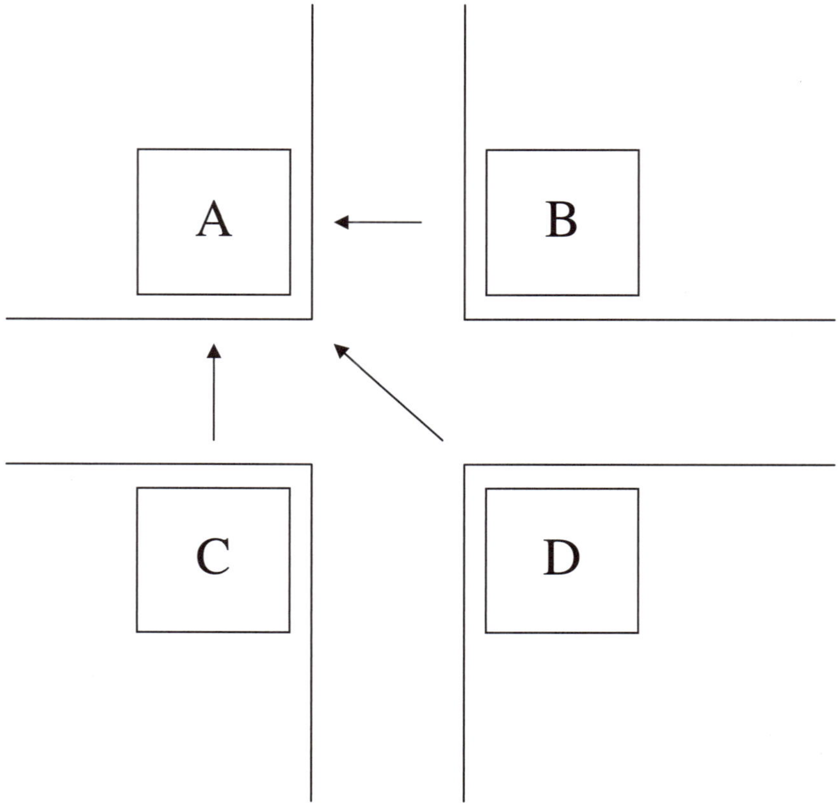

Figure 9.2 Business-stealing effect and the merger

2 WHY FIRMS MERGE: THREE HYPOTHESES

Then, why do firms merge? In my view, there are three explanations. The first is the *empire-building hypothesis* (Ravenscraft and Scherer, 1987). As discussed by Mueller in the quotation at the start of this chapter, managers may pursue goals other than shareholder wealth, such as size and growth, because these raise their power and prestige. They will satisfice, but not maximize, shareholder returns. This hypothesis is an application to mergers of the managerial theory of the firm and will be discussed in detail in section 5.

The second is the *collusion hypothesis*. With fewer firms, collusion tends to be easier to form, because the transaction cost of forming an agreement among firms is smaller. Collusion, whether it is explicit or implicit, tends to be more stable because collusive profits for each firm are larger and, hence, the gain from deviating from the collusive strategy (which equals the difference between the monopoly profits and the collusive profits) is smaller. Besides, such deviation is likely to be detected sooner. Hence, trigger strategies are more effective, resulting in an easier formation of collusion and more stability (Vives, 1999). It is for this reason that merger guidelines in the EU, Japan and USA explicitly state a need for investigating whether a proposed merger would increase the probability of an anti-competitive consequence of collusive behavior.[5]

If managers are profit-maximizers and collusion is absent, then, the merger must be explained with the *efficiency hypothesis*, namely, the hypothesis that the merger brings in an increased efficiency. This efficiency increase, one may argue, may come from economies of scale. However, if economies of scale are really substantial, natural monopoly must be the equilibrium outcome. The prevalence of an n-firm equilibrium prior to the merger is thus contradictory to the hypothesis of economies of scale.

Other reasons for efficiency enhancement are learning and complementary assets. Learning implies that the merger partners can learn better technologies and better management practices from each other. Complementary assets imply that the partners can combine their complementary assets to raise efficiency. In either explanation, it must be that the efficiency gain cannot be attained through market transactions or knowledge spillovers. The knowledge to be learned must be implicit because, if it is explicit like patented technology, then, the firm can learn from others through licensing or through knowledge spillover, with no need for merger. Similarly, if complementary assets can be purchased at markets, merger is unnecessary. Therefore, the knowledge and assets that are referred to in the learning and complementary-assets arguments must be those that are unsuitable for procurement, licensing, alliance or other market transactions. That is, they must be the types of knowledge and assets that necessitate too large a transaction cost to be transferred in markets so that internalization within a single firm is more efficient, as argued in the transaction-cost literature (Williamson, 1975, 1985). Following Nelson and Winter (1982), Chandler (1990), and Teece et al. (1997), 'capabilities' are probably a better word to describe what these knowledge and assets really imply.

In fact, almost in every major merger case, firms claim they expect a big efficiency increase and cost reduction from the proposed merger. Table 9.2 gives one such example. Japan Airlines (JAL) and Japan Air Systems (JAS) announced their merger plan in November 2001 and the merger took place in October 2002.[6] Table 9.2 is taken from their press release at

Table 9.2 Merger of Japan Airlines (JAL) and Japan Air Systems (JAS): benefits from the merger as claimed by JAL

Integration effects			
COST reduction (in FY2005)	73 billion yen	1. Facilities 2. Manpower	31 billion yen 24 billion yen
(In the first stage of integration we have to invest in information technology – about 20 billion yen a year)		3. Aircraft 4. Others	12 billion yen 6 billion yen
INVESTMENT (up to FY2005)	100 billion yen	1. Aircraft 2. Facilities	75 billion yen 25 billion yen
MANPOWER reductions (up to FY2005)	About 3000 staff	1. Main ground personnel 2. Associated companies 3. Others	840 Staff 2050 Staff
FLEET reductions	About 10 aircraft	Based on current fleet planning of both airlines.	
Group targets			
To establish stable and steady dividends at the earliest possible stage, by FY2005			
Consolidated return on earnings			15%
Repayment of interest-bearing debt			About 7 Years

Source: Japan Airlines Press Release, 29 January, 2002 (http://www.jal.com/en/press/2002/012902/012902.html).

the time of proposed merger, which shows that the firms claimed a cost reduction of 73 billion yen and a reduction of about 3000 employees. They also claimed they would be able to achieve a rate of return on equity (ROE) of 15 per cent by the fiscal year 2005, even though JAL and JAS combined was making a loss in 2001 with a ROE of −15.3 per cent.

Thus, efficiency improvement is a most commonly cited rationale for mergers. Whether such improvement is really significant will be questioned in section 4. Indeed, JAL's actual ROE in 2005 was −31.9 per cent, again negative and even worse than the pre-merger figure, contrary to their expectation at the time of merger.[7]

For the moment, however, let us assume that mergers do improve efficiency and discuss whether they would also improve social welfare.[8]

3 MERGERS WITH EFFICIENCY IMPROVEMENT

When a merger improves the firms' efficiency, it will decrease costs, increasing the social welfare, but it may also cause a price increase, decreasing the social welfare. Williamson (1968) discussed this 'welfare tradeoff' in his now classic paper. His analysis, however, assumed that all firms in the industry, that is, both merger firms and non-merger firms, would reduce their costs after the merger – an unlikely possibility because, if it were the case, merger firms would not be able to strengthen their relative position within the industry.

We therefore investigate the case in which only the merger firms are able to reduce their marginal cost by Δc. Other assumptions in the previous section still apply. Among the n firms, we assume that Firm 1 and Firm 2 merge and, after the merger, it is still called Firm 1. The constant marginal cost of the pre-merger firm is c while that of the post-merger Firm 1 is $c - \Delta c$. The marginal cost of all other firms, that is, Firm i with $i = 3, \ldots,$ n, remains at c after the merger. Then, a simple calculation shows that the post-merger Cournot equilibrium (shown with superscript 1) is as follows:

$$q_1^1 = \frac{1}{n}\left[S + (n-1)\frac{\Delta c}{b}\right] \tag{9.5}$$

$$q_1^1 = \frac{1}{n}\left[S - \frac{\Delta c}{b}\right] \quad i = 3, \ldots, n \tag{9.6}$$

$$Q^1 = q_1^1 + (n-2)q_i^1 = \frac{1}{n}\left[(n-1)S + \frac{\Delta c}{b}\right] \tag{9.7}$$

$$p^1 = a - bQ^1 = c + \frac{b}{n}\left[S - \frac{\Delta c}{b}\right] \tag{9.8}$$

and

$$\pi_1^1 = \frac{b}{n^2}\left[S + (n-1)\frac{\Delta c}{b}\right]^2 \tag{9.9}$$

Therefore, the merger changes the profits of merger firms as follows:

$$\pi_1^1 - 2\pi_1^0 = \frac{b}{n^2}\left[S + (n-1)\frac{\Delta c}{b}\right]^2 - \frac{2b}{(n+1)^2}S^2$$

$$= \frac{2(bS)^2}{b(n+1)^2} + \frac{(n-1)^2}{bn^2}\left(\Delta c - \frac{bS}{n+1}\right)\left[\left(\Delta c - \frac{bS}{n+1}\right) + \frac{4nbS}{(n-1)(n+1)}\right] \tag{9.10}$$

It can be shown that there is a level of Δc that equates the right-hand side (RHS) to zero. Let us denote it by $\Delta\hat{c}$. If $\Delta c > \Delta\hat{c}$, then RHS is positive; that is, if the merger firms can lower their marginal cost by more than $\Delta\hat{c}$, then, the merger is profitable to the firms. We know from the discussion in the previous section that the merger is unprofitable if there is no cost reduction. Also, from Equation (9.10), it is obvious that if $\Delta c = bS/(n+1)$, then RHS is positive. Hence, it must be that

$$0 < \Delta\hat{c} < \frac{bS}{n+1} \tag{9.11}$$

We can also calculate the price change by comparing equations (9.2) and (9.8):

$$p^1 - p^0 = \frac{1}{n}\left(bS - \Delta c\right) - \frac{1}{n+1}bS = \frac{1}{n}\left[\frac{bS}{n+1} - \Delta c\right] \tag{9.12}$$

Therefore,

$$p^1 < p^0 \quad \text{if and only if} \quad \Delta c > \frac{bS}{n+1} \tag{9.13}$$

That is, if the cost reduction is substantial, the equilibrium price may actually fall despite the increased market concentration. However, the required condition is strict. Recall from Equation (9.2) that

$$p^0 - c = \frac{bS}{n+1} \tag{9.14}$$

The left-hand side (LHS) is a pre-merger markup; hence, Equation (9.13) implies that the price decreases after the merger if and only if the cost reduction is more than the pre-merger markup. For instance, if the pre-merger price was 15 per cent above the marginal cost (which equals the average cost in the present model), the marginal cost has to decrease more than 15 per cent for the equilibrium price to go down after the merger. The condition for the profits of the merger firms to increase is less strict as Equation (9.11) shows.

When $\Delta c > bS/(n+1) = p^0 - c$, the price decreases and, consequently, consumers' surplus (*CS*) increases. The profit of the merger firm also increases by Equation (9.11). Even though the profits of non-merger firms can be shown to decrease under the same condition (that is, $\pi_i^1 < \pi^0$, for $i = 3, \ldots, n$), producers' surplus (*PS*), that is, total industry profits, can be shown to increase. Hence, the social welfare (*W*), namely, the sum of *CS* and *PS*, also increases; that is, $W^1 > W^0$. On the other hand, when $\Delta c = 0$, we know, from equations (9.2) and (9.3), the industry output decreases after the merger, implying that the social welfare should decrease; that is, $W^1 < W^0$. In between there must be a level of Δc, say Δc^*, that makes $W^1 = W^0$. This Δc^* can be found in the following manner.

Given the linear inverse demand function defined by Equation (9.1), consumers' surplus (*CS*) equals $(a-p)Q/2 = bQ^2/2$. Therefore, the social welfare before the merger is

$$W^0 = CS^0 + n\pi^0 = \frac{b}{2}\left(\frac{nS}{n+1}\right)^2 + nb\left(\frac{S}{n+1}\right)^2 = \frac{(n+2)nbS^2}{2(n+1)^2} \tag{9.15}$$

and, after the merger,

$$W^1 = CS^1 + \pi_1^1 + (n-2)\pi_i^1 \tag{9.16}$$

$$= \frac{b}{2n^2}\left[(n-1)S + \frac{\Delta c}{b}\right]^2 + \frac{b}{n^2}\left[S + (n-1)\frac{\Delta c}{b}\right]^2 + \frac{(n-2)b}{n^2}\left[S - \frac{\Delta c}{b}\right]^2$$

Therefore, Δc^* is the level of Δc that equates RHS of (9.15) to that of (9.16) and can be shown to satisfy the following condition (Odagiri, 2001):

$$0 < \Delta\hat{c} < \Delta c^* < \frac{bS}{n+1} = p^0 - c \tag{9.17}$$

Putting the results together, we can separate four cases as shown in Table 9.3. In Case (1), the cost reduction is so small that the profits of merger firms go down; hence, firms should have no incentive to merge (provided they maximize profits), which is good from the social viewpoint as well. In Case (4) by contrast, firms have a good incentive for mergers. This suits the consumers' and the society's interests, because the equilibrium price goes down. In Case (3), firms have an incentive for mergers because profits go up. Even though the price also goes up, hurting *CS*, the

Table 9.3 Changes in the price, consumers' surplus, profits of the merger firm, and social welfare according to the extent of reduction of merger firms' marginal cost (Δc)

Case No.: Condition:	(1) $0 \leq \Delta \hat{c} < \Delta \hat{c}$	(2) $\Delta c < \Delta c < \Delta c^*$	(3) $\Delta c^* < \Delta c < p^0 - c$	(4) $p^0 - c < \Delta c$
Price	⇑	⇑	⇑	⇓
Consumers' surplus (CS)	⇓	⇓	⇓	⇑
Profits of the merger firm	⇓	⇑	⇑	⇑
Social welfare ($CS+PS$)	⇓	⇓	⇑	⇑

Note: ⇑ indicates that the variable increases after the merger. ⇓ indicates that the variable decreases after the merger.

increase in PS outweighs the decrease in CS, increasing the total social welfare. In any of these cases, therefore, the firms' decision does not conflict with the social optimum, as long as the firms' objective is to maximize their profits and the society's goal is to maximize the social surplus, namely, the sum of CS and PS (that is, industry profits). In the remaining Case (2), however, such a conflict arises because the profits of the merger firms increase, giving them an incentive for merger, but the rising equilibrium price hurts CS, with the total effect of decreasing the social welfare.

Here is a case for government intervention. Even though the firms will have an incentive for merger, this merger is socially undesirable and should be prohibited. Note that my policy stand is weaker than a behavioral one that regards any price-raising merger as undesirable and hence will advocate that the mergers in Case (2) be also prohibited. My view agrees with Williamson's that, even if the price goes up after the merger, the social welfare may still increase. However, we have explicitly taken into consideration the fact that efficiency gains occur in merger firms only and not in other firms. Still, as in Williamson's, our theory suggests that the expected effect of the merger on price alone cannot and should not be the criterion for whether the merger should be accepted or banned.

If so, should the government be more open-minded about the efficiency arguments in evaluating merger proposals? To reach such a conclusion, however, there are substantial conditions that have to be cleared. To this topic, we now turn.

4 EMPIRICAL EVIDENCE ON MERGERS AND EFFICIENCY IN JAPAN

Do mergers really raise efficiency? Quite a few empirical studies have been made to test this question in the US as well as in other countries. Mueller (2003, Chapter 9) provides a convenient survey of these results. Also, see the collection of papers in Cosh and Hughes (1998) and Kaplan (2000), or a survey of European results in Röller et al. (2001). In my view, a general picture that emerged from these studies is twofold. First, most studies with stock-price data (or data on shareholder rate of return) suggest that the shareholders of target firms may gain (because of the premiums paid by bidders) but those of acquiring firms do not, with the total gain being positive or negative. Second, the majority of studies with accounting data found that, after the merger, profitability fails to increase, or even decreases, relative to the industrial average.

As for Japanese firms, Hase and I have compared the financial performance of 46 merger firms to that of control firms in the 1980s (Odagiri and Hase, 1989).[9] The result suggested no evidence that merger firms performed better. In fact, it rather suggested that the pre-merger profit superiority of merger firms disappeared after the merger. Similarly, in a study of 15 mergers during 1977–1995, Matsuoka (1997) found no post-merger improvement of relative profitability of merger firms.

More recently, three studies found similar evidence. Fukamachi and Makino (2004b) made event studies in which the impact on CAR (cumulative abnormal returns on stock) was studied of 10 mergers in 4 industries (petroleum products, carbon products, cement and corrugated cardboard) that occurred during 1984–1999. The result indicates negative impact in 5 out of 10 mergers and positive impact in 3 out of the 10, with the remaining 2 showing no impact. This suggests that, assuming that the stock market accurately predicts the firm's post-merger performance, mergers are more likely to cause efficiency to worsen rather than improving it.

Nagaoka (2005) used an unbalanced panel of 1988 firms and 19 years (1985–2003) and found no significant effect of mergers on profitability. For sales growth, he found that mergers tend to raise the growth rate by 2 percentage points generally. However, among equal mergers, they tended to lower the rate by 6.5 percentage points, where mergers are considered equal if the two merging firms consider themselves as equal partners, usually in terms of size and/or the composition of directors. Since many of the large-scale horizontal mergers, namely, those mergers that tend to be the target of close scrutiny by the competition policy authority, are equal mergers, the result implies that, on average, such mergers hurt the growth capability of the

Table 9.4 Changes in relative performance after mergers

	Profit rate change			Labor productivity change		
	mean	st. dev.	*t*-value	mean	st. dev.	*t*-value
1st year after merger	−0.0068	0.0294	−1.6989*	0.1115	0.6744	1.1807
2nd year after merger	−0.0046	0.0239	−1.4094	0.1112	0.7915	1.0032
3rd year after merger	−0.0053	0.0254	−1.5189	0.2148	1.0616	1.4451
Average of 1st, 2nd and 3rd years after the merger	−0.0056	0.0215	−1.8897*	0.1458	0.7097	1.4675

Notes:
(1) The profit rate change is the difference in relative profit rates between the designated post-merger year and one year before the merger, where the relative profit rate is calculated as the profit rate of the merger firm (sum of the profit rates of firms to merge, for the pre-merger figure) minus that of industrial average.
(2) The labor productivity change is the difference in relative labor productivity between the designated post-merger year and one year before the merger, where the relative labor productivity is calculated as the labor productivity of the merger firm (weighted average of labor productivities of firms to merge, for the pre-merger figure) divided by that of industrial average.
(3) * indicates 10% significance, two-tailed.
(4) Sample size: 53 for profit rate change and 51 for labor productivity change.

Source: Yoshida (2007).

firms. The effect of equal mergers on profitability was also negative but insignificant.

Finally, Yoshida (2007) studied 53 mergers during 1991–2002. These were the mergers of non-financial firms on which both of the pre-merger firms were listed in Stock Exchanges as well as the post-merger combined firm. Most of them were horizontal mergers. The results are summarized in Table 9.4. Relative profitability of merger firms tended to decline after the merger. Labor productivity tended to increase after the merger but only insignificantly. Since Nagaoka (2005) also found a decline in employment growth rate after equal mergers, both studies may suggest that firms make efforts to reduce employment after horizontal equal mergers. Such effort has not contributed to profitability increase, however.

Yoshida also found that the profitability change is an increasing function of the ratio of sales between the merger partners, with the sales of a larger firm in the numerator. That is, a merger of equal-sized firms tends to yield the poorest profitability change. This result agrees with Nagaoka's finding. A similar tendency was also found on labor productivity change.

All these results therefore found no evidence of mergers contributing to profit increase and some in fact found a negative contribution, that is, mergers hurting profitability. Therefore, among the four cases in Table 9.3, Case (1) seems to be most common in reality or, of course, the cost reduction (Δc) may have been actually negative, that is, mergers may have lowered efficiency.

In addition, Fukamachi and Makino (2004a) studied the impact of mergers on product prices, estimating price equations that also take into account the effects of factor prices and demand fluctuation. Except for the petroleum product industry, in which import is likely to be an effective competitive threat, they found that prices increased significantly after the mergers. This result suggests that, unless import threat is substantial, Case (4) is unlikely and is consistent with our speculation that Case (1) is the most common outcome.

Therefore, the welfare tradeoff shown in Case (3) in which consumers' surplus is hurt and yet the social surplus increases appears uncommon in reality. Actually, the puzzle is why firms do merge when the majority of mergers have failed. I have earlier argued two possibilities. One is the collusion hypothesis, which can be consistent with the finding of price increase after the merger. However, the lack of evidence that mergers increased profitability suggests that, even if collusion took place, its effect on profitability was probably mitigated by increased *in*efficiency. This explanation is rather in conflict with the lowered employment growth found by Nagaoka and increased labor productivity (though statistically insignificant) by Yoshida. Therefore, the collusion hypothesis does not appear to explain the majority of merger cases in Japan.

The second is the empire-building hypothesis or the managerial hypothesis. Let me discuss this issue further.

5 MERGERS AND ECONOMIC GROWTH: A MANAGERIAL PERSPECTIVE

Is the managerial behavior of firms, such as empire building and growth maximization, always bad for the economy? Are mergers based on such behavior bad for the economy? I would answer 'no' to the first question but 'yes' to the second.

In Odagiri (1981), I have offered a theory in which managerial behavior contributes to economic growth. Based on Marris's (1964) theory of 'managerial capitalism',[10] I assumed that managers intend to maximize the rate of growth of the firm, measured in terms of sales, assets or the number of employees. However, if the manager ignores the owners' interests excessively,

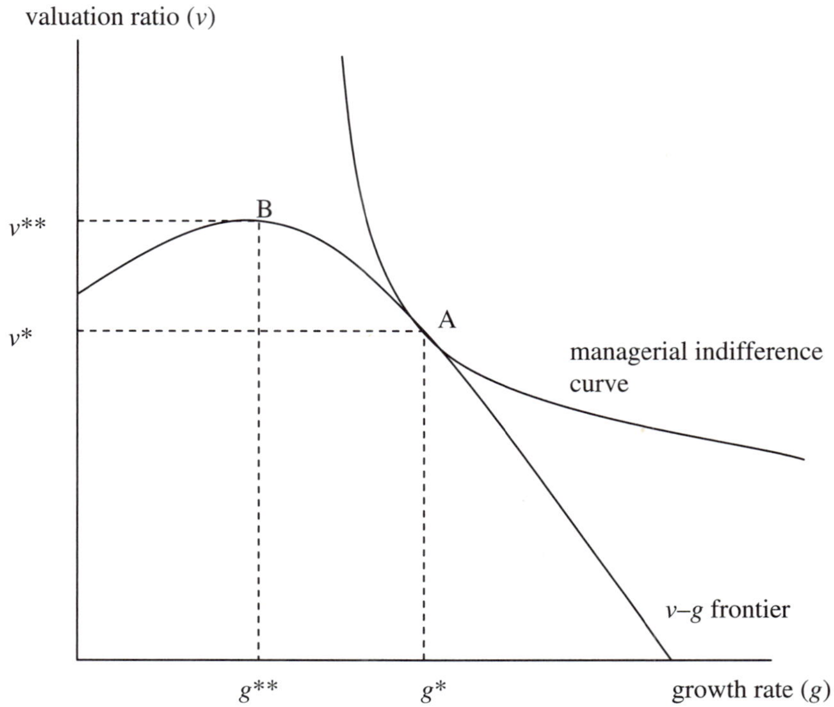

Source: Odagiri (1981), Chapters 2 and 3.

Figure 9.3 Growth-maximization behavior of managers

she (for he/she) will face an increasing threat of being taken over or being ousted from the firm. Figure 9.3 illustrates this theory.

In the vertical axis is the valuation ratio, also known as Tobin's q, which is the ratio of the market value of the firm (the sum of the market values of equity and debt) to total assets. The growth rate affects the valuation ratio in two ways. First, faster growth implies larger profits in the future, resulting in a larger net present value of profits and accordingly a larger valuation ratio. Second, faster growth necessitates a larger investment, hurting current profits and hence causing the valuation ratio to be smaller. As long as the firm aims at a modest growth rate, the first positive effect dominates. However, under an accelerating cost of investment, the second negative effect starts to dominate once the target growth rate exceeds a threshold rate, say, g^{**}. The curve depicted as the *v-g* frontier (abbreviated from the 'valuation-growth frontier') in Figure 9.3 shows this relationship. It is a frontier because, if the management is inefficient, the firm can realize only a point below the frontier, that is, a smaller valuation ratio *given* growth rate.

Clearly, g^{**} is the value-maximizing profit rate and is the optimal choice if the manager wants to (or is constrained to) maximize the shareholder wealth. By contrast, if she intends to maximize growth, subject to the anticipation that a lower valuation ratio will threaten her survival, she will have a downward-sloping indifference curve as shown in Figure 9.3 and her optimal choice has to be point A at which the two curves are tangent. The equilibrium growth rate, g^*, is of course larger than g^{**}.

Now suppose that there are two economies, the managers of one economy choosing g^{**} and those of the other choosing g^*. Then, is the latter's macroeconomic growth rate also higher than the former's? With a macroeconomic equilibrium model, Odagiri (1981) proved it is.

A crucial condition for this result to hold is that growth-maximizing firms invest in R&D to increase labor productivity because, otherwise, labor supply constraint binds the equilibrium economic growth rate to the rate of population growth. If they do invest more on such R&D, the rate of labor productivity increase becomes higher. In consequence, the rate of macro labor supply in efficiency units, that is, Harrod's (1939) natural rate of economic growth, also becomes higher, exceeding the rate of population growth. Also, the managers' choice of a higher growth rate results in higher investment in machines and plants, thereby increasing effective demand. In equilibrium, therefore, an economy with growth-maximizing firms achieves faster economic growth.

Of course, it is too simplistic to argue that the higher the rate of economic growth the better it is for the economy. However, since the socially optimal rate of economic growth is ambiguous, depending on the people's rate of time preference and intergenerational allocation of wealth among other factors, and also because economic growth is one of the key policy targets in most countries, I believe it is hard to argue that the managerial behavior of choosing a growth rate higher than the value-maximizing rate causes a socially 'excessive' rate of economic growth. This is why I said that the managerial behavior is not always bad for the economy. In fact, it does contribute to economic growth.

I emphasize that the theory critically depends on the assumption that the firm pursues growth through internal means, namely, expanding production capacity and making R&D investment. If it pursues growth externally through M&A, its expansion is offset by the contraction (or the disappearance, to be precise) of the acquired. Hence, it does not contribute to any increase in effective demand. In most cases, horizontal mergers are unlikely to lead to increased R&D investment. More usually, they tend to reduce

R&D investment, in order to eliminate duplicate R&D efforts. The efficiency hypothesis again comes to play a role, this time in relation to R&D. If they can increase R&D efficiency, they may be able to achieve the same or even better innovation with a smaller R&D investment. However, existing studies do not lend support to the hypothesis that mergers, particularly equal mergers and/or horizontal mergers, contributed to the firms' innovation performance: see Cassiman and Colombo (2006).

In conclusion, I believe that managerial behavior can contribute to economic growth and technological progress, but only if the managers' growth pursuit is made with internal means. Growth pursuit with M&A can be contributing only if it is accompanied by internal growth strategies as well. Such cases may arise in the case of non-horizontal M&As made as a means with which the firm intends to expand the scope of their capabilities and enter into new markets. Needless to say, such M&As are unlikely to increase market concentration and therefore are unlikely to be the subject of merger regulation.

6 IMPLICATIONS FOR MERGER REGULATION

In this chapter, using a Cournot oligopoly model, I discussed that a merger can be socially beneficial only if it contributes to a reduction in marginal cost through efficiency enhancement. If the cost reduction is substantial, for example, in the case of a symmetric pre-merger equilibrium with constant marginal cost, if the marginal cost is expected to be reduced by more than the pre-merger markup, the merger is not only profitable for the firms but also can result in a lower equilibrium price, thus benefiting consumers' surplus. This, I believe, is the case that competition policy authorities accept mergers on the ground of 'efficiency defense'. According to the US Merger Guidelines (1997, Section 4), 'To make the requisite determination, the Agency considers whether cognizable efficiencies likely would be sufficient to reverse the merger's potential to harm consumers in the relevant market, e.g., by preventing price increases in that market.'

The Guidelines of the European Commission (2004, Section VII) state that

> The relevant benchmark in assessing efficiency claims is that consumers will not be worse off as a result of the merger. For that purpose, efficiencies should be substantial and timely, and should, in principle, benefit consumers in those relevant markets where it is otherwise likely that competition concerns would occur.

And the Japanese Guidelines (2007, Part IV, 2(7)) state that

> When improvements of efficiency, through economy of scale, integration of production facilities, specialization of factories, reduction in transportation costs, efficiency in research and development, etc, is deemed likely to make the company group to take competitive conduct after the business combination, this factor will also be considered to determine the impact of the business combination on competition. Efficiency to be considered in this case is determined from three aspects: (i) efficiency should be improved as an effect specific to the business combination, (ii) improvement of the efficiency should be materialized, and (iii) improvement of the efficiency contributes to enhance users' welfare.

We have shown that, even if the equilibrium price goes up, there is a case (Case 3 in Table 9.3) in which the reduction of consumers' surplus is more than offset by the increase in profits, thereby raising the social surplus. The guidelines suggest that such a case is unlikely to be accepted in any of the three authorities.

I consider this attitude reasonable for two reasons. First, owing to the asymmetry of information between the merger firms and the competition policy authority, it is extremely difficult for the authority to verify the firms' claim of efficiency gains. This difficulty is particularly serious because firms tend to overemphasize the positive contribution of the merger not only to persuade the authority but also to impress the investors. I believe it essential that the authority regularly investigates the post-merger restructuring and performance and thereby accumulates their knowledge so as to increase the capability needed to make a better evaluation of the merger firms' claims.

Second, as shown in section 4, empirical evidence is not supportive of the claim that mergers tend to increase efficiency. Particularly, the effects on profitability were generally insignificant and some studies actually suggested that mergers worsen the firms' profitability. This tendency was particularly evident for equal mergers of a horizontal nature, exactly the type of mergers that tend to be the subject of close scrutiny by the competition policy authority.

Therefore, both theoretical and empirical evidence suggests that the efficiency defense of mergers should be accepted only in limited cases. Admittedly, the model I presented in this chapter is based on many assumptions. Among the most crucial is the absence of entry, including entry by imports. When the threat of entry by domestic or foreign firms is strong enough, the market price will not rise regardless of increased concentration after the merger, as the contestable market theory predicts. It is thus reasonable that the Guidelines give a detailed discussion on how the authority will examine the ease of importation, such as the transportation and distributional costs, supply capability of foreign firms, and substitutability to imported products; and the ease of entry, such as the extent of entry barriers, switching costs, and substitutability to related products.

As argued by Mueller, mergers are often pursued not to increase profitability but as a means for managers to pursue growth and size, namely, the empire-building theory. I have argued that growth-maximizing behavior of managers is not necessarily bad for the economy. It may in fact contribute to innovation and economic growth. But, for this to be the case, growth must be pursued internally and not through mergers and acquisitions.

I have once argued that such growth pursuit was indeed the key factor of post-war high economic growth in Japan (Odagiri, 1981, 1992). One may be tempted to call it *entrepreneurship*. Schumpeter (1942, p. 132) wrote that

> the function of entrepreneurs is to reform or revolutionize the pattern of production by exploiting an invention or, more generally, an untried technological possibility for producing a new commodity or producing an old one in a new way, by opening up a new source of supply of materials or a new outlet for products, by reorganizing an industry and so on. . . . To act with confidence beyond the range of familiar beacons and to overcome that resistance requires aptitudes that are present in only a small fraction of the population and that define the entrepreneurial type as well as the entrepreneurial function

Schumpeter, I trust, has never assumed that these entrepreneurs have profit maximization in mind. Probably, he thought of the type of people who would challenge innovation beyond the extent profit calculation would warrant. Such entrepreneurship was the key engine of Japan's industrialization both before and after the Second World War (Odagiri and Goto, 1996).

That mergers were relatively few during the high growth era must have been closely related to such entrepreneurship, that is, the managers' pursuit of growth through innovation and internal expansion, despite the high risk and difficult challenges they had to face in order to introduce untried technologies, adapt them to their environment, develop them further, and create markets for them. From this viewpoint, the increasing cases of mergers these days are not quite welcome, even though I accept that many of them, mostly non-horizontal ones, are made as a part of the managers' efforts to reorganize their businesses, streamline the operation, or expand into new business fields.

The attempted (and failed) takeover case of Oji Paper, the market leader, against Hokuetsu Paper in the summer of 2006 is a case in point. From Oji's statement (3 July, 2006), it is apparent that their major aim was to acquire Hokuetsu's technologically superior plant and use it as Oji's central production site, by scrapping Oji's old and inefficient plants. According to a press report (*Nihon Keizai Shimbun*, 5 August, 2006), Oji was afraid that Hokuetsu's construction of this superior plant would erode the market price and Hokuetsu's president claimed that he was under pressure from Oji to abandon the construction plan.

Not only would such a takeover have been against market competition. It might have also failed to promote innovation and economic growth. Though it may be too far-fetched, I am inclined to think that an increasing preference of M&A over own innovation and internal investment has been the real cause of Japan's problems since 1990.

NOTES

* An earlier version of this chapter was presented at the International Symposium on 'M&A and Competition Policy', Competition Policy Research Center, Fair Trade Commission, 23 March, 2007, Tokyo. This study was partly supported by the 21st Century COE Program on 'Normative Evaluation and Social Choice of Contemporary Economic Systems',1 Hitotsubashi University.

1. A report by METI's research group in 2006 (in Japanese only, http://www.meti.go.jp/press/20060519004/kyousouken-houkokusho-set.pdf) is subtitled 'Towards an improved predictability of M&A examinations under global competition' (my translation).
2. Hereafter, I will simply use the word 'merger' to indicate all types of M&A. Japan's FTC uses the word 'business combinations' to refer to them.
3. A more general analysis of mergers in Cournot models was given by Farrell and Shapiro (1990).
4. Mankiw and Whinston (1986) discussed 'business-stealing effects' to explain why, in a homogeneous oligopoly market, socially excessive entry tends to take place provided there are fixed costs.
5. We will discuss merger guidelines later in more detail.
6. To be precise, the two companies jointly established a holding company (Japan Airlines System) and both JAL and JAS were acquired by this holding company.
7. I should add that All Nippon Airways (ANA), the main and virtually only rival to JAL, earned a positive ROE of 7.7 per cent in 2005, to suggest that JAL's negative ROE was not entirely due to the factors common to the industry.
8. In the case of hostile takeovers, a *bargain hypothesis* is also proposed, suggesting that the share of the target firm is under-valued by the stock market and, hence, the acquisition appears to be a bargain to the acquirer. Since hostile takeovers have been rare in Japan (until a few years ago), we will not pursue this possibility.
9. The major part of this study is reproduced in Odagiri (1992), Chapter 5.
10. This now classic Marris book was reproduced, with editing and addition, as Marris (1998), in which he discussed Odagiri's theory as an important extension of the Marris model. For a survey of related theories, see Marris and Mueller (1980).

REFERENCES

Cassiman, Bruno and Massimo G. Colombo (2006), *Mergers & Acquisitions: The Innovation Impact*, Cheltenham, UK and Northampton, MA, USA: Edward Elgar.

Chandler, Alfred D., Jr (1990), *Scale and Scope*, Cambridge, MA: Harvard University Press.

Cosh, Andy and Alan Hughes (1998), *Takeovers*, 3 volumes, Aldershot: Ashgate Publishing Co.

Farrell, J. and C. Shapiro (1990), 'Horizontal mergers: an equilibrium analysis', *American Economic Review*, **80**, 107–26.

Fukamachi, Masanori and Mai Makino (2004a), 'Kigyo ketsugo ni yoru kakaku henka ni kansuru jissho kenkyu' ('Empirical analysis on the price effects of mergers and acquisitions'), CPRC Discussion Paper, CPDP-11-J, Competition Policy Research Center, Fair Trade Commission.

Fukamachi, Masanori and Mai Makino (2004b), 'Kigyo ketsugo ni kansuru kabuka event bunseki' ('Event studies on the competitive effects of mergers and acquisitions'), CPRC Discussion Paper, CPDP-12-J, Competition Policy Research Center, Fair Trade Commission.

Harrod, R.F. (1939), 'An essay in dynamic theory', *The Economic Journal*, **49**, 14–33.

Kaplan, Steven N. (ed.) (2000), *Mergers and Productivity*, Chicago: The University of Chicago Press.

Mankiw, N.G. and M.D. Whinston (1986), 'Free entry and social inefficiency', *Rand Journal of Economics*, **17**, 48–59.

Marris, Robin L. (1964), *The Economic Theory of 'Managerial' Capitalism*, London: Macmillan.

Marris, Robin L. (1998), *Managerial Capitalism in Retrospect*, London: Macmillan.

Marris, R.L. and D.C. Mueller (1980), 'The corporation, competition, and the invisible hand', *Journal of Economic Literature*, **18**, 32–63.

Matsuoka, Kenji (1997), 'Gappei, kigyo-ketsugo kisei' ('Regulations on mergers and business combinations'), in *Nihon no Dokusen Kinshi Seisaku 50-Nen ni Kansuru Chousa Kenkyu*, an unpublished report to Fair Trade Commission, pp. 72–90.

Mueller, Dennis C. (1986), 'United States' antitrust: at the crossroads', in H.W. de Jong and W. G. Shepherd (eds), *Mainstreams in Industrial Organization*, Book II, Dordrecht: Kluwer, pp. 215–41.

Mueller, D.C. (1989), 'Mergers: causes, effects and policies', *International Journal of Industrial Organization*, **7**, 1–10.

Mueller, Dennis C. (2003), *The Corporation*, London: Routledge.

Nagaoka, Sadao (2005), 'Gappei baishu wa kigyo seicho wo unagasuka?' ('Do mergers and acquisitions promote corporate growth?'), *Hitotsubashi Business Review*, **53**(2), 32–44.

Nelson, Richard R. and Sidney G. Winter (1982), *An Evolutionary Theory of Economic Change*, Cambridge, MA: Harvard University Press.

Odagiri, Hiroyuki (1981), *The Theory of Growth in a Corporate Economy*, Cambridge: Cambridge University Press.

Odagiri, Hiroyuki (1992), *Growth through Competition, Competition through Growth*, Oxford: Oxford University Press.

Odagiri, Hiroyuki (2001), *Atarashii Sangyo Soshikiron* (*Modern Industrial Organization*), Tokyo: Yuhikaku.

Odagiri, Hiroyuki and Akira Goto (1996), *Technology and Industrial Development in Japan*, Oxford: Oxford University Press.

Odagiri, H. and T. Hase (1989), 'Are mergers and acquisitions going to be popular in Japan too? An empirical study', *International Journal of Industrial Organization*, **7**, 49–72.

Ravenscraft, David J. and F.M. Scherer (1987), *Mergers, Sell-Offs, and Economic Efficiency*, Washington, DC: The Brookings Institution.

Röller, L.-H., J. Stennek and F. Verboven (2001), 'Efficiency gains from mergers', *European Economy*, no. 5, 31–127.

Schumpeter, Joseph A. (1942), *Capitalism, Socialism, and Democracy*, New York: Harper and Row.

Teece, D.J., G. Pisano and A. Shuen (1997), 'Dynamic capabilities and strategic management', *Strategic Management Journal*, **18**, 509–33.
Vives, Xavier (1999), *Oligopoly Pricing*, Cambridge, MA: The MIT Press.
Williamson, O.E. (1968), 'Economies as an antitrust defense: the welfare tradeoffs', *American Economic Review*, **58**, 18–36.
Williamson, Oliver E. (1975), *Markets and Hierarchy*, New York: Free Press.
Williamson, Oliver E. (1985), *The Economic Institutions of Capitalism*, New York: Free Press.
Yoshida, Kenji (2007), 'Kigyo gappei ni okeru kigyo bunka to performance' ('Corporate culture and performance in mergers'), unpublished Bachelor's thesis, Department of Economics, Hitotsubashi University.

10. UK corporate governance and takeover performance

Andy Cosh, Paul Guest and Alan Hughes

This chapter addresses the changing nature of corporate governance in the United Kingdom over recent decades and examines whether these changes have had an impact on the UK market for corporate control. The disappointing outcomes for acquiring company shareholders in the majority of corporate acquisitions, public discontent with some pay deals for top executives and some high-profile corporate scandals led in the early 1990s to a call for governance reform. The scrutiny of governance in UK companies has intensified since the publication of the Cadbury Report in 1992 and has resulted in calls for changes in the size, composition and role of boards of directors, in the role of institutional shareholders, the remuneration and appointment of executives, and in legal and accounting regulations. We review the background to these changes and the consequences of the changes since 1990 for governance structures. Finally, we examine whether these changes have affected takeover performance in recent years. Our analysis is specific to the institutional circumstances of the UK although we refer where appropriate to takeover studies in other countries.

MERGER OUTCOMES AND MANAGERIALISM

In their seminal book on the emerging modern corporation, Berle and Means demonstrated the growing separation of ownership from control with an increasing dispersion of shareholdings along with an increasing concentration of economic power. Taken together, these forces required us to question the assumption that firms would be run in the interests of their shareholders since product market competition was inadequate to limit management discretion, and dispersed shareholdings limited cohesive shareholder control (Berle and Means, 1932).

In the late 1950s and early 1960s various authors developed alternative theories of the firm, taking account of the separation of ownership from control. These models found their most developed form in the Marris model of managerial capitalism (Marris, 1964). This steady-state growth model posited a tradeoff between profit and growth maximization and explored alternative growth strategies for the firm, balancing the growth of demand with the financing of growth, and with higher growth of demand being achieved through diversification. This model gave a central role to takeovers as the ultimate constraint on excessive growth ambitions by managers as shareholder dissatisfaction would lead to falling share prices and the emergence of underpriced companies ripe for takeover. This aspect of Marris' work was echoed by Manne (1965) in his eloquent exposition of the market for corporate control.

In an important development Mueller (1969) recognized the dual role played by merger activity in a managerial world. Whilst acquisitions might be the principal method through which the abuse of managerial control might be limited, they also provided the mechanism by which managerial growth ambitions could be met, and this was most likely to be found in the case of the conglomerate merger.

> The management intent upon maximising growth will tend to ignore, or at least heavily discount, investment opportunities outside the firm, since these will not contribute to the internal expansion of the firm. . . . A growth-maximising management will then be assumed to calculate the present value of an investment opportunity using a lower discount rate than a stock-holder-welfare-maximiser would. As before, this will result in greater investment and lower dividends for the growth maximiser. (Mueller, 1969, pp. 647–8)

This line of argument clearly anticipated and is essentially the same as in the free cash flow theory of takeovers (Jensen, 1986), which explained why takeover outcomes were disappointing, particularly when they involved diversification.

These developments in the theory of the firm spawned a large number of studies examining the outcomes of merger activity in the period up to the early 1980s. It is not the purpose of this chapter to review this early evidence in depth since that has been done elsewhere (for example, Mueller, 1980; Jensen and Ruback, 1983; Magenheim and Mueller, 1988; Hughes, 1993; Gugler et al., 2003; Tuch and O'Sullivan, 2007). Instead, we will highlight some of the key points, particularly in relation to UK studies.

The first UK study of takeovers to formally address the implications for takeovers of managerial models of the firm was by Singh (1971). This study particularly focused on the natural selection role for the market for corporate control by examining the characteristics of the acquirer and the acquired. The findings cast some doubt on the workings of the market for corporate control and gave support to managerial models.

> To sum up, the take-over mechanism on the stock market, although it provides a measure of discipline for small firms with below average profitability, does not seem to meet the motivational requirements of the orthodox theory of the firm as far as the large firms are concerned. The evidence suggests that these firms are not compelled to maximise or to vigorously pursue profits in order to reduce the danger of takeover, since they can in principle achieve this object by becoming bigger without increasing the rate of profit. . . . The results of this study suggest that the fear of takeover, rather than being a constraint on managerial discretion, may also encourage them in the same direction. (Singh, 1971, p. 144)

Whilst Singh did examine the performance of the firm post-takeover, this aspect was modestly explored in comparison with the mass of studies that followed. Merger activity since the period analysed by Singh is shown in Figure 10.1. Early studies of these years for the UK examined accounting measures as a means of judging merger success (for example, Meeks, 1977; Cosh et al., 1980). These studies examined the performance of the acquirer post-merger with the weighted average performance of the acquirer and the acquired before the event. This requires a counterfactual assumption about how the acquirer and acquired would have performed in the post-merger period had they remained independent. This assumption could be drawn from the average performance of the industry, but this does not allow for individual firm characteristics, so it is more common today to use a control group of firms matched to the event firms by certain criteria. Despite the fact that accounting measures are capable of being manipulated in ways that distort the true picture and that a variety of alternative counterfactual assumptions can be made about what would have happened in the absence of merger, the findings of studies of UK takeovers up to and including the 1980s (for example, Cosh et al., 1989; Dickerson et al., 1997) generally supported the view that profitability did not improve and generally fell following a takeover.

Accounting studies were rapidly submerged by a flood of mainly US studies based on share prices, initially of their behaviour surrounding the announcement of the takeover, but subsequently over an extended event window of a few years. These event studies face the same sort of problems in tackling the counterfactual and the sophistication of the methods has increased substantially in recent years (for example, Jaffe, 1974; Mandelker, 1974; Brown and Warner, 1985; Barber and Lyon, 1997; Fama, 1998; Lyon et al., 1999). Apart from some early studies (Asquith et al., 1983; Franks and Harris, 1989), the findings concerning announcement returns for both the UK and the US are fairly consistent in showing insignificant or negative returns to acquirer shareholders and positive gains to the shareholders of the acquired. The picture becomes even more bleak if we extend the event window to a few years following the acquisition. UK studies (for example, Limmack, 1991; Gregory, 1997) provided convincing evidence of significantly negative returns on average over this period for acquirer shareholders.

In summary, the evidence available at the time of the Cadbury Report in 1992 and its successors was that the selection mechanism in the market for corporate control was highly imperfect, and that takeovers were not returning performance gains either in terms of profitability, or for their shareholders. Therefore, the conclusion of this brief review is that we are faced with a dilemma. The failure of owners to directly monitor and control managers in order to ensure that value-maximizing decisions are taken led to a reliance on the market for corporate control to discipline management. However, the evidence briefly reviewed above suggests that:

- the market for corporate control is an imperfect disciplinarian; and
- an active takeover market provides the means for greater non-value-maximizing behaviour by management, particularly amongst the largest companies.

In other words, rather than providing a check on managerial discretion, the market for corporate control was a means of exploiting it. In these circumstances the emphasis turns back on shareholders to develop governance mechanisms, to elect boards of directors, and design, monitor and enforce incentives for management as the means of ensuring that companies are run in their interests.

THE REGULATION OF CORPORATE GOVERNANCE

The concerns about the apparent failure of corporate acquisitions to deliver the promised returns to shareholders were heightened by high-profile cases of high rewards to top management that were not associated with exceptional corporate performance. These were reinforced by a series of corporate collapses and scandals in the 1980s and 1990s in the UK and abroad, and this meant that corporate governance came under increasing scrutiny. The principal concerns were about the effectiveness of the board of directors as guardians of the shareholders' interests and the transparency of company accounts and reports. The City of London has a long history of self-regulation and so the first move took the form of the Cadbury Committee set up in May 1991 by the Financial Reporting Council, the London Stock Exchange and the accountancy profession to address the financial aspects of corporate governance.

a) number of domestic and overseas acquisitions by UK acquirers 1969–2006

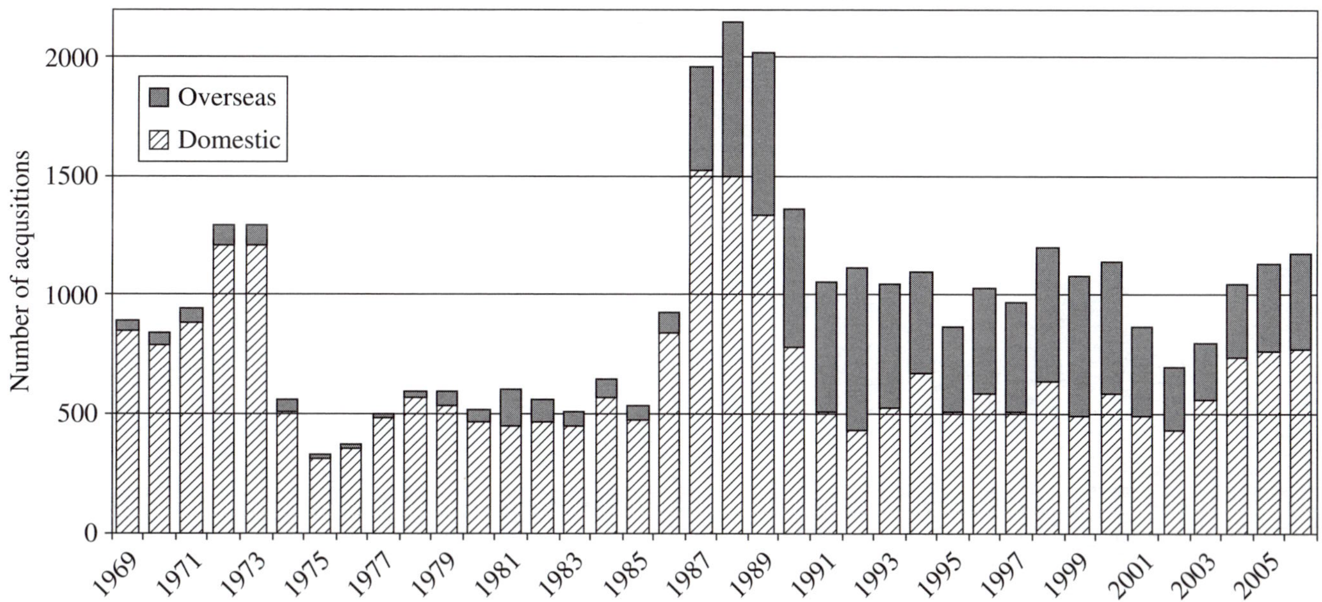

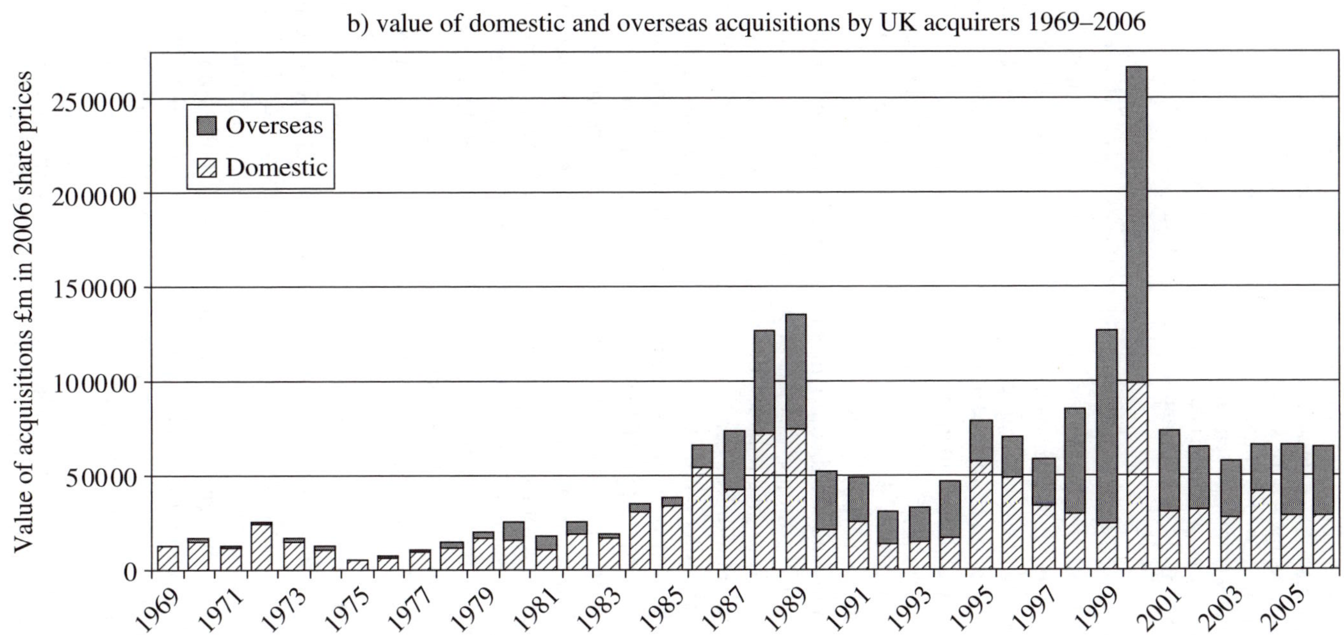

Figure 10.1 Merger activity in the United Kingdom, 1969–2006

> Its sponsors were concerned at the perceived low level of confidence both in financial reporting and in the ability of auditors to provide the safeguards which the users of company reports sought and expected. The underlying factors were seen as the looseness of accounting standards, the absence of a clear framework for ensuring that directors kept under review the controls in their business, and competitive pressures both on companies and on auditors which made it difficult for auditors to stand up to demanding boards. (Cadbury, 1992, 2.1)

The distinguished Committee established the principles that have been reinforced and securely established in the years since it was published. The governing principles are transparency in reporting and a code of practice based on 'comply or explain' rather than legislation. The report concerned the effective operation of the board of directors, the separation of the roles of chief executive and Chairman, the role of non-executives, board committees and the audit process. At the heart of the Committee's recommendations was a Code of Best Practice designed to achieve the necessary high standards of corporate governance behaviour. The London Stock Exchange required all listed companies registered in the United Kingdom, as a continuing obligation of listing, to state whether they were complying with the Code and to give reasons for any areas of non-compliance.

The recommendations of the Cadbury Committee have been refined and augmented in the intervening years. Continuing concerns about top executive remuneration led to the establishment in 1995 of the Greenbury Committee on the initiative of the CBI. Its purpose was 'to identify good practice in determining Directors' remuneration and prepare a Code of such practice'. It recommended that pay structures should be set to align the interests of directors and shareholders, reinforced the independence of remuneration committees and introduced significant reporting requirements. The guidelines have been reinforced subsequently by reports from the Association of British Insurers (ABI, 2006) and others.

The Financial Reporting Council in turn set up the Hampel Committee to review the findings and outcomes from the Cadbury and Greenbury Reports (Greenbury, 1995; Hampel, 1997). The result was the Combined Code on Corporate Governance published in 1998. In response to this Code, the accounting body, the ICAEW, commissioned the Turnbull Report, which examined internal control capabilities and mechanisms (and the guidance that emerged was later revised in 2005). Following the Enron and WorldCom scandals, the Higgs Report of 2003 led to the updating of the Combined Code. Soft regulation and shareholder performance remained at the heart of the reforms.

> The Combined Code and its philosophy of 'comply or explain' is being increasingly emulated outside the UK. It offers flexibility and intelligent discretion and

> allows for the valid exception to the sound rule. The brittleness and rigidity of legislation cannot dictate the behaviour, or foster the trust, I believe is fundamental to the effective unitary board and to superior corporate performance. (Higgs, 2003, p. 3)

> Whereas in the US most governance discussion has focused on corporate malpractice, in the UK sharp loss of shareholder value is more common than fraud or corporate collapse. The fall in stockmarkets in the period 2000–2002 has thrown up some stark examples. In recent cases of corporate under-performance in the UK, the role of the board and of non-executive directors in particular, has understandably been called into question. (Higgs, 2003, p. 16)

The revised Code 'aimed principally to advance and reflect best practice through revisions to the code' and 'to focus on the behaviours and relationships, and the need for the best people, which are essential for an effective board'. To this end it gave increased attention to non-executive directors and their recruitment, role and independence.

Throughout this fifteen-year period of development and refinement of the Code, the role of institutional shareholders has been tackled quite modestly in each of the reports. Cadbury and the subsequent reports and versions of the Code have made few meaningful suggestions in this area – mainly consisting of improvements to consultation and information flow. This may be due in part to the orientation of the Code towards aspects of corporate behaviour it is able to influence directly, but it is also due to the requirement to treat all shareholders equally. This 'equity' requirement has left these shareholders, who collectively hold over half the shares, with an often indirect influence and involvement with the company. On the other hand there is some evidence that the monitoring role of institutional investors in relation to the implementation of the Code has increased between the publication of the first guidelines by the Institutional Shareholders' Committee in 1991 and their revisions (ISC, 2007).

The current version of the Combined Code on Corporate Governance (FRC, 2006) has the following main provisions.

The Role and Composition of the Board

- A single board of appropriate size with members collectively responsible for leading the company and setting its values and standards and taking decisions in the interests of the company.
- A clear division of responsibilities for running the board and running the company with a separate chairman and chief executive.
- A balance of executive and independent non-executive directors – for larger companies at least 50 per cent of the board members should

be independent non-executive directors; smaller companies should have at least two independent directors.

- Formal, rigorous and transparent procedures for appointing directors, with all appointments and re-appointments to be ratified by shareholders.
- Regular evaluation of the effectiveness of the board and its committees.

Remuneration

- Formal and transparent procedures for setting executive remuneration, including a remuneration committee made up of independent directors and a vote for shareholders on new long-term incentive schemes.
- Levels of remuneration sufficient to attract, retain and motivate directors of quality.
- A significant proportion of remuneration to be linked to performance.

Accountability and Audit

- The board is responsible for presenting a balanced assessment of the company's position (including through the accounts), and maintaining a sound system of internal control.
- Formal and transparent procedures for carrying out these responsibilities, including an audit committee made up of independent directors and with the necessary experience.

Relations with Shareholders

- The board must maintain contact with shareholders to understand their opinions and concerns.
- Separate resolutions on all substantial issues at general meetings.

The 2006 Code also imposes obligations on institutional shareholders as follows:

- Institutional shareholders should enter into a dialogue with companies.
- Institutional shareholders have a responsibility to make a considered use of their votes.

Table 10.1 Board size and composition, 1980–2006 (large UK companies)

	1980/81	1995/96	2005/06
All directors	14	13	11
Executive directors	9	6	5
Non-executive directors	5	6	6
Proportion of non-executives	0.36	0.50	0.60

Source: 1980/81 and 1995/96 are drawn from Cosh and Hughes (1997a). 2005/06 are from the authors' calculations for the top 100 UK companies.

The key questions are whether companies have responded to these changing requirements demanded by successive Codes and, more importantly, whether this has brought the greater alignment of performance with shareholder interests that was sought.

THE IMPACT ON GOVERNANCE

The first question to be tackled is whether fifteen years of soft regulation has brought significant changes in corporate governance practice and structure in the UK. We will address this question by examining in turn: the role of non-executive directors; the separation of the roles of chief executive and chairman; the level and structure of executive remuneration; and the power and role of institutional investors.

Non-executive Directors

There is overwhelming evidence that the proportion of non-executive directors has increased substantially in the UK in the past two decades. Table 10.1 shows for a sample of the largest UK companies that the proportion of non-executive directors on the board rose from an average of about one-third in 1980/81 to one-half in 1995/96. By 2006, non-executive directors accounted for 60 per cent of the board on average in the top 100 UK-listed companies. Guest (2008b) shows for a much larger sample of UK-listed firms that it is not only amongst the largest that this has occurred. Figure 10.2 shows that much the same process has been under way for the largest 1500 companies, with the proportion of non-executives rising from 35 per cent in the early 1980s to 55 per cent in 2002 – a remarkably similar level as well as pattern to that found for the largest companies. Whilst this growth of the proportion of non-executive towards the typical proportion found in US companies (Cosh and Hughes, 1987) is undoubtedly associated with the reforms discussed in

a) board size

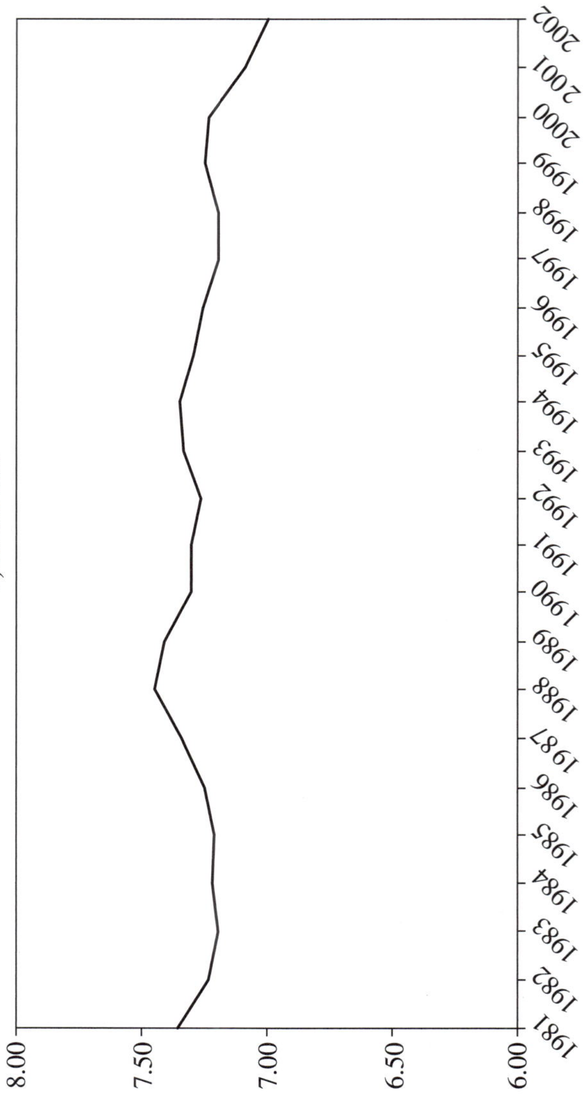

8.00
7.50
7.00
6.50
6.00
1981
1982
1983
1984
1985
1986
1987
1988
1989
1990
1991
1992
1993
1994
1995
1996
1997
1998
1999
2000
2001
2002

b) % outsiders

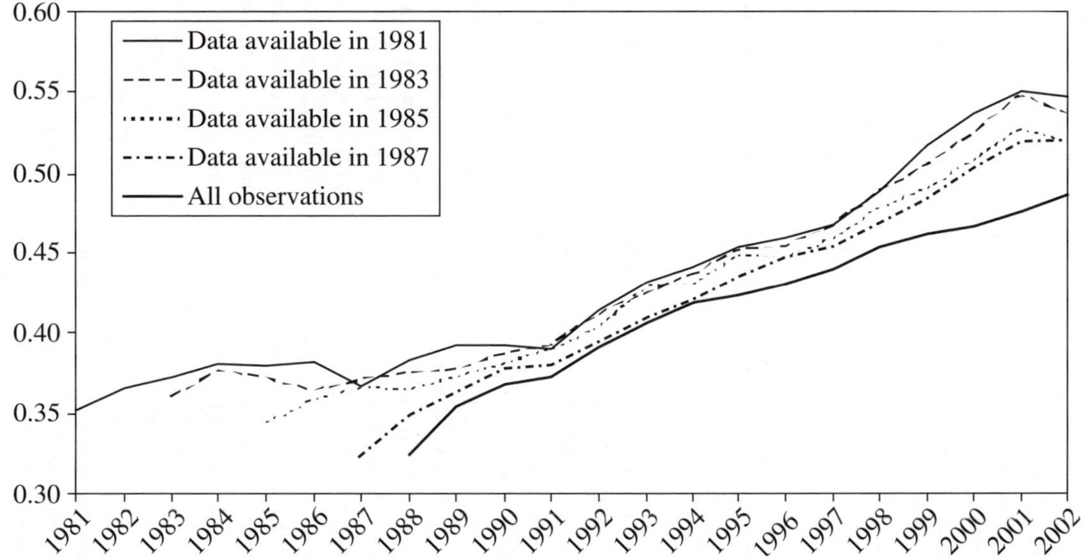

Notes: Figures a) and b) report the trends in average board size and the proportion of outsiders respectively for UK firms during 1981–2002. The bold line in each figure incorporates all firm year observations. For Figure b) this is estimated from 1988 onwards only because of changing sample composition prior to this date. For this figure earlier trends are exhibited by the fainter lines, which represent samples available in earlier years (1981, 1983, 1985 and 1987) for which new firms are not added in subsequent years.

Source: Guest (2008b).

Figure 10.2 Trends in board structure, 1981–2002

Table 10.2 Independence of non-executive directors (percentage distribution – giant UK companies)

	1981	1996
Past CEO / executive director of this company	15	10
CEO / executive director of other Times 1000	26	28
Former CEO / executive director of Times 1000	10	14
Executive director of other non-financial company	4	3
Executive director of financial company	20	13
Former civil servant or politician	12	12
Overseas	6	14
Other	7	6
	100%	100%
% 'Insider' non-executives (first four rows)	55%	55%

Source: Cosh and Hughes (1997a).

the previous section, Figure 10.2 shows that the change was already happening prior to the Cadbury Report.

Another feature of changes in board structure is the decline in the average board size shown for the largest companies in Table 10.1. This finding is supported for the larger sample that includes companies from across a wider size range. Figure 10.2 shows that this decline started in the late 1980s and is more directly associated with the intense debate about the appropriate size and composition of boards engendered by the various reports. It would appear that somewhat smaller boards could be viewed as more cohesive and effective. An alternative view is that the shortage of top quality candidates for non-executive directorships has forced board size decline as a means of raising the proportion of non-executive directors.

In some writings the terms 'non-executive directors' and 'independent directors' are used interchangeably, but this is not necessarily the case. Table 10.2 examines the background of non-executive directors amongst giant UK companies in 1981 and 1996. It shows that over half of the non-executive directors of these companies are current, or former, executive directors of the company, or of other similar companies; and there is no sign of any change in this proportion in the 1980s and 1990s. Table 10.3 examines the other directorships held by various types of directors and reinforces the picture of interlocking directorships. Current executive directors typically hold one other directorship within the Times 1000 companies, but non-executives hold more. Overall, there is a decline in the number of these outside directorships held between 1981 and 1996. This may have declined

Table 10.3 Number of outside directorships (median numbers – giant UK companies)

	1981	1996
Executive		
CEO chair	2.3	1.2
CEO not chair	0.9	1.1
Other executive chair	4.8	2.0
Other executive	0.6	0.5
Non-executive		
Past CEO / executive director of this company	2.7	2.6
CEO / executive director of other Times 1000	3.3	2.1
Former CEO / executive director of Times 1000	4.2	2.9
Executive director of other non-financial company	3.9	2.2
Executive director of financial company	4.1	2.2
Other	2.4	2.4
Summary		
All CEO	1.9	1.2
All executive directors	0.9	0.6
All non-executive directors	3.3	2.4

Source: Cosh and Hughes (1997a).

further since that time. Higgs (2003) reports that of the 3908 non-executive directors of UK-listed companies in 2002, 80 per cent hold only one directorship and only 7 per cent hold both executive and non-executive directorships in UK-listed companies. One would expect a higher proportion of the latter amongst the largest companies, but the decline in interlocking directorships does appear to have continued over the period 1996–2002.

The above concerns resulted in great emphasis being placed on the importance of the independence of non-executive directors in the Higgs Report published in 2003. It identified the circumstances in which a non-executive director's independence would be called into question; specifically, where the director:

- is a former employee of the company or group until five years after employment (or any other material connection) has ended;
- has, or has had within the last three years, a material business relationship with the company either directly, or as a partner, shareholder, director or senior employee of a body that has such a relationship with the company;

- has received or receives additional remuneration from the company apart from a director's fee, participates in the company's share option or a performance-related pay scheme, or is a member of the company's pension scheme;
- has close family ties with any of the company's advisers, directors or senior employees;
- holds cross-directorships or has significant links with other directors through involvement in other companies or bodies;
- represents a significant shareholder; or
- has served on the board for more than ten years.

It is too early to assess the impact of these new recommendations on the independence of non-executive directors in UK companies.

Separation of the CEO and Chairman

A key element of the corporate governance reforms within the UK from the Cadbury Report onwards has been the separation of the roles of chief executive and chairman.

> Given the importance and particular nature of the chairman's role, it should in principle be separate from that of the chief executive. If the two roles are combined in one person, it represents a considerable concentration of power. We recommend, therefore, that there should be a clearly accepted division of responsibilities at the head of a company, which will ensure a balance of power and authority, such that no one individual has unfettered powers of decision. Where the chairman is also the chief executive, it is essential that there should be a strong and independent element on the board. (Cadbury, 1992)

There can be little doubt that here too the governance reforms in the UK have had an impact. Cosh and Hughes (1997a) show that, for a sample of the largest UK companies, the proportion of firms combining these roles fell from 74 per cent in 1981 to 50 per cent in 1996. Conyon and Peck (1998a) examine the FT top 100 UK-listed companies and find that the proportion with the combined role of chief executive and chairman fell from 52 per cent in 1991 to 36 per cent in 1994. They also show that the proportion with a remuneration committee rose from 78 per cent to 99 per cent, and those with a nomination committee rose from 12 per cent to 72 per cent, over the same period. These findings suggest an instant structural impact of the Cadbury proposals in these areas. Today almost all large UK-listed companies have separate audit, remuneration and nomination committees.

Executive Remuneration

The Combined Code on Corporate Governance recommends that executive remuneration should be at a level sufficient to attract and retain executive talent and that a significant proportion should be directly related to corporate performance. It also seeks transparency in the reporting of executive pay to shareholders and, as a consequence, UK company reports today generally contain lengthy and detailed reports from the Remuneration Committee. However, these still fail to give a simple overall picture of the total remuneration package and its composition. In addition, it is perhaps ironic that public concern about the level of top executive pay that led to these reforms has not resulted in lower levels of executive pay on average. In fact, quite the opposite has occurred. Cosh and Hughes (1997a) show that the median level of CEO remuneration rose from £222 000 in 1981 to £827 000 in 1996 for a sample of large UK companies (in 2006 prices). The bonus element of this pay rose from a negligible proportion to 21 per cent by 1996. Amongst the top 100 UK-listed companies in 2006, the median level of CEO remuneration was £1 017 000 and the bonus element had risen to over 35 per cent of this part of the remuneration package. This rise in executive pay levels, particularly in the past decade, has been reinforced by the award of stock option and long-term incentive plans that were rare in the early 1980s (Cosh and Hughes, 1987, 1997a; and Main et al., 1996). By 2006 the inclusion of these elements raises the average pay package of CEOs of FTSE 100 companies to £3.3m and the performance-related element of the whole package has increased to about 80 per cent (*Financial Times*, 15 May 2006). Despite this rise in the level and structure of top executive pay, the debate continues to rage about whether it has had the intended effects in terms of performance (for example, Bebchuk and Fried, 2004; Kay and van Putten, 2007).

Institutional Shareholdings

The rising dominance of financial institutions as holders of UK-listed company shares is well documented. Figure 10.3 shows that the proportion of ordinary shares held by financial institutions more than doubled from 30 per cent in 1963 to 62 per cent in 1993. The figure also shows that overseas holdings have risen dramatically from 4 per cent in 1981 to 40 per cent in 2006. Most of these holdings appear to be with overseas financial institutions and so it is reasonable to allocate the overseas holdings across the other categories in the proportions in which they are found for domestic holdings. If overseas holdings are allocated in this way, the holdings of financial institutions have risen from about 30 per cent in 1963 to above 70 per cent since the 1990s.

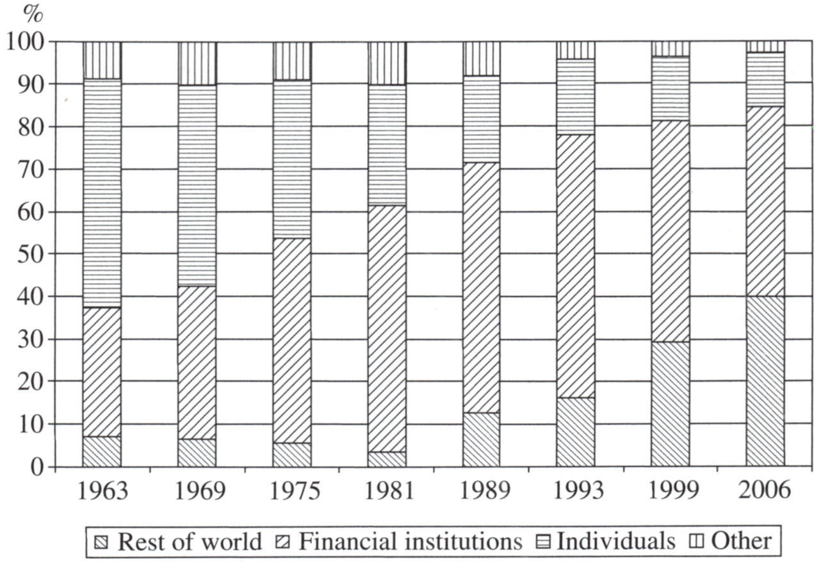

Figure 10.3 The ownership of the ordinary shares of UK-listed companies, 1963–2006

This picture of rising dominance is calculated by summing all the holdings of financial institutions, but this may give a false picture if the holdings are so dispersed that effective action is prevented. This is not the case. In a random sample of 50 of the FTSE 100 companies we found that the median number of holdings above 3 per cent of the voting stock was 3, and that the median percentage of the stock held by such holdings was 17.9 per cent (the mean figures were 3.5 holdings with 21.8 per cent). These holdings are in general dominated by the holdings of financial institutions, about half of which are foreign. This suggests a much greater dominance by institutional holders than that reported by Cosh and Hughes (1997a) for 1981 and 1996. It would appear that this type of holder clearly has the ability to directly influence management behaviour.

In conclusion, we can see that there have been many changes to these key structural aspects of corporate governance over the last two decades, at least partly in response to the evolving Code. The question remains whether this closer tie of executive pay to performance and the supposed greater scrutiny of their decisions by the board of directors have led to changed takeover behaviour. It is apparent from Figure 10.1 that despite all of these changes there has been no abatement in takeover activity. In fact, it has grown in scale and become more international in nature. In recent years the UK market has seen the rise in importance of private equity transactions.

> Our inquiry was undertaken in response to the growing significance of the private equity industry in the UK, and particularly the rising number of takeovers of very large companies by private equity firms. These are a new phenomenon; the recent £11 billion purchase of Alliance Boots was the first takeover of a FTSE 100 company by a private equity firm. The increasing size of private equity deals raises a range of issues, relating for example to the impact of private equity on jobs, pensions, financial stability, transparency and accountability and tax revenues. . . . Currently 8% of the UK's workforce (1.2 million workers) is employed in private equity owned companies and 19% work in companies which have at some stage been in private equity ownership. (Treasury Select Committee, 2007)

This phenomenon is beyond the scope of this review, but we do speculate below whether it has introduced something new into the market for corporate control. We now turn to examine whether we can observe an improved takeover performance in recent years.

UK TAKEOVER PERFORMANCE SINCE THE 1980S

Have these corporate governance changes been associated with better acquisition performance? There are different ways of addressing this question. We can examine the apparent impact on performance of individual aspects of corporate governance. We do this below but, first, in this section we ask whether the large and pervasive changes in corporate governance have been associated with overall improvements in acquisition performance. A number of UK studies have examined the performance of takeovers since 1980 in terms of both shareholder returns and accounting profitability.

These studies have shown that share returns at announcement are negative for acquirer shareholders. For example, Cosh et al. (2006) for a sample of 363 acquirers (between 1985 and 1996) acquiring UK-listed targets find that the mean announcement abnormal return is −1.13 per cent, which is statistically significant. Therefore, over the three days surrounding the acquisition announcement, the stock market overall assessment is that the average acquisition will result in a small but significantly negative effect on acquirer value. This finding is consistent with other UK studies for the time period that also report significantly negative abnormal announcement returns to acquirers (for example Sudarsanam and Mahate, 2003). Share returns for acquiring firms over the long-run post-acquisition period are also significantly negative for samples since 1980. For example, Cosh et al. (2006) find that the 36-month post-acquisition mean return is −16.26 per cent, which is statistically significant. This result is consistent with other long-run studies of UK acquirers over this sample time period such as Gregory (1997), and Sudarsanam and Mahate (2003).[1] Therefore, overall, the impact on the share price performance of acquiring firms is similar to earlier periods.

The impact of takeovers on profitability since the 1980s is somewhat more positive than in earlier periods, although it depends very much on the specific profitability measure employed. Powell and Stark (2005) and Cosh et al. (2006) use a range of measures and find consistent results. Specifically, when comparing post- and pre-takeover performance, measures based on accrual profit report a significantly positive increase in operating performance. The improvement ranges from 1.08 in the case of profit to book assets, to 1.65 in the case of profit to market value of assets. In contrast, when cash flow, rather than accrual, measures are used the impacts are positive, but smaller and statistically indistinguishable from zero. Therefore, there is some evidence that takeovers improve profitability, but this does not hold across all profitability measures.

To summarize, results post-1980 show that UK takeovers result in significant share price losses over both the short and long-run period surrounding the acquisition. Acquiring shareholders are unambiguously worse off. The effect on operating performance ranges from mildly positive for the cash flow measures, to economically and statistically significantly positive for the accrual operating performance measures. There is therefore some evidence that the considerable changes in corporate governance described above have resulted in improved takeover performance in the aggregate.[2] The fact that this result is measurement-specific suggests that caution should be exercised in placing too much weight on the accounting results. However, within the average effect it could be that those firms with 'effective' governance structures do better for their shareholders than those with less effective structures. In order to control for such factors, it is necessary to directly examine the impact of the specific corporate governance features on acquisition performance itself.

GOVERNANCE AND MERGER PERFORMANCE REVIEW

There is a large UK empirical literature on the impact of firm-specific corporate governance mechanisms on both overall firm performance as well as firm-specific actions. However, despite the importance of acquisitions within firm strategy and the market for corporate control, only one published study to date in the UK has examined the impact of internal corporate governance measures on acquisition performance. Cosh et al. (2006)

examine the impact of a wide range of corporate governance variables on takeover performance. They examine a sample of 363 domestic UK takeovers which occurred in the period 1985–96, and assess performance in terms of announcement returns, long-run share returns and a portfolio of accounting measures. In this section, we review the Cosh et al. (2006) findings, a summary of which is reported in Table 10.4. We also review the literature that examines the impact of these particular governance factors on firm performance in general.

The Impact of Cadbury

We argued above that average takeover performance and acquiring company shareholder returns do not appear to differ in the period prior to and following the 1980s. Although pressure for corporate governance change can be traced to at least the early 1980s, formal corporate governance reforms could arguably be said to commence with the Cadbury Code in 1992. Since the sample takeovers in Cosh et al. (2006) straddle the Code, the authors include a dummy variable to reflect before and after the implementation of the Cadbury Report. Table 10.4 shows that acquisitions carried out after Cadbury have more positive announcement and long-run returns, significantly so for the latter. In terms of operating performance, this is more positive following Cadbury but not significantly so. Acquisitions are more profitable following Cadbury for four of the six operating performance measures, significantly so for one of these measures. There is therefore some evidence that takeover performance improves following Cadbury.

Board Composition

A small number of UK studies examine the impact of board composition on overall firm performance. The results provide little support for the hypothesis that a greater number, or proportion, of non-executive directors is associated with enhanced performance. Vafeas and Theodorou (1998), using a cross-section of 250 UK firms in 1994, find that the proportion of non-executives has an insignificant impact on Tobin's q. Weir and Laing (2000) examine 200 UK firms in both 1992 and 1995, finding that the number of non-executives has a negative impact on profitability, but an insignificant impact on share price performance. Weir et al. (2002) find that the proportion of non-executives has an insignificant effect on Tobin's q for 311 firms over 1994–96. These results are broadly consistent with the results for outside the UK.[3] In terms of firm-specific decisions, there is evidence that a higher proportion of non-executives leads to less earnings

Table 10.4 Summary of the findings of Cosh et al. (2006) on the impact of corporate governance characteristics on UK takeover performance

Corporate governance measure	Takeover performance measure		
	Announcement share returns	Long-run share returns	Profitability
Board structure			
% non-executives	–	–	+
Board size	–	+	+
Chairman-CEO	–	–	+
Impact of Cadbury			
Post-Cadbury	+	+ *	+
Chairman-CEO post-Cadbury	– *	+	–
Ownership structure			
Board ownership (%)	+	+ *	+
Board ownership (%) squared	+	–	–
CEO ownership (%)	–	+ *	+ *
CEO ownership (%) squared	+	–	–
Executive ownership (%)	+	+	+
Executive ownership (%) squared	–	+	–
Non-executive ownership (%)	–	–	+
Non-executive ownership (%) squared	+	+	+
Largest institutional shareholder (%)	–	+	–
Largest corporate shareholder (%)	+	+	–
Largest personal shareholder (%)	–	+	–
Incentive shares & relative pay			
CEO incentive shares (%)	–	+	+
Executive incentive shares (%)	– *	– *	–
Non-executive incentive shares (%)	+	+	–
High CEO relative pay	+	–	+

Notes: This table summarizes the results from Cosh et al. (2006), who examine the impact of various firm-specific governance characteristics on the performance of 363 domestic acquisitions made by UK public firms for UK public firms between January 1985 and December 1996. % non-executives is the number of non-executive directors on the board divided by board size. Board size refers to the entire board of all executive and non-executive directors. Chairman-CEO is a dummy variable that is set equal to one if the Chairman is also the CEO, zero otherwise. Post-Cadbury is a dummy variable that is set equal to one if the year of completion is 1993 or afterwards, zero otherwise.

Chairman-CEO post-Cadbury is a dummy variable that is set equal to Chairman-CEO if the acquisition year is 1993 or afterwards, zero otherwise. Board ownership (%) is the number of beneficial and non-beneficial shares owned by the entire board, divided by total shares in issue. CEO ownership (%) is the number of beneficial and non-beneficial shares owned by the CEO, divided by total shares in issue. Executive ownership (%) is the number of beneficial and non-beneficial shares owned by all executive directors except the CEO, divided by total shares in issue. Non-executive ownership (%) is the number of beneficial and non-beneficial shares owned by all non-executive directors, divided by total shares in issue. Largest institutional shareholder (%) is the largest external shareholding held by a financial institution. Largest corporate shareholder (%) is the largest external shareholding held by another firm that is not a financial institution. Largest personal shareholder (%) is the largest external shareholding held by a private individual. CEO incentive shares (%) is the number of incentive shares owned by the CEO, divided by the total number of shares in issue. Executive incentive shares (%) is the number of incentive shares owned by all executive directors except the CEO, divided by the total number of shares in issue. Non-executive incentive shares (%) is the number of incentive shares owned by all non-executive directors, divided by the total number of shares in issue. High CEO relative pay is the highest paid director's salary divided by the board total remuneration divided by board size. Pay refers to salary, plus pensions and bonuses. Announcement share returns are the mean cumulative abnormal share return for acquirers calculated from day −1 to day +1 (where day 0 is the announcement day), relative to the Market Index. Long-run share returns are the mean buy-and-hold abnormal returns for acquirers over the 36-month period following the completion month, relative to control firms. Profitability is the post-takeover abnormal profitability (median operating profitability of the acquirer in years +1 to +3 relative to control firms) regressed on pre-takeover profitability (median operating profitability of the weighted average acquirer and target in years −1 to −3 relative to control firms). Six measures of profitability are employed (profit/total assets, profit/sales, profit/market value, cash flow/total assets, cash flow/sales, cash flow/market value), where profit is operating profit before depreciation, cash flow is operating profit before depreciation adjusted for short-term accruals, and market value is the market value of equity and book value of long and short-term debt. The profitability column here reflects the average impact on all six measures. Control firms, for both long-run returns and profitability, are non-merging firms matched on industry and pre-acquisition profitability. The results for CEO ownership, executive ownership, non-executive ownership, and incentive shares, are for a reduced sample of 178 acquisitions for which data is available. * indicates statistical significance at the 10% level or higher. For the profitability measure, significance is measured according to the average *t*-statistic across the six profitability measures.

manipulation (Peasnell et al., 2005), but little evidence it leads to more efficient decisions in terms of CEO dismissals (Cosh and Hughes, 1997b; Franks et al., 2001) or executive compensation (Cosh and Hughes, 1997b). This is in contrast to the US, where there is stronger evidence that the proportion of outside directors is associated with better specific decisions such as acquisitions, executive compensation and CEO turnover (Hermalin and Weisbach, 2003). In terms of the impact on takeover performance, Cosh et al. (2006) find that the proportion of non-executives has an insignificantly negative impact on announcement and long-run returns, and an insignificantly positive impact on five of their six operating performance measures. Therefore the impact is inconsistent across the measures and is insignificant.

Board Size

A large number of empirical studies for the US have documented a negative association between board size and firm performance (Hermalin and Weisbach, 2003).[4] In addition to these general performance effects, there is also evidence that smaller boards are more effective at specific decisions.[5] The only UK study to date is Conyon and Peck (1998b). They examine 481 listed UK firms for 1992–95 and find a significantly negative effect of board size on both market to book value and profitability. However, there is no evidence that the negative impact of board size extends to takeover performance. Cosh et al. (2006) find that board size has a statistically insignificant effect on takeover performance. Although the impact is negative for announcement returns, it is positive for long-run returns and profitability.

Separation of the CEO and Chairman

There is a relatively small body of empirical research examining the impact of whether firms have a combined CEO-Chairman or not on performance. The evidence that does exist suggests that this factor has no significant impact on performance. For the UK, studies such as Vafeas and Theodorou (1998), Weir and Laing (2000) and Weir et al. (2002) find little impact. Similar results hold elsewhere.[6] Cosh et al. (2006) find that when the chairman and CEO roles are combined, there is a negative impact on announcement and long-run returns, yet a positive effect on five of the six operating performance measures, none of which are statistically significant. The authors hypothesize that any negative impact of the combined role will be weaker following Cadbury since the Code required a transparent and specific public justification where they continued to be combined. Therefore Cosh et al. (2006) interact the CEO-Chairman dummy variable with the post-Cadbury dummy. As Table 10.4 shows, this interactive variable is significantly negative for announcement share returns, but positive for long-run returns and insignificantly negative for profitability effects. Thus in the long run, acquiring company shareholders may be better off as a result of this governance change.

Board Ownership

There is an extensive empirical literature on the impact of ownership structure on overall company performance. Until the mid-1980s, the literature in this area tested for differences between usually dichotomous groups of firms characterized as owner or manager controlled. Control status depended upon the proportion of shares owned by the board. Most such studies were concerned with testing specific predictions of the managerial theory of the firm that manager-controlled firms would have higher growth rates but lower and more volatile profit rates or return on shares than owner-controlled firms (Marris, 1964). However, this particular tradeoff was rarely supported by the data. For the UK, Radice (1971) shows that significant board ownership is associated with superior shareholder performance whilst Holl (1975), using a much larger sample and controlling for market power, finds insignificant differences. The US results are equally mixed.[7]

Later studies for both the UK and the USA have moved away from the dichotomous approach as more refined ownership data has become available, and attention has switched to testing for entrenchment-based non-linear effects. Empirical studies attempting to identify the impact of these effects in the US and UK have found evidence of a non-monotonic relation between board ownership and company performance. For the USA, Morck et al. (1988) find that the value of Tobin's q at first increases with board share ownership in the range 0 to 5 per cent, decreases between 5 and 25 per cent and then increases again above 25 per cent. They argue that the entrenchment effect takes root once certain shareholding levels are reached and increases as shareholdings rise up to a further point beyond which no further entrenchment is necessary. Once the conditions necessary for entrenchment are reached, further ownership bestows no further entrenchment and no further adverse effects in terms of shareholder welfare. The convergence-of-interests effect it is argued, in contrast, operates throughout the whole range of ownership. Therefore once entrenchment is reached, further ownership will result in an increase in company performance. McConnell and Servaes (1991 and 1995), and Hermalin and Weisbach (1991), find an inverted U-shaped relationship that is consistent with entrenchment, but do not find a second turning point beyond which alignment effects reappear. The former, for instance, report positive effects between 0 and 40–50 per cent and negative effects thereafter with no subsequent upturn. Kole (1995) argues that the difference between the first turning point in these results and those of Morck et al. (1988) may be due to the exclusion of small companies from Morck et al.'s sample. The inclusion of large numbers of smaller companies, she contends, raises the point up to which the positive effects of alignment persist because 'the positive relationship between Tobin's q and managerial ownership is sustained at higher levels of ownership for small firms than it is for large firms' (Kole, 1995, p. 426).

For the UK, Cubbin and Leech (1986) develop a continuous variable of shareholder power based on the size and location of shareholdings and the dispersion of remaining shares. In a sample of 43 large companies in the early 1970s they find no evidence of significant performance effects arising from board shareholder power. However, Short and Keasey (1999) use a random sample of 221 large UK companies for the period 1988–1992 and report similar results to Morck et al. (1988) linking board ownership to performance. They report higher turning points at around 12–15 per cent and then 41 per cent depending on the performance measure used. Although these are similar to the turning points in some of the other US studies, they interpret this as showing that board entrenchment becomes effective at higher levels of ownership in the UK compared to the US and that the entrenchment effect dominates up to much higher share ownership levels. Faccio and Lasfer (1999) analyse a much larger UK sample of all UK non-financial listed companies in 1996 and find no relationship between firm value and board ownership in general, although they report that a non-linear relationship with two turning points exists for the subset of firms with high growth prospects (proxied by high P/E ratios). They speculate that their general lack of robust findings of any entrenchment effects of board ownership on firm value or performance may reflect the effectiveness of external governance pressures in the UK. Finally, Weir et al. (2002) analyse 311 companies from the 1996 *Times 1000* list, and find evidence for an entrenchment effect in terms of an inverted U-shaped relationship between Tobin's q and CEO share ownership. They do not report the estimated turning point in this relationship.[8,9]

Cosh et al. (2006), in keeping with the existing literature on entrenchment and alignment, test the hypothesis that there will be a significant but non-linear relationship between board ownership and takeover performance. They experiment with various functional forms. They find no evidence of a relation between board ownership and announcement period share returns, strong evidence of a positive linear relation between board ownership and long-run share returns, and weak evidence of a positive linear relation between board ownership and operating performance. They find no evidence of negative entrenchment effects although they do find that the effect of board ownership is more acute at low (less than 5 per cent) levels of holdings, and some evidence of diminishing effects at higher levels of ownership.

The scope for entrenchment and the exercise of discretionary power to pursue non-shareholder welfare strategies may be imperfectly measured by focusing on board ownership in aggregate and by focusing on board ownership alone. Aggregate board ownership is one component of the anatomy of corporate control and should be disaggregated and located in a wider range of factors which will condition its impact (Cosh and Hughes, 1987 and 1997a; Deakin and Hughes, 1997; Vafeas, 1999; Weir et al., 2002). Where a substantial aggregate board holding is made up of several smaller holdings, entrenchment requires coordination of action and a clear community of interests between the holders. This may weaken the power of the entrenchment effect, and at the same time strengthen the incentive effect because ownership is dispersed across more board members. Conversely, where board ownership in aggregate is dominated by one, or a few, large holdings, the entrenchment effect will be more likely to emerge and the incentive effect will be more muted because fewer directors are involved.

Stronger entrenchment effects for CEO and executive shareholdings are predicted than for board ownership as a whole and for non-executive shareholdings. In a US study focusing on CEO ownership, Griffith (1999) reports results similar to Morck et al. (1988) in having two turning points. He shows that Tobin's q rises with CEO ownership between 0 and 15 per cent, declines for values between 15 and 50 per cent, and rises again when the CEO has over 50 per cent of the stock. For the UK, Weir et al. (2002) find that Tobin's q initially rises with CEO ownership and then declines. It is also important to distinguish between non-executive and executive directors' shareholdings. The former, in principle, play a key role in monitoring executive directors and are expected to have objectives aligned with shareholder interests. We would therefore expect entrenchment effects based on ownership to be weaker for this group compared to executive shareholdings.

Cosh et al. (2006) also take a disaggregated view of board shareholdings, paying particular attention to the composition of board shareholdings as well as their size. They analyse the separate impact of CEO shareholdings and the pattern of non-executive and executive holdings within the board. Much stronger effects are found when the overall board measure is split into CEO, executive and non-executive directors. They find strong evidence of a positive relation between CEO ownership and both the long-run return and operating performance impact of takeover on acquiring firms. The positive effect declines as CEO ownership increases to high levels of about 20 per cent. These findings are consistent with the existence of discretion to pursue non-shareholder welfare maximization takeovers, and with an incentive impact of CEO shareholdings that prevents it from occurring when substantial CEO holdings are present. This 'corrective' power appears to be subject to diminishing returns. It is not, however, subverted by potential entrenchment effects at higher CEO shareholding levels. In contrast, shareholdings of other executive directors, non-executive directors and non-board holdings are found to have no significant effect on takeover performance.

The intra-board emphasis is in keeping with a more general interest in the governance and agency literature, of conflicts of interest within corporate elites and the potential role of CEO power and hubris in driving corporate strategic decision taking (Allen, 1981; Baysinger and Hoskisson,

1990; Hayward and Hambrick, 1997; Jensen and Zajac, 2004). Cosh et al. (2006) investigate the impact that CEO dominance may have in affecting takeover outcomes where dominance is proxied by the ratio of CEO to other directors' remuneration. The authors predict a negative relationship between takeover performance and the ratio of CEO to average board pay. However, the coefficient for the CEO pay over average pay measure is of indeterminate sign and statistically insignificant. This is consistent with corporate governance restrictions on CEO discretion.

As noted above, incentive shares increased dramatically in the bull markets of the 1990s and potentially increase the incentive alignment effects of share ownership since in principle the shares should yield gains conditional on meeting specified shareholder welfare-creating activities. The extent to which this is the case clearly depends upon the design of the contracts and the extent to which executives can manipulate them in their favour. Cosh et al. (2006) consider the impact of incentive shares on takeover performance, by examining the number of incentive shares as a proportion of number of shares in issue. The hypothesis is that takeover performance will be enhanced in the presence of CEO, executive and non-executive incentive shares. They find that neither CEO nor non-executive director incentive shares have a consistent or significant effect on takeover performance. However, they do find that executive director incentive shares have a consistently negative impact, significantly so in the case of announcement returns, long returns, and for two of the six operating performance measures. This is a curious finding which is inconsistent with expectations.

Institutional Shareholdings

As noted above, takeover performance is hypothesized to be more closely aligned with shareholder interests where substantial off-board holdings by financial institutions exist. Filatotchev et al. (2007) review the literature on large external shareholders and overall firm performance and conclude that there is no robust link between more concentrated external holdings and better firm performance. The only previous UK study examining the impact of financial institutions on merger performance is Cosh et al. (1989). They examine two UK merger samples. In the first sample drawn from the low merger period 1981–1983, pre- and post-merger differences are found between merging companies with and without a significant institutional presence. However, in the takeover boom year of 1986, from which the second sample is drawn, all such distinctions become blurred. Cosh et al. (2006) also assess the impact of non-board holdings by financial institutions, as well as by corporations and persons. The effect of these external shareholders is indeterminate and rarely significant. For example, the largest institutional shareholder has an insignificantly positive impact on announcement and long-run returns, yet a negative impact for three (significantly so in one case) of the operating performance measures, and a positive impact for the other three of these measures.

Summary

Our review of the literature on the relationship between internal corporate governance mechanisms and the performance of UK companies in both a general sense and in terms of takeover performance shows that there is a weak relationship between internal governance mechanisms and performance. The exception is board and, more specifically, CEO ownership. Acquirers whose CEOs own a larger proportion of equity, consequently carry out acquisitions which perform significantly better in terms of both long-run returns and operating performance, and these impacts are stronger at lower levels of board ownership, reflecting diminishing returns to alignment at higher ownership levels. There is no evidence of entrenchment effects within the levels of board ownership examined. Furthermore, acquisition performance is not only better, but significantly positive for such acquirers. This key finding on CEO ownership in the context of acquisitions is robust to a number of potential biases. Firstly, a potentially serious problem with many corporate governance studies is that of reverse causality, whereby governance changes because of past or expected performance, not the other way round. One possibility in the context of acquisitions is that at low levels of ownership, CEOs purchase stock in anticipation of good takeover performance. Cosh et al. (2006) carry out two-stage least squares regressions but find that this approach yields results that are very similar. They therefore conclude that the positive effect of CEO ownership on takeover performance is the result of higher CEO shareholdings leading to improved takeover performance rather than CEOs buying shares in anticipation of good takeover performance. The finding is also robust to controlling for other factors that determine takeover performance (acquirer performance, relative size, means of payment, hostility, industrial direction) and a variety of other constraints which may influence director behaviour arising from debt-related lender power and the product market. The fact that CEO ownership leads to higher acquisition performance potentially has important implications for the effect of acquisitions involving private equity firms. In particular, given that such acquisitions frequently result in CEOs taking a large ownership stake, they may, *ceteris paribus*, perform better than other types of acquisition.

CONCLUSION

We have shown that waves of takeover activity have occurred with increasing intensity in recent decades in the UK, unabated by the significant changes to share ownership and corporate governance. Initially, the poor average outcomes for shareholders of these bouts of takeover activity could be argued to follow from the separation of ownership from control, the lack of alignment of management with shareholder interests, and the inability of boards of directors to monitor and control the strategies of their management teams. We have shown the massive structural changes in each of these features over the last 40 years and yet, takeover performance for the acquiring shareholders shows little sign of improving, and positive profitability performance effects depend upon the choice of particular performance measures. In addition, the specific changes to board structures and executive pay cannot be shown to have had much impact on takeover outcomes. It still appears to be the case that, as Dennis Mueller argued in 1969, the directors of large corporations invest in acquisitions beyond the point at which the welfare of their shareholders will be maximized. It may be the case that both management and shareholder representatives are overly optimistic about the gains they can make from acquisitions and about the premiums they can afford to pay. We have pointed out above that it is possible that private equity firms bring a new type of player on to the market for corporate control, one for whom the rewards for effective takeovers are greater and more direct. It would be ironic if this turned out to be the means for improved takeover performance given the conglomerate nature of private equity acquisitions and their rather poor record on corporate governance.

NOTES

1. It is important to note that studies which examine the impact of acquisitions of private targets (for example, Conn et al., 2005) do not find evidence of negative returns. Earlier studies (that is, pre-1980) do not examine this type of acquisition.
2. Despite the overall performance of acquisitions over the period, Guest (2008a) shows that acquisitions on average have a significantly positive impact on executive pay. Therefore acquiring firm directors benefit in terms of higher pay, even if their shareholders do not.
3. For the US, most studies (for example, Hermalin and Weisbach, 1991; Yermack, 1996; Dalton et al., 1998; Klein, 1998) find no association, whilst a smaller number (for example, Agrawal and Knoeber, 1996; Bhagat and Black, 2002; Coles et al., 2008) find a negative relation. Outside the US, Hossain et al. (2001) and Choi et al. (2007) find a positive relation for New Zealand and Korea respectively, Beiner et al. (2004; 2006), and Haniffa and Hudaib (2006) find no relation for Swiss and Malaysian firms respectively, whilst Bozec (2005) finds a negative relation for Canadian firms.
4. For the US, see Yermack (1996), Huther (1997), and Coles et al. (2008). Evidence from other countries is broadly consistent but less robust. Eisenberg et al. (1998) provide similar evidence for small private firms in Finland, whilst Mak and Kusnadi (2005) and Haniffa

and Hudaib (2006) do so for Malaysian firms. For Belgium, Dehaene et al. (2001) find that board size has an insignificantly negative impact on profitability. For Switzerland, Loderer and Peyer (2002) find a significantly negative impact on Tobin's q (although not on profitability) whilst Beiner et al. (2004 and 2006) find no negative impact. Bozec (2005) finds a significantly negative effect on sales margin but not profitability for Canadian firms.

5. For example, Yermack (1996) finds that firms with smaller boards have a stronger relationship between firm performance and CEO turnover, and higher sensitivity of CEO cash compensation to stock returns.
6. See, for example, Daily and Dalton (1992; 1994), Beatty and Zajac (1994), Boyd (1994), and Ocasio (1994). In their meta-analysis of 31 studies of links between separation and financial performance, Dalton et al. (1998) do not establish any significant causal relationship.
7. Profit and share price performance differences alone proved equally elusive, although studies which corrected returns for risk, controlled for market power constraints and allowed for some disaggregation between board and non-board holdings produced more robust results. For the USA, Kamerschen (1968), Larner (1970), Sorensen (1974), Qualls (1976), Kania and McKean (1976), Zeitlin and Norich (1979), and Herman (1981) find insignificant shareholder performance differences between high board shareholder (owner controlled) and low board shareholder (manager controlled) groups. In contrast, Monsen et al. (1968), Boudreaux (1973), Palmer (1973 and 1975), Stano (1975 and 1976), McEachern (1975 and 1978) do find superior shareholder welfare performance. Palmer (1973 and 1975), in particular, show the importance of market power in allowing managerial discretion and performance differences to emerge.
8. A number of studies have related ownership characteristics not to overall performance, but to specific observable firm actions. These include US papers analysing the impact of board ownership on the premiums paid in takeover bids, the method of takeover payment and post-acquisition executive job retention (Martin, 1996; Hayward and Hambrick, 1997; Ghosh and Ruland, 1998), executive pay around acquisitions (Wright et al., 2002), and the likelihood of paying greenmail or excessive bid premia (Kosnik, 1987 and 1990). These studies provide mixed evidence in identifying significant ownership impacts. For the UK, Guest (2008a) finds that ownership structure has no impact on executive pay awards following acquisition.
9. There are also some direct estimates of the impact of board ownership on takeover performance outcomes for the acquiring company shareholders. These have focused on announcement effects, and relate only to the USA. Conn (1980) using a dichotomous approach finds no differences in merger pricing or share returns between owner- and manager-controlled groups. However, Slutsky and Caves (1991) show that as acquiring board holdings increase, a lower premium is paid for the target. Lewellen et al. (1985), Loderer and Martin (1998) and Shinn (1999) using a more continuous approach, report a positive linear relationship between board ownership and announcement returns. These latter three studies suggest that the detrimental effects of entrenched management observed with company performance in general do not apply in the case of corporate takeovers. Hubbard and Palia (1995), however, provide evidence of a U-shaped relationship. They argue that at sufficiently high levels of managerial ownership, managers hold a large non-diversified financial portfolio in the firm. Such management will pay a premium for risk-reducing acquisitions, even if the value of the acquiring firm decreases.

REFERENCES

ABI (2006), *Executive Remuneration – ABI Guidelines on Policies and Practices*, London: Association of British Insurers.

Agrawal, A. and C.R. Knoeber (1996), 'Firm performance and mechanisms to control agency problems between managers and shareholders', *Journal of Financial and Quantitative Analysis*, **31**, 377–97.

Allen, M.P. (1981), 'Managerial power and tenure in the large corporation', *Social Forces*, **60**, 482–94.

Asquith, P., R.F. Bruner and D.W. Mullins (1983), 'The gains to bidding firms from merger', *Journal of Financial Economics*, **11**(1–4), 121–39.

Barber, B.M. and J.D. Lyon (1997), 'Detecting long run abnormal stock returns: the empirical power and specification of test statistics', *Journal of Financial Economics*, **43**, 341–72.

Baysinger, B. and R.E. Hoskisson (1990), 'The composition of boards of directors and strategic control: effects on corporate strategy', *Academy of Management Review*, **15**, 72–87.

Beatty, R.P. and E.J. Zajac (1994), 'Managerial incentives, monitoring and risk bearing: a study of executive compensation, ownership, and board structure in initial public offerings', *Administrative Science Quarterly*, **39**, 313–35.

Bebchuk, Lucin and Jesse Fried (2004), *Pay without Performance: The Unfulfilled Promise of Executive Compensation*, Cambridge, MA: Harvard University Press.

Beiner, S., W. Drobetz, M.M. Schmid and H. Zimmermann (2004), 'Is board size an independent corporate governance mechanism?', *Kyklos*, **57**, 327–56.

Beiner, S., W. Drobetz, M.M. Schmid and H. Zimmermann (2006), 'An integrated framework of corporate governance and firm valuation', *European Financial Management*, **12**, 249–83.

Berle, A.A. and G.C. Means (1932), *The Modern Corporation and Private Property*, New York: Macmillan.

Bhagat, S. and B.S. Black (2002), 'The non-correlation between board independence and long-term firm performance', *Journal of Corporation Law*, **27**, 231–73.

Boudreaux, K.J. (1973), 'Managerialism and risk-return performance', *Southern Economic Journal*, **29**, 366–72.

Boyd, B.K. (1994), 'Board control and CEO compensation', *Strategic Management Journal*, **15**, 335–44.

Bozec, R. (2005), 'Boards of directors, market discipline and firm performance', *Journal of Business Finance & Accounting*, **32**, 1921–60.

Brown, S.J. and J.B. Warner (1985), 'Using daily stock returns, the case of event studies', *Journal of Financial Economics*, **14**, 3–31.

Cadbury, Sir A. (1992), *The Financial Aspects of Corporate Governance*, London: Financial Reporting Council.

Chatterjee, R. and G. Meeks (1996), 'The financial effects of takeover: accounting rates of return and accounting regulation', *Journal of Business Finance & Accounting*, **23**, 851–68.

Choi, J.J., S.W. Park and S.S. Yoo (2007), 'The value of outside directors: evidence from corporate governance reform in Korea', *Journal of Financial and Quantitative Analysis*, **42**, 941–62.

Coles, J.L., N.D. Daniel and L. Naveen (2008), 'Boards: does one size fit all?', *Journal of Financial Economics*, **87**, 329–56.

Conn, R.L. (1980), 'Merger pricing policy by owner-controlled versus manager-controlled firms', *Journal of Industrial Economies*, **28**, 427–38.

Conn, R.L., A. Cosh, P.M. Guest and A. Hughes (2004), 'Why must all good things come to an end? The performance of multiple acquirers', in D.H. Nagao (ed.), *Proceedings of the Sixty-third Annual Meeting of the Academy of Management*, Briarcliff Manor, NY: Academy of Management, ISSN 1543–8643.

Conn, R.L., A. Cosh, P.M. Guest and A. Hughes (2005), 'The impact on UK acquirers of domestic, cross-border, public and private acquisitions', *Journal of Business Finance & Accounting*, **32**, 815–70.

Conyon, M.J. and S.I. Peck (1998a), 'Board control, remuneration committees and top management compensation', *Academy of Management Review*, **41**, 146–57.

Conyon, M.J. and S.I. Peck (1998b), 'Board size and corporate performance: evidence from European countries', *The European Journal of Finance*, **4**, 291–304.

Cosh, Andy and Alan Hughes (1987), 'The anatomy of corporate control: directors, shareholders and executive remuneration in giant US and UK corporations', *Cambridge Journal of Economics*, **11**, 285–313.

Cosh, A. and A. Hughes (1997a), 'The changing anatomy of corporate control and the market for executives in the United Kingdom', *Journal of Law and Society*, **24**, 104–23.

Cosh, A. and A. Hughes (1997b), 'Executive remuneration, executive dismissal and institutional shareholdings', *International Journal of Industrial Organisation*, **15**, 469–92.

Cosh, A., P.M. Guest and A. Hughes (2006), 'Board share ownership and takeover performance', *Journal of Business Finance & Accounting*, **33**, 459–510.

Cosh, Andrew, Alan Hughes and Ajit Singh (1980), 'The causes and effects of takeovers in the United Kingdom: an empirical investigation for the late 1960s at the microeconomic level', in D.C. Mueller (ed.), *The Determinants and Effects of Mergers: An International Comparison*, Cambridge, MA: Oelgeschlager, Gunn & Hain, pp. 227–70.

Cosh, A., A. Hughes, K. Lee and A. Singh (1989), 'Institutional investment, mergers and the market for corporate control', *International Journal of Industrial Economics*, **7**(1), 73–100.

Cubbin, J. and D. Leech (1986), 'Growth versus profit-maximisation: a simultaneous equation approach to testing the Marris model', *Managerial and Decision Economics*, **7**, 123–31.

Daily, C.M. and D.R. Dalton (1992), 'The relationship between governance structure and corporate performance in entrepreneurial firms', *Journal of Business Venturing*, **7**, 375–86.

Daily, C.M. and D.R. Dalton (1994), 'Bankruptcy and corporate governance: the impact of board composition and structure', *Academy of Management Journal*, **37**, 1603–17.

Dalton, D.R., C.M. Daily, A.E. Ellstrand and J.L. Johnson (1998), 'Meta-analytic reviews of board composition, leadership structure and financial performance', *Strategic Management Journal*, **19**, 269–90.

Deakin, S. and A. Hughes (1997), 'Comparative corporate governance: an interdisciplinary research agenda', *Journal of Law and Society*, **24**, 1–9.

Dehaene, A., V. De Vuyst and H. Ooghe (2001), 'Corporate performance and board structure in Belgian companies', *Long Range Planning*, **34**, 383–98.

Dickerson, A., H. Gibson and E. Tsakalotos (1997), 'The impact of acquisitions on company performance: evidence from a large panel of UK firms', *Oxford Economic Papers*, **49**, 344–61.

Eisenberg, T., S. Sundgren and M.T. Wells (1998), 'Larger board size and decreasing firm value in small firms', *Journal of Financial Economics*, **48**, 35–54.

Faccio, M. and M. Lasfer (1999), 'Managerial ownership, board structure and firm value: the UK evidence', City University, Working Paper.

Fama, E.F. (1998), 'Market efficiency, long-run returns, and behavioral finance', *Journal of Financial Economics*, **49**, 283–306.
Filatotchev, I., G. Jackson, H. Gospel and D. Allcock (2007), 'Key drivers of "good" corporate governance and the appropriateness of UK policy responses', January, London: Department of Trade and Industry.
Franks, J. and R.S. Harris (1989), 'Shareholder wealth effects of corporate takeovers: the UK experience 1955–1985', *Journal of Financial Economics*, **23**, 225–49.
Franks, J., C. Mayer and L. Renneboog (2001), 'Who disciplines management in poorly performing companies?', *Journal of Financial Intermediation*, **10**, 209–48.
FRC (2006), *The Combined Code on Corporate Governance*, London: Financial Reporting Council.
Ghosh, A. and W. Ruland (1998), 'Managerial ownership, the method of payment for acquisitions and executive job retention', *Journal of Finance*, **53**, 785–98
Greenbury, Sir R. (1995), *Directors' Remuneration*, London: CBI.
Gregory, A. (1997), 'An examination of the long run performance of UK acquiring firms', *Journal of Business Finance & Accounting*, **24**, 971–1002.
Griffith, J.M. (1999), 'CEO ownership and firm value', *Managerial and Decision Economics*, **20**, 1–8.
Guest, P.M. (2008a), 'The impact of mergers and acquisitions on executive pay in the United Kingdom', *Economica*, forthcoming, doi:10.1111/j.1468-0335.2007.00674.x.
Guest, P.M. (2008b). 'The determinants of board size and composition: evidence from the UK', *Journal of Corporate Finance*, **14**, 51–72.
Gugler, K., D.C. Mueller, B.B. Yurtoglu and C. Zulehner (2003), 'The effects of mergers: an international comparison', *International Journal of Industrial Organisation*, **21**, 625–53.
Hampel, R. (1997), *Committee on Corporate Governance, Final Report*, London: Gee Publishing Ltd.
Haniffa, R. and M. Hudaib (2006), 'Corporate governance structure and performance of Malaysian listed companies', *Journal of Business Finance & Accounting*, **33**, 1034–62.
Hayward, M.L.A. and D.C. Hambrick (1997), 'Explaining the premiums paid for large acquisitions: evidence of CEO hubris', *Administrative Science Quarterly*, **42**, 103–27.
Hermalin, B.E. and M.S. Weisbach (1991), 'The effects of board composition and direct incentives on firm performance', *Financial Management*, **20**(4), 101–12.
Hermalin, B.E. and M.S. Weisbach (2003), 'Boards of directors as an endogenously determined institution: a survey of the economic evidence', *Economic Policy Review*, **9**, 7–26.
Herman, E.S. (1981), *Corporate Control, Corporate Power*, New York: William Morrow.
Higgs, D. (2003), 'Review of the role and effectiveness of non-executive directors', London: Department of Trade and Industry.
Holl, P. (1975), 'Effect of control type on the performance of the firms in the UK', *Journal of Industrial Economics*, **23**, 257–71.
Hossain, M., A.K. Prevost and R.P. Rao (2001), 'Corporate governance in New Zealand: the effect of the 1993 Companies Act on the relation between board composition and firm performance', *Pacific-Basin Finance Journal*, **9**, 119–45.
Hubbard, R. and D. Palia (1995), 'Benefits of control, managerial ownership, and

the stock returns of acquiring firms', *Rand Journal of Economics*, **26**, 782–92.
Hughes, Alan (1993), 'Mergers and economic performance in the UK: a survey of the empirical evidence 1950–90', in M. Bishop and J. Kay (eds), *European Mergers and Merger Policy*, Oxford: Oxford University Press.
Huther, J. (1997), 'An empirical test of the effect of board size on firm efficiency', *Economics Letters*, **54**, 259–64.
ISC (2007), 'The responsibilities of institutional shareholders and agents – Statement of principles', Institutional Shareholders Committee, June, http://institutionalshareholderscommittee.org.uk/library.html.
Jaffe, J.F. (1974), 'Special information and insider trading', *Journal of Business*, **47**, 305–60.
Jensen, M.C. (1986), 'Agency costs of free cash flow, corporate finance and takeovers', *American Economic Review*, **76**, 323–9.
Jensen, M. and R. Ruback (1983), 'The market for corporate control: the scientific evidence', *Journal of Financial Economics*, **11**, 5–50.
Jensen, M.C. and E.J. Zajac (2004), 'Corporate elites and corporate strategy: how demographic preferences and structural position shape the scope of the firm', *Strategic Management Journal*, **25**, 507–24.
Kamerschen, D.R. (1968), 'The influence of ownership and control on profit rates', *American Economic Review*, **58**, 432–47.
Kania, J.J. and J.R. McKean (1976), 'Ownership, control and the contemporary corporation: a general behavioural analysis', *Kyklos*, **29**, 272–91.
Kay I. and S. Van Putten (2007), *Myths and Realities of Executive Pay*, Cambridge: Cambridge University Press.
Klein, A. (1998), 'Firm performance and board committee structure', *Journal of Law and Economics*, **41**, 275–303.
Kole, S.R. (1995), 'Measuring managerial equity ownership: a comparison of sources of ownership data', *Journal of Corporate Finance*, **1**, 413–35.
Kosnik, R.D. (1987), 'Greenmail: a study of board performance in corporate governance', *Administrative Science Quarterly*, **32**, 163–85.
Kosnik, R.D. (1990), 'Effects of board demography and directors' incentives on corporate greenmail decisions', *Academy of Management Journal*, **33**, 129–50.
Larner, R.J. (1970), *Management Control and the Large Corporation*, New York: Dunellen.
Lewellen, W., C. Loderer and A. Rosenfeld (1985), 'Merger decisions and executive stock ownership in acquiring firms', *Journal of Accounting and Economics*, **7**, 209–31.
Limmack, R.J. (1991), 'Corporate mergers and wealth effects: 1977–86', *Accounting and Business Research*, **21**, 239–51.
Loderer, C. and K. Martin (1998), 'Executive stock ownership and performance: tracking faint changes', *Journal of Financial Economics*, **45**, 223–55.
Loderer, C. and U. Peyer (2002), 'Board overlap, seat accumulation and share prices', *European Financial Management*, **8**, 165–92.
Lyon, J.D., B.M. Barber and C. Tsai (1999), 'Improved methods for tests of long-run abnormal stock returns', *Journal of Finance*, **54**, 165–201.
Magenheim, E.B. and D.C. Mueller (1988), 'Are acquiring-firm shareholders better off after an acquisition?', in John C. Coffee Jr, Louis Lowenstein and Susan Rose-Ackerman (eds), *Knights, Raiders and Targets*, Oxford: Oxford University Press, pp. 171–93.

Main, B., A. Bruce and T. Buck (1996), 'Total board remuneration and company performance', *Economic Journal*, **106**, 1627–44.
Mak, Y.T. and Y. Kusnadi (2005), 'Size really matters: further evidence on the negative relationship between board size and firm value', *Pacific-Basin Finance Journal*, **13**, 301–18.
Mandelker, G. (1974), 'Risk and return: the case of merging firms', *Journal of Financial Economics*, **1**, 303–35.
Manne, H. (1965), 'Mergers and the market for corporate control', *Journal of Political Economy*, **73**, 110–20.
Marris, Robin L. (1964), *The Economic Theory of Managerial Capitalism*, London: Macmillan.
Martin, K.J. (1996), 'The method of payment in corporate acquisitions, investment opportunities, and management ownership', *Journal of Finance*, **51**(4), 1227–46.
McConnell, J. and H. Servaes (1991), 'Additional evidence on equity ownership and corporate value', *Journal of Financial Economics*, **27**, 595–612.
McConnell, J. and H. Servaes (1995), 'Equity ownership and the two faces of debt', *Journal of Financial Economics*, **39**, 131–57.
McEachern, William A. (1975), *Managerial Control and Performance*, Lexington, MA: D.C. Heath.
McEachern, W.A. (1978), 'Corporate control and growth: an alternative approach', *Journal of Industrial Economics*, **26**, 257–66.
Meeks, Geoffrey (1977), *Disappointing Marriage: Gains from Mergers*, Cambridge: Cambridge University Press.
Monsen, R.J., J.S. Chiu and D.E. Cooley (1968), 'The effects of separation of ownership and control on the performance of the large firm', *Quarterly Journal of Economics*, **82**, 435–51.
Morck, R., A. Shleifer and R. Vishny (1988), 'Management ownership and market valuation: an empirical analysis', *Journal of Financial Economics*, **20**, 293–315.
Mueller, D.C. (1969), 'A theory of conglomerate mergers', *Quarterly Journal of Economics*, **83**, 643–59.
Mueller, D.C. (ed.) (1980), *The Determinants and Effects of Mergers: An International Comparison*, Cambridge, MA: Oelgeschlager, Gunn & Hain.
Ocasio, W. (1994), 'Political dynamics and the circulation of power: CEO succession in US industrial corporations 1960–1990', *Administrative Science Quarterly*, **39**, 285–312.
Palmer, J. (1973), 'The profit performance effects of the separation of ownership from control in larger US industrial corporations', *Bell Journal of Economic and Management Science*, Spring, pp. 293–303.
Palmer, J. (1975), 'A further analysis of profitability and managerialism', *Economic Training*, **13**, 127–30.
Peasnell, K.V., P.F. Pope and S. Young (2005), 'Board monitoring and earnings management: do outside directors influence abnormal accruals?', *Journal of Business Finance & Accounting*, **32**, 1311–46.
Powell, R. and A. Stark (2005), 'Does operating performance increase post-takeover for UK takeovers? A comparison of performance measures and benchmarks', *Journal of Corporate Finance*, **11**, 293–317.
Qualls, D.P. (1976), 'Market structure and managerial behaviour', in R.T. Masson and D.P. Qualls (eds), *Essays on Industrial Organisation in Honour of J.S. Bain*, Cambridge, MA: Ballinger.

Radice, H.K. (1971), 'Control type, profitability and growth in large firms: an empirical study', *Economic Journal*, **81**, 547–62.

Shinn, E. (1999), 'Returns to acquiring firms: the role of managerial ownership, managerial wealth, and outside owners', *Journal of Economics and Finance*, **23**, 78–89.

Short, H. and K. Keasey (1999), 'Managerial ownership and the performance of firms: evidence from the UK', *Journal of Corporate Finance*, **5**, 79–101.

Singh, Ajit (1971), *Take-overs: Their Relevance to the Stock Market and the Theory of the Firm*, Cambridge: Cambridge University Press.

Slutsky, A. and R. Caves (1991), 'Synergy, agency, and the determinants of premia paid in mergers', *Journal of Industrial Economics*, **39**, 277–96.

Sorensen, R. (1974), 'The separation of ownership and control and firm performance: an empirical analysis', *Southern Economic Journal*, **41**, 145–8.

Stano, M. (1975), 'Executive ownership interests and corporate performance', *Southern Economic Journal*, **42**, 272–8.

Stano, M. (1976), 'Monopoly power, ownership control, and corporate performance', *Bell Journal of Economics*, **7**, 672–9.

Sudarsanam, S. and A.A. Mahate (2003), 'Glamour acquirers, method of payment and post-acquisition performance: the UK evidence', *Journal of Business Finance & Accounting*, **30**, 299–341.

Treasury Select Committee (2007), 'Private equity', House of Commons Treasury Committee, Tenth Report of Session 2006–07, July, London: The Stationery Office.

Tuch, C. and N. O'Sullivan (2007), 'The impact of acquisitions on firm performance: a review of the evidence', *International Journal of Management Reviews*, **9**, 141–70.

Turnbull, N. (1999), *Internal Control: Guidance for Directors on the Combined Code*, London: Financial Reporting Council.

Vafeas, N. (1999), 'Board meeting frequency and firm performance', *Journal of Financial Economics*, **53**, 113–42.

Vafeas, N. and E. Theodorou (1998), 'The relationship between board structure and firm performance in the UK', *British Accounting Review*, **30**, 383–407.

Weir, C. and D. Laing (2000), 'The performance–governance relationship: the effects of Cadbury compliance on UK quoted companies', *Journal of Management and Governance*, **4**, 265–81.

Weir, C., D. Laing and P.J. McKnight (2002), 'Internal and external governance mechanisms: their impact on the performance of large UK public companies', *Journal of Business Finance & Accounting*, **29**, 579–611.

Wright, P., M. Kroll and D. Elenkov (2002), 'Acquisition returns, increase in firm size and chief executive officer compensation: the moderating role of monitoring', *Academy of Management Journal*, **45**, 599–608.

Yermack, D. (1996), 'Higher market valuation of companies with a small board of directors', *Journal of Financial Economics*, **40**, 185–221.

Zeitlin, M. and S. Norich (1979), 'Management control, exploitation, and profit maximization in the large corporation: an empirical confrontation of managerialism and class theory', *Research in Political Economy*, **2**, 33–62.

11. Mergers and alliances in pharmaceuticals: effects on innovation and R&D productivity

Henry Grabowski and Margaret Kyle

I INTRODUCTION

The pharmaceutical industry provides a good laboratory to investigate the effects of mergers and alliances on innovation and R&D productivity. Over the past few decades, the industry has been characterized both by significant consolidation of large pharma firms as well as the vertical disintegration of the R&D process. The latter is associated with significant entry into the discovery and development process by early stage biopharmaceutical firms. Since the early 1990s, an evolving marketplace for new technologies through licensing agreements and joint ventures has emerged, accompanied by the growth of contract research organizations that specialize in implementing clinical trials for new drug candidates.

To put some of these changes in historical perspective, it is useful to chronicle some of the key dynamic forces affecting the pharmaceutical industry since the early 1980s. While the 1980s were a period of rising prices and profits for the industry, many challenging developments also occurred for the vertically integrated, multinational drug industry. These developments included rising R&D costs (DiMasi et al., 1991; 2003), the expiration of patents on major commercial products, and the beginning of intensive price competition from generics. The passage of the Waxman–Hatch Act in 1984 was a key legislative change that allowed generics to enter the market by demonstrating bioequivalence (that is without the need to do clinical tests of safety and efficacy) (Grabowski, 2007). These dynamic forces intensified in the 1990s with the rise of buyer-side market power in the form of managed care organizations and pharmacy benefit managers in the US, and increasingly stringent price controls in other major world markets. Market and political pressures have caused declining growth in sales and profits that have been particularly evident on an industry-wide basis since the mid-1990s.

There has been increasing attention over recent years to whether the pharmaceutical industry is now in an R&D productivity crisis. Several observers have pointed to a pattern of rising R&D expenditures accompanied by a declining trend in new molecular entities since the mid-1990s. The productivity crisis idea is subject to various qualifications relating to the quality of NMEs, the long lags that characterize the R&D process in pharmaceuticals, and a gradual shift to a new R&D paradigm based more on biology than chemistry (Cockburn, 2006). Nevertheless, the declining trend in new products from the R&D labs, along with continuing patent expirations on prior 'blockbuster' products has created a replacement problem for many large pharma firms.

The structural response to these dynamic forces has included both large horizontal mergers as well as a growing number of development-stage agreements between large pharma firms and smaller, research-based biopharmaceutical firms. The first merger wave began in the 1989–1990 period. The annual value of pharmaceutical mergers in these two years exceeded that of any prior year in the 1980s by a considerable margin (Ravenscraft and Long, 2000). This was followed by an even larger merger wave beginning in the mid-1990s and continuing into the 2000s (Danzon et al., 2007; Koenig and Mezick, 2004). Combinations have included not only mergers between large pharma firms but also the acquisitions of biotech firms by pharma firms and mergers between firms of different sizes in the emerging biotech sector.

Table 11.1 shows how the global market shares in the pharmaceutical firms have changed between 1989 and 2004. All the companies shown in bold consummated a major merger in the period between the prior rankings shown in Table 11.1. Correspondingly, the starred companies were combined into larger entities in the period between rankings. If one looks across the full 15-year span between 1989 and 2004, eight of the top ten ranked companies by 2004 had consummated major mergers with other biopharmaceutical firms (Merck and J&J being the notable exceptions). There were also many smaller scale mergers and acquisitions over this period.

Global shares for top ten firms increased to 48.3 per cent by 2004, compared to 28.3 per cent in 1989. Despite the increased merger activity, the pharmaceutical industry is still relatively unconcentrated compared to many other industry sectors. Many changes in company rankings also occur over time as a result of both new product introductions and patent expirations. This is reflected by the rapid growth of dedicated biotech firms like Amgen[1] and also of primarily generic firms like Teva.[2] These firms were part of the top 20 biopharmaceutical firms in 2004.

While mergers and acquisitions (M&A) have tended to occur in waves, there has been continued growth in the number and value of alliances

Table 11.1 Global shares and mergers in pharmaceuticals, 1989–2004

Rank	2004		1999		1989	
	Company	Share (%)	Company	Share (%)	Company	Share %
1	**Pfizer**	**9.8**	Merck	4.5	Merck	4.0
2	**GlaxoSmithKline**	**6.3**	**Astra Zeneca**	**4.4**	**BMS**	**3.5**
3	**Sanofi-Aventis**	**5.2**	**Glaxo Wellcome***	**4.1**	Glaxo*	3.1
4	J&J	4.7	Pfizer*	4.1	**SKB**	**3.0**
5	Merck	4.6	BMS	4.0	Ciba-Geigy*	2.9
6	Novartis	4.4	**Novartis**	**4.0**	**AHP***	**2.7**
7	AstraZeneca	4.2	**Aventis**	**3.9**	Hoechst*	2.4
8	Roche	3.4	J&J	3.8	J&J	2.3
9	BMS	3.0	**AHP**	**3.1**	Bayer	2.3
10	Wyeth	2.7	**Roche**	**3.0**	Sandoz*	2.1
11	Abbott	2.7	Lilly	2.9	Lilly	2.1
12	Lilly	2.4	SKB*	2.8	Pfizer	2.0
13	Amgen	2.1	Warner Lambert*	2.8	Roche*	1.9
14	Takeda	1.7	Abbott	2.6	Schering-Plough	1.6
15	Boehringer Ingel	1.6	Schering-Plough	2.5	MMD*	1.6
16	Schering-Plough	1.3	Bayer	2.0	Upjohn	1.5
17	Bayer	1.2	Pharmacia Upjohn*	1.8	Boehringer Ingel	1.5
18	Schering AG	0.9	Takeda	1.5	Warner Lambert	1.4
19	Eisai	0.9	Boehringer Ingel	1.4	Cyanamid*	1.4
20	Teva	0.8	Sanofi Synthélabo*	1.3	Abbott	1.4
21			Monsanto (Searle)	1.2	Zeneca (ICI)*	1.4
22			Sankyo	1.0	Wellcome*	1.2
23			Amgen	1.0	Shiongi	1.2
24			Schering AG	1.0	Takeda	1.2
25			Otsuka	0.8	Rhône-Poulenc Rorer	1.2

Source: IMS Health Care Market Share Data, based on merger histories compiled by Jon Northrop in Burns et al. (2005), p. 228.

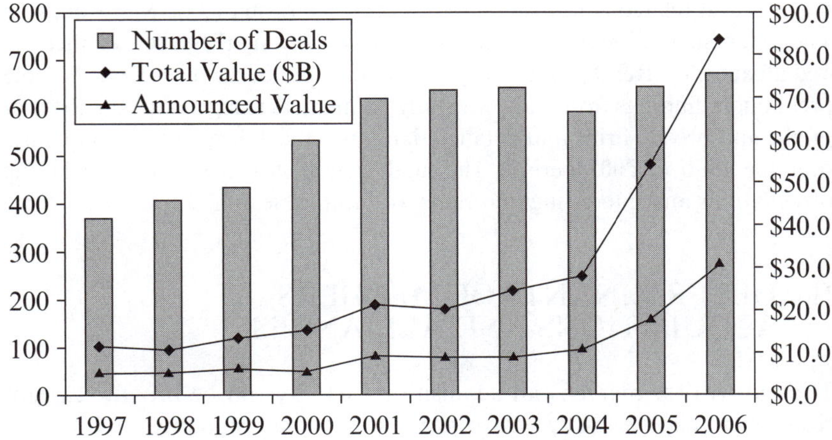

Figure 11.1 Number and value of biotech out-licensing deals, 1997–2006

between biopharmaceutical firms over time. Alliances can be a substitute for mergers and acquisitions, but can also be a forerunner to a future merger or acquisition between partners. A prototypical development stage agreement would involve payments of milestones and/or royalties and some sharing of R&D expenses in the exchange for rights to develop and/or market the new products covered under the agreement. The extent of integration at the R&D stage associated with these agreements varies considerably, ranging from true joint development agreements, to transfers of development stage products from licensors to licensees, to marketing options in exchange for development stage funding and future payments.

Figure 11.1 shows the number and potential value (including upfront payments, milestones and equity investments) of out-licensing deals from the biotech sector between 1997 and 2006. The number of annual out-licensing deals has more than doubled over this period, while the potential value has grown several fold (Recombinant Capital, 2007). The rapid growth in potential value in recent years reflects the fact that many deals are now frequently broader in scope than a single compound or a related family of compounds. It also reflects increasing potential values for licensors associated with the intense competition for deals in hot therapeutic areas like oncology (Ernst and Young, 2007).

In this chapter, our primary focus is on the effect of mergers and acquisitions on innovation and R&D productivity. However, since alliances can be either a substitute or longer-term complement to mergers, we also consider the empirical literature on the effects of alliances on these output measures. In the next section of the chapter we consider the motives for pharmaceutical mergers and related empirical studies on the determinants of M&A activity. The following section summarizes evidence concerning the effects of mergers and alliances on R&D productivity and innovation. Section IV presents some preliminary findings from our own study on mergers using a large database of public and private firms and detailed data on clinical development outcomes over the 1990 to 2007 period. The final section provides some concluding observations and interesting questions for future research.

II DETERMINANTS OF MERGERS, ACQUISITIONS AND ALLIANCES

The motives for merger and acquisitions activity can be broadly categorized into adaptive or defensive rationales, versus proactive or offensive ones (Burns et al., 2005). In this section, we utilize this classification to consider the economic drivers of mergers and acquisitions in the pharmaceutical industry. It is important to understand the rationales for mergers before attempting to evaluate studies that are focused on the effects of mergers. We also consider the role of alliances as a substitute or complement to M&A activity.

A Defensive Motives: Strategic Response to Environmental Change

The hypothesis that industry-wide shocks can precipitate merger waves appears to be a useful concept in understanding pharmaceutical mergers. The original hypothesis goes back to Michael Gort (1969). Industry-wide shocks appear to explain merger waves in other industries such as banking and telecommunications in the 1990s (Andrade et al., 2001). In the case of pharmaceuticals, the economic environment became more difficult and pipeline gaps emerged throughout the industry by the late 1980s. With stock prices under pressure, many affected drug firms were motivated to use their accumulated cash flows to acquire another firm's products and pipeline. The bidder could often pay the premium associated with these acquisitions by consolidating operations and cutting out the excessive infrastructure capacity. Various researchers have made the point that mergers and acquisitions facilitate disruptive organizational change that would otherwise meet with substantial internal inertia and resistance (Ravenscraft and Long, 2000). However, mergers are also associated with substantial integration costs that can affect the productivity of the firm in the post-merger period (Clark, 2001; Larsson and Finkelstein, 1999).

Ravenscraft and Long (2000) performed one of the first analyses of pharmaceutical mergers. Their analysis covered mergers of significant value undertaken between 1985 and 1996. Using event studies, Ravenscraft and Long found that the large horizontal mergers and cross-border mergers created gains in overall stock market value. As in other industry studies, however, target firms captured most of the returns. Their findings are consistent with the response to the industry shocks, excessive capacity hypothesis. Their analysis of cost cutting for large horizontal pharmaceutical mergers found a reduction in total headcount in the post-merger period ranging from 8 per cent to 20 per cent of the combined workforce in the pre-merger period. While cost-cutting in manufacturing and marketing personnel was proportionately greater than for R&D employees, there was also a consolidation of R&D laboratories and the elimination of marginal R&D projects by several firms.

A subsequent analysis by CenterWatch of 11 large mergers (22 pharmaceutical companies) that occurred between 1989 and 1998 reported a 34 per cent average reduction in development projects three years after the merger was consummated (CenterWatch, 2000). Neither the Centerwatch study nor Ravenscraft and Long's analysis, however, examined subsequent effects on the firms' R&D productivity or the probability of success. To the extent that these reductions in R&D activities eliminated duplicate efforts or projects with low probability of success, or facilitated more external alliances, the companies' R&D performance could have increased in the post-merger period compared to the pre-merger one. This issue is considered further below.

Other researchers also find evidence that firms under economic stress are more likely to engage in mergers. An often cited firm-specific motivation for pharmaceutical mergers and acquisitions (M&A) is to fill in gaps in a company's pipeline to maintain growth in the face of a major product's patent expirations. Patent expirations on major projects can produce rapid losses in unit sales to generic entrants and leave firms with substantial excess capacity in their marketing and sales forces. Pharmaceutical products exhibit a highly skewed distribution of revenues and returns (Grabowski et al., 2002).

Two recent analyses have found that pipeline gaps and issues continue to be a key driver of merger activity. A study of 202 biotechnology and pharmaceutical mergers between 1998 and 2001 found that pharmaceutical firms that have a relatively old portfolio of marketed drugs exhibit a higher propensity to acquire another firm (Danzon et al., 2007). A second study of 160 pharmaceutical mergers between 1994 and 2001 found that firms with lower scores in the strength of their R&D pipeline and fewer years of exclusivity on their marketed drugs had a greater probability of engaging in a merger (Higgins and Rodriguez, 2006).

The fact that firms in economic stress are more likely to engage in mergers creates methodological issues in evaluating pharmaceutical merger activity. In particular, one can not simply compare merging entities to overall industry performance. Rather, it is important to construct control groups with similar firm characteristics in evaluating the effects of a merger. This issue is considered further below.

B Economies of Scale and Scope and Other Proactive Rationales for Mergers

Proactive motives for mergers include increases in size to achieve critical mass and economies of scale in R&D and other firm activities. Firms may also engage in mergers to increase the number of therapeutic areas in their R&D programs in order to take advantage of economies to scope. Furthermore, firms may undertake mergers and acquisitions to bring new technologies and research tools into the firm to enhance their research productivity. Mergers may also reflect management goals to increase firm size and growth rates, even if this is not associated with increased profitability or productivity (Mueller, 1986).

A series of papers by Cockburn and Henderson (Cockburn and Henderson, 2001; Henderson and Cockburn, 1996) focusing on economies of scale and scope in drug R&D provide some insight on the effects of increased size on R&D productivity. They looked for the effect of scale and scope on productivity at a research program level, for ten large firms. The advantage of these papers is that they use extremely detailed data (including program-level R&D spending) over a very long time period. They conclude that firms engaged in a broader scope of research activities are more productive than focused firms, but that scale doesn't matter much once the scope is controlled for. A recent paper by Danzon et al. (2005) finds benefits from a company's development experience as measured by the number of drugs in clinical trials, but these benefits are also subject to diminishing returns. This study is discussed further in terms of the effects of alliances on R&D productivity.

The consolidation of the larger pharmaceutical firms shown in Table 11.1 has been accompanied by increasing breadth in the R&D activities of the leading firms in the industry across therapeutic categories. For example, Pfizer, as a result of its large-scale mergers with Warner Lambert and Pharmacia, now has R&D programs in new fields such as oncology, endocrinology and ophthalmology. This complements the company's historical strengths in cardiovascular, depression, anti-infectives and erectile dysfunction (Burns et al., 2005). This increased breadth may produce economies of scope benefits over time as described in the academic literature by Cockburn and Henderson. However, Pfizer, along with some of the other leading pharmaceutical firms, now have annual R&D budgets of over

$5 billion to manage. At this size, companies may have entered a region of diminishing returns from the standpoint of managing and motivating creative individuals and coordinating their activities. It is notable that Pfizer, GlaxoSmithKline, and other firms with multi-billion dollar R&D programs and several hundred R&D projects are instituting more flexible organizational structures, and delegating more decision-making authority to the heads of the various therapeutic areas (Dorey, 2001; Mathieu, 2007).[3]

Beyond economies to scale, biopharmaceutical firms may engage in mergers to gain a presence in an emerging therapeutic category that represents significant future growth opportunities. For example, the oncology class has been characterized by several new 'first in class' drugs in recent years (DiMasi and Grabowski, 2007). The oncology class is now the fastest-growing therapeutic category among all major drug classes. The novel entities in this class have emerged primarily from the biotech sector, utilizing molecular biology techniques (for example, new monoclonal antibody products and other targeted agents). Mergers provide a more expeditious way to enter such high opportunity fields relative to internal expansion. It can take several years or even decades to build the internal scientific capability to enter a new therapeutic area or implement a new research platform in an emerging scientific field. This appears to be an important motivation underlying both acquisitions and alliances of developing biotechnology firms by established pharmaceutical firms.

C Alliances as Substitutes or Complements to Mergers

As discussed in section I, larger firms are also increasingly looking to alliances and partnerships with smaller biotechnology firms as the source of new products. This suggests that scale requirements, at least in the discovery and early stages of the development process, remain modest. At these earlier stages, small research-oriented boutique firms may enjoy a number of advantages relative to their larger rivals. These include the fact that they are closer to cutting edge technology emerging from universities and public-supported basic research, are more willing to take risks on disruptive technologies, and are less bureaucratic in organizational structure (Scherer, 1999). By contrast, larger pharmaceutical and biotechnology firms may have advantages in the more advanced stages of development, where large-scale clinical trial design and regulatory coordination become important. This rationale for R&D specialization based on different comparative advantages in research versus development was advanced by Kenneth Arrow (1983) in a more general model of the R&D process.

While alliances and partnerships are an alternative to mergers as a means to acquire new technological platforms and R&D pipeline candidates, they also pose their own set of issues. Arora et al. (2001) find support for gains from a division of labor at alternative stages of the R&D process. There are also positive network effects associated with alliances and partnerships (Pammolli and Riccaboni, 2004; Powell et al., 1996). On the other hand, partnership deals may be susceptible to a 'lemons' problem arising from agency and information problems (Akerlof, 1970; Pisano, 1997). Partnerships also raise challenging bargaining, management and governance issues (Teece, 1998; Arora et al., 2001).

Many mergers and acquisitions in the pharmaceutical area have occurred between firms that had first engaged in some type of alliance or partnership (Higgins and Rodriguez, 2006). This may help merging firms overcome pitfalls associated with agency problems and information asymmetries. In particular, the information gathered over time from an alliance may allow the acquiring firm better to assess the value of the acquired firm's intangible capital. It may also provide information on the resulting organization's ability to integrate the strengths of the two companies successfully. The difficulty of integrating firms with different cultures and organizational structures is an oft-cited reason for failures in mergers in the management literature (Larsson and Finkelstein, 1999; Smith and Quella, 1995; Haspeslagh and Jemison, 1991). There is at least some preliminary evidence consistent with these hypothesized benefits from alliances. Higgins and Rodriguez (2006), for example, find that acquisitions involving alliance partners had higher abnormal stock market returns than other pharmaceutical acquisitions. This study is discussed further below, in terms of assessing effects on R&D performance.

D Increasing Market Share and Antitrust Considerations

A traditional economic motive for mergers, of course, can be to increase market share and market power to gain competitive advantage. This has not been a major issue in the case of the large pharmaceutical mergers depicted in Table 11.1. In the United States and elsewhere mergers are subject to scrutiny prior to their implementation by the antitrust authorities (Mueller, 1996). There are well-known Department of Justice guidelines on what economic parameters can trigger challenges. In the case of pharmaceuticals, markets are defined in terms of therapeutic categories, since a drug product to alleviate pain, for example, does not compete with one that is approved by the Food and Drug Administration (FDA) for hypertension. Horizontal mergers of significant consequence, therefore, must go through a vetting process before implementation. These negotiations can result in a settlement where competitive products in the same therapeutic category are spun off as a condition for allowing the merger.

Nevertheless, one of the distinctive areas of antitrust concerns for R&D-intensive pharmaceutical firms is in the area of innovation markets. In particular, this issue arises when two merging parties have potentially competing drug candidates in their R&D pipelines. The concern is that this merger could result in the combined firms suppressing one of the research paths in order to avoid cannibalizing the economic performance with the candidate that is carried forward. The idea that antitrust authorities should concentrate on these dynamic effects of mergers on R&D activities or innovation markets was first advanced in a paper in the economics literature by Gilbert and Sunshine (1995). To date, there have been ten challenges for mergers in innovation markets, and eight of these challenges have involved the pharmaceutical industry (Carrier, 2008).

While the innovation market concept in antitrust enforcement has its supporters, its applications have been criticized by many economists and lawyers (Carlton, 1995; Rapp, 1995; Carrier, 2008). For pharmaceuticals, with their long and uncertain development process, critics argue that antitrust authorities should focus on drug candidates in the late stage of development where potential competition is more easily assessed. Early stage development activities involve relatively low costs and barriers to entry, and are also subject to high levels of uncertainty.[4] Many firms take a portfolio approach to obtaining new product introductions at the early stages of R&D. There are also typically many parallel R&D efforts across firms searching for promising new therapeutic approaches (DiMasi and Pacquette, 2004). When a drug progresses to the final phase III of clinical testing, however, the probability of success increases to approximately 70 per cent, while costs of clinical trials also increase significantly. Traditional anti-competitive concerns about potential competition effects then become more relevant, particularly when there are a small number of late stage competitors for these product candidates.

Carrier (2008) has done an analysis of each of the eight innovative market cases in pharmaceuticals. He finds that some of the challenges by the antitrust authorities are warranted, but others are more problematic given the relevant characteristics of the market and an analysis of the potential costs and benefits. In the questionable cases, he argues that the Federal Trade Commission (FTC) has attempted to protect innovation where future outcomes are uncertain and many years away from the market. By contrast, the EU has taken a less stringent approach to some of these innovation market cases (Morgan, 2001). This is clearly an evolving area of antitrust policy that warrants more research and attention by scholars.

III THE EFFECTS OF PHARMACEUTICAL MERGERS AND ALLIANCES ON R&D AND INNOVATION

To date, there have only been a handful of studies that have examined the specific effects of mergers or alliances on innovative activity and R&D productivity in pharmaceuticals. As discussed below, the results are mixed in nature and raise a number of issues and questions for further research.

A Mergers and Acquisitions

Danzon et al. (2007) look directly at the effect of mergers in pharma/biotech on various measures of performance. They focus on mergers with $500 million or more of market value. They find that these mergers are frequently a response to distress, so it is important to compare outcomes for merging firms to outcomes for other firms with similar characteristics, and they create propensity scores for this purpose. They conclude that mergers result in slower growth and a reduction in operating profit, though these effects are rather small. They also find smaller R&D growth for small merging firms. This doesn't speak to productivity directly, and they only look at performance in the first three years following a merger.

Ornaghi (2006) also looks at post-merger performance in the industry, but focuses on productivity. He does not use the propensity score or economic distress index for developing a 'control group' with which to compare the performance of merging firms. He finds that in the three years following a merger, there is a decline in R&D spending as well as productivity, as measured by patents. Koenig and Mezick (2004) focus on a relatively small number of high-profile mergers consummated between 1989 and 1996 (a sample of seven large mergers). Comparing the performance of companies in the industry that undertook these mergers with a control group of firms that didn't, they find that companies that merged were able to achieve more favorable post-merger productivity scores.

To summarize, although prior studies by Henderson and Cockburn (1996), Cockburn and Henderson (2001) and Danzon et al. (2005) generally find some advantage to R&D scale and scope, the studies analyzing merger effects find a weakly negative effect on R&D performance. This may be because there is no additional advantage to size at the level for most mergers, and/or because mergers are a response to distress, in which case the counterfactual is hard to determine. These studies also leave open many questions for further research. First, none of them look at the long-run impact of mergers on a firm's productivity. Three years is unlikely to be enough time to pick up many changes in patenting activity, much less progression through the phases of development. Second, as Cockburn notes, patents and new chemical entities are not necessarily the best measure of output, though almost all the evidence on productivity centers on these two measures. Third, the focus is on the larger mergers between public firms, and there is little attention paid to heterogeneity in outcomes. The management and finance literatures are concerned with what drives a successful merger, such as whether the R&D activities of merging firms are substitutes or complements, similarities in culture or corporate structure, the integration process, and other economic and organizational characteristics (Hitt et al., 2001). These issues remain important questions for future research.

B Alliances

The most extensive published study evaluating the performance of alliances has been done by Danzon et al. (2005). They examine the productivity at each phase of drug development (that is, success probabilities) for 900 firms over the period 1988 to 2000. They focus on experience, measured by the number of drugs a firm has in development, rather than sales in looking at economies of scale. They find that the effect of experience on productivity (advancing a drug through a phase) is positive with diminishing returns for phases 2 and 3, with the max occurring at 25 drugs in development. Products developed in an alliance tend to have a higher probability of success, at least for phases 2 and 3 trials, and especially when the licensee is a large firm.

Arora et al. (2007) also examine the role of licensing and alliances in a recent working paper using data from 3000 R&D projects in pre-clinical and clinical trials in the United States in the 1980s and 1990s. After controlling for selection effects, they find licensing improves the probability of success when the licensee is a pharmaceutical firm. Their results are therefore generally consistent with the results of Danzon et al. (2005) on the positive benefits of alliances. Both studies are inconsistent with a 'lemons' hypothesis by Pisano (1997), at least for the typical development-oriented licensing arrangement between biotech and advanced pharmaceutical firms.

In contrast to the work on mergers, the studies of alliances find positive effects on R&D performance. These studies indicate that development experience is generally associated with higher success probabilities, especially in later R&D stages. Hence, there appears to be a potentially important role for specialization across R&D stages. An advantage of the studies is that they are performed with R&D project-level data with a large number of observations.

These leading studies on the effects of alliances and innovation, however, also raise many issues for further research. The business alliance literature suggests a rich array of contractual terms and an evolving landscape of ventures. In this regard, Danzon et al. (2005) do not explicitly consider the contractual terms, the extent of integration of the R&D process, or the characteristics of the firms involved in the agreement beyond a few simple attributes relating to a firm's size and experience in performing clinical trials. Arora et al. (2007) adjust for product selection effects, but their analysis only considers a few characteristic variables. Both studies raise a number of issues about the underlying drivers of successful alliances for further research analysis.

Higgins and Rodriguez (2006) is the only study we are aware of that examines the interactive effects between pharmaceutical alliances and acquisitions. They analyze a sample of 160 pharmaceutical and biotechnology firms engaging in acquisitions between 1994 and 2001. As discussed earlier, with regard to the issue of motivation, they find that firms in economic distress with weak pipeline 'scores' and fewer years of (sales weighted) exclusivity for their marketed drugs, were more likely to engage in an acquisition. For the acquisitions involving an alliance partner, they find that the acquiring firms' pipeline scores improve in the immediate post-merger period. These pipeline scores are based on the count of drugs at each stage of development weighted by the average probability of success for projects at that stage. However, their analysis is short run in nature and only looks at changes in pipeline scores one year post-acquisition. This paper raises interesting issues concerning the long-run interactions between alliances and acquisitions for R&D performance.

IV A NEW RESEARCH STUDY ON THE EFFECT OF MERGERS ON R&D OUTCOMES

A Objectives and Background

In this section we report on some preliminary results from a new research project we recently initiated on the effects of pharmaceutical mergers on R&D outcomes. In contrast to other merger studies, our analysis focuses on the effects at the R&D project level of observation. R&D outcomes are measured in terms of advancement through the various phases of drug research and market launch. It utilizes a large database of more than 4500 firms engaging in pharmaceutical R&D between 1990 and 2007. Our work is therefore closer in character to the research that has been done on alliances. At this point, we report on the data sample and some preliminary findings regarding research scale effects for merged and non-merged firms in our sample. Eventually, we hope to incorporate information on prior alliances and other firm- and project-level characteristics, including the commercial performance of new product candidates that advance to market launch.

Since data is categorized by stage of development, we give a brief description of the new drug development process here (DiMasi et al., 2003; US Food and Drug Administration, 1999). New drug discovery and development is an information-generating process that passes through well defined stages. Discovery programs involve the application of basic biomedical knowledge to develop drug candidates for specific disease targets. Pre-clinical testing is then done in assay and animal modules. Clinical (human) testing is typically divided into three basic phases. Phase I involves a small number of healthy volunteers (typically fewer than 100 individuals) to gather information on safe dosages, toxicity and pharmacokinetic effects. Phase II involves testing in patients (usually several hundred) to obtain the initial evidence on safety and efficacy for a drug's intended indication(s). Phase III tests are designed to establish efficacy, and to uncover less frequent side-effects, with sufficiently large patient populations (usually in the thousands) to satisfy regulatory criteria at accepted levels of statistical significance. The regulatory authorities then review the data and decide whether a drug can be marketed.

The R&D process from a candidate's synthesis to marketing approval typically takes more than a decade. There is significant attrition at each stage of the process as shown in our analysis below and in other research studies. Project costs also increase substantially for candidates that advance across the different stages of the R&D process. This is driven by the increasing number of subjects and tests that are performed in each successive stage (DiMasi et al., 2003).

B Data on Drug Development Projects

Our primary source for information on drug projects in development comes from IMS R&D Focus. This dataset, typically used by pharmaceutical firms to monitor the research activities of their competitors, provides a history of *all* projects known to be in development from the mid-1980s to present. This includes projects that failed in clinical trials during this period, those that were successfully launched, and those that are still in development (since projects normally take between 3 and 10 years to complete clinical trials before reaching the market).

Each record in this dataset is a drug project, which can target multiple indications and have multiple firms participating in its development. A history of the project's progression through each stage of development is compiled from patent and regulatory filings, presentations at medical conferences, press releases, and information disclosed to financial analysts. Other significant events, including mergers, are also recorded. We identify mergers between private firms using this source, as such mergers would not normally be included in datasets such as SDC Platinum.

When a merger occurs, IMS updates the record of a drug project with the name of the merged firm. In order to examine the performance of a firm prior to a merger, therefore, it is necessary to identify which of the merging firms originated each project that existed prior to the merger. To do so, we rely on patent information (as typically, the patent assignee is the originating firm) as well as the text summary of research for each record. This text summary includes the source of information about a drug's status; if the source is one of the merging firms, we assume that the project was originated by that source. We can successfully assign about 80 per cent of drug projects that began prior to a merger to one of the merging firms.

Because most of the 4500+ firms in this dataset are not publicly traded in the US, we lack consistent time-series financial data such as R&D spending, total asset size, and other important control variables used in most other studies of mergers in this industry. Those studies focus on the performance of large firms. Our data has the advantage of including firms of varying size, at the cost of poorer information on financial data for non-public firms. To measure firm size, we use the firm's count of active drug development projects each year, and create 4 size categories: small (fewer than 5 projects under way in a year); medium (5–20 projects); large (20–50 projects); and very large (more than 50 projects).

C Results

We begin by graphing the fraction of projects that advance to the next stage of development by size of firm and by merging firms. Figures 11.2 to 11.4 show the distribution of advancements for phase I–III, respectively (advancement out of phase III means the drug was registered, approved or launched). In each case, the figure includes projects that entered each phase between 1990 and 2003. We assume a five-year window for advancement; this implies some truncation for recent projects (which we observe through the first quarter of 2007), but most projects that advance do so in less than four years.

The effect of size appears to vary across development stages. For drugs in phase I and II, the effects of size on the success probabilities for the firms that did not undergo a merger are relatively small in magnitude. However, there is a strong positive relationship between size and performance in

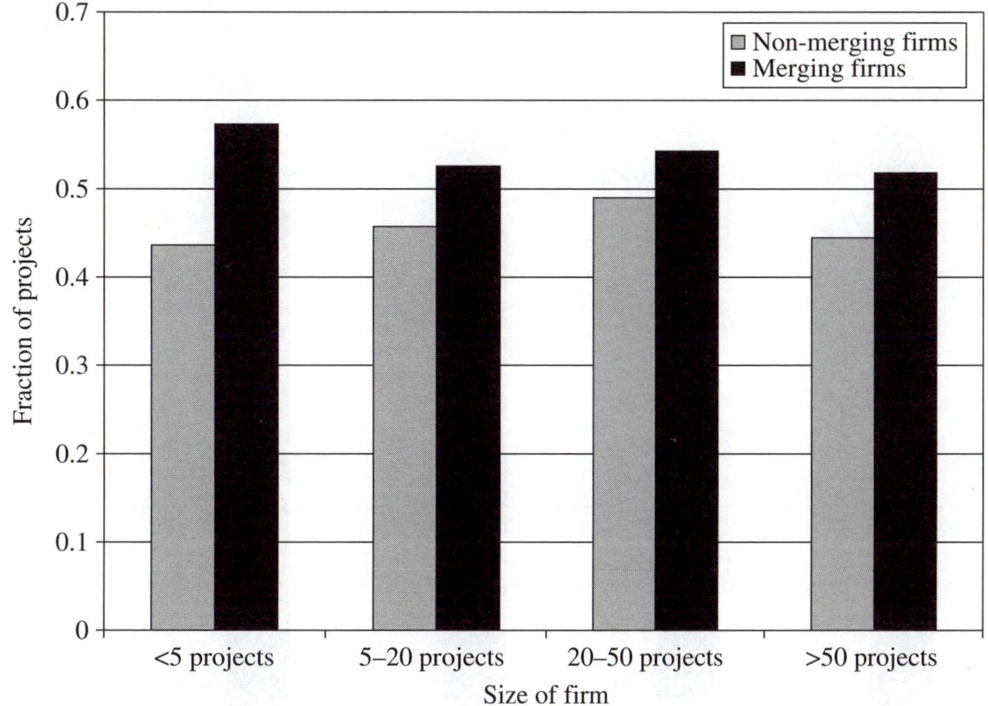

Source: Authors' analyses using IMS R&D Focus data.

Figure 11.2 Fraction of projects advanced within 5 years, phase I to phase II

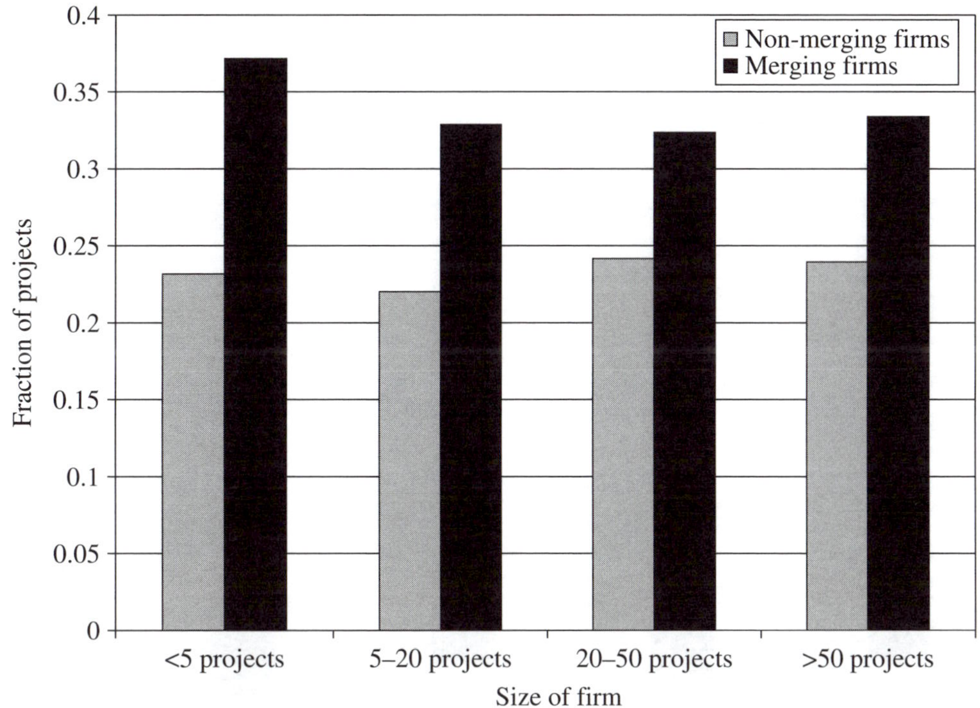

Source: Authors' analyses using IMS R&D Focus data.

Figure 11.3 Fraction of projects advanced within 5 years, phase II to phase III

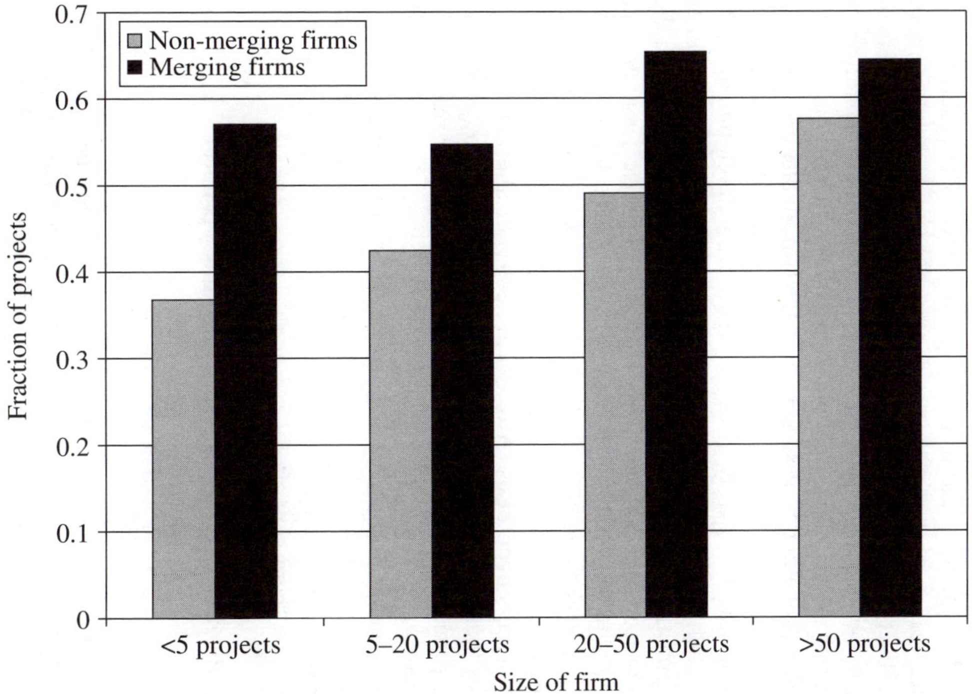

Source: Authors' analyses using IMS R&D Focus data.

Figure 11.4 Fraction of projects advanced within 5 years, phase III to launch

phase III. In particular, there is a monotonically increasing relationship and non-merging very large firms launch about 60 per cent more of their phase III projects than small firms.

In all figures, a higher fraction of projects of firms that experienced a merger during the 1985–2006 period progress to the next phase. This leaves open the question of whether high-performing firms are more likely to merge, or whether mergers lead to higher performance. The differences in advancement rates are greater for the smaller firms at each research stage. In addition, the effect of size for merging firms displays a different pattern than that for non-merging firms. However, the most substantial size difference also occurs for phase III. In this final phase, the largest two size classes have distinctly higher probabilities of success than the two smaller classes.

Although we refer to a higher rate of advancement as higher 'performance', this is not necessarily true. Because drug development costs increase with each stage, it is better to identify likely failures earlier rather than later. Firms that are better able to make this judgment early on in the development process may advance a lower fraction of projects in phase I or II, but have a higher probability of success for projects that progress to phase III. The higher probabilities of success for phase III for the largest-scale firms are consistent with their comparative advantage at later stages of the R&D process hypothesis (Arora et al., 2001) or alternatively, with the hypothesis that large firms are better at weeding out unlikely successes earlier in the process (Guedj and Scharfstein, 2004). Further research on this issue is warranted.

We next examine the probability that a project advances to the next stage of development within five years, controlling for firm size and the year the project entered its current stage. For projects that entered phase k in year t, we estimate a logit regression of:

$$\text{Advance}_k = \beta_0 + \beta_1\text{Small} + \beta_2\text{Medium} + \beta_3\text{Large} + \sum_{t=1990}^{2003} \tau_t \text{I}(\text{Year} = t) + \varepsilon$$

where small, medium and large correspond to dummy variables for the size categories defined above, and very large size (that is, more than 50 projects) is the omitted category; and $k = 1$ for phase I, 2 for phase II, and 3 for phase III. We estimate a similar regression for each phase including a dummy variable equal to 1 if the project was initiated by a firm that merged after starting the project, and a separate dummy variable equal to 1 if the project was initiated by a firm after merging.

Results are presented in Table 11.2. The coefficients of interest are those on the dummy variables for the size categories and whether the project was

Table 11.2 Logit regression analyses of R&D projects advanced within five years by phase of research, size, and merger experience

Dependent variable	Advanced within five years					
	Phase I		Phase II		Phase III	
Intercept	−0.276*	−0.717**	−1.41**	−2.14**	0.260	−0.296
	(0.119)	(0.140)	(0.199)	(0.227)	(0.254)	(0.288)
<5 drugs in development	−0.063	0.176	−0.106	0.242	−0.658**	−0.439*
	(0.097)	(0.105)	(0.123)	(0.133)	(0.172)	(0.183)
5–20 drugs in development	−0.083	0.104	−0.174	0.090	−0.562**	−0.357
	(0.098)	(0.103)	(0.126)	(0.132)	(0.176)	(0.183)
20–50 drugs in development	0.013	0.241*	−0.207	0.144	−0.123	0.108
	(0.110)	(0.116)	(0.132)	(0.139)	(0.193)	(0.201)
Pre-merger project		−0.050		−0.262		−0.293
		(0.112)		(0.150)		(0.211)
Post-merger project		0.508**		0.795**		0.707**
		(0.085)		(0.112)		(0.154)
Log likelihood	−2292.4	−2268.9	−1465.3	−1422.2	−714.5	−695.1
Number of observations used	3327	3327	2444	2444	1065	1065
Number of projects advanced	1683	1683	731	731	586	586

Note: Year indicator variables corresponding to the year the project entered a particular phase are included, but not separately reported.

Source: Authors' analyses using data from IMS R&D Focus.

pre- or post-merger. Year dummies corresponding to the year the project started are also included, but not presented in the table. The table also shows the number of projects analyzed at each stage and the number advanced within five years.[5]

The pattern of coefficients on the size categories is generally consistent with Table 11.1 and Figures 11.1 and 11.2. Size appears most important, both in terms of the magnitude and statistical significance, for phase III projects. Small and medium-sized firms are significantly less likely to launch their phase III projects relative to large and very large firms. For the earlier development phases, the coefficients on size are usually insignificant and much smaller. When we do not control for projects involved in mergers, smaller firms appear less likely to advance their projects, but the effect of size is non-monotonic.

The second column for each developmental phase considers the effects of mergers. When we include dummy variables for projects that were initiated before or after a merger (the omitted category corresponds to projects of firms that did not merge), the signs of the coefficients on size change, but still are not statistically significant. What is interesting is that projects initiated after a merger are much more likely to advance from each stage of development. This suggests a benefit to merging that is independent of size alone.

An important question for further research is the source of such benefits. Do mergers combine complementary skills of two firms, leading to better project selection? Do mergers reduce potential competition within a disease area, raise expected profits for a project, and therefore lead to more advancement? Are mergers necessary for the realization of these benefits, or could strategic alliances be used instead? Are firms that enter into alliances before mergers more likely to have higher probabilities of success in their R&D projects? These are among the issues we hope to address in future research.

V SUMMARY AND CONCLUDING COMMENTS

As is the case in other industries, mergers in pharmaceuticals are driven by a variety of company motives and conditions. Given this is the case, it is important to take account of firm characteristics and motivations in evaluating merger performance rather than using a broad aggregate brushstroke. Research to date on pharmaceuticals suggests considerable variations and heterogeneity of outcomes.

The empirical research on mergers is generally focused on the larger public companies. There is evidence that the mergers involving these pharmaceutical firms were driven in significant part by a series of industry-wide and firm-specific shocks. These shocks left many firms with an R&D pipeline gap associated with patent expirations and the increased leverage of payors during the 1980s and 1990s. While these mergers apparently have achieved cost reductions and addressed short-run pipeline problems, there is little evidence to date that they increased long-term R&D performance or outcomes. Many of the larger pharmaceutical firms listed in Table 11.1 continue to deal with a persistent R&D productivity problem.

By contrast, the empirical research on alliances between smaller biotech firms and larger pharmaceutical entities is more encouraging in nature. There is evidence of a positive relation between a firm's experience in clinical development and the probability of successful outcomes. This suggests a role for small and large firm specialization at different R&D stages. In particular, the 'R&D boutique' firms with a small number of research projects can apparently benefit from alliances with larger, more experienced firms, especially at the later stages of the R&D process. The work on alliances provides some support for this hypothesis but also raises a number of issues for further research.

Our preliminary analysis of the effect of mergers on R&D project advancement stages is generally consistent with these results from the alliance literature. In particular, using data on R&D projects from a large sample of public and private firms, we find that a company's development experience is significantly related to the likelihood of success, especially for the large pivotal phase III trials. Moreover, there is suggestive evidence that very small firms with only a few projects in their R&D portfolio can gain the most benefits from mergers with more experienced firms in developing new drug introductions.

Our results, and those of other studies, are subject to various qualifications and raise many questions for further research. The economic literature indicates, for example, that many acquisitions of smaller companies by larger firms are preceded in time by development stage partnerships. This opens a fruitful line of research in terms of when alliances are a desirable alternative to mergers, and where they can be complementary in nature. More generally, there are a host of interesting research questions to be addressed relating to the various drivers of mergers and the conditions and firm characteristics that produce successful versus unsuccessful mergers. These are important issues from both a business strategy and economic efficiency standpoint. We plan to address some of these questions in our future research agenda by augmenting our large R&D project database with other informational sources.

From an antitrust policy standpoint, the larger horizontal mergers in pharmaceuticals have run into few challenges by the regulatory authorities in the United States and the European Union, given the option to spin off competing therapeutic products to other drug firms. However, the issue of innovation markets, where firms have potentially competing development programs at very early stages of the R&D process, remains a more controversial area of antitrust policy for industries like pharmaceuticals. This remains an important area for future research by law and economics scholars.

NOTES

1. The sales of a second major biotech firm, Genentech, are included in Roche's sales in 1999 and 2004, since Roche acquired a majority equity interest in Genentech in 1990. Under the agreement, Genentech has operated as a free-standing company in the United States, with options on foreign licensing rights going to Roche on several of Genentech's products. The two companies recently signed a joint development, co-licensing option agreement that is currently being implemented for new drug product candidates.
2. The United States is the only major market without some form of price and utilization controls, but also has the largest generic drug market of any country. Generic drug products in the United States now account for more than half of all dispensed prescriptions (Grabowski, 2007).
3. Based on the R&D Focus database from IMS, the top five companies in Table 11.1 in the latest ranking averaged more than 250 projects across the various stages of the R&D process in 2006.
4. More than 75 per cent of the drugs entering phase I fail to reach the market for safety, efficacy or competitive reasons (DiMasi et al., 2003).
5. As in other studies of success rates, the lowest success rate is at phase II when the first tests of safety and efficacy in patients are performed (DiMasi et al., 2003).

REFERENCES

Akerlof, G.A. (1970), 'The market for "lemons": quality uncertainty and the market mechanism', *Quarterly Journal of Economics*, **84**, 488–500.

Andrade, G., M. Mitchell and E. Stafford (2001), 'New evidence and perspectives on mergers', *Journal of Economic Perspectives*, **15**(2), 103–20.

Arora, Ashish, Andrea Fosfuri and Alfonso Gambardella (2001), *Markets for Technology: The Economics of Innovation and Corporate Strategy*, Cambridge, MA: MIT Press.

Arora, Ashish, Alfonso Gambardella, Laura Magazzini and Fabio Pammolli (2007), 'A breath of fresh air? Firm types, scale, scope and selection effects in drug development', unpublished paper (available from the authors).

Arrow, Kenneth J. (1983), 'Innovation in large and small firms', in J. Ronen (ed.), *Entrepreneurship*, Lexington, MA: Lexington Books.

Burns, Lawton R., Sean Nicholson and John Evans (2005), 'Mergers, acquisitions and the advantages of scale in the pharmaceutical industry', in Lawton R. Burns (ed.), *The Business of Healthcare*, Cambridge: Cambridge University Press, pp. 223–70.

Carlton, Dennis W. (1995), 'Antitrust policy towards mergers when firms innovate: should antitrust recognize the doctrine of innovation markets?', testimony before the Federal Trade Commission on Headings on Global and Innovation Based Competition, 24 October.

Carrier, Michael J. (2008), 'Two puzzles resolved: of the Schumpeter–Arrow stalemate and pharmaceutical innovation markets', *Iowa Law Review*, **93**(2), 393–450, available at: http://papers.ssrn.com/sol3/papers.cfm?abstract_ id= 977603.

CenterWatch (2000), 'Troubling numbers for big pharma consolidation', reported in *In Vivo*, July/August, pp. 2–3.

Clark, Iain (2001), 'Drug discovery – Resolving the bottlenecks', *Horizons*, pharmaceutical issue 1, December.

Cockburn, Iain (2006), 'Is the pharmaceutical industry in a productivity crisis?', in Adam Jaffe, Joshua Lerner and Scott Stern (eds), *Innovation Policy and the Economy*, vol. 7, Cambridge, MA: MIT Press, pp. 1–32.

Cockburn, Iain and Rebecca Henderson (2001), 'Scale and scope in drug development: unpacking the advantages of size in pharmaceutical research', *Journal of Health Economics*, **20**(6), 1033–57.

Danzon, Patricia, Andrew Epstein and Sean Nicholson (2007), 'Mergers and acquisitions in the pharmaceutical and biotech industries', *Managerial and Decision Economics*, **28**(4/5), 307–28.

Danzon, Patricia, Sean Nicholson and Nuno Sousa Pereira (2005), 'Productivity in pharmaceutical-biotechnology R&D: the role of experience and alliances', *Journal of Health Economics*, **24**(2), 317–39.

DiMasi, Joseph and Henry Grabowski (2007), 'The economics of new oncology drug development', *Journal of Clinical Oncology*, **25**(2), 209–16.

DiMasi, Joseph and Cherie Pacquette (2004), 'The economics of follow-on drug research and development: trends in entry rates and the timing of development', *PharmcoEconomics*, **22**, suppl. 2, 1–14.

DiMasi, Joseph, Ronald Hansen and Henry Grabowski (2003), 'The price of innovation: new estimates of drug development costs', *Journal of Health Economics*, **22**, 141–85.

DiMasi, Joseph, Ronald Hansen, Henry Grabowski and Louis Lasagna (1991), 'The cost of innovation in the pharmaceutical industry', *Journal of Health Economics*, **10**, 107–42.

Dorey, Emma (2001), 'GlaxoSmithKline present a biotech façade', *Nature Biotechnology*, **19**(4), 294–5.

Ernst & Young Online (2007), 'Beyond borders: global biotechnology report 2007'; available at www.ey.com/beyondborders.

Gilbert, Richard J. and Steven C. Sunshine (1995), 'Incorporating dynamic efficiency concerns in merger analysis: the use of innovation markets', *Antitrust Law Journal*, **63**, 569–602.

Gort, Michael (1969), 'An economic disturbance theory of mergers', *Quarterly Journal of Economics*, **83**, 624–42.

Grabowski, Henry (2007), 'Competition between generic and branded drugs', in Frank A. Sloan and Chee-Ruey Hsieh (eds), *Pharmaceutical Innovation: Incentives, Competition, and Cost–Benefit Analysis in International Perspective*, Cambridge: Cambridge University Press, pp. 153–73.

Grabowski, Henry, John Vernon and Joseph DiMasi (2002), 'Returns on research and development for 1990s new drug introductions', *PharmacoEconomics*, **20**, suppl. 3, 11–29.

Guedj, Ilan and David Scharfstein (2004), 'Organizational scope and investment: evidence from the drug development strategies and performance of biopharmaceutical firms', NBER Working Paper 10933, Cambridge, MA.

Haspeslagh, Philippe and David Jemison (1991), *Managing Acquisitions: Creating Value through Corporate Renewal*, New York: Free Press.
Henderson, Rebecca and Iain Cockburn (1996), 'Scale, scope, and spillovers: determinants of research productivity in the pharmaceutical industry', *RAND Journal of Economics*, **27**(1), 32–59.
Higgins, Matthew. J. and Daniel Rodriguez (2006), 'The outsourcing of R&D through acquisition in the pharmaceutical industry', *Journal of Financial Economics*, **80**, 351–83.
Hitt, Michael, R. Duane Ireland and Jeffrey Harrison (2001), 'Mergers and acquisitions: a value creating or value destroying strategy?', in Michael A. Hitt, R. Edward Freeman and Jeffrey S. Harrison (eds), *The Blackwell Handbook of Strategic Management*, Malden, MA: Blackwell Business, pp. 384–408.
Koenig, Michael and Elizabeth Mezick (2004), 'Impact of mergers and acquisitions on research productivity within the pharmaceutical industry', *Scientometrics*, **59**(1), 157–69.
Larsson, Rikard and Sydney Finkelstein (1999), 'Integrating strategic, organizational, and human resource perspectives on mergers and acquisitions: a case survey of synergy realization', *Organization Science*, **10**(1), 1–26.
Mathieu, Mark (ed.) (2007), *Parexel's Bio/Pharmaceutical R&D Scoreboard 2007/2008*, Waltham, MA: Parexel International Corporation, pp. 77–87.
Morgan, Eleanor J. (2001), 'Innovation and merger decisions in the pharmaceutical industry', *Review of Industrial Organization*, **19**, 181–97.
Mueller, Dennis C. (1986), *The Modern Corporation: Profits, Power, Growth and Performance*, Brighton, UK: Wheatsheaf Books.
Mueller, Dennis C. (1996), 'Lessons from the United States' antitrust history', *International Journal of Industrial Organization*, **14**, 415–45.
Ornaghi, Carmine (2006), 'Mergers and innovation: the case of the pharmaceutical industry', University of Southampton, Working Paper.
Pisano, Gary (1997), 'R&D performance, collaborative arrangements, and the market for know-how: a test of the "lemons" hypothesis in biotechnology', Harvard Business School, Cambridge, MA, mimeo.
Pammolli, Fabio and Massimo Riccaboni (2004), 'Technological competencies in networks of innovators', in J. Cantwell, A. Gambardella and O. Grandstrand (eds), *The Economics and Management of Technological Diversification*, London and New York: Routledge.
Powell, Walter, Kenneth Koput and Laurel Smith-Doerr (1996), 'Interorganizational collaboration and the locus of innovation: networks of learning in biotechnology', *Administrative Science Quarterly*, **41**, 116–45.
Rapp, Richard T. (1995), 'The misapplication of the innovation market approach to merger analysis', *Antitrust Law Journal*, **64**, 19–47.
Ravenscraft, David J. and William F. Long (2000), 'Paths to creating value in pharmaceutical mergers', in Steven N. Kaplan (ed.), *Mergers and Productivity*, Chicago: University of Chicago Press.
Recombinant Capital (2007), 'Analysts notebook – Value of biotech out-licensing deals with pharma and biotech', available at http://www.recap.com/consulting.nsf/ContentWebPublish/46C030923BB918ED882572A4006A58C5?OpenDocument.
Scherer, F.M. (1999), *New Perspectives on Economic Growth and Technological Innovation*, Washington, DC: The Brookings Institution.

Smith, Kenneth and James Quella (1995), 'Seizing the moment to capture value in a strategic deal', *Mergers and Acquisitions*, **29**(4), 25–30.

Teece, David J. (1998), 'Capturing value from knowledge assets: the new economy, markets for know-how and intangible assets', *California Management Review*, **40**(3), 55–79.

US Food and Drug Administration, Center for Drug Evaluation and Research (1999), 'From test tube to patient: improving health through human drugs (special report)', US Government Printing Office, Washington, DC, September.

12. Endogenous horizontal mergers in dynamic markets

Engelbert J. Dockner, Andrea Gaunersdorfer and Steffen Jørgensen

1 INTRODUCTION

Traditionally, the consequences of mergers are studied in a static framework where a merger is modeled as an exogenous change of the number of firms in the industry. In terms of horizontal mergers, one of the first papers studying the welfare consequences of an increase in market concentration was Salant, Switzer and Reynolds (1983) (SSR). They show that in a static Cournot game with linear demand and cost functions, mergers are unprofitable unless they involve at least 80 per cent of the firms in the industry. Following this somewhat counter-intuitive result, a series of papers have analyzed the profitability of exogenous mergers and found that the SSR conclusion rests on two assumptions. First, Deneckere and Davidson (1985) show that if firms produce differentiated products and set prices instead of quantities, any price increase by the merging firms is matched by the outsiders and hence a merger becomes profitable. Second, the conclusion of SSR is linked to the modeling of the cost structures. If the merging entity can exploit scale economies of the merging firms, cost reductions ensure the profitability of mergers. Perry and Porter (1985) present a model that builds on these arguments: merging firms own a tangible asset, acquired from the merging partners, so that a merged firm can increase output at a given level of average costs and hence benefit from the merger. Dockner and Gaunersdorfer (2001) study exogenous mergers in a dynamic Cournot market. Their conclusion is in sharp contrast to the SSR analysis: if firms compete over an infinite planning horizon, a Markov perfect equilibrium exists in which it is profitable for firms to merge even if there are no scale economies.

In this chapter we present a two-stage game in which an equilibrium ownership structure is determined in the first stage and in the second stage firms compete in a dynamic Cournot game. In this way we endogenize the merger process. The literature on endogenous mergers contains three approaches to model a merger process. The first was developed by Kamien and Zhang (1990, 1991) who use a multistage normal form game in which the merger decision is based on simultaneous postings of bids and asking prices. This process eventually results in an equilibrium ownership structure. The second approach was used, for example, by Chatterjee et al. (1993) and employs non-cooperative bargaining theory to model merger formation. In such a game the formation of market (coalition) structures and the distribution of profits are simultaneous. A third approach uses cooperative game theory to study merger formation (Horn and Persson, 2001). This approach is suitable if firms can communicate freely and are able to make binding contracts. This approach will be followed in this chapter. Thus, our assumption will be that the decision to merge is irrevocable.

A model of dynamic endogenous mergers was published in 1999 by Gowrisankaran. Building on the classical model by Ericson and Pakes (1995) he looks at dynamic firm decisions and industry evolution within the framework of four actions: (i) mergers; (ii) exit of the industry; (iii) production; and (iv) investment and entry. In this general setting, equilibrium behavior of firms with and without mergers is analyzed. It turns out that allowing for mergers changes the structure of an industry, not only by making it more concentrated, but also by increasing its capacity to respond to external shocks. Moreover, mergers generally increase producer surplus, not because of an anticompetitive force, but because of the ability of the merged firms to, for example, prevent a possible deadweight loss arising from an exit.

The contribution of this chapter is to combine the cooperative game model of Horn and Persson (2001) with dynamic Cournot competition in the second stage of a game. We show that dynamic Cournot competition has the feature that any equilibrium ownership structure determined in the first stage involves mergers.

The chapter is organized as follows. Section 2 introduces the ownership model and formulates the dynamic Cournot game. In section 3 we review the benchmark equilibrium of the Cournot game in which every owner acts independently. In section 4 we study the equilibrium ownership structure of a four firm industry when all possible coalitions are permitted. Section 5 summarizes our findings and points out some future research issues.

2 THE MODEL

2.1 Ownership Stage

Consider an industry in which initially every owner possesses a unit of the productive asset that is necessary to run his own firm. Let there be N owners and hence N firms in the industry. Owners of these assets can form coalitions and hence merge the productive units of capital. The game has two stages. In the first stage, owners can form coalitions that determine the market structure in the second stage. In the second stage, the after-merger firms in the industry play a dynamic Cournot game over an infinite horizon.

We follow Horn and Persson (2001) and use cooperative game theory to model the ownership stage. Let $\mathbf{N} = \{1, \ldots, N\}$ be the set of owners and M_k a partition of $\mathbf{N}$ which describes an ownership (market) structure. Furthermore, let K_k be the number of coalitions in M_k, and O_k the number of outsider firms in M_k. Denote by $\mathbf{M}$ the set of all possible market structures and by $\mathbf{K}_k$ the set of all firms (coalitions) in a market structure M_k. Let N_{kj} be the number of firms in coalition j of market structure M_k. It follows that $\sum_{j=1}^{K_k} (N_{kj} + O_k) = N$.

Example Consider the case of four owners of productive assets so that $\mathbf{N} = \{1, 2, 3, 4\}$. The set $\mathbf{M}$ includes, for example, the market structures $M_0 = \{1, 2, 3, 4\}$, $M_1 = \{12, 3, 4\}$, and $M_2 = \{12, 34\}$.[1] Market structure M_1 is an oligopoly with three firms, one coalition $K_1 = 1$, and two outside firms $O_1 = 2$. The set of all firms $\mathbf{K}_1$ in this oligopoly consists of the firm resulting from the merger from 1 and 2 and the outsiders 3 and 4. Market structure M_2 is a duopoly with $K_2 = 2$ and $O_2 = 0$.

We assume sequential rationality of owners. That is, when owners decide which coalition to join (if any) in the first stage, they take into account what the profits will be in the (second) production stage.

We need to introduce a relation that, roughly speaking, compares the outcome of one market structure to another. For this purpose we use a binary relation: market structure M_l is dominated by M_k, $M_k > M_l$, if those firms in market structures M_k and M_l which have the power of enforcing either of the two market structures, prefer M_k over M_l. This definition requires a specification of who is a decisive group of owners.

Following Horn and Persson (2001) we employ the concept of decisive owners. These are owners who can influence the ranking of two market structures. Let $\mathbf{H}_k \subset \mathbf{K}_k$, be a subset of the firms (coalitions) in market structure M_k and let $O(\mathbf{H}_k)$ be the set of owners participating in the firms in $\mathbf{H}_k$.

Definition 1 (Horn and Persson, 2001) *A group of owners, D_{kl}, with respect to market structures M_k and M_l, and the corresponding sets of firms $\mathbf{H}_k^d$ and $\mathbf{H}_l^d$ that comprise these owners in the respective structures, is said to be decisive if*

1. $D_{kl} = O(\mathbf{H}_k^d) = O(\mathbf{H}_l^d) \neq \emptyset$
2. $\mathbf{H}_k^d \cap \mathbf{H}_l^d = \emptyset$
3. $\nexists\, D \subset D_{kl}$ *such that D satisfies 1 and 2.*

Example (continued) $\mathbf{H}_1^d = \{3, 4\}$ and $\mathbf{H}_2^d = \{34\}$ with the decisive owners $D_{12} = \{3, 4\}$. On the basis of Definition 1 we can define the binary relation $>$.

Definition 2 (Horn and Persson, 2001) *We say that market structure M_k dominates market structure M_l, $M_k > M_l$ if*

$$\sum_{j \in \mathbf{H}_k^d} \Pi_j^l > \sum_{j \in \mathbf{H}_l^d} \Pi_j^k$$

for each decisive group with respect to M_k and M_l, where Π_j^k is the profit of coalition (firm) j in market structure k.

Having defined a dominance relation that ranks all feasible market structures we can define an equilibrium ownership structure.

Definition 3 (Horn and Persson, 2001) *The set of Equilibrium Ownership Structure (EOS) is given by the core, i.e.*

$$\mathbf{M} \backslash \{M^s \in \mathbf{M} \mid \exists\, M^k \in \mathbf{M} \text{ such that } M^k > M^s\}.$$

With these definitions we have characterized the ownership structure and the merger (coalition formation) process. Let us next look at the production stage that has been analyzed in detail by Dockner and Gaunersdorfer (2001).

2.2 Production Stage

Initially we discuss the production stage under the assumption that each owner runs its independent firm, that is, we consider a dynamic oligopolistic market with N individual owners. Firms (owners) are symmetric and supply a homogeneous product. They produce with quadratic cost functions

$$C(q_i(t)) = cq_i(t) + \frac{1}{2}q_i^2(t), \quad i = 1, \ldots, N, \tag{12.1}$$

where $q_i(t) \geq 0$ is the output rate of firm i at time t and c is a positive constant. The product price $p(t)$ is related to industry output by the inverse demand function

$$p(t) = a - \sum_{i=1}^{N} q_i(t), \tag{12.2}$$

where the slope of the demand curve has been normalized to -1 and a is a positive constant. Combining (12.1) and (12.2), the instantaneous profit of firm i is given by

$$\pi_i(q_1(t),\ldots,q_N(t)) = \left[a - \sum_{j=1}^{N} q_j(t)\right]q_i(t) - cq_i(t) - \tfrac{1}{2}q_i^2(t). \quad (12.3)$$

Equation (12.3) represents a standard Cournot game played at time t. It is well known that this game has a unique, symmetric Nash equilibrium with equilibrium quantities and profits, respectively, given by

$$q_i = \frac{a-c}{N+2} \quad \text{and} \quad \pi_i = \frac{3}{2}\left(\frac{a-c}{N+2}\right)^2. \quad (12.4)$$

We use a continuous time dynamic version of the above Cournot game and apply the 'sticky price' model analyzed by Fershtman and Kamien (1987). In this game, firm i maximizes its discounted infinite stream of profits given by

$$\Pi_i = \int_0^\infty e^{-rt}\left[p(t)q_i(t) - cq_i(t) - \tfrac{1}{2}q_i^2(t)\right]dt \quad (12.5)$$

subject to

$$\dot{p}(t) = s\left[a - \sum_{j=1}^{N} q_j(t) - p(t)\right];\ p(0) = p_0, \quad (12.6)$$

where $r>0$ is the constant discount rate. Equation (12.6) implies that the actual market price deviates from its level given by the demand function (12.2) but moves towards it with a constant speed of adjustment s $(0<s\leq\infty)$. In this sense the model reflects 'sticky prices'.[2] Rewriting the state equation (12.6) as a dynamic demand function results in an objective function given by

$$\Pi_i = \int_0^\infty e^{-rt}\left[\left(a - \sum_{j=1}^{N} q_j(t)\right)q_i(t) - \frac{1}{s}\dot{p}(t)q_i(t) - cq_i(t) - \tfrac{1}{2}q_i^2(t)\right]dt. \quad (12.7)$$

In the limiting case $s\to\infty$ (instantaneous price adjustment) the payoff of each firm becomes

$$\Pi_i = \int_0^\infty e^{-rt}\left(\left[a - \sum_{j=1}^{N} q_j(t)\right]q_i(t) - cq_i(t) - \tfrac{1}{2}q_i^2(t)\right)dt, \quad (12.8)$$

which is a repeated Cournot game in continuous time.[3]

Since owners are sequentially rational, they understand and take into account that the outcome of the production stage influences the equilibrium ownership structure. We use backward induction to find the equilibrium of the two-stage game and derive the equilibrium of the production stage first. On the basis of this, we can calculate the individual profits of firms (dividends for owners), that in turn will determine the equilibrium in the ownership subgame.

3 CHARACTERISTICS OF THE BENCHMARK EQUILIBRIUM OF THE PRODUCTION STAGE

We first review optimal quantity setting in the production stage under the assumption that each firm is independent, which has been studied by Dockner and Gaunersdorfer (2001). This gives us information about the structure of the production subgame. Then we are able to exploit the structure of the production stage equilibrium to derive an equilibrium for the entire game.

We assume that the equilibrium in the production stage is identified as a Cournot/Nash equilibrium in Markovian strategies. This means that firms employ price-dependent decision rules when maximizing their discounted profits. Thus, changes in the market price stimulate responses by all players, being reflected in their optimal quantity choices. This reflects the interdependence recognized in oligopolistic markets.

Proposition 1 (Dockner and Gaunersdorfer, 2001) *There exists a stationary Markov perfect equilibrium (MPE) of the continuous-time Cournot game with independent owners, resulting in a market price*

$$p^* = \frac{a + N(c - \gamma)}{N + 1 - N\beta}, \tag{12.9}$$

with β *and* γ *defined as*

$$\beta = \frac{N + 1 - \sqrt{N^2 + 2}}{2N - 1}, \quad \gamma = \frac{c - a\beta - Nc\beta}{N + 1 - (2N - 1)\beta}.$$

The output rates are given by the Markovian strategies

$$q^* := q_i^* = p^*(1 - \beta) + \gamma - c. \tag{12.10}$$

The equilibrium output of any firm is

$$q^*(N) = (a-c)\frac{N^2 - N + 1 + (N-1)\sqrt{N^2+1}}{N(N^2+2) + (N^2-1)\sqrt{N^2+2}} \tag{12.11}$$

and the corresponding instantaneous profit rate is

$$\pi^*(N) = (a-c)^2\,\frac{2N^4 + 1 + 2N(N^2-1)\sqrt{N^2+2}}{2(N^3 + 2N + (N^2-1)\sqrt{N^2+2})^2}. \tag{12.12}$$

There is an interesting feature of the MPE that relates the equilibrium outcome of a dynamic game with Markovian strategies to that of a static conjectural variations equilibrium (see Dockner, 1992). Consider the Markovian decision rule (12.10). It represents a direct relationship between the market price and the quantity supplied by every firm. Further, assume that one of the firms – for any reason – increases its quantity. This increase reduces the price and thus triggers a response of the rival firms who decrease their quantities. In equilibrium this action and reaction pattern, as expressed by the price-dependent decision rules, is taken into account by the firms. Therefore, when considering an action, firm i knows that its rivals will react by making opposite moves and firm i will take this behavior into account when deciding its action. This, however, corresponds to a conjectural variations model. Dockner (1992) shows that in a dynamic Cournot model with quadratic adjustment costs, the use of Markovian strategies results in a steady state equilibrium price which coincides with the price of a conjectural variations equilibrium of a static Cournot game, with similar demand and production cost structures, and with negative constant conjectures that are smaller than the consistent conjectural variations.[4]

Proposition 2 (Dockner and Gaunersdorfer, 2001)[5] *The stationary Markov perfect equilibrium price* (12.9) *coincides with a conjectural variations equilibrium price of the static Cournot game*

$$\max_{q_i}\left\{\left(a - \sum_{j=1}^{N} q_j\right)q_i - cq_i - \frac{1}{2}q_i^2\right\} \tag{12.13}$$

where all players have (constant) conjectures given by

$$q_j'(q_i) =: \chi = \frac{2 - N - \sqrt{N^2+2}}{N^2 - N + 1 + (N-1)\sqrt{N^2+2}} < 0. \tag{12.14}$$

The constant conjecture is below the consistent conjecture.

The results in Proposition 2 are crucial for the next section where we characterize endogenous mergers. The reason is that we can use a conjectural variations equilibrium framework to characterize essential features of dynamic competition over an infinite horizon.

4 ENDOGENOUS HORIZONTAL MERGERS

Section 3 characterizes the benchmark equilibrium for the production stage supposing that all firms act independently. It will be our reference case when we determine an equilibrium in the production and ownership stages. Let us start with a formulation of the Cournot model after the formation of coalitions, that is, consider a given market structure. If such a market structure M_k is formed, firms are faced with the following production game. There are K_k coalitions with N_{kj} firms in coalition ($j = 1, \ldots, K_k$) and O_k outsiders. Imposing this market structure on our production game (12.5)–(12.6) results in the following dynamic Cournot model

$$\bar{\Pi}_j^k = \max_{\bar{q}_{kj1}, \ldots, \bar{q}_{kjN_{kj}}} \left\{ \int_0^\infty e^{-rt} \left[(p-c) \sum_{s=1}^{N_{kj}} \bar{q}_{kjs} - \frac{1}{2} \sum_{s=1}^{N_{kj}} \bar{q}_{kjs}^2 \right] dt \right\} \quad j = 1, \ldots, K_k \tag{12.15}$$

$$\Pi_i^o = \max_{q_{ki}} \left\{ \int_0^\infty e^{-rt} \left[(p-c) q_{ki} - \frac{1}{2} q_{ki}^2 \right] dt \right\} \quad i = 1, \ldots, O_k \tag{12.16}$$

subject to

$$\dot{p} = s\left(a - \sum_{j=1}^{K_k} \sum_{s=1}^{N_{kj}} \bar{q}_{kjs} - \sum_{i=1}^{O_k} q_i - p \right), \tag{12.17}$$

where $\bar{\Pi}_j$ and Π_i^o denote profits of coalition j and of an outsider firm, respectively, and $\bar{q}_{kjs}$ and q_{ki} are corresponding quantities.

It is now straightforward to derive an equilibrium in linear Markovian strategies for every market structure. However, before doing so, it is useful to review some results for purely concentrative mergers, that is, mergers where there is only one coalition of merging firms ($K_k = 1$) and some outsiders.

Proposition 3 (Dockner and Gaunersdorfer, 2001)

1. *A purely concentrative merger, creating a monopoly (the grand coalition) in a dynamic market, is profitable to each individual firm.*

2. *If a purely concentrative merger in a dynamic market does not result in a monopoly, then both insider and outsider firms benefit. The profit increase for an outsider firm is always larger than that for an insider firm.*

Item 2 of Proposition 3 states that in a process of coalition formation (outside) firms always have an incentive to be outsiders when a single coalition is formed.[6] Hence this result cannot explain endogenous mergers. For an endogenous merger to occur we have to show that there exist coalitions such that it pays to be an insider instead of an outsider. This, however, means that then there cannot be purely concentrative mergers with outsider firms.

We establish the main result of this chapter for the case of four symmetric firms and derive the firms' individual profits in each of the five market structures that are possible when firms are symmetric. Proposition 3 shows that a merger into a monopoly is a unique equilibrium ownership structure if there are no regulatory constraints that prevent such a merger. If a monopoly merger is prohibited, and with the results of Proposition 3 we have to show that $M_2 > M_3$, where $M_2 = \{12, 34\}$ and $M_3 = \{123, 4\}$.

Section 3 has demonstrated that the equilibrium of the dynamic game can be reproduced as a conjectural variations equilibrium of a corresponding static game. We shall employ this result to derive individual profits for any constant and negative conjectures $\chi < 0$.

Proposition 4 *Consider an industry with four owners and assume that firms play a dynamic Cournot game in the second stage with negative conjectures χ. Let $A = a - c > 0$.*

1. *In market structure M_2 profits for each individual firm are given by*

$$\bar{\Pi}_i^2 = \frac{A^2(5 + 4\chi)}{2(7 + 2\chi)^2}.$$

2. *In market structure M_3 profits for an individual firm in the coalition are given by*

$$\bar{\Pi}_j^3 = \frac{A^2(2 + 3\chi)}{9(6 + 10\chi + 3\chi^2)^2}(7 + 9\chi^2 + 16.5\chi). \tag{12.18}$$

whereas profits of an outsider

$$\Pi_i^3 = \frac{A^2\left(4+3\chi\right)}{9\left(6+10\chi+3\chi^2\right)^2}\left(6+9\chi^2+16.5\chi\right). \qquad (12.19)$$

Proof We identify the equilibrium of the dynamic game as a conjectural variations equilibrium of a corresponding static game.

1. The static game in the case of market structure M_2 is given by

$$\max_{q_i,q_j}\{(A-Q)(q_i+q_j)-0.5(q_i^2+q_j^2)\} \quad i,j=1,2; i \neq j,$$

where Q is total industry output. Applying constant conjectures $\chi<0$ results in (symmetric) equilibrium quantities given by

$$q=\frac{A}{7+2\chi}$$

which results in equilibrium profits $\bar{\Pi}_i^2$.

2. In case of market structure M_3 we have the problem for the coalition

$$\max_{q_1,q_2,q_3}\{(A-Q)(q_1+q_2+q_3)-0.5[q_1^2+q_2^2+q_3^2]\}$$

and the problem for the outsider

$$\max_{q_o}\{(A-Q)q_o-0.5q_o^2\}.$$

Applying first order conditions results in the equilibrium quantity for an individual firm belonging to coalition

$$q_c=\frac{A(2+3\chi)}{3[(1+\chi)(7+3\chi)-1]},$$

and the outsider's quantity is

$$q_o=\frac{A(4+3\chi)}{3[(1+\chi)(7+3\chi)-1]}.$$

Substituting these into the profit functions results in the equilibrium profits stated as $\bar{\Pi}_j^3$ and Π_i^3. **QED**

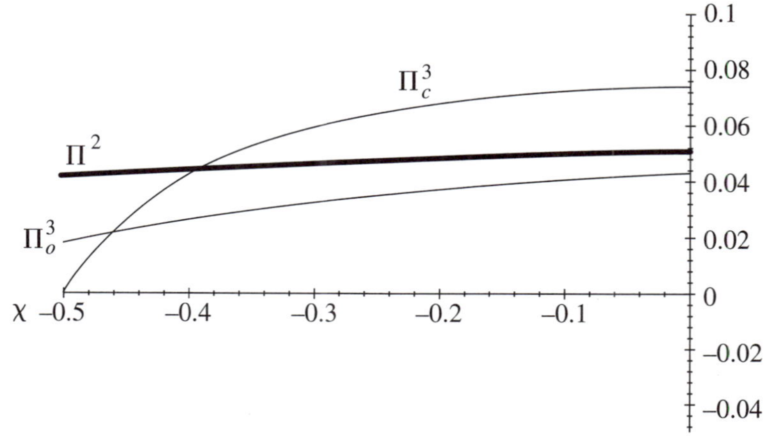

Figure 12.1 Profits of individual firms in market structures M_2 and M_3

On the basis of the individual profits given in Proposition 4 we derive the main result of the chapter.

Proposition 5 *If the negative conjectures χ are strictly lower than the consistent conjectures of the static Cournot game with linear demand and quadratic costs, $\chi < (-3 + \sqrt{5})/2$, market structure M_2 dominates market structure M_3, i.e., $M_2 > M_3$.*

Proof We present a graphical proof of Proposition 4. The relationship between profits of individual firms in the two market structures is depicted in Figure 12.1. From this figure it is clear that $\Pi^2 > \Pi_o^3 > \Pi_c^3$.

Note that the negative conjectures (12.14) do satisfy the assumption of Proposition 5.

Lemma 1 *If a monopoly merger is not feasible, the equilibrium ownership structure (EOS) in case of a four firm industry is two mergers to form a duopoly.*

The main conclusion of this result is that for all four owners in the industry it is beneficial to join a coalition. In particular, being part of a two-firm merger increases the profits of all firms in the industry. The interesting part of this result is that it is never profitable for a firm to be an outsider to a merger. Hence, we have established that the EOS is one that corresponds to endogenous mergers.

5 CONCLUSIONS

We presented a two-stage game where in the first stage firms are able to form coalitions with other firms in the industry. In the second stage, the resulting firms (coalitions or outsiders) play a dynamic Cournot game over an infinite horizon. We characterized the properties of the equilibrium in the production stage and then derived the EOS. We have shown in the case of an industry with initially four firms, that it is always optimal to form a coalition. If a monopoly (the grand coalition) is feasible, it is the unique EOS. If not, the EOS is characterized by two mergers so that the market is a duopoly. These duopolists then play a dynamic Cournot game.

NOTES

1. Other possible market structures are, for example, $M_3 = \{123, 4\}$, $M_4 = \{1, 2, 3, 4\}$ and $M_5 = \{1234\}$.
2. Fershtman and Kamien (1987) point out that the price dynamics (12.6) can be viewed as a dynamic demand function that results from rational consumption choices when consumer preferences exhibit habit persistence.
3. Instead of deriving the continuous-time repeated game (12.8) as the limit of the sticky price model of Fershtman and Kamien (1987), we could use a dynamic Cournot game with adjustment costs and obtain the repeated game in the limit when adjustment costs vanish. Both formulations provide the same qualitative results.
4. The concept of consistent conjectural variations has been introduced by Laitner (1980) and Bresnahan (1981). It refers to conjectures that are consistent with the actual responses taken by the rivals after a quantity (price) decision of firm i.
5. See Dockner et al. (1994) for a proof of this result in the case of a two firm industry.
6. In a recent paper Cesi (2007) formulates a 'stick and carrot' strategy to solve this 'insider's dilemma'.

REFERENCES

Bresnahan, N.F. (1981), 'Duopoly models with consistent conjectures', *American Economic Review*, **71**, 934–45.

Cesi, B. (2007), 'Horizontal mergers: a solution of the insider's dilemma', preprint.

Chatterjee, K., B. Dutta and K. Sengupta (1993), 'A theory of noncooperative coalitional bargaining', *Review of Economic Studies*, **60**, 463–77.

Deneckere, R. and C. Davidson (1985), 'Incentives to form coalitions with Bertrand competition', *The Rand Journal of Economics*, **16**, 473–86.

Dockner, E.J. (1992), 'A dynamic theory of conjectural variations', *The Journal of Industrial Economics*, **40**, 377–95.

Dockner, E.J. and A. Gaunersdorfer (2001), 'On the profitability of horizontal mergers in industries with dynamic competition', *Japan and the World Economy*, **13**, 195–216.

Dockner, E.J., J. M. Hartwick and G. Sorger (1994), 'Dynamic duopolistic competition with sticky prices: a note', preprint.

Dockner, E.J., S. Jørgensen, N. V. Long and G. Sorger (2000), *Differential Games in Economics and Management Science*, Cambridge: Cambridge University Press.
Ericson, R. and A. Pakes (1995), 'Markov-perfect industry dynamics: a framework for empirical work', *Review of Economic Studies*, **62**, 53–82.
Fershtman, C. and M.I. Kamien (1987), 'Dynamic duopolistic competition with sticky prices', *Econometrica*, **55**, 1151–64.
Gowrisankaran, G. (1999), 'A dynamic model of endogenous horizontal mergers', *The Rand Journal of Economics*, **30**, 56–83.
Horn, H. and L. Persson (2001), 'Endogenous mergers in concentrated markets', *International Journal of Industrial Organisation*, **19**, 1213–44.
Kamien, M.I. and I. Zang (1990), 'The limits of monopolization through acquisition', *The Quarterly Journal of Economics*, **105**(2), 465–99.
Kamien, M.I. and I. Zang (1991), 'Competitively cost advantageous mergers and monopolization', *Games and Economic Behaviour*, **3**(3), 323–38.
Kamien, M.I. and I. Zang (1993), 'Monopolization by sequential acquisition', *Journal of Law, Economics and Organization*, **9**, 205–29.
Kwoka, J. E. Jr. (1989), 'The private profitability of horizontal mergers with non-Cournot and maverik behavior', *International Journal of Industrial Organisation*, **7**, 403–11.
Laitner, J. (1980), 'Rational duopoly equilibria', *Quarterly Journal of Economics*, **95**, 641–62.
Perry, M.K. and R.H. Porter (1985), 'Oligopoly and the incentive for horizontal merger', *American Economic Review*, **75**, 219–27.
Salant, S.W., S. Switzer and R.J. Reynolds (1983), 'Losses from horizontal merger: the effects of an exogenous change in industry structure on Cournot–Nash equilibrium', *Quarterly Journal of Economics*, **98**, 185–99.
Stigler, G.J. (1950), 'Monopoly and oligopoly by merger', *American Economic Review*, **40**, 23–34.

13. Vertical mergers in markets with network effects

Gerhard Clemenz

INTRODUCTION

This chapter investigates the impact of vertical mergers between producers and retailers on social welfare and consumer surplus if the goods under consideration display network effects and are not compatible with each other. It is shown that vertical integration is indeed harmful for consumers because the integrated firm is able to exploit the network effect in such a way that the other producer is effectively kept out of the market and consumers have to pay higher retail prices. Formally we analyze a model with two producers, each of them producing a network good which is not compatible with the other good. Consumers buy one of the products from a retailer and enjoy utility from a network effect which is increasing in the number of consumers who buy the same brand. There are two retailers who engage in spatial competition which is modeled in the fashion of Hotelling's linear city model.

We compare three different market configurations. In the first scenario all four firms are independent. There exist two types of equilibrium. In a symmetric non-standardization equilibrium both brands are sold and have equal market shares. In contrast to several models in the literature on network goods (for example Shy, 2001; Farrell and Saloner, 1992) such an equilibrium exists also if the network effect dominates the traveling costs. In an asymmetric standardization equilibrium one brand captures the entire market. Due to spatial competition between retailers the price is the same in both equilibria, but consumers are better off in the standardization equilibrium.

In the second scenario each retailer merges with one producer and the two integrated firms compete with each other. It is shown that in equilibrium each integrated firm sells only her own brand, and if the mergers are *ex ante* profitable then consumers are worse off than in scenario 1.

In the third scenario one retailer merges with one producer, and the two other firms remain independent. If the marginal utility of the network effect is smaller than the marginal traveling costs, then the brand of the integrated firm will take over the entire market, but the independent retailer will be offered a wholesale price that ensures a profit for her which is equal to the one she could get if she only sold the other brand. Consumers are worse off than without any vertical integration. If the marginal network utility is larger than the marginal traveling costs an analogous equilibrium exists, but consumers may be better off than in the symmetric non-standardization equilibrium without any vertical integration. If the network effect is even greater, then the two independent firms will either merge as well or at least act as if they were merged, and in equilibrium only one brand will prevail. Consumers are again worse off than without mergers.

The chapter brings together two strands of literature, that on vertical integration and that on network goods. As far as vertical integration is concerned it offers a new possible reason for a negative effect on consumer surplus. The main reason given in the literature is the possibility that an integrated firm may be able to raise the costs of her rivals as was already recognized by Ordover et al. (1990). They have been criticized, however, for having to assume that the integrated firm can commit to a high price of her intermediate product, even though this would not be part of a subgame perfect equilibrium (Reiffen, 1992). More recently Schrader and Martin (1998) and Gaudet and Long (1996), extending the model of Salinger (1988), have shown that an integrated firm can raise the costs of an independent retailer by buying the intermediate good even though its price is higher than its marginal cost. Whereas Salinger (1988) and Schrader and Martin (1998) assume that the number of integrated and independent firms is exogenously given, the decision whether to merge or not to merge is endogenous in Gaudet and Long (1996). In an earlier paper Comanor and Frech (1985) have argued that exclusive dealing forces entrants to use more expensive distribution channels, thus reducing consumer surplus. Clemenz (2002) considers a model with spatial competition in the downstream market in which merging firms are not only able to raise rivals' costs, but also reduce the variety of products thus decreasing the utility of consumers. Finally, Riordan (1998) has shown that the acquisition of an upstream firm by a dominant downstream firm leads to an increase of the consumer price. Since at the same time production costs are reduced, the overall welfare effect, however, is ambiguous.

Like Gaudet and Long (1996), the present chapter endogenizes the number of vertical mergers. In particular, it is assumed that a merger takes place if and only if the expected profit of the integrated firm is at least as great as the sum of the two firms' profits if they remain independent. The main difference to all of the papers mentioned above concerns the market structure and the mode of competition. In these models downstream firms buy the product of the upstream firm and sell it to consumers, thereby engaging in Cournot competition in the retail market. Similarly, there is either Cournot competition (Salinger, 1988; Gaudet and Long, 1996; Schrader and Martin, 1998) or Bertrand competition (Ordover et al., 1990) for a homogeneous intermediate good between the upstream firms. Valetti (2000, 2004) has modified these models by introducing switching costs. In the present chapter, in contrast, retailers engage in spatial competition, and the goods display a positive network effect which benefits only the consumers of the same brand. One consequence is that in the present model the integrated firm has an incentive to sell also to the independent retailer, in contrast to many models of vertical integration (for example Neumann et al., 2005).

As far as goods with positive network effects are concerned an important question concerns the incentive of producers to make their products compatible. A fairly robust result, at least in models with only two producers, is that identical firms would like to make their products compatible in order to soften competition. Consumers, however, would suffer from compatibility because the disutility caused by higher prices is greater than the utility gain due to a larger network effect (Shy, 2001; Farrell and Saloner, 1992). In several of these models versions of Hotelling's linear city model have been used in order to capture the preferences of consumers for different brands (for example, Farrell and Saloner, 1992; Church and Gandal, 1992; 1993; Clements, 2004). The present model is similar in spirit, though Hotelling competition does not take place between producers, but between retailers.

The plan of the chapter is as follows. In the next section the formal model is set up and the main assumptions are stated. In the ensuing sections the four-stage game is solved in the usual way, starting with competition between retailers for various ownership structures. The chapter concludes with a summary and discussion of results and suggestions for further research.

1 THE BASIC MODEL

1.1 Firms and Consumers

Consider an industry with two producers, labeled A and B, and two retailers, labeled 1 and 2. Each upstream firm produces a good at constant marginal costs which are assumed to be equal to zero. The two goods are displaying network effects, but only for users of the same brand, that is they are incompatible. The downstream firms engage in spatial competition which is modeled as a linear city. The length of the street is normalized to equal one, and retailer 1 is located at the beginning and retailer 2 at the end of the street. There is a continuum of consumers who are uniformly distributed along the street. Each consumer has a linear transport cost function equal to δz, where z denotes the distance from the retailer she is visiting, and δ is a constant. Each consumer buys one unit either of good A or of good B as long as her utility is positive, or nothing otherwise. The utility of buying a good depends on the number of consumers who buy the same good, and on the distance between the location of the consumer and the retailer from whom she buys. Denoting the price of good i bought from retailer j as p_{ij}, $i=$A,B, and $j=1,2$, the distance from retailer j as z, and the number of consumers buying good i as s_i, the utility function is given by

$$u(p_{ij},z,s_i) = \beta + \alpha s_i - p_{ij} - \delta z \tag{13.1}$$

Retailers have to incur fixed costs (hence there is no market entry), but their marginal costs are equal to zero.

The four firms participate in the following four-stage game:

Stage 1: Each firm decides whether to remain independent or to merge vertically (horizontal mergers are not permitted). Mergers require the consent of both firms involved, that is the sum of the equilibrium profits of both firms must be smaller then the profit of the integrated firm.

Stage 2: Each firm decides whether to enter the wholesale market or not. Integrated firms may enter as seller, as buyer, as both, or not at all.

Stage 3: Producers who have entered the wholesale market make price offers and are committed to sell any quantity demanded at that price.

Stage 4: Given their costs (wholesale prices and production costs of the own output of an integrated firm) retailers compete on the consumer market via prices.

In the following sections we analyze the subgames beginning with stage 2, that is after the number of merged and independent firms has been decided. Clearly, there are three such subgames, namely (i) all firms remain independent; (ii) there are two integrated firms; and (iii) one integrated firm is facing one independent retailer and one independent producer. Each of these subgames is solved in the usual way by working backwards from the final stage. Once this exercise is completed it is possible to show which equilibrium will rule in stage 1.

1.2 The Retail Market

Recall that the two retailers, denoted as 1 and 2, are located at the endpoints of a street which has a length normalized to equal one. Consumers are indifferent between good A and good B, but if prices are equal they prefer the good with the larger market share because the network effect is greater. In contrast to the standard Hotelling model there are now two indifference conditions: one with respect to the brand of a good (A or B), and one with respect to the location of the retailer from whom to buy. Suppose the retailer has been chosen. A consumer who has to travel a distance z is indifferent between A and B if the following condition holds:

$$\beta + \alpha s_A - p_A - \delta z = \beta + \alpha s_B - p_B - \delta z \tag{13.2}$$

or

$$\alpha(s_A - s_B) = p_A - p_B.$$

If this condition holds then a consumer buys either A or B, each with probability 1/2. It is assumed that the effect of each consumer on s_i is negligible. When a consumer decides which brand to buy she does not know the market shares and has to form expectations. It seems reasonable to assume that she expects all other consumers who buy from the same retailer to choose the cheaper brand which is therefore expected to have a larger market share and therefore to yield greater utility due to the network effect. Consequently, a retailer will sell positive quantities of both brands only if their prices are equal.

We assume that neither retailers nor consumers can coordinate their decisions in order to agree on one brand.

Suppose next consumers have decided which brand to buy and now choose the retailer. The fraction of consumers visiting retailer 1 in order to buy brand i is a function of retail prices. Let x_i denote the fraction of consumers buying brand i from retailer 1. It can be obtained from the following indifference condition.

$$\beta + \alpha s_i - p_{i1} - \delta x_i = \beta + \alpha s_i - p_{i2} - \delta(1 - x_i) \tag{13.3}$$

implying

$$x_i = 1/2 + [p_{i2} - p_{i1}]/2\delta. \tag{13.4}$$

In equations (13.3) and (13.4) it is assumed that $\beta + \alpha s_i$ is large relative to δ and the prices and that therefore all consumers buy one unit of output.

Note that (13.4) is exactly the same as in the standard Hotelling model for a homogeneous good without network effect. Consequently, the price in a symmetric equilibrium, denoted as p_i^*, is given by

$$p_i^* = c_i + \delta. \tag{13.5}$$

Equation (13.5) holds in an equilibrium for any market share $s_i > 0$ if both firms have identical marginal costs c_i. This is the case if there is no vertical integration and both retailers buy brand i at the same price.

2 ALL FIRMS INDEPENDENT

We turn next to the equilibrium of the wholesale market if all firms are independent. Since (13.5) holds for any market share of the two brands, retailers have no reason to promote any of the two. Consequently, producers are engaged in Bertrand competition and since costs of production are assumed to be equal to zero, we get

$$c_A^* = c_B^* = 0. \tag{13.6}$$

Suppose, to the contrary, $c_A^* > c_B^*$. By (13.5) $p_A^* > p_B^*$ and $s_A = 0$. Similarly, if $c_A^* = c_B^* > 0$ then either firm could almost double their profit by reducing their price marginally.

There exist three equilibria:

1. $s_A = s_B = 1/2$.
2. $s_A = 1$, $s_B = 0$,
3. $s_A = 0$, $s_B = 1$.

In the first equilibrium both brands sell the same quantity because each consumer is indifferent between the two, and the probability of buying A is the same as the one for buying B. Retailers have no incentive to change their price and make a profit equal to $\delta/2$; the profit of producers is equal to zero. Consumer surplus equals $\beta + \alpha/2 - \delta - \delta/4$, where the last term denotes average traveling costs. It is noteworthy that $\delta > \alpha$ is not required for a symmetric non-standardization equilibrium to exist, in contrast to similar models analyzed in the literature on network goods (Farrell and Saloner, 1992; Shy 2001, ch. 2).

In an asymmetric standardization equilibrium prices and profits are the same, but consumers enjoy a greater network effect since all buy the same brand. Consumers are better off with standardization if

$$\beta + \alpha - \delta - \delta/4 > \beta + \alpha/2 - \delta - \delta/4 \text{ or}$$
$$\alpha > 0. \tag{13.7}$$

With a strictly positive network effect standardization is better than the symmetric non-standardization equilibrium regardless of whether consumer surplus or total surplus is taken as the objective function. This is an interesting contrast to standard results in the literature on network externalities in which it is shown that consumers do not benefit from compatibility of machines or standardization because the increased network effect is dominated by the softening of competition and the price increase. The reason is that in the present model retailers have some monopoly power due to spatial competition which is not affected by the compatibility of machines and the size of the network externality.

3 TWO INTEGRATED FIRMS

Without loss of generality we assume that producer A merges with retailer 1 and is labeled A1, and similarly, we label the other integrated firm as B2.

The first thing to note is that entering the wholesale market only as a buyer is a dominated strategy. If an integrated firm, say A1, buys brand B machines and offers them on the retail market, whereas B2 can only sell brand B machines, it is reasonable to assume that consumers believe that the market share of B is larger than that of A, and therefore consumers would be hesitant to buy brand A from A1. Consequently, if B2 does not sell brand A in the retail market the best response of A1 is not to sell brand B, and vice versa.

But the same is true if B2 does sell brand A: if A1 only sells A then it is plausible for consumers to expect brand A to gain a larger market share and they will all buy brand A.

Consequently, both integrated firms will only sell their own brand, and we are in the standard model of incompatible network goods (for example Farrell and Saloner, 1992).

3.1 Marginal Traveling Costs Greater than Marginal Network Effect

We consider first the case with $\delta > \alpha$. Assuming that A1 is located at the beginning and B2 at the end of the unit interval we now get $x = s_A$ and $1 - x = s_B$. The indifference condition becomes

$$\delta x + p_A - \alpha x = \delta(1 - x) + p_B - \alpha(1 - x) \tag{13.8}$$

implying

$$x = 1/2 + (p_B - p_A)/2(\delta - \alpha) \text{ and}$$
$$1 - x = 1/2 + (p_A - p_B)/2(\delta - \alpha).$$

It is straightforward to show that with $\delta > \alpha$ there exists a symmetric equilibrium with

$$p^* = \delta - \alpha. \tag{13.9}$$

Total profits are therefore also equal to $\delta - \alpha$, hence a vertical merger is not profitable if the two other firms merge as well. It is instructive, nevertheless, to consider the effect of full integration on consumer surplus.

For consumers, two mergers are an improvement as compared to the symmetric equilibrium with four independent firms: the utility due to the network effect is still $\alpha/2$, but the price is now reduced to $\delta - \alpha$.

Denote consumer surplus in an asymmetric equilibrium with all firms independent as u_{ai} and consumer surplus in a symmetric equilibrium with full integration as u_{sf}. In the asymmetric equilibrium the network effect equals α; in the symmetric equilibrium it is only $\alpha/2$. The utility of owning the network good is in both cases β, and the traveling costs are $\delta/4$. But the price equals δ in the asymmetric equilibrium without integration, and $\delta - \alpha$ in the symmetric equilibrium with full integration. Compared to an asymmetric equilibrium with four independent firms the two mergers are an improvement for consumers if

$$u_{ai} := \beta + \alpha - \delta - \delta/4 < \beta + \alpha/2 - \delta + \alpha - \delta/4 =: u_{sf}$$

which holds for $\alpha > 0$.

We can summarize our findings so far in the following:

Proposition 1 *Suppose $\delta > \alpha$. If each producer merges vertically with one retailer then there exists a unique symmetric equilibrium with the equilibrium price $p^* = \delta - \alpha$. Consumers would be better off than in an equilibrium with four independent firms, but the firms would have no incentive to merge.*

3.2 Marginal Network Effect Greater than Marginal Traveling Costs

If $\alpha > \delta$ then only an asymmetric equilibrium exists with either $s_A = 1$ and $s_B = 0$ or $s_A = 0$ and $s_B = 1$. Suppose without loss of generality that $s_A = 1$. The corresponding equilibrium price p_A^{**} is obtained from

$$\alpha - \delta - p_A^{**} = 0 \text{ or}$$
$$p_A^{**} = \alpha - \delta. \tag{13.10}$$

If (13.10) holds then firm B2 would not be able to attract the consumer located at her end of the interval (who incurs traveling costs of δ when buying from the other firm) at a strictly positive price. Now according to (13.7), $\alpha > 0$ implies that consumer surplus is greater in the asymmetric equilibrium than in the symmetric one if all firms are independent. Hence, a double merger resulting again in an asymmetric equilibrium would benefit consumers if

$$\beta + \alpha - \alpha + \delta - \delta/2 > \beta + \alpha - \delta - \delta/4 \text{ or}$$
$$7\delta/4 > \alpha. \tag{13.11}$$

The interpretation of condition (13.11) is as follows. If α is large, consumers enjoy a larger network benefit, but if δ is relatively small, this implies that the victorious firm can charge a high price, thus reducing consumer surplus. Interestingly, in an asymmetric equilibrium with integrated firms, the positive effect of a large δ dominates the disutility of greater traveling costs. Furthermore, in contrast to a symmetric equilibrium, a larger δ reduces rather than increases the equilibrium price.

As far as the profit of the successful integrated firm is concerned, it is equal to $p^{**} = \alpha - \delta$. Recall that the profit in any equilibrium with two independent retailers is $\delta/2$. Vertical integration is profitable for the successful firm if

$$\alpha - \delta > \delta/2 \text{ or}$$
$$\alpha > 3\delta/2. \tag{13.12}$$

Condition (13.12) states that vertical integration resulting in an asymmetric equilibrium, requiring $\alpha > \delta$, is profitable for the successful firm if the network effect is large in comparison to the traveling costs. The increased profit has two sources: (i) the successful firm serves the entire market and therefore doubles its sales; and (ii) a large network effect enables it to charge a high price.

A comparison between (13.11) and (13.12) reveals that the two conditions are not incompatible, as it is possible to have

$$7\delta/4 > \alpha > 3\delta/4. \tag{13.13}$$

The question is whether α satisfying (13.13) would induce retailers to agree to a vertical merger with one of the two producers. The answer is no if they are not risk-lovers since it is not clear which of the two integrated firms would prevail in equilibrium. Assuming that the probability is the same for both, that is 1/2, the condition for a merger to occur is that the expected profit is greater than in an equilibrium with independent firms, hence

$$[\alpha - \delta]/2 > \delta/2 \text{ or}$$
$$\alpha > 2\delta. \qquad (13.14)$$

But (13.14) is not compatible with (13.11), and therefore a vertical merger which yields an increase of expected profits and results in an asymmetric equilibrium is not beneficial for consumers. We summarize these results in

Proposition 2 *Suppose $\delta < \alpha$. With two integrated firms only asymmetric equilibria exist with either brand A or brand B prevailing, and the equilibrium price is given by $p^{**} = \alpha - \delta$. There exist values of δ and α for which the prevailing firm makes a higher profit than in the equilibrium with independent firms and consumers are also better off. If, however, the expected profit of two merging firms is greater than their joint profits in the pre-merger equilibrium, then consumers are worse off after the merger.*

4 ONE INTEGRATED FIRM

4.1 Marginal Traveling Costs Greater than Marginal Network Effect

Finally we look at a situation with only one integrated firm, labeled A1, facing the independent retailer 2 and the independent producer B. We start again with the case in which $\delta > \alpha$. First we show that the integrated firm has a strong incentive to supply the independent retailer 2 with their product. If they do not then retailer 2 will only sell brand B and we are essentially in the same situation as with two integrated firms. Consequently, the merger would result in a loss as compared to the pre-merger equilibrium. If retailer 2 is supplied with brand A at wholesale price equal to zero then chances are that all consumers buy brand A and the profit of the integrated firm equals $\delta/2$ which is equal to the profit of retailer 1 in the pre-merger equilibrium. Note that retailer 2 has no incentive to merge with producer B in response to a merger of producer A and retailer 1, since this would reduce their profits as shown above.

However, the integrated firm A1 can do better than offering retailer 2 a wholesale price equal to marginal costs. Suppose they offer a wholesale price $c_A > 0$. If retailer 2 only sells brand A the resulting equilibrium price is greater than δ which is the symmetric equilibrium price. Of course, the market share of retailer 2 would be less than 1/2, but this could be compensated by the higher price. Consequently, firm A1 should try to find some

$c_A > 0$ such that the profit of retailer 2 is greater or equal to $[\delta - \alpha]/2$, which is the profit retailer 2 could ensure for themselves by selling only brand B. We show next that such a wholesale price always exists. Consider first once more the indifference condition if both retailers sell only brand A:

$$\beta + \alpha - p_1 - \delta x = \beta + \alpha - p_2 - \delta(1 - x)$$

implying

$$x = 1/2 + [p_2 - p_1]/2\delta,$$
$$1 - x = 1/2 + [p_1 - p_2]/2\delta,$$

where subscript A is omitted for the sake of convenience. The profits of A1 and retailer 2 are given by

$$\pi_1 = p_1 x,$$
$$\pi_2 = [p_2 - c_A](1 - x).$$

Differentiating π_i with respect to p_i yields the first order conditions

$$p_2 + \delta - 2p_1 = 0,$$
$$p_1 + \delta + c_A - 2p_2 = 0,$$

yielding the solutions

$$p_1^* = \delta + c_A/3 \tag{13.15a}$$
$$p_2^* = \delta + 2c_A/3. \tag{13.15b}$$

The market shares are

$$x = 1/2 + c_A/6\delta,\ 1 - x = 1/2 - c_A/6\delta.$$

Substituting into π_2 and setting it equal to $[\delta - \alpha]/2$ implicitly defines c_A^*, the wholesale price of brand A offered to retailer 2 which is incentive compatible with the desire of A1 that only brand A is sold:

$$[\delta + 2c_A/3 - c_A][1/2 - c_A/6\delta] = [\delta - \alpha]/2 \text{ or}$$
$$c_A{}^2 - 6c_A\delta + 9\alpha\delta = 0. \tag{13.16}$$

The explicit solution of (13.16) is given by

$$c_A^* = 3\delta \pm \{36\delta^2 - 36\alpha\delta\}^{1/2}/2 = 3\delta \pm 3\{\delta[\delta - \alpha]\}^{1/2} \tag{13.17}$$

An economically meaningful solution must satisfy $3\delta > c_A > 0$, and since $\delta > \alpha$ there exists a solution of (13.17) which has this property. Consequently the integrated firm A1 will charge the wholesale price c_A^* which satisfies the incentive compatibility constraint, that is which yields a profit that does not make it profitable for retailer 2 to sell brand B.

A problem arises if A1 has to commit to a price before retailer 2 is committed to sell only brand B. Since p_{1A} is greater than δ, retailer 2 could offer brand B at a price below p_{1A}, get more than 50 per cent market share and make a profit greater than $[\delta - \alpha]/2$. This could be avoided if retailers have to make a down payment on their orders or have to buy a certain quantity before competition in the retail market starts. For simplicity we assume that retailers have to place their orders with the producers before competition in the retail market takes place.

Consumers are worse off in the equilibrium with only one integrated firm than in an equilibrium with four independent firms. This is obvious if the latter equilibrium is asymmetric with all consumers buying the same brand. The network effect is the same, but retail prices go up. In a symmetric equilibrium with independent firms the consumer surplus, denoted as u_{si}, equals

$$u_{si} := \beta + \alpha/2 - \delta - \delta/4. \tag{13.18}$$

The consumer surplus of clients of A1 in the equilibrium with partial vertical integration, denoted as u_{Ap}, equals

$$u_{Ap} := \beta + \alpha - \delta[1/2 + c_A/6\delta]/2 - \delta - c_A/3, \tag{13.19}$$

where $\delta[1/2 + c_A/6\delta]/2$ are the average traveling costs of consumers buying from the integrated firm A1 whose market share is the expression in square brackets. Subtracting (13.19) from (13.18) yields

$$\begin{aligned}\Delta := u_{si} - u_{Ap} &= -\alpha/2 + 5c_A/12 \\ &= -\alpha/2 + [5/12]3\{\delta - [\delta^2 - \delta\alpha]^{1/2}\}.\end{aligned} \tag{13.20}$$

For $\alpha = 0$ we get $\Delta = 0$, and $\alpha = \delta$ implies $\Delta > 0$. Differentiating Δ with respect to α yields

$$d\Delta/d\alpha = -1/2 + [5/4]\delta[\delta^2 - \delta\alpha]^{-1/2} > 0 \text{ since } \delta/[\delta^2 - \delta\alpha]^{1/2} > 1. \tag{13.21}$$

The intuition behind this result is that an increase of α relative to δ weakens the market power of retailer 2 since traveling costs are becoming less important as compared to the network effect. This in turn allows firm A1 to charge a higher wholesale price, which is reflected in a greater retail price. Consumers buying from the independent retailer 2 are even worse off since they pay the price $\delta + 2c_A/3$, which dominates the reduction of average traveling costs.

Summing up the results of this section we state

Proposition 3: *If* $\delta \geq \alpha$ *then there exists an equilibrium with partial vertical integration and standardization in which the integrating firms have a higher total profit than in the equilibrium with four independent firms. The profit of the remaining independent retailer is smaller than in the equilibrium with no vertical integration at all, but it is the same as they would get if they merged with producer B in response to the merger of A and 1. Consumers are worse off, even though the network effect is greater than in the symmetric equilibrium without vertical integration.*

4.2 Marginal Network Effect Greater than Marginal Traveling Costs

The vertically integrated firm A1 has two options: they can try to capture the entire market, thereby provoking a response from retailer 2 who would fight back by trying to get the entire market for brand B. Essentially we would have the same situation as described in section 3(b), regardless of a formal merger between 2 and B or their remaining independent. The second option is similar to the one analyzed in section 4(a), that is to offer retailer B a wholesale price which yields a profit equal to the expected profit if there is competition for the entire market. Turning to the second possibility first note that the expected profit of retailer 2 when attempting to capture the entire market equals $[\alpha - \delta]/2$. Thus, firm A1 has to offer a wholesale price c_A, which satisfies

$$[\delta + 2c_A/3 - c_A][1/2 - c_A/6\delta] = [\alpha - \delta]/2 \text{ or}$$
$$c_A^2 - 6c_A\delta + 9\delta[2\delta - \alpha] = 0. \tag{13.22}$$

The explicit solution of (13.22) is given by

$$c_A^{**} = 3\delta \pm 3\{\delta[\alpha - \delta]\}^{1/2}. \tag{13.23}$$

Again we impose the condition $0 < c_A^{**} < 3\delta$, as a negative wholesale price does not make any economic sense and a wholesale price greater than 3δ would imply a loss for retailer 2. From (13.23) it can be seen that such a c_A^{**} exists if and only if $\delta < \alpha < 2\delta$. For $\alpha > 2\delta$ it is profitable for each retailer to merge with one of the producers and we are back in the situation described in section 3(b). As far as consumer surplus is concerned the situation is slightly different from the one described in section 4(a). Consider again the first part of (13.20):

$$\Delta := u_{si} - u_{Ap} = -\alpha/2 + 5c_A/12. \qquad (13.20a)$$

But now c_A is obtained from (13.23) instead of (13.17), and $\delta < \alpha < 2\delta$. For $\alpha = \delta$ we get $c_A = 3\delta$, thus $\Delta > 0$, but $\partial c_A/\partial\alpha < 0$ and therefore $\partial\Delta/\partial\alpha < 0$. In fact, for $\alpha = 2\delta$ we get $c_A = 0$ and $\Delta < 0$. The intuition is that a larger network effect makes it more attractive to capture the entire market, and firm A1 must offer a smaller wholesale price in order to prevent retailer 2 from fighting for the market. But this benefits consumers who enjoy the total network benefit as the price approaches δ, the one ruling in the equilibrium with four independent firms. Compared to the asymmetric equilibrium without any vertical integration, however, this equilibrium is still worse for consumers.

In summing up this section we state:

Proposition 4
(i) *If $\delta < \alpha < 2\delta$ then there exists an equilibrium with partial vertical integration and standardization in which the integrating firms have a higher total profit than in the equilibrium with four independent firms. The profit of the remaining independent retailer is smaller than in the equilibrium with no vertical integration at all, but it is the same as their expected profit if they merged with producer B in response to the merger of A and 1. Consumers are worse off than in the equilibrium without any vertical integration for α close to δ, but as α approaches 2δ, their consumer surplus is increased and they are better off than in the symmetric non-standardization equilibrium with four independent firms.*
(ii) *If $\alpha > 2\delta$ then it is a dominant strategy to merge and try to capture the entire market for one brand. Consumers are worse off than in an equilibrium with four independent firms.*

5 SUMMARY AND CONCLUSIONS

We have shown that vertical integration between producers and retailers increases consumer prices, thus reducing the consumer surplus. Profitable mergers lead to standardization which has a positive effect on the utility of consumer, but at the same time it allows an increase of the consumer price, and this negative effect dominates the positive one.

The following extensions of the basic model seem desirable in order to see how robust these results are.

a) Consumers usually have a preference for a particular brand as well as for certain retailers, and the former may be more important than the latter. Hence the model could be extended along the lines of Matutes and Regibeau (1988, 1992), who consider a model with two strictly complementary goods and consumers who can buy the components from different firms.

b) Results obtained from models with duopolies frequently cease to hold for more than two downstream and/or upstream firms, hence the model should be extended in this direction.
c) Since it is important for producers of network goods to create a large installed base, dynamic considerations should be taken into account as has been done, for example, by Valetti (2000, 2004) for goods with switching costs which have many similarities with network goods (Farrell and Klemperer, 2006).

It remains to be seen whether these and other extensions affect the main conclusions of the present analysis which, if nothing else, suggests some caution with respect to vertical mergers.

BIBLIOGRAPHY

Besanko, D. and M.K. Perry (1993), 'Equilibrium incentives for exclusive dealing in a differentiated product oligopoly', *RAND Journal of Economics*, **24**, 257–65.

Bolton, P. and M.D. White (1991), 'The "Foreclosure" effect of vertical mergers', *Journal of Institutional and Theoretical Economics*, **147**, 207–26.

Bonanno, G. and J. Vickers (1988), 'Vertical separation', *Journal of Industrial Economics*, **36**, 257–65.

Church, J. and N. Gandal (1992), 'Network effects, software provision, and standardization', *Journal of Industrial Economics*, **40**, 85–103.

Church, J. and N. Gandal (1993), 'Complementary network externalities and technological adoption', *International Journal of Industrial Organization*, **11**, 239–60.

Clements, M.T. (2004), 'Direct and indirect network effects: are they equivalent?', *International Journal of Industrial Organization*, **22**, 633–45.

Clemenz, G. (2002), 'A model of vertical integration between producers and retailers', in W. Franz, H.J.Ramser and M. Stadler (eds), *Fusionen*, Tübingen: Mohr Siebeck.

Comanor, W.S. (1990), 'The two economics of vertical restraints', *Review of Industrial Organization*, **5**, 99–126.

Comanor, W.S. and H.E. Frech III (1985), 'The competitive effects of vertical agreements', *American Economic Review*, **75**, 539–46.

Farrell, J. and P. Klemperer (2006), 'Coordination and lock-in: competition with switching costs and network effects', from: www.paulklemperer.org.

Farrell, J. and G. Saloner (1992), 'Converters, compatibility, and the control of interfaces', *Journal of Industrial Economics*, **40**, 9–35.

Gaudet, G. and N.V. Long (1996), 'Vertical integration, foreclosure, and profits in the presence of double marginalization', *Journal of Economics and Management Strategy*, **5**, 409–32.

Hart, O. and J. Tirole (1990), 'Vertical integration and market foreclosure', *Brookings Papers on Economic Activity, Microeconomics*, pp. 205–86.
Klass, M.W. and M.A. Salinger (1995), 'Do new theories of vertical foreclosure provide sound guidance for consent agreements in vertical merger cases?', *Antitrust Bulletin*, **40**, 667–98.
Matutes, C. and P. Regibeau (1988), 'Mix and match: product compatibility without network externalities, *RAND Journal of Economics*, **19**, 221–34.
Matutes, C. and P. Regibeau (1992), 'Compatibility and bundling of complementary goods in a duopoly', *Journal of Industrial Economics*, **40**, 37–54.
McAfee, R.P. and M. Schwartz (1994), 'Opportunities in multilateral vertical contracting: nondiscrimination, exclusivity, and uniformity', *American Economic Review*, **84**, 210–30.
Neumann, M., U. Fell and R. Reichel (2005), 'Successive oligopolies, vertical downstream integration and foreclosure', *Journal of Industry, Competition and Trade*, **5**, 59–77.
O'Brien, D.P. and G. Shaffer (1992), 'Vertical controlling with bilateral contracts, *RAND Journal of Economics*, **23**, 299–308.
Ordover, J., G. Saloner and S. Salop (1990), 'Equilibrium vertical foreclosure', *American Economic Review*, **80**, 127–42.
Reiffen, D. (1992), 'Equilibrium vertical foreclosure: comment', *American Economic Review*, **82**, 694–7.
Rey, P. and J.E. Stiglitz (1995), 'The role of exclusive territories in producers' competition', *RAND Journal of Economics*, **26**, 431–51.
Riordan, M. (1998), 'Anticompetitive vertical integration by a dominant firm', *American Economic Review*, **88**, 1232–48.
Salinger, M.A. (1988), 'Vertical mergers and market foreclosure', *Quarterly Journal of Economics*, **103**, 345–56.
Salop, S.C. and D.T. Scheffman (1983), 'Raising rivals' costs', *American Economic Review*, Papers and Proceedings, **73**, 267–71.
Salop, S.C. and D.T. Scheffman (1987), 'Cost raising strategies', *Journal of Industrial Economics*, **36**, 19–34.
Schrader, A. and S. Martin (1998), 'Vertical market participation', *Review of Industrial Organization*, **13**(3), 321–31.
Shy, O. (2001), *The Economics of Network Industries*, Cambridge: Cambridge University Press.
Valetti, T.M. (2000), 'Switching costs in vertically related markets', *Review of Industrial Organization*, **17**, 395–409.
Valetti, T.M. (2004), 'Vertical integration and exclusivity contracts when consumers have switching costs', *Southern Economic Journal*, **71**(1), 36–59.

14. The impact of competition on macroeconomic performance[1]

Karl Aiginger

1 INTRODUCTION AND OBJECTIVE

The competition–innovation–performance triangle is investigated at the micro level from the days of Schumpeter to the works of Aghion today. This chapter investigates the impact of the toughness of competition on the macroeconomic performance of countries. The relation between the degree of competition and a company's performance is at the heart of competition policy, and the relation between competition and innovation is discussed and investigated intensely in industrial economics. The impact of competition on innovation started with Schumpeter's hypothesis[2] that monopoly profits were necessary for innovation, leading then to u-curve relationships where innovation is largest for a medium-range degree of competition, but lower for very tough as well as for very lax competition. Empirical studies on the growth differences between countries increasingly stress the role of institutions,[3] but refer more often to regulation than to competition. Conventional macroeconomic growth models did not model the impact of competition, but assumed perfect competition. This changed in the New Growth Theory, where growth depends on purposeful and maximizing activities for which competitive pressure plays an important role. However, this has not resulted – with very few exceptions (see Griffith and Harrison (2004) or Salgado (2002) – in the inclusion of competition variables in empirical growth equations.

We use a set of thirteen indicators on the toughness of competition. The set combines survey data from managers, but also from experts, with the data on the regulation of product markets being provided by the OECD. We have added '*ex post* indicators' on effective price–cost margins at the industry level and profit shares on the national level, and also added an indicator on the openness of countries to trade. As a special tribute to the work of Dennis Mueller, we have also included an indicator on the persistence of profit hierarchies in about 100 three-digit industries between 1990 and 2000. For 14 EU member countries, we ranked price–cost margins at the start of the 1990s, and then looked at how similar the hierarchies were one decade later. A high persistency of profit differences could be the outcome of technical factors, but high and persistent profits in a specific industry may also indicate market power, the abuse of a dominant position, low mobility or the lack of grip of the competition authorities.

We then related the toughness of competition to economic performance. It is an innovation, following other papers of the author, to define performance as a concept broader than economic growth. The performance evaluation also includes the employment rate (positively); unemployment (with negative impact); furthermore the dynamics of employment and unemployment and an indicator on the income distribution (with more equality as better performance of the socio-economic system). Measuring the impact of competition on macroeconomic performance is a rather new territory (albeit a very old question). We start from rather simple techniques (from descriptive statistics, correlations and single regressions). Due to the categorical character of many of the competition indicators (and extreme outliers in others), we prefer an ordinal ranking of countries and rely on rank correlations. This may be a serious limitation, specifically in our final test. We estimate primitive stylized growth models in which performance depends on the starting level of income, investment ratio, human capital and innovation. Then we add the competition indicators to the best model. The surprisingly robust result is that the competition indicator by far outperforms the usual determinants of growth in our preferred model. This encouraging result could be the starting point for further research with more elaborate econometric techniques.

2 COMPETITION: THE IMPACT IN THEORY

The Impact of Regulation and Innovation in Empirical Studies

The most elaborate literature exists on the impact of product market regulation on economic growth. This research profited heavily from the construction of indicators by the OECD (Nicoletti et al., 2003). The literature is developed, published and stimulated specifically in publications by the OECD (Nicoletti and Scarpetta, 2002; 2003) and in studies commissioned by the European Commission.

There are three channels through which product market regulation impacts growth: (i) competition; (ii) entry and exit; and (iii) innovation. All three channels provide indirect links between product market regulation and growth, via the effect on the toughness of competition.

In theories, the link is established by the new growth theory and by industrial organization. The endogenous growth theory provides an increasing number of models that render endogenous the optimal level of innovation and make it dependent on structural variables. For theoretical reasons, but also because of their flexibility as a basis for empirical research, models of monopolistic competition dominate in endogenous growth theory.

The relationship between market concentration and growth stimulated by industrial organization dates back to the 1940s. Based on the insights gained from the theoretical model of perfect competition, it has been widely recognized that competition is an important force in achieving a better allocation of resources, providing incentives for the efficient organization of production, and pushing forward innovation activities.

Incentives for improved efficiency are provided by competition and can be divided into allocation efficiency, productive efficiency and dynamic efficiency (cf. Armstrong et al., 1994). While the (positive) effects of product market reforms on macroeconomic performance achieved through an increase in allocation and productive efficiency represent one-off changes to the level of output and productivity, improvements in dynamic efficiency through innovation are expected to have a much larger impact on long-term macroeconomic performance.

According to Schumpeter (1942), an atomistic firm operating in a perfectly competitive market may be a perfect vehicle for static resource allocation, but a large firm with substantial market power is the most powerful engine of progress and long-run expansion of total output. He identified two effects of market power on innovation. First, he argued that the expected *ex post* market power, even though it will be transient, induces firms to have an incentive to innovate. If firms expect excessive rivalry after the innovation, they will have little incentive for innovation. Second, Schumpeter also argued that an *ex ante* oligopolistic market structure and the possession of *ex ante* market power are favorable to innovation. This is because it is easier for firms to predict rivals' behavior under an oligopolistic market structure and therefore there is less uncertainty of excessive rivalry. Schumpeter believed that profit from *ex ante* market power could serve as a source of internal financial resources for innovation activity by implicitly assuming an imperfect capital market (cf. Cohen and Levin, 1989).

Market competition takes place as a 'process of creative destruction' (Schumpeter, 1942) and can be interpreted as a 'search and discovery process' (von Hayek, 1968). Competition as a perpetual search and discovery process ensures that producers are forced to adapt their products continuously to changing consumer preferences in order to keep their customers. Existing products and processes are challenged by innovations and will be driven out of the market if innovative products and processes fit customer needs better. In contrast to Schumpeter's view, a number of theoretical studies show that increased competition stimulates innovation activities. For instance, Arrow (1962) shows that innovating firms benefit more from innovations when competition is strong.

A series of studies in the tradition of principal–agent theory show that competition induces a firm to be more efficient by reducing its agency problems (Hart, 1983; Nalebuff and Stiglitz, 1983; Mookerjee, 1984; Willig, 1987; Hermalin, 1992).

Competition and Innovation in New Growth Models

Aghion et al. (2001) demonstrate in a model with step-by-step innovation that competition has a positive effect on growth by pointing out that a technological leader in a more competitive industry earns higher profits relative to other firms in the industry. In this institutional setting, a strong motive for innovation and/or investment in R&D comes from the opportunity to escape from competition with 'neck-and-neck' rivals ('escape-competition effect').

Empirical evidence for the assertion that competition forces firms to innovate and to be more efficient, thereby raising productivity and enhancing growth, is presented by Nickell (1996), Blundell et al. (1995) and Geroski (1990, 1995).

Porter (2000) found empirical evidence for both the intensity of local competition and the effectiveness of national antitrust policy[4] having a positive relationship with the level as well as the growth rate of GDP per capita. The argument that more competition has a positive impact on growth is also confirmed by the fact that the OECD countries, having begun to deregulate network industries most ambitiously in the early 1990s, enjoyed the highest GDP growth per capita in the late 1990s.

By further exploring Schumpeter's basic propositions in the context of endogenous growth theory (for example Aghion and Howitt, 1992; Grossman and Helpman, 1991; Romer, 1990), no compelling evidence for the negative tradeoff between competition and growth was found. Schumpeter's results rather proved to be very sensitive to the underlying assumptions (cf. Aghion and Howitt, 1998).

In an attempt to 'reconcile' both lines of argumentation, more recent research in the Schumpeterian tradition provides evidence that starting from a monopoly, competition enhances efficiency (only) until a certain level of market concentration is reached, while competition hampers efficiency if it is too intense. This non-monotonic relationship between competition and efficiency (or productivity and growth) is known in the literature as the 'Inverted U-Shape' hypothesis. According to Aghion et al. (2002), the relationship between product market competition and innovation is inverted U-shaped because at low levels of competition, the 'escape-competition effect' tends to dominate, while the Schumpeterian effect tends to dominate at higher levels of competition.

Empirical evidence for the 'inverted U' is presented in older literature, but also in recent studies (for example Scherer, 1967; Scott, 1984; Levin et al., 1985; Caves and Barton, 1992; Aghion et al., 2005; Griffith and Harrison, 2004). For less favorable evidence on the impact of product market competition on innovation see Ahn and Hemmings (2000) and Cohen and Levin (1989). Aghion et al. (2005) show additionally that the optimal level of competition – for maximizing the incentive for innovation – lies rather near to the position of perfect competition.

By using data for UK manufacturing industries, Aghion et al. (2002) found that negative 'Schumpeterian' effects of competition on innovation (and growth) only materialize at very high competition intensity levels. According to this research, the escape-competition effect is the strongest in industries with a small technology gap ('neck-and-neck' industries) and the appropriability effect is the strongest in industries with a large technology gap. However, in the case of really strong competition, not too many industries will remain neck-and-neck (composition effect). On the other hand, weak competition leads to many industries remaining neck-and-neck where the escape-competition effect dominates, while strong competition makes them less even, leading to the predominance of the appropriability effect.

By finding confirmation on the existence of an inverted-U relationship between product market competition and R&D expenditure for both the manufacturing and the service sector by using data for twelve EU countries, recent research strengthens the hypothesis that the relationship between product market competition and innovation/growth is non-linear, with both very high and very low levels of competition providing lower incentives for innovation.

On the Empirical Relation between Product Market Regulation and Performance

Empirical research on the relation between regulation and growth had been boosted by the availability of data sets on market regulation, specifically that of the OECD (Nicoletti et al., 1999). Unfortunately research on the impact of product market regulation has been less intensive than research on labor market regulation. One of the reasons is that the main set of indicators on product market regulation had originally been available only for one year in the 1990s (1998), so that it could not be used for studies on regulatory change or in panel analysis. The general finding is that product market deregulation is supportive of growth. However, this result is stronger if product market regulation is interrelated with labor market regulation and the regulation of the financial sector. For the impact of regulation on multi-factor productivity see Nicoletti and Scarpetta (2003).

Aiginger (2004a) concentrated on the relative importance of innovation policy and regulation strategy on economic performance at the country level, specifically investigating the performance differences between European countries since the mid-1990s. Economic performance is measured according to a set of indicators including growth of output, employment and productivity, which is thought to be important insofar as European countries had placed divergent emphasis on increasing competitiveness and productivity, on one hand, and to spread employment with the objective to decrease unemployment, on the other hand. Regulation is measured by indices on the product market and the labor market; innovation is measured by a set of 16 indicators on input and output of innovation, education and information technology. The overall finding is that countries did very well if they followed a strategy of liberalization, while at the same time boosting investment in the future (R&D, education, ICT). In univariate comparisons, the starting level of (de) regulation and the dynamics of investment in the future seem to be most important for economic performance at the country level, with the impact of innovation still being stronger.

3 MEASURING THE TOUGHNESS OF COMPETITION

Defining Competition

Even at the micro level it is not easy to define competition and to measure the different aspects of competition. There are at least two approaches to defining competition. Competition can be defined as a theoretical model, namely as a market in which the number of firms is indefinite, the price–cost margin is zero, and firms are mechanistic price-takers. Or competition can be defined as an evolutionary search process, in which firms enter, grow and exit, with entrepreneurs exploring chances and solving problems in a constantly changing environment (Mueller, 1977).

Measures for competition are often divided into structural variables and conduct variables. Structural variables are the number of firms, their size, market shares, or the size distribution of firms. Different 'rates of concentration' can be calculated, be they the share of the largest firms, Herfindahl rates, Gini-coefficients or entropy indices. The market delineation – that is, the question of where a market ends, how restrictive or broad it should be defined – is itself a never-ending question, and market shares and numbers of companies do not tell the whole story. Dynamic considerations in general and game theory in particular have shown that the importance of the number of companies might be overridden by behavioral or dynamic aspects. Conduct variables have always been considered important, but became even more important in game theory models. If there is one firm, this may be a boon, but the monopoly could also be 'contested', quick exit and entry might prevent any behavior different from the competitive model and the monopoly firm may get lazy (Aiginger and Pfaffermayr, 1997). If there are two firms, they may earn no profits (zero margins as in the competition model) or they may collude up to the shared monopoly profits. Collusion itself depends on conduct, but also on objective facts, specifically the length of the game. This makes the design of the game the most important issue, as acknowledged by the 2007 choice for the Nobel prize. If structure as well as conduct and the unknown design of the game are important, it pays to look at *ex post* indicators, for example price–cost margins, mobility and turnover indicators, the stability of rankings in market shares and profits. Tough competition is not consistent with high margins, stable rankings, low entry and exit, whatever the true model might be.

The evasiveness of competition is aggravated if we switch from specific markets to the aggregate level of an economy. The degree of competition is different between manufacturing and services, between sectors dominated by small firms and those with large firms. Competition is restricted in economies where up to half of GDP is supplied or at least intensively influenced or regulated by public authorities. It is limited if public schools and hospitals dominate, also in sectors with a large share of government procurement or state firms. Competition is high – independent from lenient domestic competition authorities – in small open economies, where 50 per cent of domestic consumption is supplied by foreign firms and half of production is exported.

Indicators Chosen

We used competition indicators from surveys, mainly from the assessments of managers as published in the WEF Global Competitiveness Report and the IMD World Competitiveness Yearbook, but also from a rating of the Competition Authorities by an external agency. We added indicators provided by the OECD on product market regulation. Finally we added statistics on the *ex post* outcomes on markets (profits shares, price–cost margins, openness); see Table 14.1.

Table 14.1 Toughness of competition and country performance

Indicator	Source	Q or C	Correlation (R) with		t-value in preferred performance model
			Performance	Growth	
1 Intensity of local competition	WEF	C	0.288	−0.177	0.12
2 Effectiveness of antitrust policy	WEF	C	0.514	−0.197	1.37
3 Extent of market dominance	WEF	C	0.479	−0.269	1.61
4 Time required to start a business[1]	WEF	C	0.485	−0.100	1.32
5 Government subsidies[1]	IMD	C	−0.026	0.192	0.56
6 State ownership of enterprises	IMD	C	0.586	0.068	2.82
7 Competition legislation	IMD	C	0.649	−0.133	2.79
8 Rating Competition Authority	Star Rating	C	0.351	−0.158	1.00
9 Wage share 2003–2005	Eurostat; AMECO	Q	0.440	−0.242	0.16
10 Price–cost margin (PCM), average 1998–2000[1]	OECD; STAN	Q	−0.410	0.189	−1.40
11 Persistence PCM (2000 relative to 1990)[1]	Eurostat; New Cronos	Q	0.020	0.549	0.43
12 Openness 2006 (export plus import share/GDP)	Eurostat; AMECO	Q	0.073	0.540	1.13
13 Product Market Regulation 2003[1]	OECD	Q	0.561	−0.007	1.83
Composite indicator[2]	WIFO	C	0.603	−0.062	2.06

Notes:
1. For these indicators the ranking had to be inverted relative to the original data published (since a high price–cost margin indicates a low degree of competition).
2. Average rank over the 13 indicators on toughness of competition. This unweighted average is then ranked again.

Q: quantitative data.
C: categorical data (rating).

Source: WEF The Global Competitiveness Report 2005–2006; IMD World Competitiveness Yearbook 2007; Star Rating (www.GlobalcompetitionReview.com).

Survey data are available on the intensity of local competition (indicator 1), on the effectiveness of antitrust policy (indicator 2) and on the extent of market dominance (indicator 3). Additionally, we used an assessment of competition legislation (indicator 5) and a rating of the National Competition Authority by the Global Competition Review (indicator 8).

As indicators of product market regulation, we used the time needed to start a business (indicator 4), the share of government subsidies as a percentage of GDP (indicator 5), the state ownership of enterprises (assessment; indicator 6), and again a survey on competition legislation (indicator 7). Finally, we used the summary indicator on product market regulation published by the OECD (indicator 10).

As indicators of effective competition (*ex post* indicators), we calculated the profit shares at the macroeconomic level (more exactly we calculated the 'non-wage share' in value added, a variable usually labeled income share of workers; indicator 9). Secondly, we calculated the average price–cost margin over 99 industries (PCM 1998–2000; indicator 10). Countries in which profits in the general economy as well as the margins in manufacturing industries are high and trade is low relative to GDP will probably have less rivalry on the domestic markets than those with opposite characteristics.

Dennis Mueller has intensively investigated the persistency of profit differences. While persistently above-normal profits can be the result of specific assets and of a tremendous ability to innovate and to react proactively to the changing environment at specific firms, in general, the persistence of high margins and large differences between industries may indicate some kind of slack, barriers to competition and leniency regarding competition policy. We therefore ranked the price–cost margins of 99 three-digit industries in each country (EU-15 members) and compared the ranking of the margins at the beginning of the 1990s and one decade later (persistency, indicator 11; for specific results see Table 14.2). Countries in which the correlation between the profit ranking at the beginning and at the end of the 1990s was high are presumed to have less domestic and foreign competition. Countries in which the ranking between the industries changed a lot face a tougher competition regime (indicator 12). Finally, we added the general indicator on product market regulation by the OECD (indicator 13). It partly overlaps with the assessment in indicator 6, since state ownership is one of 10 indicators used to assess product market regulation.

These indicators are combined into a 'composite competition indicator'. This is done by ranking the countries for the 12 individual indicators and then taking average ranks over the indicator set. While there are clearly more technically advanced methods available to combine noisy indicators

Table 14.2 Persistence of profit differences at EU level

		1990		2000	
			Rank		Rank
Top 10 industries					
N265	Cement, lime and plaster	0.649	1	0.718	4
N223	Reproduction of recorded media	0.698	2	0.798	1
N160	Tobacco products	0.622	3	0.748	3
N23	Coke, refined petroleum and nuclear fuel	0.673	4	0.785	2
N242	Pesticides, other agro-chemical products	0.702	5	0.602	10
N154	Vegetable and animal oils and fats	0.649	6	0.583	14
N181	Leather clothes	0.659	7	0.673	6
N156	Grain mill products and starches	0.638	8	0.594	12
N159	Beverages	0.613	9	0.646	7
N362	Jewellery and related articles	0.620	10	0.592	13
Bottom 10 industries					
N312	Electricity distribution and control apparatus	0.402	90	0.399	10
N342	Bodies for motor vehicles, trailers	0.382	91	0.395	9
N323	TV, radio and recording apparatus	0.401	92	0.345	3
N332	Instruments for measuring, checking, testing, navigating	0.411	93	0.435	22
N296	Weapons and ammunition	0.401	94	0.309	2
N352	Railway locomotives and rolling stock	0.375	95	0.252	1
N283	Steam generators	0.365	96	0.360	5
N363	Musical instruments	0.305	97	0.393	8
N272	Tubes	0.200	98	0.500	58
N333	Industrial process control equipment	−0.082	99	0.440	24

Source: Eurostat (New Cronos).

for the construction of a more comprehensive one, this is a first step to condense a large set of diverse information and to look at the impact of competition on performance.

To measure performance, we added the data on economic growth (average growth rate of GDP between 1996 and 2005), the employment rate and the unemployment rate of 2005, as well as changes in these two rates between 1996 and 2005 (see Table 14.3). We added the level of GDP in 2005, since high GDP per capita is at least as important in the assessment of the performance of an economy as short-run growth (which tends to be higher if starting from low levels); and finally we added as an equity measure, the relation between the top 20 per cent income and the bottom

Table 14.3 Indicators for macroeconomic performance (and ranking)

	Growth of GDP 1996–2005		Employment rate 2005		Employment change 1995–2005		Unemployment rate 2005		Unemployment change 1995–2005		GDP per capita 2005		Equity ranking Highest 20%/lowest 20%		Performance indicator	
	%	Rank	%-points	Rank	%-points	Rank	%	Rank	%-points	Rank	1,000 €	Rank	Ratio	Rank	Average[1]	Rank
Scandinavian countries	**2.8**	**17.3**	**73.0**	**7.0**	**3.8**	**13.0**	**7.0**	**16.0**	**−3.3**	**9.3**	**27.2**	**10.7**	**4.1**	**5.7**	**11.3**	**6.3**
Denmark	2.1	24	77.2	2	2.6	16	4.8	8	−1.9	10	28.6	7	4.3	8	10.7	5
Finland	3.6	11	68.6	13	8.4	3	8.4	22	−7.0	3	25.9	13	3.8	3	9.7	3
Sweden	2.8	17	73.3	6	0.5	20	7.8	18	−1.0	15	26.9	12	4.0	6	13.4	11
Small open economies	**2.3**	**21.3**	**68.1**	**13.7**	**3.4**	**11.7**	**6.1**	**13.0**	**−0.6**	**15.3**	**28.7**	**7.0**	**4.8**	**12.3**	**13.5**	**12.7**
Austria	2.2	21	68.6	14	0.5	19	5.2	11	1.3	21	28.8	6	4.4	10	14.6	16
Belgium	2.1	25	62.1	22	3.7	10	8.4	22	−1.3	14	27.7	10	4.9	13	16.6	20
Netherlands	2.6	18	73.6	5	6.0	6	4.7	6	−1.9	11	29.5	5	5.1	14	9.3	2
Continental countries	**1.6**	**26.0**	**64.7**	**18.3**	**4.4**	**11.0**	**9.0**	**22.3**	**−1.1**	**13.7**	**24.9**	**15.7**	**5.5**	**17.0**	**17.7**	**21.7**
Germany	1.3	27	70.3	11	3.0	14	9.5	25	1.5	23	25.8	14	4.3	9	17.6	22
France	2.1	23	61.3	23	2.8	15	9.7	26	−1.4	13	25.4	16	5.6	18	19.1	24
Italy	1.3	28	62.4	21	7.4	4	7.7	16	−3.5	5	23.6	17	6.5	24	16.4	19
Southern countries	**3.3**	**12.7**	**64.0**	**19.0**	**6.8**	**8.7**	**8.9**	**22.0**	**−2.8**	**12.7**	**19.8**	**20.3**	**6.7**	**23.7**	**17.0**	**19.3**
Greece	3.9	8	55.5	28	2.3	17	9.8	27	0.6	19	19.7	20	6.2	22	20.1	26
Spain	3.7	10	64.3	19	13.7	1	9.2	24	−9.2	1	23.0	18	6.0	21	13.4	11
Portugal	2.4	20	72.1	10	4.5	8	7.6	15	0.3	18	16.8	23	7.9	28	17.4	21
Catching-up countries	**3.7**	**12.3**	**60.3**	**22.0**	**−1.4**	**21.4**	**9.9**	**19.1**	**0.4**	**18.9**	**15.2**	**24.0**	**4.7**	**11.3**	**18.4**	**21.3**
Czech Republic	2.6	19	66.8	15	−4.7	27	7.9	19	2.1	27	17.3	22	3.5	2	18.7	23

Table 14.3 (continued)

	Growth of GDP 1996–2005		Employment rate 2005		Employment change 1995–2005		Unemployment rate 2005		Unemployment change 1995–2005		GDP per capita 2005		Equity ranking Highest 20%/lowest 20%		Performance indicator	
	%	Rank	%-points	Rank	%-points	Rank	%	Rank	%-points	Rank	1,000 €	Rank	Ratio	Rank	Average[1]	Rank
Estonia	6.9	2	66.5	16	−0.8	23	7.9	19	−1.8	12	14.0	25	5.5	17	16.3	18
Hungary	4.2	6	55.9	26	4.1	9	7.2	14	−2.8	7	14.7	24	3.8	4	12.9	9
Lithuania	1.3	28	62.4	21	7.4	4	7.7	16	−3.5	5	23.6	17	6.5	24	16.4	19
Poland	4.2	5	52.6	29	−5.4	28	17.7	29	4.5	29	11.7	28	5.6	19	23.9	29
Romania	2.2	22	55.5	27	−8.4	29	7.7	16	1.6	26	8.0	29	4.8	12	23.0	28
Slovak Republic	4.0	7	57.5	25	−2.6	26	16.3	28	3.1	28	13.4	26	4.0	5	20.7	27
Slovenia	3.9	9	65.2	17	−0.9	25	6.5	12	−0.4	17	19.2	21	4.1	7	15.4	17
Liberal countries	**4.0**	**11.8**	**70.2**	**10.7**	**5.4**	**10.0**	**4.9**	**7.0**	**−3.5**	**7.3**	**28.8**	**8.7**	**6.8**	**23.8**	**11.3**	**8.0**
United Kingdom	2.8	16	72.2	9	3.4	12	4.7	6	−3.8	4	27.6	11	7.2	27	12.1	8
Ireland	7.7	1	68.9	12	13.6	2	4.3	3	−8.0	2	32.6	3	5.7	20	6.1	1
USA	3.3	14	72.6	8	0.4	21	5.1	10	−0.5	16	34.7	2	8.5	29	14.3	15
Canada	3.3	13	73.8	4	4.7	7	6.8	13	−2.8	7	28.4	8	5.5	16	9.7	3
Australia	3.6	12	73.2	7	3.4	13	5.0	9	−3.1	6	28.3	9	7.0	26	11.7	7
New Zealand	3.1	15	60.6	24	7.0	5	3.7	1	−2.6	9	21.4	19	6.8	25	14.0	14

Note: 1. Average over the rankings of the seven individual performance indicators.

Source: Eurostat (AMECO); IMD World Competitiveness Yearbook 2007.

20 per cent. This combination of indicators similar – sets had been used in Aiginger (2004b) in studies on successful macroeconomic strategies – implicitly assume that the welfare of individuals as well as of an economy depends on income (growth and level), employment chances (levels and changes) and equity. Possibly, it would be nice to add indicators on the environment, or on other non-material goods (health, security and so on). Similar to the construction of the overall indicator on the toughness of competition, we combined the individual indicators by ranking and averaging them over the ranks. Implicitly, this assumes that the individual arguments in the welfare function have the same weight and are related in a similar way (for example, same degree of redundancy); see Table 14.4.

4 TENTATIVE RESULTS ON THE RELATION BETWEEN COMPETITION AND THE ECONOMIC PERFORMANCE OF A COUNTRY

Descriptive Evidence

The correlation between the individual indicators and the macroeconomic performance is surprisingly strong. The correlation is highest for the managers' evaluation of competition legislation (indicator 7; R = 0.65). The competition legislation is rated as effective by managers in several European countries (Austria, Netherlands, Luxemburg and Denmark), where economic performance is good too, and, as expected, in Anglo-American countries (United Kingdom, Australia, New Zealand). Competition legislation is assessed as poor in former European transition countries and in the South European economies.

Many countries with large state ownership (see indicator 6) have a lower performance ranking. Besides the transition countries, Japan and France support this relationship since they have both high state ownership and low performance. The third best correlation exists between performance and the general OECD indicator on product market regulation (indicator 13).

This is followed by three indicators, with correlation coefficients still being around 0.50, namely, the effectiveness of antitrust policy (indicator 2), extent of market dominance by large firms (indicator 3) and the time required to establish a business (indicator 4). Thus, performance depends on the degree of competition with regard to entry – which is specifically relevant for new and small firms as well as conditions monitoring the behavior of large firms. The indicator on the intensity of local competition does not prove to be significant, and neither does it for government subsidies.

Table 14.4 Toughness of competition indicators (and ranking)

	Intensity of local competition		Effectiveness of antitrust policy		Extent of market dominance	
	Rating[1]	Rank	Rating[2]	Rank	Rating[3]	Rank
Scandinavian countries	**5.6**	**12.7**	**5.7**	**8.3**	**5.4**	**9.3**
Denmark	5.5	14	5.7	7	5.7	7
Finland	5.7	10	6.0	3	5.9	4
Sweden	5.5	14	5.3	15	4.7	17
Small open economies	**5.9**	**6.0**	**5.7**	**8.3**	**5.7**	**6.7**
Austria	5.8	8	5.7	7	5.9	4
Belgium	6.0	4	5.6	11	5.6	8
Netherlands	5.9	6	5.7	7	5.6	8
Continental countries	**5.6**	**12.7**	**5.4**	**11.0**	**5.0**	**14.3**
Germany	6.2	2	6.3	1	6.3	1
France	5.6	12	5.7	7	5.3	13
Italy	4.9	24	4.2	25	3.5	29
Southern countries	**5.2**	**18.7**	**4.8**	**19.0**	**4.4**	**20.3**
Greece	5.0	22	4.6	22	4.2	23
Spain	5.5	14	4.9	18	4.7	17
Portugal	5.1	20	5.0	17	4.3	21
Catching-up countries	**5.1**	**20.1**	**4.3**	**24.1**	**4.2**	**23.1**
Czech Republic	5.2	18	4.9	18	4.2	23
Estonia	5.6	12	4.8	20	4.0	26
Hungary	5.5	14	4.6	22	4.2	23
Lithuania	5.2	18	4.1	27	3.6	28
Poland	5.0	22	4.3	24	4.5	19
Romania	4.3	29	3.4	29	4.3	21
Slovak Republic	4.9	24	3.9	28	4.0	26
Slovenia	4.9	24	4.2	25	4.5	19
Liberal countries	**5.8**	**7.7**	**5.9**	**6.3**	**5.6**	**9.0**
United Kingdom	6.1	3	6.0	3	6.0	3
Ireland	5.1	20	5.5	13	5.4	12
USA	6.3	1	5.9	6	6.3	1
Canada	5.7	10	5.6	11	5.5	10
Australia	6.0	4	6.1	2	5.2	14
New Zealand	5.8	8	6.0	3	5.2	14

The *ex post* indicators in general fare worse probably because of feedbacks and reverse causality. Better macro performance seems to be related to a higher wage share. Denmark, Switzerland, Finland and Sweden have low macro profit ratios and good performance. All are small open

Table 14.4 (continued)

Time required to start a business 2005		Government subsidies		State ownership of enterprises		Competition legislation	
Rating[4]	Rank	Rating[5]	Rank	Rating[6]	Rank	Rating[7]	Rank
11.3	**8.0**	**1.8**	**21.3**	**6.8**	**12.0**	**7.0**	**7.0**
4.0	3	2.3	25	8.1	1	7.5	2
14.0	10	1.8	22	6.3	17	7.0	7
16.0	11	1.4	17	6.0	18	6.5	12
24.7	**14.3**	**2.0**	**20.3**	**7.2**	**6.7**	**7.3**	**5.7**
29.0	17	3.0	27	7.4	6	8.0	1
34.0	20	1.7	20	6.8	11	6.5	13
11.0	6	1.3	14	7.4	3	7.5	3
22.0	**12.3**	**1.2**	**13.0**	**5.7**	**18.7**	**6.1**	**15.3**
45.0	23	1.2	12	6.8	10	6.8	10
8.0	5	1.4	18	5.7	20	6.6	11
13.0	9	0.9	9	4.7	26	4.8	25
74.7	**26.0**	**0.9**	**10.3**	**5.2**	**23.7**	**5.3**	**21.7**
38.0	21	0.1	1	5.6	22	4.9	23
108.0	29	1.0	11	4.5	27	5.2	22
78.0	28	1.6	19	5.6	22	5.6	20
45.3	**21.5**	**2.3**	**17.6**	**5.6**	**19.3**	**5.0**	**24.0**
40.0	22	7.9	29	6.3	16	5.3	21
72.0	27	1.0	10	7.2	9	6.0	19
52.0	24	1.4	16	7.6	2	6.1	18
26.0	15	0.8	8	5.4	24	4.7	26
31.0	18	0.5	5	4.3	28	4.4	27
28.0	16	2.0	24	5.6	21	4.8	24
52.0	24	1.9	23	5.0	25	4.3	28
61.0	26	3.0	26	3.3	29	4.1	29
10.7	**6.8**	**0.7**	**7.2**	**6.7**	**10.8**	**6.6**	**10.8**
18.0	12	0.5	4	6.3	14	6.3	14
24.0	14	0.6	6	6.3	15	6.1	17
5.0	4	0.5	3	6.5	12	6.3	16
3.0	2	1.2	13	6.5	13	6.9	9
2.0	1	1.3	15	7.4	3	7.2	4
12.0	8	0.3	2	7.2	8	7.0	5

economies. We could not establish a relation between the average price–cost margin across industries of a country and performance, and in fact, countries with higher profit margins show a somewhat better performance. This might indicate a reverse causality, or just the fact that both channels work

Table 14.4 (continued)

	Rating Competition Authority	Wage share 2003–2005		Price–cost margin (1998–2000)	
	Rating	%	Rank	Margin	Rank
Scandinavian countries	**9.3**	**73.8**	**8.0**	**0.152**	**23.0**
Denmark	6.0	77.6	3	0.133	21
Finland	7.0	66.7	17	0.182	25
Sweden	15.0	77.1	4	0.141	23
Small open economies	**16.3**	**68.0**	**13.7**	**0.140**	**17.7**
Austria	18.0	67.1	16	0.127	20
Belgium	21.0	69.4	10	0.042	5
Netherlands	10.0	67.4	15	0.250	28
Continental countries	**6.0**	**65.4**	**14.3**	**0.072**	**10.7**
Germany	5.0	69.1	11	−0.038	1
France	4.0	70.3	9	0.218	27
Italy	9.0	56.7	23	0.036	4
Southern countries	**18.7**	**58.9**	**20.3**	**0.148**	**13.3**
Greece	25.0	42.7	29	0.120	7
Spain	14.0	65.0	19	0.204	26
Portugal	17.0	68.9	13	0.120	7
Catching-up countries	**13.4**	**57.5**	**21.6**	**0.090**	**7.8**
Czech Republic	11.9	65.1	18	−0.037	2
Estonia	11.9	64.7	20	0.120	7
Hungary	11.9	48.6	27	0.135	22
Lithuania	11.9	52.7	25	0.120	7
Poland	24.0	51.8	26	0.120	7
Romania	11.9	45.4	28	0.120	7
Slovak Republic	11.9	55.8	24	0.017	3
Slovenia	11.9	75.5	5	0.120	7
Liberal countries	**6.3**	**67.4**	**14.0**	**0.143**	**13.3**
United Kingdom	1.0	70.5	7	0.155	24
Ireland	8.0	62.8	22	0.120	7
USA	2.0	70.4	8	0.061	6
Canada	11.0	69.0	12	0.120	7
Australia	3.0	68.0	14	0.120	7
New Zealand	13.0	63.6	21	0.285	29

Notes:

1. 7.01: competition in the local market is (1=limited in most industries and price-cutting is rare, 7=intense in the most industries as market leadership changes over time).
2. 7.02: Anti-monopoly policy in your country is (1=lax and not effective at promoting competition, 7=effective and promotes competition).
3. 7.03: Corporate activity in your country is (1=dominated by a few business groups, 7=spread among many firms).
4. 7.11: number of days required to register a business.
5. 2.4.08 Government subsidies.

Table 14.4 (continued)

Persistence PCM industrial ranking		Openness 2006		Product Market Regulation 2003		Composite competition indicator	
Rating	Rank	%	Rank	Rating	Rank	Average[8]	Rank
0.313	**5.0**	**92.5**	**14.0**	**1.2**	**6.7**	**11.1**	**9.7**
0.199	2	100.8	12	1.1	4	8.2	2
0.367	6	82.3	16	1.3	9	11.8	13
0.372	7	94.4	14	1.2	7	13.4	14
0.335	**10.3**	**141.6**	**7.3**	**1.4**	**12.0**	**11.2**	**9.3**
0.087	1	109.6	11	1.4	12	11.4	11
0.362	5	174.6	3	1.4	12	11.0	8
0.555	25	140.6	8	1.4	12	11.2	9
0.550	**20.7**	**65.5**	**21.3**	**1.7**	**20.7**	**14.7**	**16.3**
0.614	26	84.5	15	1.4	12	9.9	4
0.419	9	55.6	25	1.7	23	14.1	16
0.615	27	56.5	24	1.9	27	20.1	29
0.386	**7.3**	**59.9**	**23.0**	**1.7**	**22.7**	**18.8**	**25.0**
0.452	10	51.4	26	1.8	26	19.8	28
0.404	8	58.4	23	1.6	21	19.2	25
0.303	4	70.0	20	1.6	21	17.6	22
0.452	**10.0**	**134.6**	**8.9**	**1.8**	**20.0**	**17.8**	**22.3**
0.452	10	148.9	6	1.7	23	16.8	19
0.452	10	169.3	4	1.5	16	14.8	18
0.452	10	155.1	5	2.0	28	17.1	20
0.452	10	129.3	10	1.5	16	17.4	21
0.452	10	82.0	17	2.8	29	19.7	27
0.452	10	76.9	18	1.5	16	19.6	26
0.452	10	176.0	2	1.5	16	18.8	24
0.452	10	139.1	9	1.5	16	18.2	23
0.506	**14.3**	**68.9**	**20.8**	**1.0**	**3.3**	**10.1**	**6.3**
0.523	24	61.6	21	0.9	1	10.1	6
0.297	3	148.1	7	1.1	4	11.4	11
0.861	29	28.0	29	1.0	3	9.2	3
0.452	10	70.4	19	1.2	7	10.3	7
0.452	10	44.5	27	0.9	1	8.1	1
0.452	10	60.7	22	1.1	4	11.3	10

6. 2.4.10 State ownership of enterprises: State ownership of enterprises is a threat to business activities/is not a threat to business activities.
7. 2.4.11 Competition legislation: Competition legislation is not effective in preventing unfair competition/is efficient in preventing unfair competition.
8. Average rank over the 13 indicators of toughness of competition. This unweighted average is then ranked again.

Source: WEF The Global Competitiveness Report 2005–2006; IMD World Competitiveness Yearbook 2007; Star Rating (www.GlobalcompetitionReview.com); Eurostat (AMECO); OECD (STAN).

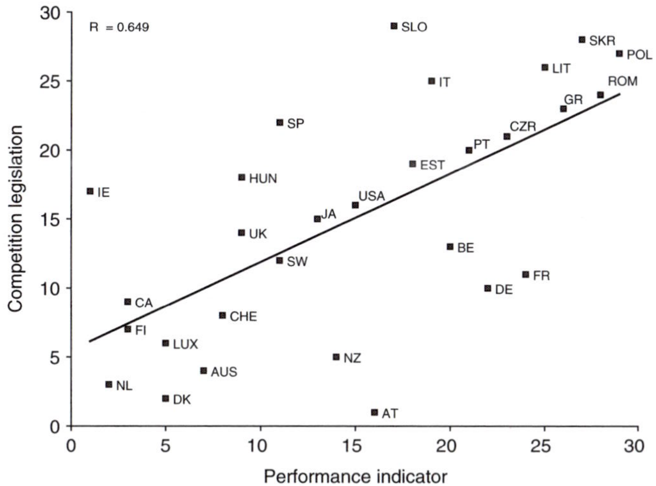
R = 0.649
Competition legislation
Performance indicator
0
5
10
15
20
25
30
IE
NL
CA
FI
LUX
DK
AUS
CHE
HUN
UK
SP
SW
JA
NZ
USA
AT
SLO
EST
IT
BE
PT
DE
CZR
FR
LIT
GR
SKR
ROM
POL

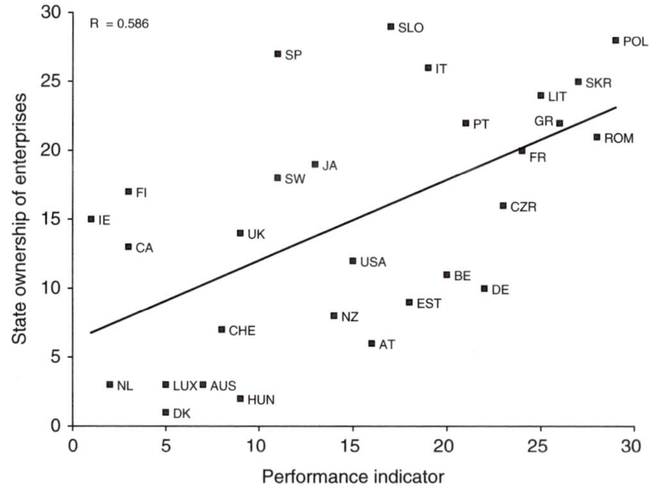
R = 0.586
State ownership of enterprises
Performance indicator
0
5
10
15
20
25
30
IE
NL
FI
CA
LUX
DK
AUS
CHE
HUN
UK
SP
SW
JA
NZ
USA
AT
SLO
EST
IT
BE
PT
DE
CZR
FR
LIT
GR
SKR
ROM
POL

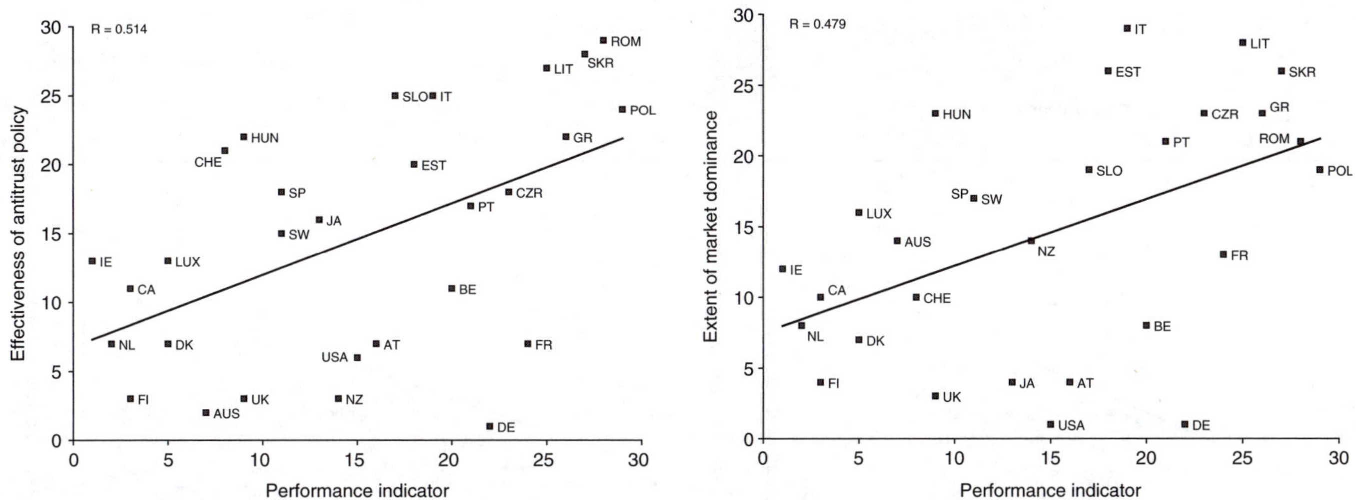

Source: WEF The Global Competitiveness Report 2005–2006; IMD World Competitiveness Yearbook 2007; Star Rating (www.GlobalcompetitionReview.com).

Figure 14.1 Rating of competitiveness indicators and country performance

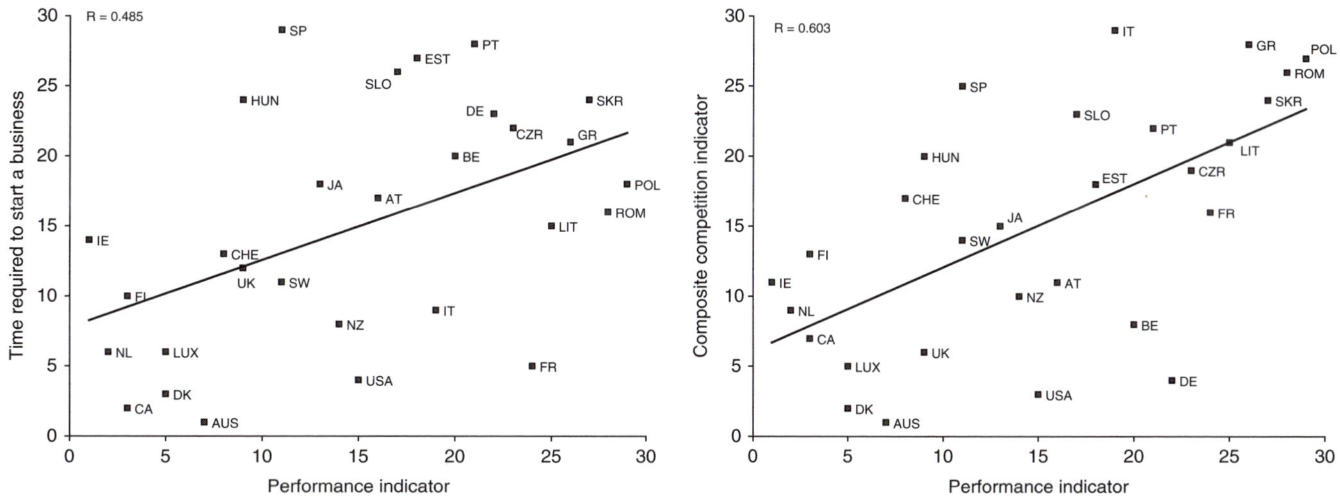

Figure 14.1 (continued)

and cannot be disentangled: competition increases performance, but performance increases or keeps high the level of margin. Non-linearity – as stressed by competition and innovation might play a role, since all these countries have high shares of R&D in GDP. There is no correlation between performance and openness and persistency of profit differences.

Out of all of the 13 indicators we used, 11 have the correct sign, and eight are larger than 0.4. If we combine the 13 indicators (including the insignificant ones and those with the wrong sign, assuming that these nevertheless carry some useful information), we obtain a composite indicator on the toughness of competition. Its correlation with the performance ranking is 0.60, which is a very close relation. The relation is driven by the Anglo-Saxon and the Scandinavian countries (with the exception of Sweden which lies in the upper half, but is not leading in competition toughness) and Canada and Australia; the US and New Zealand have tough competition, but only medium performance according to our performance indicator. On the other hand, the southern European countries and the new member countries of the EU have both low competition and low general performance. The single largest outsider is Germany with a very tough regime in competition (position 4), but low performance in the specific decade.[5]

As far as persistency is concerned, we did not find a good relation to economic performance. Some good performers have low persistency (Ireland, the Netherlands and Denmark) but others like Australia have a high persistency of profit rankings. Correlation of persistency with economic growth, on the other hand, is rather close. The data also indicate that persistency is high in large countries and that the causality might run in both directions.

If we combine all indicators (the significant and the insignificant, even including those with a negative sign), we obtain an overall composite indicator. The correlation between this composite indicator and the performance ranking is $R = 0.60$, which is highly significant. The positive relation is established by a high ranking in competition and performance in the Netherlands, Denmark and Finland (three Scandinavian European countries) and Canada. With the United Kingdom, Ireland and Australia, three more countries from the Anglo-Saxon world follow. Australia and the United Kingdom are placed a little bit lower in performance than in competition, and Ireland is better in performance (it is only number 15 in competition). Low performance is combined with low competition in the new EU member countries of Romania, Slovakia, Lithuania and Czech Republic, and in the three southern European countries, notably Greece, but also Portugal and Italy. Outsiders which reduce the fit are Spain, which has enjoyed a better-than-average performance in the past decade, but has the worst competition regime of all 29 countries; on the other hand, Germany excels in all rankings of competition, but has had an unsuccessful decade as far as economic performance is concerned. Both countries show that while competition is important, there are overriding issues. Germany suffered from the costs and the attention given to the unification as well as from its placing insufficient emphasis on high-tech industries,[6] education and information technology. Spain enjoyed the construction boom initiated by EU membership and liberalized labor markets (but did not promote domestic competition in product markets).

The Impact of Competition in a Stylized Model

Testing simple correlations does not prove causality. One way to tackle this problem is to start from a standard model of economic growth or performance and then to add the variable of interest and test its explanatory power and its effect on the coefficients of the 'standard model'. We started from the presumption that a standard model explaining growth or performance (in our case we emphasize performance) should try to model the impact of at least four variables: physical investment, starting income, human capital and research expenditures.

We applied this 'starting model' to our specific dataset. We have 29 countries and mainly data for the 1990s. As in other models, the multi-collinearity between human capital and research proved to be a problem, irrespective of whether we chose life expectancy or years of schooling as an indicator for human capital. The second negative result was that we did not get the expected negative impact of the starting level of per capita GDP. As best performing model we obtained the result that performance (more exactly our country composite ranking on performance) was dependent on physical investment and on research. We added to this 'preferred model' human capital, but there is the same strong multi-collinearity with research, as in other papers. To this very parsimonious 'preferred model', which alone was able to explain a quarter of the performance differences, we added the 13 competition indicators individually and then the combined indicator.

The result was rather encouraging. The individual competition indicators had the right sign in 12 out of 13 regressions. It was significant (with t-values above 2) for state ownership and competition legislation, and fairly significant for product market regulation and market dominance.

The result for the composite indicator was especially impressive. The coefficient is significant at the 5 per cent level ($t = 2.06$); see Table 14.5. Its inclusion reduces the coefficients (in effect it destroys the significance) of the other determinants. Specifically important seems to be the interrelation

Table 14.5 Preferred model with and without competition variable

Dependent variable: Performance ranking		Investment share in GDP		R&D ratio		Human capital (life expectancy)		Dummy 1		Dummy 2		Composite competition indicator	
		Coeffi-cient	t-value	Coeffi-cient	t-value	Coeffi-cient	t-value	Coeffi-cient	t-value	Coeffi-cient	t-value	Coeffi-cient	t-value
perf = f (investment share, R&D ratio, dummy 1, dummy 2)	Model 1	0.35	1.54	0.69	2.76			4.83	1.27	8.70	1.66		
perf = f (investment share, R&D ratio, human capital, dummy 1, dummy 2)	Model 2	0.28	1.22	0.63	2.47	0.32	0.97	−0.03	0.00	9.78	1.83		
perf = f (investment share, R&D ratio, dummy 1, dummy 2, composite competition indicator)	Model 3	0.24	1.09	0.39	1.45			2.74	0.74	7.97	1.62	0.44	2.06
perf = f (investment share, R&D ratio, human capital, dummy 1, dummy 2, composite competition indicator)	Model 4	0.09	0.40	0.20	0.73	0.59	1.92	−6.91	−1.13	9.74	2.05	0.57	2.69

Note: Dummy 1: New member countries; Dummy 2: Slow-growing countries (Germany, Japan, Switzerland).

between competition and R&D. This confirms the complex relationship suggested in the industrial organization literature. If we then extend the regression by the other determinants (eliminated in the course of choosing the preferred model), the result proves to be robust. The composite competition indicator is the single most significant explanatory variable for the performance ranking.

Of course this result is the starting point rather than the end of research on this interesting question, calling for much more elaborated econometric work: enlarging the time period, testing for endogeneity and multicollinearity, and a panel approach are called for. We should test whether the result depends on our performance measure, and whether it holds if we combine quantitative and categorical data (we transformed all indicators into categorical variables). And we should study the different impact of competition on growth performance and on our broader performance measure as well as indirect effects of competition on growth via innovation in sub-segment research.

The Relation Between Competition Policy and Socio-economic Models

The economic performance of European countries since the mid-1990s has been disappointing. Economic growth was lower than in the past and than in the US; the productivity gap with the US, which had narrowed over the past decades (with some European countries surpassing the US in GDP per hour), widened again; the employment rate which had been higher in Europe in the 1970s is now trailing the US rate by nearly 10 percentage points; and the unemployment rate, which used to be lower in Europe, is now higher than in the US. One factor suspected behind the disappointing performance of Europe between 1995 and 2005 was the 'European Socioeconomic Model', with its emphasis on social inclusion, big government and tight regulation of product and labor markets. This explanation never proved easy, since most of these conditions had been different also in periods of higher European growth. But against this argument, the importance of 'interaction effects' was invoked: big government, high costs and rigid rules are more important in more turbulent times of globalization and rapid technological changes.

However, European countries are different. The literature distinguishes three to five types of European socio-economic models. The surprising result is that of the different versions of the European socio-economic models, the two extreme ones have enjoyed a better performance since the 1990s. This holds for growth comparisons, but even more for the broader approach taken here to measure performance by income, employment, unemployment plus income distribution. The Anglo-Saxon model in

Europe is applied in Ireland and the United Kingdom and most resembles the US model, for example, because of low regulation and social costs as one extreme. The Scandinavian model, at the other end of the spectrum, has high taxes, big government and high welfare payments (for example, replacement ratios for unemployed or retired persons).

In our performance indicator, Ireland and the United Kingdom take position 1 and 8 among the 29 countries, and the Scandinavian countries (Denmark, Finland and Sweden) hold positions 5, 3 and 11. The unweighted average across the 'model members' of the overall performance rank is therefore 5 for Anglo-Saxon Europe and 6.3 for the Scandinavian model. In contrast, the big European economies (Germany, France and Italy) are ranked as 22, 24 and 19 (average rank 21.7). There are many explanations for what the successful Scandinavian countries did and especially what they have done differently since the 1990s (after severe crises in the late 1980s or early 1990s).[7] And there are also good arguments that Ireland's catching-up was a specific case (enabled by European transfers, low taxes and inward investment by US firms), and that the United Kingdom was rebuilding infrastructure after a strong period of austerity. But let us now look at the difference in toughness of competition.

Both successful countries groups are leaders in the indicators on the toughness of competition. The United Kingdom is ranked as number 6 and Ireland as 11. Ireland has the lowest regulation of product markets, but managers assess local competition as low and state ownership as rather high; profits are high. As for the Scandinavian countries, Denmark is ranked as the country with the second-highest degree of competition (second only to Australia). Finland and Sweden are ranked as number 13 and 14, with good rankings for competitive legislation and low product market regulation. Rankings of both are adversely affected by state ownership and subsidies, which are two elements that had been reduced in the past years and where the assessment was different for these countries according to other indicators (see Aiginger and Sieber, 2006). It looks as if a combination of medium toughness of competition and attempts to increase the degree of competition, plus the strong emphasis on innovation (see Aiginger, 2004a; Aiginger and Guger, 2006), play an important role in these countries regarding the achievement of a good performance despite a still large government sector and high taxes.

The lowest competitive pressure of all countries is in Italy (rank 29), and the competitive regime is below average in France. Germany is an outlier: in most respects it has to be considered as an economy with a high degree of competition, specifically as regards antitrust regulation. However, the process of starting a new business is rather long and costly. The average ranking for the countries of the continental model is 16.3 (an average over the very different regimes in Germany and Italy). The situation is very uniform in the southern European countries with a low degree of competition (average rank 19.3), and in the catching-up countries (new members), with an average rank of 25.3. The small European countries have an above-average degree of competition.

Thus, the Anglo-Saxon countries in Europe and outside add a high degree of competition to their model of low social cost and taxes. The Scandinavian countries reduced the potential burden of high taxes to competitiveness by a medium to tough regime on competition, and they seemed to have enforced competition over the past decade. In conjunction with the factors of excellence in innovation, education and lifelong learning, they are now able to stay competitive in a globalizing world, despite high taxes and big government. France and Italy, on the other hand, have failed to strengthen internal competition and are laggards in performance and toughness of competition.

5 CONCLUSIONS AND OUTLOOK

The importance of competition is well established in industrial economics; models and research results in this field have been the basis for competition policy. The relationship between rivalry and cooperation is investigated in regional analyses and impacts on regional policy in the tradition of Porter's diamond and cluster policy, and the – probably non-linear – relation between innovation and competition and its impact on performance is a perennial topic in innovation theory. The impact of competition on economic growth and overall macroeconomic performance is far less investigated. Although empirical growth models now include more institutional variables, they very seldom include indicators on the toughness of competition and there are very few studies relating performance differences of countries and regions in the past decade to the degree of competition. The only indicators used sometimes are trade openness and – primarily in studies by OECD researchers – product market regulation.

We collected 13 indicators on the toughness of competition for 29 countries. Some are survey indicators for example on the legislative regime (intensity of competition, effectiveness of antitrust and so on); other indicators on product market regulation were gathered by OECD experts (time to start a business, state ownership and so on). We added *ex post* indicators to the price–cost margins in industries, on aggregate profits, and finally, and as a tribute to the works of Dennis Mueller, on the persistence of profit differences between industries. The usual indicator on trade openness complements the set. Since all indicators relate on a narrow aspect of the broad notion of 'toughness of competition', since they are noisy, and contain measurement errors, we combined the information delivered by the individual indicators by ranking and then averaging them, to arrive at a 'composite indicator on competition'.

We define economic performance of a country more broadly than usual, combining data on income (per capita level and macroeconomic growth), employment, unemployment (rates and change over ten years) and equity (relation of top 20 per cent income to bottom 20 per cent). Similar performance measures had been used in Aiginger (2004a) to analyze performance differences between countries and models since the mid-1990s. Combining several aspects of performance (rather than concentrating on economic growth alone), mitigated the problem that a period of ten years is influenced by many country-specific problems (from the catching-up of Ireland to German unification).

Eleven of the 13 indicators on competition are positively related to performance in the cross-country correlation, with close relations to the assessment of the competition legislation, the extent of state ownership and product market regulation (the latter two with a negative sign). Most importantly, the relationship between the performance ranking and the combined indicator on competition was proven to be very close.

As a stronger test, we add the competition indicators to a small parsimonious 'preferred model' explaining performance differences across countries. The preferred model explains country performance over the past ten years by innovation (R&D ratio) and investment (share of physical investment in GDP). If we add the competition variables, all but one have the correct sign, two are significant by the usual standards, and for two the impact is marginally below significance. The overall indicator is robustly significant. Its inclusion reduced the explanatory power of innovation, thus indicating the same complex relation between innovation and competition, as modeled on the micro level. The overall impact of competition seems to be the most important and most robust indicator in explaining performance differences.

The degree of competition is strongest in the Anglo-Saxon countries: complementing low taxes and social costs by a tough competition regime seems to be favorable for competitiveness and growth. Most of these countries (specifically Ireland, Canada and Australia) are also front-runners in the performance ranking. Equally high performance was achieved in the Scandinavian countries. This has to be considered as a surprise, since these countries have high taxes and big government. It is explained by Aiginger (2004a) and Aiginger and Guger (2006), first, by their excellence in research and education (the countries are surpassing the Lisbon goals with respect to R&D ratios and are leading the Pisa education ratings); secondly, by changes in the labor market regimes (flexicurity and re-qualification, carrot-and-stick strategies); and thirdly, by prudent public finance (long-term pension reforms, budget surplus goals, concerns about equity and fairness). What may have been overlooked is that these countries are encouraging competition too (even in public services). Denmark is at the top in the rating of competition, Finland and Sweden (despite big government) lie in the middle of the bulk, with tendencies to the upper half and to increasing competition over time (encouraging entry, reducing regulation). The Scandinavian countries demonstrate that strong emphasis on innovation plus medium or strong competition is good for performance; this combination can outweigh the high costs for the social and environmental system. France and Italy are negative extremes: low competition in the domestic market and a low degree of openness, together with low investment in the future (research, education, new technologies) is bad for economic performance. Germany excels in competition policy, but this positive effect is overridden by the costs of German unification and the insufficient attention to research and education. This is an important problem for the country with the highest wages in manufacturing. Spain, on the other hand, shows that for a certain period of time, the negative effects of low competition and low innovation may be hidden by strong investment in housing and construction and high transfers by the EU. How long this will last must be monitored.

In the long run, innovation plus competition seem to be a good double strategy for improving performance and staying competitive in a globalizing world. The interrelation between competition and innovation may be as complex at the macro level as indicated in the micro models, since competition means private appropriation of inventions and patents, while innovation at the country level will profit from external effects, spillovers and synergies. The relation between innovation and competition and their combined effect of persistence of profit differences and on country performance will remain a fascinating research topic.

NOTES

1. The author acknowledges research assistance by Dagmar Guttmann and critique of earlier versions by Michael Böheim, Martin Falk, Klaus Friesenbichler, Werner Hölzl, Michael Peneder, Andreas Reinstaller and Gunther Tichy.
2. It is interesting to note that this point occurred specifically in his later papers.
3. Rodrik (2000) highlights five key institutions: property rights, regulatory institutions, macro stability, social insurance, and conflict management. He does not mention competition.
4. Since 'intensity of local competition' and 'effectiveness of national antitrust policy' are both qualitative 'soft indicators' that have been constructed on the basis of interviews with a sample group of (national) business managers, any far-reaching conclusions derived from these indicators have to be treated with due care.

5. We have intentionally not chosen economic growth alone as measure of success, since we wanted to include the starting level and the employment performance as well as equality. Furthermore countries might excel for growth more easily in a short-run period than in a long one. If we had taken growth in general the correlations would have been weaker. The exceptions are that persistence of profit ranking across industries is closely related with growth, and openness is related to growth. The composite indicator does not correlate with growth rankings, however.
6. See Aiginger (2003, 2004b).
7. Aiginger (2003, 2004b) and Aiginger and Guger (2006) find that the main reforms were related to labor markets (flexicurity, carrot and stick, deregulation of irregular contacts and part-time), investments into the future (excellence in R&D, education, lifelong learning) plus prudent fiscal policy (long-run surplus, output and distribution-oriented budget techniques, pension reforms with long-term as well as equity concerns).

REFERENCES

Aghion, P. and P. Howitt (1992), 'A model of growth through creative destruction', *Econometrica*, **60**, 323–51.

Aghion, Philippe and Paul Howitt (1998), *Endogenous Growth Theory*, Cambridge, MA: MIT Press.

Aghion, P., C. Harris, P. Howitt and J. Vickers (2001), 'Competition, imitation and growth with step-by-step innovation', *Review of Economic Studies*, **68**, 467–92.

Aghion, P., N. Bloom, R. Blundell, R. Griffith and P. Howitt (2002), 'Competition and innovation: an inverted U relationship', London: The Institute of Fiscal Studies, WP02/04.

Aghion, P., N. Bloom, R. Blundell, R. Griffith and P. Howitt (2005), 'Competition and innovation: an inverted U relationship', *Quarterly Journal of Economics*, **120**(2), 701–28.

Ahn, S. and Ph. Hemmings (2000), 'Policy influences on economic growth in OECD countries: an evaluation of the evidence', Paris: OECD, Economics Department Working Paper No. 246.

Aiginger, K. (2003), 'The contribution of labour market reforms, macroeconomic policy and growth drivers to economic growth', in *Fostering Economic Growth in Europe*, Vienna: Austrian National Bank, Proceedings of the 31st Economics Conference of the OeNB, pp. 120–31.

Aiginger, K. (2004a), 'The three tier strategy followed by successful European countries in the 1990s', *International Review of Applied Economics*, **18**(4), 399–422.

Aiginger, K. (2004b), 'The economic agenda: a view from Europe', in 'Economic Agenda of the 21st Century', Special Issue: *Review of International Economics*, **12**(2), 187–206.

Aiginger, K. (2005), 'Labour market reforms and economic growth – the European experience in the nineties', *Journal of Economic Studies*, **32**(6), 540–73.

Aiginger, K. (2007a), 'Industrial policy: past, diversity, future', Introduction to the special issue on the Future of Industrial Policy, *Journal of Industry, Competition and Trade*, **7**(3+4), 143–6.

Aiginger, K. (2007b), 'Industrial policy: A dying breed or a re-emerging phoenix', special issue on the Future of Industrial Policy, *Journal of Industry, Competition and Trade*, **7**(3+4), 297–323.

Aiginger, K. and A. Guger (2006), 'The ability to adapt: why it differs between the Scandinavian and Continental models', *Intereconomics – Review of European Economic Policy*, **41**(1), 14–23.

Aiginger, K. and A. Guger (2005), 'The European Social Model: from an alleged barrier to a competitive advantage', *Journal of Progressive Politics*, **4**(3), 40–47.

Aiginger, K. and M. Pfaffermayr (1997), 'Looking at the cost side of "monopoly"', *Journal of Industrial Economics*, **45**(3), 245–67.

Aiginger, K. and S. Sieber (2006), 'The matrix approach to industrial policy', *International Review of Applied Economics*, **20**(5), December, 573–603.

Armstrong, Mark, Simon Cowan and John Vickers (1994), *Regulatory Reform: Economic Analysis and British Experience*, Cambridge, MA: MIT Press.

Arrow, Kenneth J. (1962), 'Economic welfare and the allocation of resources for invention', in *The Rate and Direction of Inventive Activity: Economic and Social Factors*, National Bureau of Economic Research, Princeton University Press, pp. 609–26.

Bassanini, A., S. Scarpetta and P. Hemmings (2001), 'Economic growth: the role of policies and institutions. Panel data evidence from OECD Countries', Paris: OECD, Economics Department Working Paper No. 283.

Bayoumi, T., D. Lexton and P. Pesenti (2004), 'Benefits and spillovers of greater competition in Europe: a macroeconomic assessment', Cambridge, MA: NBER Working Paper Series No. 10416, April.

Blanchard, O. (2004), 'The economic future of Europe', *Journal of Economic Perspectives*, **18**(4), Fall, 3–26.

Blundell, R., R. Griffith and J.V. Reenen (1995), 'Dynamic count data model of technological innovations', *Economic Journal*, **105**, 333–44.

Caves, Richard E. and David R. Barton (1992), *Efficiency in US Manufacturing Industries*, Cambridge, MA: MIT Press.

Cohen, W.M. and R.C. Levin (1989), 'Empirical studies of innovation and market structure', in Richard Schmalensee and Robert Willig (eds), *Handbook of Industrial Organization*, Amsterdam: North-Holland, vol. 2, pp. 1060–107.

Esping-Andersen, Gosta (1990), *The Three Worlds of Welfare Capitalism*, Cambridge, UK: Polity Press.

Esping-Andersen, Gosta (ed.), (2002), *Why We Need a New Welfare State*, Oxford: Oxford University Press.

Geroski, P.A. (1990), 'Innovation, technological opportunity, and market structure', *Oxford Economic Papers*, **42**, 586–602.

Geroski, Paul A. (1995), *Market Structure, Corporate Performance and Innovative Activity*, Oxford: Oxford University Press.

Griffith, R. and R. Harrison (2004), 'The link between product market reform and macro-economic performance', European Commission, Economic Paper No. 209.

Grossman, Gene M. and Elhanan Helpman (1991), *Innovation and Growth in the Global Economy*, Cambridge, MA: MIT Press.

Guger, A., M. Marterbauer and E. Walterskirchen (2004), 'Growth policy in the spirit of Steindl and Kalecki', Vienna: WIFO Working Papers, No. 240.

Hart, O.D. (1983), 'The market mechanism as an incentive scheme', *Bell Journal of Economics*, **14**, 366–82.

Hayek, Friedrich A. (1968), *Der Wettbewerb als Entdeckungsverfahren*, Kiel: Kieler Vorträge.

Hermalin, B.E. (1992), 'The effects of competition on executive behavior', *Rand Journal of Economics*, **23**, 350–65.

Leibfried, Stephan (2000), 'Towards a European welfare state?', in Chris Pierson and Francis G. Castles (eds), *The Welfare State Reader*, Cambridge, UK: Polity Press, pp. 190–206.

Levin, R.C., W.M. Cohen and D.C. Mowery (1985) 'R&D appropriability, opportunity, and market structure: New evidence on some Schumpeterian hypotheses', *American Economic Review*, Proceedings, **75**, 20–24.

Mookerjee, D. (1984), 'Optimal incentive schemes with many agents', *Review of Economic Studies*, **51**, 433–46.

Mueller, D. (1977), 'The persistence of profits above the norm', *Economica*, **44**, 369–80.

Nalebuff, B.J. and J.E. Stiglitz (1983), 'Prizes and incentives: towards a general theory of compensation and competition', *Bell Journal of Economics*, **14**, 21–43.

Nickell, S.J. (1977), 'Unemployment and labour market rigidities: Europe versus North America', *Journal of Economic Perspectives*, **11**(3), 55–74.

Nickell, S.J. (1996), 'Competition and corporate performance', *Journal of Political Economy*, **104**, 724–66.

Nickell, S.J. (2003), 'Labour market institutions and unemployment in OECD countries', Munich: CESifo Dice Report 2/2003, pp. 13–26.

Nicoletti, G. and S. Scarpetta (2002), 'Regulation, productivity and growth: OECD evidence', Paris: OECD.

Nicoletti, G. and S. Scarpetta (2003), 'Regulation, productivity and growth: OECD evidence', Paris: OECD, Economics Department Working Paper No. 347.

Nicoletti G., S. Scarpetta and O. Boylaud (1999), 'Summary indicators of product market regulation with an extension to employment protection legislation', Paris: OECD, Economics Department Working Paper No. 226.

Nicoletti, G.A., E. Bassanini, S. Ernst, P. Jean and P. Santiago Swaim (2001), 'Product and labour markets interactions in OECD countries', Paris: OECD, Economics Department Working Paper No. 312.

Pisani-Ferri, J. (2005), 'Only teamwork can put the eurozone on a steady course', *Financial Times*, 31 August.

Porter, M.E. (2000), 'The current competitiveness index: measuring the economic foundations of prosperity', Geneva: World Economic Forum, The Global Competitiveness Report.

Pryor, F.L. (2002), 'Quantitative notes on the extent of governmental regulations in various OECD nations', *International Journal of Industrial Organization*, **20**(5), 693–714.

Rodrik, D. (2000), 'Institutions for high-quality growth: what they are and how to acquire them', London: CEPR Discussion Paper No. 2370.

Romer, P.M. (1990), 'Endogenous technological change', *Journal of Political Economy*, **98**, 71–102.

Salgado, R. (2002), 'Impact of structural reforms on productivity growth in industrial countries', Washington, DC: IMF Working Paper No. 02/10.

Sapir, André, Philippe Aghion, Guiseppe Bertola, Martin Hellwig, Jean Pisani-Ferry, Dariusz Rosati, José Vinals and Helen Wallace (2004), *An Agenda for a Growing Europe: Sapir Report*, Oxford: Oxford University Press.

Scarpetta, S. (1996), 'Assessing the role of labour market policies and institutional settings on unemployment: a cross-country study', Paris: *OECD Economic Studies*, **2**(26), 43–82.

Scherer, F.M. (1967), 'Market structure and the employment of scientists and engineers', *American Economic Review*, **57**, 524–31.

Schettkat, R. (2003), 'What impact do welfare state institutions have on economic performance?', Munich: CESifo Dice Report 2/2003, pp. 27–33.

Schumpeter, Joseph (1942), *Capitalism, Socialism, and Democracy*, London: Allen and Unwin.

Scott, J.T. (1984), 'Firm versus industry variability in R&D intensity', in Zvi Griliches (ed.), *R&D, Patents, and Productivity*, NBER Conference Proceedings, Chicago: University of Chicago Press, pp. 233–45.

Tichy, Gunther (2005), 'Die "Neue Unsicherheit" als Ursache der europäischen Wachstumsschwäche', *Perspektiven der Wirtschaftspolitik*, **6**(3), 385–407.

Willig, Robert D. (1987), 'Corporate governance and market structure', in Assaf Razin and Efraim Sadka (eds), *Economic Policy in Theory and Practice*, London: Macmillan, pp. 481–94.

Index